ACUTE MELANCHOLIA

and Other Essays

GENDER, THEORY, AND RELIGION

GENDER, THEORY, AND RELIGION

Amy Hollywood, Editor

The Gender, Theory, and Religion series provides a forum for interdisciplinary scholarship at the intersection of the study of gender, sexuality, and religion.

Martyrdom and Memory: Early Christian Culture Making, Elizabeth A. Castelli

When Heroes Love: The Ambiguity of Eros in the Stories of Gilgamesh and David, Susan Ackerman

Abandoned to Lust: Sexual Slander and Ancient Christianity, Jennifer Wright Knust

Bodily Citations: Religion and Judith Butler, Ellen T. Armour and Susan M. St. Ville, editors

Naming the Witch: Magic, Ideology, and Stereotype in the Ancient World, Kimberly B. Stratton

Dying to Be Men: Gender and Language in Early Christian Martyr Texts, L. Stephanie Cobb

Tracing the Sign of the Cross: Sexuality, Mourning, and the Future of American Catholicism, Marian Ronan

Between a Man and a Woman? Why Conservatives Oppose Same-Sex Marriage, Ludger H. Viefhues-Bailey

Promised Bodies: Time, Language, and Corporeality in Medieval Women's Mystical Texts, Patricia Dailey

Christ Without Adam: Subjectivity and Difference in the Philosophers' Paul, Benjamin H. Dunning

Electric Santería: Racial and Sexual Assemblages of Transnational Religion, Aisha M. Beliso-De Jesús

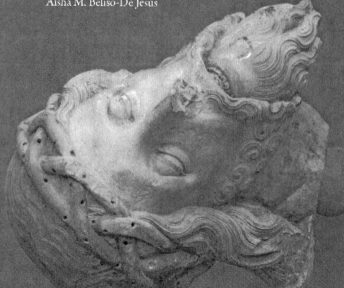

ACUTE
MELANCHOLIA
and Other Essays

MYSTICISM,
HISTORY, AND
THE STUDY
OF RELIGION

AMY HOLLYWOOD

COLUMBIA UNIVERSITY PRESS
NEW YORK

Columbia University Press
Publishers Since 1893
New York   Chichester, West Sussex
cup.columbia.edu
Copyright © 2016 Columbia University Press
All rights reserved

Library of Congress Cataloging-in-Publication Data
Names: Hollywood, Amy M., 1963–
Title: Acute melancholia and other essays : mysticism, history,
    and the study of religion / Amy Hollywood.
Description: New York : Columbia University Press, 2016. |
    Series: Gender, theory, and religion | Includes bibliographical references and index.
Identifiers: LCCN 2015027599 | ISBN 9780231156431 (cloth : alk. paper) |
    ISBN 9780231156448 (pbk. : alk. paper) | ISBN 9780231527439 (e-book)
Subjects: LCSH: Christianity—Philosophy. | Experience (Religion) | Mysticism. |
    Religion—Philosophy.
Classification: LCC BR100 .H6155 2016 | DDC 270—dc23
LC record available at http://lccn.loc.gov/2015027599

Cover and book design: Lisa Hamm
Cover image: *Two Fragments of a Pietà*, Prague, around 1400 © Staatliche Museen
zu Berlin, Skulpturensammlung und Museum für Byzantinische Kunst / Fabian Fröhlicich

In memory of my brothers and sister, Pedro, Michael, Mary, and Daniel, and of friends dead too young:

> *. . . and with each a limb of our own lives cut off. Exactly why we should be expected to talk about it, I don't know.*

—Henry Adams

CONTENTS

List of Illustrations   ix

Acknowledgments   xi

A Triptych   1

    On the True, the Real, and Critique; By Way of an Introduction   2

    Henry Adams, Clover Adams, and the Death of the Real   19

    The Unspeakability of Trauma, the Unspeakability of Joy   44

PART I   65

1   Acute Melancholia   67

PART II. HISTORY   91

2   Feminist Studies in Christian Spirituality   93

3   Gender, Agency, and the Divine in Religious Historiography   117

4   Reading as Self-Annihilation: On Marguerite Porete's
    Mirror of Simple Souls   129

PART III. SEXUALITY   147

5   Sexual Desire, Divine Desire; Or, Queering the Beguines   149

6   The Normal, the Queer, and the Middle Ages   163

7   "That Glorious Slit": Irigaray and the Medieval Devotion
    to Christ's Side Wound   171

PART IV. PRACTICE   189

8   Inside Out: Beatrice of Nazareth and Her Hagiographer   191

9   Performativity, Citationality, Ritualization   213

10   Practice, Belief, and Feminist Philosophy of Religion   233

PART V   251

11   Love of Neighbor and Love of God: Martha and Mary in
the Christian Middle Ages   253

Notes   *271*
Sources   *375*
Index   *377*

ILLUSTRATIONS

0.1   *The Mystery of the Hereafter and the Peace of God that Passeth Understanding*, from the memorial to Marian "Clover" Hooper Adams   20

0.2.   The mother of Jesse, depicted on the ceiling of the Sistine Chapel   21

0.3   *White-robed Bodhisattva of Compassion*   23

0.4   Mourners (*Pleurant*), from the Tomb of John the Fearless and Margaret of Bavaria   24

0.5   The Tomb of Philippe Pot, Lord of La Roche-Pot   25

0.6   *Madonna of Bruges*   26

0.7   *Medici Madonna*   27

0.8   *Pietà*   28

0.9   Funerary statue from Laurel Hill Cemetery   31

7.1   Passional of Abbess Kunigunde of Bohemia   174

7.2   *Vision des Heiligen Bernhard (sogenanntes Blutkruzifixus)*   177

7.3   Villers Miscellany   180

7.4   *Psalter of Bonne of Luxembourg*   181

7.5   *The Wounds of Christ with the Symbols of the Passion*   183

ACKNOWLEDGMENTS

THERE IS no way that I can thank all the students, colleagues, and friends who heard, read, questioned, criticized, bemoaned, applauded, or otherwise contributed to these pages. A litany of the people, places, and institutions that provided space and time to work out the ideas contained within them would also be boring for everyone. So I will just say thank you—all of you—who helped.

I do have to thank by name Rhodes College, Dartmouth College, the University of Chicago, and Harvard Divinity School for the jobs; the Henry Luce III Fellowship in Theology Program for the grant; Michael Motia for the technical assist; Paul Iappini and Ken Fox for the oasis; and Reed Lowrie—for everything.

ACUTE MELANCHOLIA

and Other Essays

A TRIPTYCH

Without Mary, man had no hope except in Atheism, and for Atheism the world was not ready. Hemmed back on that side, men rushed like sheep to escape the butcher, and were driven to Mary; only too happy in finding protection and hope in a being who could understand the language they talked, and the excuses they had to offer. How passionately they worshipped Mary, the Cathedral of Chartres shows; and how this worship elevated the whole sex, all the literature and history of the time proclaim. If you need more proof, you can read more Petrarch; but still one cannot realize how actual Mary was, to the men and women of the middle-ages, and how she was present, as a matter of course, whether by way of miracle or as a habit of life, throughout their daily existence. The surest measure of her reality is the enormous money value they put on her assistance, and the art that was lavished on her gratification, but an almost equally certain sign is the casual allusion, the chance reference to her, which assumes her presence.

—Henry Adams, *Mont Saint Michel and Chartres* (1904)

Ellen I'm not real—oh make me real—You are all of you real!

—Marian ("Clover") Hooper Adams (1885)

They were avoiding the serious, standing off, anxiously, from the real.

—Henry James, *The Golden Bowl* (1904)

On the True, the Real, and Critique; By Way of an Introduction

At the beginning of the twentieth century, Henry Adams wrote the history of an earlier century through the study of what he believed to be its major accomplishments—Mont Saint Michel, Chartres, the life of Francis of Assisi, and the theology of Thomas Aquinas. For Adams, the years 1150 to 1250 expressed the essence of a time that was to be fundamentally transformed by the forces of modernity. An age is defined, Adams argues, by the site from which force emanates: hence his distinction, in *The Education of Henry Adams* (1907), between the Virgin—the Mary of the Christian Middle Ages—and the Dynamo.[1] Both, as centers of force, are real.

At the beginning of the twenty-first century, I found myself preoccupied with the question of what it might mean to say that the Virgin is real—actual, present, palpable—in one time and place and not in another. The question is vital, I think, to writing the history of religion. For Adams, history is always the history of forces. The Virgin was a force; hence the Virgin was real. In positing the reality of the Virgin in the Middle Ages, Adams suggests her veridicality: she exists in the world, able to effect the actions of human beings. Adams does not say whether her veridicality depends on the creative power of the human imagination or is, instead, independent of human desires, practices, and aspirations. In *Mont Saint Michel and Chartres*, he points to these crucial theological and philosophical questions when he asks whether Mary is actual "by way of miracle or as a habit of life." (As we will see, he is significantly less reticent—or rather, his characters are—about answering these questions in his earlier novel *Esther*, published in 1884.)

In most of the essays collected here I too focus on medieval Christianity, particularly on texts in which people claim that they or others around them encounter, talk to, see, smell, taste, feel, and hear spirits, saints, angels, demons, and, of course, God. Any attempt to understand the claims made by these writings immediately opens onto vital ontological and epistemological questions. What does it mean to say that the object of religious devotion is real? If something is real, are propositions about it also true? If such propositions are true, in what way are they so?[2] If we posit the veridicality of the saints, angels, demons, and God encountered by medieval Christians, and hence the truth of claims about them, are we simply acknowledging the creative power of the human imagination or are we asserting that these entities exist independently of human practice?

Today, those working in the human sciences have become adept at distinguishing between what is real for the people they study and what is real for some putatively generalizable "us." Calls for imagination, empathy, and respect generally fall short, explicitly or implicitly, from assertions that what is real for religious people is also true, at least in the sense of that term generally presumed by contemporary historians, anthropologists, sociologists, textual critics, philosophers—even often theologians. A number of scholars in religious studies argue that for medieval people, Mary is real; they cede, furthermore, that premodern Christians believed Mary to be irreducible to human knowledge, practice, or desire. Yet the methodological skepticism and agnosticism of modern Western scholarship (mirroring that of much modern Western philosophy) generally require that we deny or bracket the question of whether it is true *for us* that Mary, as Virgin Queen of Heaven, exists or existed—of whether she is or was an ontological force in the world independent of human practices and relationships. In Adams's terms, the modern world is ready for atheism, perhaps even unable to think critically and coherently outside of its terms. Mary may be very real for believers, but the claim that Mary existed or exists as an independent being is at worst untrue and at best one the historian, given the constraints of her field and its methodologies, cannot answer.

Lest we think that the distinction between the real and the true—between that which an individual palpably experiences and hence inexorably takes to be the case and what is the case from the standpoint of a third-party witness—is a thoroughly modern one, there is ample evidence that such a distinction was operative within the Christian Middle Ages. Not every vision was understood to be a vision of God or of demons; sometimes, medieval authors view the visionary as sick, deluded, or insane.[3] (Sometimes, even, people made up stories to entertain and astonish others; and sometimes, of course, they lied.)[4] And yet the desire to move from compelling experience—what is palpably real for the one who undergoes it—to claims for independently verifiable truth of that which is experienced seems inexorable. History, the human science on which I focus most attention in the essays collected here, is, as a discipline, premised on a critical engagement with this movement. It is precisely here that the following essays pause.

The true and the real are intimately tied in the modern human sciences—or, in terms more often used in the contemporary academy, in the humanities and social sciences—to the practice of critique.[5] So with the questions outlined above also comes the question of whether history is necessarily a *critical* endeavor, with critique understood in a quite specific way.[6] The critical historian, for example, stubbornly pushes against unreflective acceptance of her sources, continually testing them against one another in order to sort out the true from the false.

This is work in which I have an enormous investment, as a number of the essays collected here attest. For Adams, it is one of the crucial distinctions between what he calls the science of history and antiquarianism. The other key factor for Adams is that history, to be scientific, must be theoretical. It must, he insists, give an account of history as a unified whole—hence be philosophical; the antiquarian, on the other hand, is content with fragments.[7] Adams did not hesitate to argue for the reality, the actuality, and the truth of Mary *for* medieval Christians, but he is able to do so because he assumes that she is no longer an active presence in the world.

As should be obvious to contemporary readers, Henry Adams's insistence that Mary was a real force in the Christian Middle Ages but that she is not in early-twentieth-century America ignores the persistence, in his own time, of claims that spirits, ancestors, saints, angels, and deities are present in the world and that they play a vital role in the experience of those who encounter them.[8] Of course, such claims persist into the present. Christianity did not lose all of its force in modernity, nor have other religious traditions that have come into contact with the modernizing and secularizing power of certain forms of modern Western rationality. Nor did Christianity become, as some hoped, a fully rational or naturalized religion. So while it may be true, as Charles Taylor argues, that in the premodern West atheism was not a live option and that the modern West is governed by a social imaginary in which what Taylor calls the supernatural does not necessarily play a role, the fact remains that in almost every part of the world people continue to engage in religious practices and to make claims about their experience of and encounters with modes of being irreducible to the human.[9] Questions Adams thought he could relegate to the past are very much alive in the present; for many in modernity, both the Virgin and the Dynamo are real.

In a number of the essays collected here, I ask what it might look like if we were to entertain the notion that what others encounter as real might also be true, not just for them and not solely as a force generated by acts of the human imagination. Most importantly, I want to ask whether the methods others—in this case religious people of a particular sort, those who encounter and interact with ghosts, spirits, saints, demons, or God—use to determine what is real and what is true might challenge the ontological and epistemological presuppositions of modern history, themselves grounded in central presumptions of modern Western philosophy.[10] For whether we acknowledge it or not, there *is* a theory—there are many theories—underlying contemporary historical work and the study of religion, most prominently a kind of naturalism that assumes everything in human history can be explained in terms of the operations of the natural world and of human beings, themselves a part of that world.[11] Truth is unquestioningly identified with empirical truth, which in discussions of the human means either scientific or historical truth, a historical truth that is assumed to operate in naturalistic terms. (I discuss this further in "Gender, Agency, and the Divine.")

To push against these presumptions—or in my case to allow the texts I study to push against them—entails real risks; we know that the presences—and absences—that populate the worlds in which we live give rise to confusion, conflict, and violence, as well as to the certainty, security, and joy for which Adams was nostalgic. Reason, articulated broadly within Western modernity as entailing the verifiability of belief by independent observers, has been essential to keeping certain kinds of conflict in check. From this standpoint, many contemporary scholars of religion assume that the best we can do is to acknowledge that religion is the product—often the very vital and active product—of human acts of the imagination; this is as real, many imply, as we can allow religion to be.

This is probably closer to what I think than my argument thus far would suggest, and yet there is an important, if subtle, difference. The clearest articulation of my current views can be found in "Acute Melancholia." It appears in the form of a fiction that insists on leaving room for something irreducible to individual or collective acts of the imagination. I there tentatively hold out the possibility of a transcendence that occurs between people, or between people and the world around them, and yet is irreducible to the various parties in the relationship, perhaps even to the relationship itself.[12] I hesitate to give a solely humanist or naturalizing account of religion because of my own experience, as "Acute Melancholia" attempts to show, but also because of my study of Christianity and my desire to understand what it is in Christianity, as in other religious traditions, that resists such accounts.

My project in these essays, then, is not governed in any simple sense by nostalgia for a lost historical past; the vitality of Christianity—and of many other religions—surrounds me, even if I do not share in its practices and often find them, in their contemporary forms, dull or repugnant. Like the anthropologist Saba Mahmood, whose work plays an important role in my thinking, my concerns are political and ethical—I would add, given my own training and predilections, theological and philosophical. As an anthropologist, Mahmood takes the living women and men whom she studies not only as objects of analysis, but also as subjects able to offer meaningful accounts of their own practices. Again, at stake is not nostalgia for some putatively lost religious past, but instead an ethically and politically motivated encounter with living religious subjects. Mahmood asks, together with a host of other scholars in the study of religion, whether we can have a meaningful engagement with subjects whose self-understanding we *presume from the outset* to be false or misguided. How can we begin with such assumptions and ever hope to understand?

In a recent issue of the *Journal of the American Academy of Religion*, Elizabeth A. Pritchard condemns a number of scholars who pursue this line of inquiry (although curiously not Mahmood). Pritchard argues that Robert Orsi and I abnegate the responsibility of critique. Rather than contending with the crucial *differences* between religious people, she argues, the stance of openness to the other is in danger of becoming merely another liberal plea for tolerance in which real conflict is ignored or—even worse—a self-satisfied and self-satisfying exercise in intellectual masochism.[13] Focusing her attention on my essay "Gender, Agency, and the Divine in Feminist Historiography," collected here, and Orsi's "Snakes Alive: Resituating the Moral in the Study of Religion," to which I refer in a note in that essay, Pritchard generalizes from quite specific cases.[14] In the two essays, Orsi and I both ask questions about what it might mean to suspend judgment, at least temporarily, as part of an ethical mode of listening.

In his discussion of Appalachian snake handlers, Orsi may be subject to Pritchard's first charge. He asks his readers to defer judgments about his subjects, even as they voice and enact virulent misogyny. Yet Orsi is a historian and he argues that the historian must bracket the phenomena to be studied in order to come to as rich an understanding of them as possible. Easy judgments, he contends, stand in the way of understanding. On this reading, Orsi does not claim that critique is impossible, but simply that it is not what historians do. (I raise questions about the possibility of maintaining that distinction in a number of essays, as does Orsi himself.) He also suggests, quite rightly, that any well-grounded critique must be premised on as rich an understanding of the phenomena in question as possible and that such understanding depends on a suspensive moment like that undertaken in good historical work.[15] As to the second charge, my word choice in "Gender, Agency, and the Divine in Religious Historiography," in which I urge scholars of religion to allow themselves to be "pierced" by the presumptions of those they study, is the subject of Pritchard's criticism and the Christian resonances of self-sacrifice are, perhaps, a little too strong. Yet while "challenged" might have done the trick argumentatively, it doesn't suffice affectively. The language of affect does not denote simply or primarily how I feel, as Pritchard seems to assume, but instead points to the complex interplay between how I affect those whom I encounter, they affect me, and what happens in our interactions. I am not looking for some kind of self-sacrificial *jouissance*, but instead trying to find a way to hear those whose voices are often unheard or muted into naturalistic, reasoned—in recognizable modes of Western rationality—speech.

This cuts to the heart of Pritchard's argument, for she insists that in "Gender, Agency, and the Divine in Religious Historiography" I renounce critique. (She is careful to note that the historian Dipesh Chakrabarty, with whose work I engage in the essay, does maintain the necessity of critique even as he asks what it would mean to occupy the time of those for whom the gods are active in history.) This is inaccurate, but in an interesting and a telling way. I do maintain the necessity of critique in the ways in which Chakrabarty uses the term; for Chakrabarty critique is essential to emancipatory political projects. But I also ask—and at that point it appears very much in the form of a question—whether religious practice and discourse might *themselves* be sites from which critique emanates. Unlike Chakrabarty, who suggests that critique is the result of a particular historical moment, in his case rendered in explicitly Marxist terms, I ask whether critical challenges to the way things are and creative hope for how the world might be—all fundamental, on my view, to critique—might not come from religion itself.

For not all critique is secular, nor is it always grounded in secular accounts of what constitutes reason. My views on the topic became clearer to me a number of years ago, when I was invited by Saba Mahmood to participate in the symposium "Is Critique Secular?" My most immediate response was that it was a provocative—and a provocatively stupid—question.[16] This is precisely why it is such a crucial one; hence also the importance of Pritchard's essay. A lot of people will think the answer to the question—"Is critique secular?"—is obvious. Yet whether that obvious answer is "no" or "yes" depends entirely on who is answering the question and what they take the terms "critique" and "secular" to mean, as well as how they understand religion. Many within the academy, as I suspected when I first approached the question and as subsequent commentary demonstrates, find the question redundant, presuming that critique is defined in terms of its secularity and vice versa.[17] For those who presume that critique is always the critique of something, that this something is associated with a putatively unquestioned authority, and that religion is, in its very nature, grounded in an unquestioned and unquestioning appeal to such an authority, critique and secularity are mutually interdependent phenomena.[18] One might even push this a step further and suggest that, for those who would answer the question "Is critique secular?"

with an unqualified "yes," the appeal to any authority other than reason is always, in some way, religious. From this perspective the transmutation of physical force into authority has been called theological or mystical, and hence has been seen as participating in an irrationality associated with religion.[19]

There are those, then, who insist that critique is antithetical to religion, given the putative rationality of the former and irrationality of the later. To these secularist critics of religion I find myself asking how anyone can possibly look at Christianity—just to give an example close to home—and claim that its practitioners do not engage in critique.[20] One can think very quickly of examples across the political spectrum, from the long history of Christian protest against war to Christian activism in pursuit of the repeal of *Rowe v. Wade*. And of course, there are Christians who embrace and make religious arguments for war and Christians who pursue the cause of women's reproductive freedom.[21] The diversity and complexity of Christian positions on any given topic render assumptions about what Christians, as a putative whole, think or do moot and my examples will seem painfully obvious to scholars of the tradition. Yet the lack of care with which many in the academy and beyond it discuss Christianity requires that the record be, continually, set straight. Moreover, a certain kind of secularist interlocutor might respond that the social, political, moral, and theoretical critique of authority leveled by Christians is always tendered either on grounds other than those specific to Christianity or on the unquestioned authority of Christianity itself. (Hence either with the help of a truly critical enterprise or, even worse, on uncritical grounds.) Yet the first assertion is false. Christians critique that which lies outside the domain of Christianity on the basis of specifically Christian claims all the time—this is precisely what bothers so many about Christianity in the contemporary United States.

To the second, one must ask what it means to talk about the authority of Christianity. The authority of the Bible, some might be tempted to reply. Yet there is not now nor has there ever been any agreement among Christians about what it means to speak of the authority of the Bible or even about what constitutes the Bible, to say nothing of what this contested entity tells Christians they ought to do or think (or even whether it does so and, if it does so, how). Some of the earliest Christian creedal formulations claim explicitly that the Bible is *not* the ultimate source of authority for Christians. (A number of other candidates are put forward, including the very formulae themselves—just the kind of putative circularity religion's contemporary despisers love to exploit. Note that I am not making any claim here for the rationality of Christian belief, but simply for its critical and self-critical capacities.) Every one of these issues has been and continues to be contested among those who call themselves Christians.

In other words, Christians continually critique Christianity and that which lies outside its boundaries. They constantly contest even what it means to be a Christian. And the same can be said for every other religion about which I know anything. It is difficult to see how a tradition could stay alive and vital without such contestation, however implicit and unremarked on it might be. As for the boundary between Christianity and the world, in the Latin West a distinction was made early on between the "city of God" and the "city of humanity," but Augustine, who most famously argues the point, insists that the former can never fully be known as long as we are residents in the latter.[22] For Augustine, the two can never be entirely disentangled in the present time (*saeculum*, the temporal realm, as opposed to the eternal, of which we only have obscure glimpses). What this means concretely is that Christians stand in a critical relationship to the temporal realm from the perspective of hope given in things as yet only dimly known, not from the standpoint of fully present and authoritative knowledge.[23] (There are, of course, Christians who will disagree, who claim that there is a self-evident and inerrant source of Christian teaching and that they know exactly what it is and what it demands. Some of those about whom I write in the following essays stand among this group, although far fewer than one might suppose. Furthermore, I am not a Christian and so might be judged by some incompetent to participate in the debate. Yet the Christian tradition and contemporary Christian practice—which do not always align with what contemporary Christians say about what they do—bear out my view.)[24]

Yet despite all of the evidence to the contrary, the position persists, even within the study of religion, that religion is inherently uncritical, authoritarian, and ideological. This is the primary assumption of those who insist that the study of religion purify itself of all theological remnants and that it be rigorously social scientific or historical. In an extremely helpful intervention, *Encountering Religion: Responsibility and Criticism After Secularism*, Tyler Roberts makes the cogent point that these arguments depend on a notion of religion as locative.[25] Roberts borrows the term from J. Z. Smith, who uses it to describe Mircea Eliade's understanding of religion as "affirming and repeating the basic order of the world, firmly locating or placing people by repressing the creativity of chaos, denying change, and stressing 'dwelling within a limited world.' "[26] Yet Roberts points out that Smith also offers another account of religion, for Smith distinguishes between a locative vision of religion, like that he finds in Eliade, and a utopian one. To cite Roberts once again, for Smith, "the second vision emphasizes rebellion against and freedom from established order. Smith calls it a 'utopian' vision of the world: where the locative vision focuses on place, the utopian affirms the value of being in no place. Both, he claims, are 'coeval existential possibilities.'"[27] According to Roberts, Smith's second understanding of religion shifts across the essays collected in *Map Is Not Territory* from utopian to liminal. Roberts is most compelled by Smith's account of religion as capable of engaging with disorder, incongruity, and excess; religion understood in this way, according to Roberts, "neither rejects one order for another nor revises an old order." It is "neither locative or utopian" but instead "relativizes *all* order."[28] The utopian and the excessive, I think, are very closely related, for the utopian rejection of an old order of necessity relativizes all order and the relativization of order can itself be understood as utopian. But Roberts's primary point—that religion operates in ways that are both locative and excessive—is enormously helpful in the context of contemporary debates in the study of religion.

Against those scholars of religion who assume that religion is always about order, stability, and authority, then, Roberts asks whether an overemphasis on "locative religion" has

> prevented us from pursuing more fully other questions: Can religious people play religiously? Can they recognize absurdity in and through their religious thought and practice and, if so, how? Do they always, necessarily, "speak" with transcendent and eternal authority when they speak of God or about their religious beliefs? Can they think critically when they think religiously? Finally, if so, where and how, exactly, do we draw the boundary between religion and the academic study of religion?[29]

My answer to these questions is obvious: of course religious people play religiously, recognize absurdity, and think critically while thinking religiously. The essays collected here show numerous examples of religious people doing precisely these things, all the while both claiming and subverting their own claims to transcendent and eternal authority in their talk about God. Roberts also uses the conception of religion as excessive, as unsettling boundaries, norms, and authorities, to show that locative accounts of religion are inadequate to their object and that forms of critique embraced by many locativists can be found among religious people, even theologians. (His favorite example here is Rowan Williams, who continually emphasizes the need for humility in claims about God and the nature of reality.)[10] This is a vital contribution to the study of religion, for it enables scholars to articulate the different ways in which religious texts, practices, and communities work, and to see and name the vast array of sometimes discordant things that religions do.

I also agree with Roberts's assertion that the study of religion can and should be not only descriptive, but also constructive. (This is not to say that every scholar of religion will bring together the various aspects of its study, but instead that constructive theological and philosophical work is properly part of the study of religion and cannot and should not be ejected from the conversation.) To this end, Roberts turns to the work of Hent de Vries, Eric Santner, and Stanley Cavell to think through what an "affirmative criticism" might entail. There are powerful accounts of responsibility, responsiveness, and gratitude in these pages, all of which speak to our work as scholars and to the broader question of how we might best live. The pages on Cavell and gratitude are particularly important, yet they are also the most distant from religion. Perhaps more crucially, Roberts embraces de Vries's conception of philosophy itself as a form of "minimal theology," a "restless wakefulness" and "infinite responsibility" in which thought is always in excess of itself.[31] Although Roberts deploys Santner and Cavell in an attempt to overcome the seemingly hopeless and unending task of critique to which we are enjoined by de Vries, the resources for doing so come primarily from outside of religion.[32] This leads to the unfortunate implication, surely not what Roberts intends, that the only religion useful to the secular critic is excessive and destabilizing. Religion as locative, as providing a space in which to live and to breath, has once again effectively been banished; it is here that I would like to press on and expand Roberts's argument.

With Roberts, we seem to be far from those who insist that critique is, of necessity, secular, since for both de Vries and Roberts, religion, at its best, *is* critique. What de Vries and Roberts share with secular advocates of critique is an understanding of critique as always destabilizing and unsettling. De Vries, Roberts, and secular advocates of critique may dispute the role theology and religion play in critique, but they come from the same lineage of Western thought. The critics of Christianity most often cited as the source of contemporary Western philosophical conceptions of critique—Immanuel Kant, Ludwig Feuerbach, Karl Marx, and Friedrich Nietzsche, among others—all understood Christianity itself as a vital *source* of the impulse toward critique. A presumption runs through parts of the modern European philosophical tradition that the self-critical nature of Christianity leads—or will lead—to the radical revision of Christianity or to its dissolution (and, with it, the dissolution of all religion). (This final turn of the screw appears most explicitly in Feuerbach, Nietzsche, and Sigmund Freud. John Locke and Immanuel Kant, for example, had no intention of dissolving Christianity, which both of them believed to be congruent with rational claims.) Embedded here are assertions of both the supremacy of Christianity (sometimes Judaism instead or as well) over all other religious traditions and an association of Christianity with the emergent secular realm, one in which rational argument is said to take the place of irrational faith. (In the terms provided by Augustine, then, Christian self-critique leads to the recognition that all we have is the temporal [*saeculum*]; there is no eternal realm and it is irrational to believe that there is.) Christianity, according to this account, is both irrational and the ground out of which rationality emerges.

In one version of this argument, the secular looks a lot like liberal Protestant Christianity—sometimes shorn of its explicitly Christian trappings, sometimes not. Irrational, authoritarian, bad Christianity is then identified with Roman Catholicism and, often, the radical reformation. Since the early modern period, the battle has also been staged as one between irrational fanaticism (Catholics again are among the chief culprits) and rational belief. Yet regardless of the distinctions made—between rationality and fanaticism, paganism and true religion, Protestantism and Roman Catholicism—a paradox remains at the center of some of the most influential modern accounts of the dissolution of religion, for in Feuerbach, Marx, Nietzsche, and Freud somehow the irrational begets the rational. On this account, critique is *both* secular and theological, for religion (or at least Christianity) gives rise to—even fuels—that which stands in opposition to it.[33]

Despite the desire that rational discourse be undertaken in a spirit of calm and order, modern Western rationality bears within it the marks of a purificatory fervor. (Roberts sees this clearly in his uneasy alliance with de Vries.) In its endless demands, critique is itself fanatical. From this standpoint, a certain implacability is visible even in Mahmood's capacious account of what constitutes critique. Mahmood urges "an expansion of . . . normative understandings of critique." Whereas on the old view criticism "is about successfully demolishing your opponent's position and exposing the implausibility of her argument and its logical inconsistencies," she argues that "critique . . . is most powerful when it leaves open the possibility that we might also be remade in the process of engaging with another's worldview, that we might come to learn things that we did not already know before we undertook the engagement. This requires that we occasionally turn the critical gaze upon ourselves, to leave open the possibility that we may be remade through an encounter with the other."[34] Note here that critique as critique of something does not disappear, but instead is turned against one's own presuppositions. I stand by my assertion that the move is essential to contemporary political and cultural criticism, and yet, from whence this relentlessness? Are there times when critique, understood as a form of intellectual, political, and ethical—dare I say religious—ascesis, is not enough?

Roberts, who follows de Vries in positing a theological and religious origin for the relentlessly destabilizing force of critique, turns to philosophy for remedy and respite. Within this context, religion is most compelling as critical and excessive, less so as locative; the two aspects of religion seem at odds with each other in ways Roberts does not fully explore.[35] What I want to suggest here is that a different deployment of the concept of excess, one that draws directly on the work of the philosopher Jacques Derrida as well as on the Christian tradition, might help us think about the relationship between the locative and the critical aspects of religion in fresh ways. Religion might then be understood as providing rich resources with which to do the work of responsive criticism in which Roberts is interested.

For Roberts reading de Vries reading Derrida, "the religious exceeds the historical" in the very process of handing down, that is, of tradition itself:

> One responds to the past, as tradition or heritage, in a repetition that, if it is to be responsible, is faithful to the past even as it exceeds and betrays it in a performance of singularity, an "event" of "irreducible prescriptivity." Such testimony involves a complex performative, or a "perveraformative," speech act that is both a following of or adhering to *and* a perversion of this past, a faithful interpretation and a singular invention.[36]

There are at least two problems with this account in addition to the worry Roberts himself has with its purely negative conception of critique and responsibility. (Again this worry runs parallel to my own concern about the relentlessness of critique.) First, de Vries's reading of Derrida is one-sided in much the same way that locativist readings of religion are one-sided, although what is emphasized and what is ignored differ. Whereas the locativist takes religion as solely upholding order, stability, and authority, de Vries finds religion of value only in its excessive, destabilizing, antiauthoritarian form. The move is premised on a reading of Derrida in which the claim that repetition always involves both sameness and difference (this is the movement of what Derrida calls differance, in which spatial and temporal otherness is recognized as intrinsic to repetition itself) is understood as perversion and infidelity.

Yet in Derrida's work from the 1960s, differance is not marked by perversion and infidelity—or if it is, it is a perversion and an infidelity that Derrida embraces. Across his corpus, moreover, he insists that tradition exists because of the human capacity to repeat, whether linguistic signs, visual images, or bodily practices.³⁷ As I argue in "Performativity, Citationality, Ritualization," included here, for Derrida repetition always entails both sameness (a practice must be sufficiently like other practices to be recognizable as the same practice) and different (the practice, to be repeated, occurs in a different time and place than other instances of its enactment).³⁸ The difference internal to repetition both enables a tradition to be handed down and requires that it change, whether that change is recognized or not. Only if we believe that we can know the absolute origin of signification—a term I use here in its broadest possible sense to include practices and images as well as language—can we be said to betray a tradition and our responsibilities to it merely through the act of repetition itself.³⁹ But Derrida argues forcefully that we can never know a pure origin; this is something about which a large part of the Christian tradition agrees with Derrida.

As Roberts notes in his use of Rowan Williams's work, many if not most Christians insist we can never know God with fullness or surety. (For some we can never have this knowledge while living; for others, we will never have it; and for a very few, those, not surprisingly, most interesting to Derrida, it is possible that God Godself does not know God.) The unsaying of the names of God— what the sixth-century Syriac monk who goes under the name of Dionysius the Areopagite first called apophasis—marks the recognition that all human concepts and practices are inadequate to the divine.⁴⁰ God is without limits and so escapes all our attempts to know God. Derrida spent a considerable amount of energy pointing to the similarities and emphasizing the differences between his work and that of apophasis.⁴¹ What is of most interest to me here, however, is that for Dionysius, as for the Christian tradition as a whole, apophasis always comes together with what Dionysius called cataphasis, the saying or naming of God. For Dionysius, cataphasis and apophasis are two moments in the movement toward God, two moments that together constitute Christianity. Until something has been ascribed *of* God, we cannot unsay it; without some conception of God's goodness or being or love, we cannot move to the claim that God is beyond goodness or being or love, or that God is unbounded goodness or being or love, or that God's goodness or being or love is so unlimited that we cannot think it within human conceptions of these attributes.

There is no "apophatic theology" within Christianity, then, but only the interplay between cataphasis and apophasis. Some emphasize one movement over the other. Some bury or forget the one movement in favor of the other. Yet when this happens, the *liveness* of the tradition—its very capacity to signify and to be handed down—is in danger.[42] Arguably this is the problem with much academic theology at the moment, whether it be Christian or post-Christian, an ugly term that I take to mean secular philosophers and theologians deeply influenced by the Christian tradition, not unlike myself; too many insist that theology be solely cataphatic or solely apophatic. In the first instance, the tradition is idolized and becomes a dead and inert thing; in the second, all ties to a living tradition of practice and faith are lost and with them the vitality of human life within those traditions. (There are enormous problems with the very language of this claim, grounded as it is in the Christian dismissal of non-Christian religions as idolatrous and the refusal to recognize other religions as worshiping anything other than dead and inert things. One of the most crucial tasks before us now is to find language with which to name the liveness of a tradition and whatever the opposite of that liveness might be. The language most likely will not be new in some absolute sense, but handed down from traditions other than Christianity.)[43]

Santner and Cavell, on Roberts's reading, both point to the possibility of a secular theology or philosophy of religion in which we look to the everyday world and our critical engagements with it as the site of theological and existential meaning. As I suggested above, in many ways my own work is moving in just that direction. Yet because Roberts is intent on following out a certain kind of philosophical argument, he remains focused on abstractions; from whence do we receive the concrete traditions that enable us to live? Santner and Cavell turn to psychoanalysis, literature, and film as sites for reflection on how we might live;[44] for many people, literature, music, film, television, and the visual arts *are* their tradition—and the source of its unsettling. Yet the resources of Christianity and Judaism, as of many other religions, are also available to us if we can find ways to keep them alive, even in—always necessarily in—beautifully altered forms.

This leads to my second worry about Roberts's argument, which is that what is truly excessive within religion may be lost. (Above I posited this in terms of a question about whether naturalizing humanistic accounts of religion, like the one Roberts ultimately embraces, are adequate to their object.) One way to read my understanding of the cataphatic and the apophatic into Roberts's work is to argue that the cataphatic is locative and the apophatic excessive. In terms of Derrida's understanding of signification, the cataphatic and the locative would be that which remains the same in the act of repetition, whereas the apophatic and the excessive would be the movement of difference. Yet I am uneasy with these analogies even as I make them. I am not at all sure that the cataphatic naming of God and of worlds is purely locative or the apophatic purely destabilizing, for the distinction between cataphasis and apophasis, unlike that between the locative and the excessive, does not depend on their opposition. Instead, the two work in relationship to each other; the one always requires the other. Put in Derridean terms, you cannot repeat without both sameness and difference. Hence the importance of Derrida's neologism, differance, which entails *both* sameness and difference, naming and unnaming, fidelity and infidelity—or better, fidelity *as* infidelity. (Derrida's inability or refusal to properly understand the interplay between the cataphatic and the apophatic fuels his own agonized relationship to Christianity in particular and religion in general.)

Derrida's writing from at least the 1980s until his death, work in which he worries about singularity, rests on his recognition that what is released in the interplay between sameness and difference is irreducible to any particular instantiation of signification or to its general movement. Both history and philosophy, insofar as they are governed by the logic of the particular and the general (and hence of the generalizable), are inadequate to the experience of the gift, of givenness, of grace. Yet this does not mean that we can stop trying to name what we receive, what we value, and what we desire. We can never free ourselves from our debts, yet we can work to understand them and to live in the space of creative transformation that is the intertwined tasks of tradition and critique, of tradition as critique and as always irreducible to critique.

For the real and the true are not determined only through the process of critique as it has been understood within the modern West; finding and creating the real and the true, articulating when they converge and when they diverge, demand attention to the interplay between sameness and difference so vital to the handing down, acceptance, and rejection of tradition. To do this work we need to be willing to listen, to hear, and to try to understand what is; to articulate how what is and what was and what will be are always intertwined, even as our political and moral commitments may require us to disentangle them; and to recognize that there are aspects of human experience we will never fully capture, never fully understand, never fully name. (A different kind of thinker than I am might call this grace.) We always and inevitably receive what is handed down, whether religious practices, philosophical texts, or *Double Indemnity* (my mother used to make me watch it with her when I was far too small to know what it was about). If we are very, very lucky—extraordinarily lucky—we are given worlds in which we can thrive. Yet our reception of tradition is always also a critical engagement with it, and it is that gap—the gap between what is handed down and what is received—that makes life possible *and* that makes possible the more robust and self-conscious forms of critique on which most of our lives and any livable future depend. Critique emerges as a self-conscious modality in those moments when we realize that we occupy the world differently—or desire to occupy the world differently—than at least some part of the traditions into which we have been born demand.[45] (The multiplicity of tradition is also in play here, for there is always, of necessity, more than one way of being handed down, hence opening further the space to live differently and to live in critical relationship to the traditions that form us.)

The essays collected here all, in one way or another, touch on my preoccupation with the real, the true, and critique; they explore the ways in which we make real the worlds in which we live; they attempt to demonstrate the inescapably intertwined work of imagination and critique through which we create and discover the true. In the second panel of this triptych, I will return to Henry Adams and to the question of the real as it preoccupied him at the turn of the last century. Adams was a master critic, often overwhelmed by the annihilatory power of critical reason, which is fundamentally tied to melancholy. His work and life are full of crypts in which he attempts both to keep alive and to cover over a now-dead reality. After exploring the complexity of Henry Adams's relationship to Christianity and to religion, in the triptych's third panel I will argue that the emphasis on trauma as the site of the real at the turn of *our* century marks particular, often unspoken, assumptions about what is real and what is true. The late-nineteenth- and early-twentieth-century pursuit of the real, then, a pursuit in which Adams was one of the most vital players, can be seen reenacted in the late twentieth century in related yet new ways. Through the engagement with a medieval text that has been read in terms of hysteria and trauma, I will ask about the limitations of these contemporary preoccupations, posing the question of whether joy might also be a site of the real, as Adams hoped it might be. The question, then, is whether this is a joy we can recapture—or perhaps better, one that contemporary political and ethical concerns, including the politics of academic discourse, can allow or enable us to name, even to celebrate and explore.

This opening triptych lays out the issues of crucial concern across the volume. The second essay turns to a reflection on how God is made real in late medieval religious practice and in contemporary life, even as I suggest that the ability to make God real does not mean God is necessarily a human construction. (I return to these questions in part 4.) The essays in part 2 focus most explicitly on the historiographical issues around reality and truth, particularly as they are raised in the study of medieval women's religious writings. My contention here and throughout the book is that these texts offer particularly useful sites for reflecting on reality, truth, and critique precisely because these issues are, in ways not often recognized, explicitly thematized within them.

Part 3 is also about the writing of history and the question of what is real, here with a focus on the issue of sexuality in medieval mystical and devotional texts. The historiographical questions that frame the essays and the very brief essay that stands between them focus less directly on the realness of the objects of religious experience than on the realness of experiences of desire, pleasure, and *jouissance* with and in those others. If we say that the experiences described or enacted in medieval texts are real, where do we locate that reality in relationship to sex, sexed and sexualized bodies, sexed and sexualized psyches, and perhaps—what this might mean is precisely the issue—sexed and sexualized souls? Finally the essays in part 4 are more theoretically and philosophically oriented attempts to think about what it means to say that bodily and spiritual practices constitute, at least in part, the complex worlds in which we live. I argue in these essays that ritualized practices are performative—that they make real that which they enact. Yet at the same time, I do not think that the performative force of ritualized practice can be taken as resolving ontological claims. Monastic and other forms of devotional practice in the Middle Ages are premised precisely on the view that God is ontologically distinct from and preexistent to humans and yet, at the same time, that God can be made palpable, experiential, present, even overwhelming—in a word, real—to those who engage in certain types of practice. These issues lead into the single essay in part 5, in which I lay out the history of allegorical readings of Luke 10:38–42, the story of Mary and Martha, as the prelude to a reading of Meister Eckhart's decidedly novel engagement with the Lukan passage and the accepted forms of allegoresis that he inherited as a preacher, biblical commentator, and university-trained theologian. The question Eckhart poses, once again, is what it means for a reading or a set of religious claims or an experience to be real, what it means for them to be true, what it means to engage with the other that is history. It asks, finally, whether there are moments in which our responsibility to history fades in the face of our responsibilities to one another, living, now.

Many of the questions I pose in these essays cannot be definitively answered, at least not by me. The relationships between them, the persistence of a line of questioning that is always a little ahead of itself, never entirely sure at what moment to retreat and when to press forward, only become visible when they are read together. At the same time, almost all were written within specific contexts, in response to particular scholarly conversations and intellectual demands. I think that the framework of each essay is vital to how they are read as a whole. They appear here with only the most pressing of corrections attended to and little substantive revision of my arguments. As is inevitably the case with work produced over a twenty-year period—and by someone as dogged as myself—some material is repeated across the essays, most notably key moments in the writing of and about Beatrice of Nazareth, Marguerite Porete, Margaret Ebner, and the contemporary historian Caroline Walker Bynum. I think the passages do different work in each of the essays, however, and will allow the repetitions to stand.

The essays presented here remain, of necessity, fragmented. I see them—individually and as a whole—as part of conversations in the study of religion, philosophy, theology, medieval studies, and feminist and queer studies. The work has a persistent eye on issues of sex, gender, and sexuality in ways that I hope will make it useful to feminist and queer scholars across a broad array of disciplines. I begin and end with texts central to the Christian mystical tradition. One of my ongoing goals is to bring these diverse, daring, and, often, dangerous texts into conversation with what, for lack of a better word, I will call the present.

Henry Adams, Clover Adams, and the Death of the Real

Shortly before his death in 1910, the artist John La Farge gave an interview with Gustav Kobbe of the *Evening Star* (Monday, January 17, 1910). He famously describes his friend and traveling companion, Henry Adams, commissioning the sculptor Augustus Saint Gaudens to make a Memorial for the grave of Adams's late wife, Marian Hooper Adams, known by her family and friends as Clover. (See figure 0.1.)

In 1886, shortly after La Farge and Adams had returned from a trip to Japan, Adams approached Saint Gaudens. According to La Farge,

0.1 *The Mystery of the Hereafter and the Peace of God that Passeth Understanding.*
Augustus Saint Gaudens, ca. 1890. From the memorial to Marian "Clover" Hooper
Adams, Rock Creek Cemetery, Washington, D.C. Photo credit: Jerry L. Thompson/
Art Resource, N.Y.

Mr. Adams described to him [Saint Gaudens] in a general way what he wanted,
going, however, into no details, and really giving him no distinct clue, save the
explanation that he wished the figure to symbolize "the acceptance, intellectually, of the inevitable." Saint Gaudens immediately became interested, and
made a gesture indicating the pose which Mr. Adams' words had suggested in

his mind. "No," said Mr. Adams, "the way that you're doing that is a Penseroso." Thereupon the sculptor made several other gestures until one of them struck Mr. Adams as corresponding with the idea. As good luck would have it, he would not wait for a woman model to be brought in and posed in accordance with the gesture indicated by the sculptor, so Saint Gaudens grabbed the Italian boy who was mixing clay, put him into the pose, and draped a blanket over him. That very blanket, it may be stated here, is on the statue, and forms the drapery of the figure. "Now that's done," said Mr. Adams, "the pose is settled. Go to La Farge about any original ideas of Kwannon. I don't want to see the statue till it's finished."[46]

Of course, Adams did intervene further, both at this meeting and subsequently. He asked on that day that Saint Gaudens consider not only Buddhist devotional art, but also photographs of Michelangelo's Sistine Chapel, in particular the mother of Jesse. (See figure 0.2.)

0.2 The mother of Jesse, depicted on the ceiling of the Sistine Chapel, Rome. Michelangelo, 1508–12. Photo credit: Scala/Art Resource, N.Y.

Saint Gaudens's notebook record of the meeting is suitably telegraphic: "Adams. Buhda. Mental Repose. Calm reflection in contrast with the violence or force in nature." He added a sketch showing a seated figure posed facing front, with the legs slightly ajar. The word "reflect" appears again on the other side of the sketch.[47] In 1891, Saint Gaudens's sculpture, which he apparently liked to call "The Mystery of the Hereafter and the Peace of God That Passeth All Understanding," was erected at Rock Creek Cemetery in what is now Northwest Washington, D.C., with an architectural setting designed by Stanford White. The bronze figure of a seated, hooded figure stands over six feet tall. Adams was in the South Seas, again with La Farge, but received favorable reports from friends. When he returned to Washington in February 1892, he immediately went to see it.

Although what is most often noted by scholars and guidebooks is the references to Buddhist images of Kannon (Japanese) or Guan Yin (Chinese), the female Buddha of Compassion, Adams's immediate response on seeing the monument was to write that "Saint Gaudens is not the least Oriental and is not even familiar with Oriental conceptions." He later decided that this didn't matter—"The whole meaning and feeling of the figure is its universality." Yet as we have seen, Adams himself had pointed Saint Gaudens not only to Japanese images of Kannon, but also to medieval and Renaissance figures. La Farge seems to have taken Saint Gaudens to see an early sixteenth-century Kannon, given by the Orientalist Ernest Fenellosa to the Boston collector Charles Goddard Weld and on display at Boston's Museum of Fine Arts. (Although still owned by the museum, it is not currently on display.) (See figure 0.3.)

Saint Gaudens was also familiar with late medieval funerary sculpture, which resonates powerfully with the Adams Memorial, despite Henry Adams's own desire that the statue not bring grief to mind. (He objected strenuously to those, among them Mark Twain, who so dubbed it the "Memorial." Twain called it, simply, "Grief"). So Saint Gaudens's image calls to mind the exquisite mourning figures (*pleurant*) made by Jean de la Huerta and Antoine le Moiturier for the tomb of John the Fearless (1371–1419), the second Duke of Burgandy, and his wife, Margaret of Bavaria, and the more widely seen, albeit less accomplished, figures from the tomb of Philippe Pot, Lord of La Roche-Pot. (See figures 0.4 and 0.5.) One cannot help but also see in the Memorial Michelangelo Madonnas: the Bruges Madonna of 1501–05; the late Medici Madonna of 1524–34; and, what again would no doubt arouse strenuous objections from Henry Adams, the *Pietà* of 1499. (The Adams Memorial resembles nothing more than the *Pietà* without Christ.) (See figures 0.6, 0.7, and 0.8.)

0.3 *White-robed Bodhisattva of Compassion.* Kano Motonobu, Muromachi period,
first half of the sixteenth century, Japan. Museum of Fine Arts, Boston. Fenellosa-Weld
Collection, 1911. Photograph © Museum of Fine Arts, Boston.

0.4 Mourners (*Pleurant*), from the Tomb of John the Fearless and Margaret of Bavaria. Jean de la Huerta and Antoine le Moiturier, 1443–1445. Musée des Beaux-Arts, Dijon, France. Photo credit: Gianni Dagli Orti/Art Archive at Art Resource, N.Y.

0.5 The Tomb of Philippe Pot, Lord of La Roche-Pot. Late 15th century. Musée du Louvre, Paris. Photo credit: akg-images.

0.6 *Madonna of Bruges*. Michelangelo, 1501–05. Onze Lieve Vrouwekerk, Bruges. Photo credit: akg-images.

0.7 *Medici Madonna.* Michelangelo, 1524–34. On the tombs of the dukes Giuliano de'
Medici and Lorenzo de' Medici. Sagrestia Nuova, Basilica of San Lorenzo, Florence.

0.8 *Pietà*. Michelangelo, 1499. Basilica of San Pietro, Vatican City.

Perhaps because Adams did not begin his systematic study of medieval art, particularly the Marian imagery of Chartres, until after Clover Adams's death and the completion of the monument, many do not mention the medievalism of the memorial, even as they associate Henry's medievalist turn in *Mont Saint Michel and Chartres* and *The Education of Henry Adams* with his intense mourning in the face of Clover's seemingly senseless suicide. (Clover poisoned herself with potassium cyanide, a chemical she had on hand as a photographer. It is perhaps worth mentioning that *Mont Saint Michel and Chartres* continually refers to photographs—and never to Clover. Nor does *The Education of Henry Adams*, in which Henry quietly passes over his years with her.) These late works are often read in isolation from Henry's other writing and seen as marking a new turn in his thinking, away from the history of the United States from Jefferson to Madison, his commentaries on contemporary political life, and his novels. Yet the attraction to Buddhism and to Kannon or Guan Yin begins before Clover Adams's death and in connection with Adams's interest in diplomatic efforts in the Far East, and it is intimately related to his travels to the Far East and return to medieval Europe after her death. (He had, of course, taught medieval history at Harvard in the 1870s.)

One can better understand what Adams wanted from the Memorial when it is seen against the background of nineteenth-century American Christianity. Describing the Laurel Hill Cemetery in Philadelphia, like Rock Creek a privately owned enterprise, the historian of American religion Colleen McDannell points to the ubiquity not only of non-Christian symbols from Egypt, Greece, and Rome, but also of Christian symbols—the cross, the book, and the angel. As McDannell notes, "A popular marker for graves at Laurel Hill and other Victorian cemeteries was a statue of a robed woman draping her arm around a cross or mournfully leaning against it." (See figure 0.9.) According to McDannell, the image is not biblical, but comes from the most popular Victorian hymn, found in hymnals in every Christian denomination (even a Catholic one)—"Rock of Ages."[48] From a medievalist's perspective, the image is deeply biblical, as the hymn makes clear. Based on a poem by the Anglican priest Augustus Montague Toplady from 1776 and set to music in 1830 by Thomas Hasting, it is rife with biblical language and images:

Rock of Ages, cleft for me,
Let me hide myself in Thee;
Let the water and the blood,
From Thy wounded side which flowed,
Be of sin the double cure,
Save from wrath and make me pure.

Nothing in my hand I bring,
Simply to Thy cross I cling;
Naked, come to Thee for dress;
Helpless, look to Thee for grace;
Foul, I to the fountain fly;
Wash me, Savior, or I die.

While I draw this fleeting breath,
When my eyes shall close in death,
When I rise to worlds unknown,
And behold Thee on Thy throne,
Rock of Ages, cleft for me,
Let me hide myself in Thee.[49]

Henry Adams, as a student of medieval Christianity, would have recognized the tropes—if they can even be described as such. Bernard of Clairvaux in his sixty-first sermon on the Song of Songs comments on verse 2:14—"My dove in the clefts of the rock." Bernard follows Cassiodorus and Gregory the Great in understanding the clefts in the rock as the wounds of Christ. "And quite correctly," Bernard adds, "for Christ is the rock" (1 Cor 10:4).[50] One could go on—certainly the image of the soul or the believer clinging to the cross is ubiquitous in the high and late Middle Ages, as in this devotional image, generated through a complex interweaving of biblical and extrabiblical sources, from around 1300.

But that is not really my point. My point is that this image—of a woman clinging to the cross, with its implicit feminization of Christianity and its promise of a familial immortality—stands in stark contrast to Saint Gaudens's Memorial. Moreover, as I will show, the version of Christianity depicted in the hymn is precisely the one Henry Adams has his character, Esther, reject in the 1884 novel that bears her name. Again, McDannell is helpful here, aptly describing nineteenth-century American Protestant conceptions of the afterlife—found in

0.9 Funerary statue from Laurel Hill Cemetery, Philadelphia. Figure 79 in Colleen
McDannell, *Material Christianity: Religion and Popular Culture in America* (New Haven:
Yale University Press, 1995). Courtesy of the author.

religious tracts, hymns, novels, funerary monuments, photographs, and a variety of other cultural forms—as a "continuation and perfection of what made this life good." For the affluent nineteenth-century Protestants who populated cemeteries like that at Laurel Hill, Rock Creek, and Mount Auburn, this meant "love, family, friendship, work, progress, conversation—all these familiar earthly involvements continued in the next life."[51] The cemetery was a site of memorialization, but also one of pilgrimage, a pilgrimage on which the living came to see representations of their loved ones—or is it the loved ones themselves?—in the bucolic and familial space and place of the afterlife.

The natural setting of the Adams Memorial in Rock Creek Cemetery is very like that found in cemeteries throughout the nineteenth century, which were designed to evoke the beauties of the afterlife.[52] Yet the Adams Memorial bears no name, there is no cross and no child, and little to evoke a familial afterlife. In discussing the memorial with Saint Gaudens and with friends, Henry disavows the peculiarly American conception of heaven. The pilgrims to Rock Creek—and there were many in the years following the Memorial's erection—were not meant, Henry insists, to find meaning there.

Again, we see the full force of the forms of Christianity rejected by Henry Adams in *Esther*, written before the death of Clover's father, her final depression, and her suicide.[53] Henry's novel was published without any publicity and under the pseudonym Frances Snow Compton.[54] He explained to friends that he was interested in how a novel might make its way in the world without advertisement and without a famous name attached to it. Yet the uncanny resemblance between the title character and Clover Adams raises questions as to Henry's true motives. Esther's restless skepticism, her thwarted artistic ambitions, and her intense love of her father can all be seen in Clover Adams. Read in this way, the novel's depiction of Esther's overwhelming despair in the face of the death of a beloved father seems both uncanny and cruel.[55] At the same time, it is through Esther's despair that Henry Adams voices his own fear of submission to any creed, his rejection of Christianity, and his simultaneous attraction to and repulsion from alternative conceptions of the infinite.[56] (Aspects of Henry can, of course, be seen in a number of the novel's characters.)

Esther is an example of both a thwarted marriage plot and of the Victorian novel of doubt.[57] Unlike other fictional and autobiographical protagonists within this literature, Esther never has faith; she struggles to attain it only because of her love for the clergyman, Stephen Hazard. (Hazard is a thinly veiled version of Henry Adams's second cousin, Philips Brooks, rector of Boston's Trinity

Church.) The novel depicts Esther at the moment she finds herself confronted with a Christianity that she cannot accept, a form of Christianity made, so the narrative tells us, as attractive and intellectually rigorous as possible by the intellectual, aesthetically sophisticated Hazard. Esther cannot reconcile herself to being a clergyman's wife without sharing his faith. She listens to Hazard's sermons, she reads theology, she questions him and all of those around her, but she cannot believe. In the closing pages of the novel, against the vivid background of the Niagara Falls, Esther and Hazard engage in the dispute that will end their relationship.[58] Esther's fear that she will give in to Hazard is likened to a suicidal leap into the abyss of the falls.

> She sat some moments silent while he gazed into her face, and her eyes wandered out to the gloomy and cloud-covered cataract. She felt herself being swept over it. Whichever way she moved, she had to look down into the abyss and leap.
>
> "Spare me!" she said at last. "Why should you drive and force me to take this leap? Are all men so tyrannical with women? You do not quarrel with a man because he cannot give his whole life."
>
> "I own it!" said Hazard warmly. "I am tyrannical! I want your whole life, and even more. I will be put off with nothing else. Didn't you see that I can't retreat. Put yourself in my place! Think how you would act if you loved me as I love you!"[59]

Hazard insists that in his love for Esther and his duty to the church, he must win both her love and her soul. "You are," he insists, "trembling on the verge of what I think destruction. If I saw you tossing on the rapids yonder, at the edge of the fall, I could not be more eager to save you."[60] Yet for Esther, to submit to Hazard's Christianity would itself entail a suicidal submission. "She fancied," Adams writes, "that the thunders of the church were already rolling over her head, and that her mind was already slowly shutting itself up under the checks of its new surroundings."[61] Esther must save the self she simultaneously claims to despise.

At the heart of Esther's disbelief lies the doctrine of the resurrection.

> "Do you really believe in the resurrection of the body?" she asked.
>
> "Of course I do!" replied Hazard stiffly.
>
> "To me it seems a shocking idea. I despise and loathe myself, and yet you thrust self at me from every corner of the church as though I loved and

admired it. All religion does nothing but pursue me with self even into the next world."[61]

It is not simply that Esther cannot believe in the resurrection of the body, but that the very idea of such a resurrection is horrible to her. She despises and loathes herself and so despises and loathes a Christianity whose highest aspiration is that the self should live eternally. Esther "can see nothing spiritual in the church. It is all personal and selfish."

Hazard is appalled by Esther's response, not because of its self-hatred, but because it implies that she hates those around her. He has, he tells her, heard all of the criticism leveled against Christianity. He believes that it hits on nothing vital. The one thing that is essential, the one point on which he cannot brook disagreement with Esther, regardless of their love for each other, is familial love and the desire for reunion it, for him at least, necessarily entails. "You say the idea of the resurrection is shocking to you. Can you, without feeling still more shocked, think of a future existence where you will not meet once more father or mother, husband or children? surely the natural instincts of your sex must save you from such a creed!"[63] Women's putatively natural instincts should, Hazard suggests, triumph over self-doubt; their love for others should lead them to desire the other's eternal life; most crucially, Esther's love for *him* should enable her not only to submit to him and his beliefs but to desire that they be true.

> "Ah!" cried Esther, almost fiercely, and blushing crimson, as though Hazard this time had pierced the last restraint on her self control: "Why must the church always appeal to my weakness and never to my strength! I ask for spiritual life and you send me back to my flesh and blood as though I were a tigress you were sending back to her cubs. What is the use of appealing to my sex? the atheists at least show me respect enough not to do that!"[64]

Esther refuses to be tied down by the expectations for her sex; she refuses what she sees as the reduction of women to the bodily and the familial. But even more, she refuses the conception of the human on which Hazard's arguments rest. She wants the spirit, and the spirit—what she calls her strength—cannot thrive within the conceptions of resurrection and redemption that appeal to her love for other human beings.

Buddhism, at least as Henry understood it, lurks here, for Esther desires a spiritual life that is an escape from the confines not only of the flesh, but also of the self. In his conversation with Saint Gaudens about the memorial for Clover, Henry insists that the statue evoke an acceptance of the inevitable, which is for him the essence of Buddhism.[65] Neither joyful nor mourning, the statue, in its putative universality, is at peace. Again, *Esther*, written before Clover's death, gives some indication of what Henry was looking for after that sad event. Esther's first encounter with Niagara Falls does not evoke the fear of submission and submersion articulated in her final discussion with Hazard. Instead, for Esther, the Falls were a "tremendous, rushing, roaring companion, which thundered and smoked under her window as though she had tamed a tornado to play." In a steady, frank, and sympathetic voice, it "rambled on with its story."[66]

> She fell in love with the cataract and turned to it as a confidant, not because of its beauty and power, but because it seemed to tell her a story which she longed to understand. "I think I do understand it," she said to herself as she looked out. "If he could only hear it as I do," and of course "he" was Mr. Hazard; "how he would feel it!" She felt tears roll down her face as she listened to the voice of the waters and knew that they were telling her a different secret from any that Hazard could ever hear. "He will think it is the church talking!"[67]

For Esther, the Falls are better than any sermon; they mock any sermon, as Esther herself mocks Hazard's sermons throughout the novel. "When eternity, infinity and omnipotence seem to be laughing and dancing in one's face," how can one worry about love affairs or the paltry claims of Christianity?

The extent of Esther's submission to the eternity, infinity, and omnipotence of the Falls becomes clear in a conversation she has with her cousin and friend, the paleontologist George Strong, just before her final encounter with Hazard. In her attempt to make sense of religion, she repeatedly asks Strong what he believes. (Strong is loosely based on Adams's close and intensely idealized friend Clarence King.) He evades the question for much of the novel, not wanting to take it or Esther's compunction about marrying Hazard too seriously. (Strong, in fact, tries not to take anything too seriously.) Finally, at the Falls, Strong makes a bid to be true to his own beliefs and to attempt to help Hazard's cause. "There is evidence amounting to strong probability," he tells Esther, "of the existence of two things," namely "mind and matter." This does not render belief in the future moot, Strong insists. "If our minds could get hold of one abstract truth," he explains, "they would be immortal so far as that truth is concerned."[68] Strong argues that the only difference between his view and Hazard's is that he does not believe he has yet gotten hold of a single bit of truth, whereas Hazard insists the church contains it. As the historian Jackson Lears points out in his reading of *Esther*, the ensuing exchange is crucial. Esther asks,

> "Does your idea mean that the next world is a sort of great reservoir of truth, and that what is true in us just pours into it like raindrops?"
>
> "Well!" said he, alarmed and puzzled: "the figure is not perfectly correct, but the idea is a little of that kind."
>
> "After all I wonder whether that may not be what Niagara has been telling me!" said Esther, and she spoke with an outburst of energy that made Strong's blood run cold.[69]

As Lears notes, late Victorian Orientalist conceptions of Nirvana often use the image of a drop of water dissolved into an ocean to evoke the loss of the self into the all. (Earlier in the novel, Nirvana is evoked by the painter Wharton as paradise and eternal life, a state of peace attained after passion has been experienced and subdued.)[70] Lears argues that Henry rejects this view, a reading suggested by Strong's repellant response to Esther's energetic embrace of the idea of annihilation. Yet Esther, I think, remains true to this vision in her final confrontation with Hazard.

For the peace that follows her final meeting with Hazard is an ominous and terrible one. As Hazard leaves Esther, an awful silence descends: "It was peace, but the peace of despair."[71] Strong, meanwhile, has fallen in love:

> "Esther, I meant it! you have fought your battle like a heroine. If you will marry me, I will admire and love you more than ever a woman was loved since the world began."
>
> Esther looked at him with an expression that would have been a smile if it had not been infinitely dreary and absent; then she said simply and finally:
>
> "But George, I don't love you. I love him."

These, the closing lines of the book, point to the intractability of Esther's dilemma and the inevitability of her despair, no matter how accepting it might appear to be. She loves Hazard, with fierceness and implacability, yet she refuses to be defined by that love, its "personal and selfish" nature. She cannot accept an account of reality in which human beings are reduced to personal relations.

She tells Hazard that she wants a religion that appeals to what is stronger, more spiritual, more pure than that. On one reading, we might see Esther as a figure for the rational subject. As with the scientist and intellectual Strong, on this reading, Esther's rejection of Christianity is a principled refusal to discard reason for religion, the truth for fantasy, the reality of the abyss into which all humans will eventually fall from the dream of an eternal life in which the family is reborn. Having internalized her dead father's rational skepticism, she refuses herself the comforts offered by Hazard. Peace, however full of despair, is the fruit of intellectual rigor and honesty.

Yet the argument between Esther and Hazard about the resurrection does not hinge on the rationality or irrationality of the belief; the issue is not whether or not the resurrection is real and its promise a truthful one, but rather whether it is a promise and a hope worthy of human beings. On this reading, Esther refuses to allow her love for a single human being to annul her desire for something more than her body and herself. Within the terms of the novel, Esther's love for Hazard and her desire for something more are *both* real; she insists that both are true, but also that they are not both equally worthy of humanity at its strongest.[72] Even as she refuses to allow her love of Hazard to sweep her away into the doctrine and practice of the church, she remains committed to the story Niagara Falls tells her. Hence the forbidding sense I have every time I read the novel that Esther will throw herself into the Falls, into an eternal, infinite, and omnipotent force worthy of the human spirit. (Is this the fear that makes Strong's blood run cold?)

Of course, this doesn't happen in the novel. Henry provides a picture of how Esther will live on, stoic in the face of her suffering, having come through passion to seek peace in the company of the infinite. It is Clover, Henry's wife, who will die and it is surely a mistake to read her fate into the novel. Yet the ubiquity of the Falls and of Esther's imagined—whether fearfully or energetically—submersion in them continues to feel like a prediction of Clover's death. The ominously proleptic quality of the novel is rendered even sharper when we turn back to the moment when Hazard first fully elicits Esther's love. During her father's final illness, Hazard comes to offer help.

> "I want to help you," he said. "I am used to such scenes and you are not. You need help though you may not ask for it."
> She shook her head: "I am a miserable coward," she said; "but we are beyond help now, and I must learn endurance."

"You will over-tax your strength," he urged. "Remember, there is no excitement so great as to stand for the first time in face of eternity, as you are doing."

"I suppose it must be so," she answered. "Everything seems unreal. I can't realize my father's illness. Your voice sounds far-off, as though you are calling to me out of the distance and darkness. I hardly know what you are saying, or why you are here. I never felt so before."[73]

Henry seems again to predict Clover's response to her father's death. (Perhaps his experience of her earlier depressions gave him insight into what might occur.) For according to her sister Ellen, Clover's "constant cry" in the summer following her father's death, the summer leading up to her suicide, was, "Ellen I'm not real—oh make me real—You are all of you real!"[74]

This elicits an even more complex reading of the novel's final scenes, for what Adams's narrator calls "mysticism" provides the way to a new reality for Esther, one she discovers *with* Hazard but that will ultimately lead her to reject him. When the always skeptical but intensely loving William Dudley dies—like Clover's father, a widower who had raised his daughter with keen attention—Esther is desolate. "At twenty-six to be alone, with no one to interpose as much as a shadow across her path, was a strange sensation; it made her dizzy, as though she were a solitary bird flying through mid-air, and as she looked ahead on her aerial path, could see no tie more human than that which bound her to Andromeda or Orion."[75] What follows is an acute description of the experience of mourning. To the "moral strain" of finding herself alone in the world, Henry writes,

> was added the reaction from physical fatigue. For a week or two after her father's death, Esther felt languid, weary and listless. She could not sleep. A voice, a bar of music, the sight of any thing unusual, affected her deeply. She could not get back to her regular interests. First came the funeral with its inevitable depression and fatigue; then came the days of vacancy, with no appetite for work and no chance for amusement. She took refuge in trifles, but the needle and scissors are terrible weapons for cutting out and trimming not so much women's dresses as their thoughts. She had never been a reader, and perhaps for that reason her mind had all the more run into regions of fancy and imagination. She caught half an idea in the air, and tossed it for amusement. In these days of unrest, she tossed her ideas more rapidly than ever. Most women are more or less mystical by nature, and Esther had a vein of mysticism running through her practical mind.[76]

In this mental and physical state, the only person outside of her family Esther sees is Hazard.

Hazard comes to the house daily, taking care of practical arrangements and "talking mysticism" with Esther. Unlike the artist Wharton, who during a similar crisis finds reality only in looking on at moments of extreme suffering and physical death,[77] Esther "learned to look on the physical life, the daily repetition of breakfast and dinner, as the unreal part of existence." "Her illusions were not serious; perhaps she had for this short instant a flash of truth, and by the light of her father's deathbed, saw life as it is; but, while the mood lasted, nothing seemed real except the imagination, and nothing true but the spiritual."[78] The passage is difficult to decipher. Her "illusions" seem tied, paradoxically, to "a flash of truth" in which she "saw life as it is"—namely, as ending in death. On this reading the illusion seems not an illusion, but a flash of the truth. But perhaps the illusion is her subsequent sense that nothing "seemed real except the imagination, and nothing true but the spiritual." Is the narrator telling us that death is the only true, the only real thing and that, in the face of this reality, Esther recoils, finding a false truth and reality in the illusions of the imagination and spirit? Regardless, Hazard revels in this side of Esther's character: "His great eyes shone with the radiance of paradise, and his delicate thin features expressed beatitude, as he discussed with Esther the purity of the spirit, the victory of spirit over matter, and the peace of infinite love."[79] The lines are remarkably for the intensity of their focus on Hazard's physical beauty, even as he purportedly rejoices in the spiritual ambitions he shares with Esther.

For the love into which Esther and Hazard fall is not purely spiritual, but also intensely physical. Death is not the only thing real about bodily life, despite the narrator's protestations. As long as Hazard is physically present to her, within reach of her touch, Esther does not feel scruples about her lack of religion. But when she sits in the congregation of his church, listening to him preach his version of their mystical talk, she rebels. Going to the service, mixing with the crowd, itself irritates Esther. "By the time the creed was read, she could not honestly feel that she believed a word of it, or could force herself to say that she ever should believe it."

> With fading self-confidence she listened to the sermon. It was beautiful, simple, full of feeling and even of passion, but she felt that it was made for her, and she shrank before the thousand people who were thus let into the secret chambers of her heart. It treated of death and its mystery, covering ignorance

with a veil of religious hope, and ending with an invocation of infinite love so intense in feeling and expression that, beautiful as it was, Esther forgot its beauties in the fear that the next word would reveal her to the world. This sort of publicity was new to her, and threw her back on herself until religion was forgotten in the alarm. She became more jealous than ever. What business had these strangers with her love? Why should she share it with them?[80]

Esther's intellectual critique, spiritual refusal, and physical repulsion are densely intertwined. She can't accept Hazard's beliefs on intellectual grounds; her deeply felt sense of the mystical or eternal, of the unreality of daily life in the face of the realness of the imagination and the spiritual, is offended by the materialism and egotism of Hazard's conception of resurrection and paradise; and, most brutally and frankly, she does not want to share him physically or spiritually.

In the final confrontation between Hazard and Esther discussed above, I left out one crucial point. The narrator notes that when Hazard admits that he wants to save Esther's soul as much as he wants to win her as his wife, his "speech was unlucky." "She seemed to feel now," the narrator continues, "what she had only vaguely suspected before, the restraint which would be put upon her the moment she should submit to his will."[81] Against the torrents of Niagara Falls, these constraints seem meant to check the unleashed power of Esther and Hazard's passion for each other, both physical and spiritual. Hazard requires, demands, the safeguard of the church to keep his own and Esther's passion in check. Esther can't believe in the church, but more importantly, she doesn't want to; her appeal to mysticism, to the Falls, and the narrator's evocation of the intensity of her physical desire all, paradoxically, point in the same direction. Esther does not want what is excessive in her desire to be curtailed. She isn't afraid of being subsumed by the spiritual *or* by the physical force of desire. What she cannot stand is the purportedly spiritual, but in fact intensely physical, constraints of the church and of its expectations about love between men and women putting a limit on her passion.

Henry Adams writes this character, in all of her recalcitrance, and yet the narrator seems uncomfortable with the excessiveness of her desire—both for things of the spirit, about which he overtly speaks, and for things of the body. Bodily desire is evoked by the powerful effect on Esther of Hazard's physical presence—his glance, the sound of his voice, his touch; by the narrator's descriptions, often through Esther's eyes, of Hazard's physical beauty; and, perhaps most keenly, through the imagery of the torrential Falls.

Lears argues that Henry Adams rejects the appeals to Buddhism and Nirvana found in *Esther* and in his other writings and perhaps this is right. It is difficult to say how we would know what is Adams, what the narrator, what Hazard, what Strong, what Esther. For Esther herself does not reject Nirvana as she hears it in the Falls. Late-Victorian conceptions of the pure spirituality of Buddhism are not all that is at stake, for Esther's singular love for Hazard, in all of his physicality, and her desire to merge with the spirit are not at odds with each other. In the terms presented by the artist Wharton within the novel, one attains Nirvana only by living through physical passion and coming to accept its transience. Both *Esther* and the Adams Memorial are monuments to this melancholic peace, a peace always unsettled by the still living dead encrypted within it.

There are good reasons to accept Lears's claims that Henry, after the completion of the monument, sought something more. For Henry lived on, grouchy and sardonic, vital and vitriolic, until his death at the age of ninety. His life and writing after Clover's death might be understood as a ceaseless attempt—through travel, study, friends, work—to uncover, recapture, or create a reality not mired in melancholy. The desire to live on marks his return to the Middle Ages, his fascination with the South Seas and the Far East, and his attempt to find a reality beyond the mere brute force of the Dynamo. He wants to experience the joy and sensuality of life he ascribes to the South Sea Islanders, to the great old Norman landowners, to the saints and the mystics of the Christian Middle Ages. He seeks a return to innocence, yet continually enacts his own mourning at its passing. For all of this work is haunted by the specter of Clover's death. The ubiquitous references to photography in *Mont Saint Michel and Chartres* continually recall her. The twenty years passed over in *The Education of Henry Adams* mark her grave as surely as the monument on which her name does not appear. Henry never names Clover in his published work and only rarely spoke of her or wrote about her in his letters, yet she lives on, encrypted within all that he did. Her physical presence—her physical absence—haunts him.

We will never know what led Clover to take her own life. But Henry fears the reality and finality of Clover's death; he can't let her go, but, like all good melancholics, he buries her inside of himself and inside of his work. Yet he also fears the excessiveness of the love she elicits in him. Henry simultaneously desires and fears the abyss of love toward which his character, Esther, ceaselessly strives, both spiritually and physically, for in that abyss life and death lie, forever intertwined. After Clover's death, Henry listens for life, joy, and the real in the actual, yet the echoing cataracts of the fall, evoking beauty, movement, and eternity, always also threaten death, a death and a finality of loss against which Henry continually, persistently, obdurately rebels.

In a letter to his friend Henry James, written some months after the death of James's brother William, Adams writes:

> I did not write to you about your brother William, because I fancied that letters were a burden to you. The other reason is that I felt the loss myself rather too closely to talk about it. We all began together, and our lives have made more or less of a unity, which is, as far as I can see, about the only unity that American society in our time has shown. Nearly all are gone. Richardson and St. Gaudens, LeFarge, Alex Agassiz, Clarence King, John Hay, and at the last, your brother William; and with each, a limb of our own lives cut off. Exactly why we should be expected to talk about it, I don't know.[82]

As George Monteiro points out in his introduction to the collected letters of Henry Adams and Henry James, the importance of the friendship between the two men is signaled by one of the rare moments in which Henry mentions Clover after her death. In a letter to his close friend Elizabeth Cameron, written after Henry James himself had died, Adams explains the extent of his mourning: "Not only was he a friend of mine for more than forty years, but he also belonged to the circle of my wife's set long before I knew him or her, and you know how I have clung to all that belonged to my wife."[83]

James was the recipient of Adams's "melancholy outpouring" on at least one other occasion in the final years of their lives. Adams's letter does not survive, although it appears to have been a remonstrance over James's *Notes of a Son and Brother* (1914), in which James writes of his life in Cambridge as a young man, precisely the time at which he first knew Clover and Henry. To Elizabeth Cameron, Adams writes,

> I've read Henry James' last bundle of memories which have reduced me to a dreary pulp. Why did we live? Was that all? Why was I not born in Central Africa and died young. Poor Henry James thinks it all real, I believe, and actually still lives in that dreamy, stuffy Newport and Cambridge, with papa James and Charles Norton—and me! Yet, why! It is a terrible dream, but not so weird as this here which is quite loony. Never mind![84]

Adams and James tended to disagree about their shared history, but in this instance, James's response marks a present concern for Adams more than a desire to be right about the past. On March 21, 1914, writing from Cheyne Walk, James remonstrates with his "dear Henry":

> *I have your melancholy outpouring of the 7th, & I know not how to acknowledge it than by the full recognition of its unmitigated blackness. Of course we are lone survivors, of course the past that was our lives is at the bottom of an abyss—if the abyss has any bottom; of course too there's no use talking unless one particularly wants to. But the purpose, almost, of my printed divagations was to show you that one can, strange to say, still want to—or at least can behave as if one did. Behold me therefore so behaving—& apparently capable of continuing to do so. I still find my consciousness interesting—under cultivation of the interest. Cultivate it with me, dear Henry—that's what I hoped to make you do; to cultivate yours for all that it has in common with mine. Why mine yields as interest I don't know that I can tell you, but I don't challenge or quarrel with it—I encourage it with a ghastly grin. You see I still, in presence of life (or of what you deny to be such,) have reactions—as many as possible—& the book I sent you is a proof of them. It's, I suppose, because I am that queer monster the artist, an obstinate finality, an inexhaustible sensibility. Hence the reactions—appearances, memories, many things go on playing upon it with consequences that I note & "enjoy" (grim word!) noting. It all takes doing—& I do. I believe I shall do yet again—it is still an act of life. But you perform them still yourself—& I don't know what keeps me from calling your letter a charming one! There we are, & it's a blessing that you understand—I admit indeed alone—your all-faithful*
> *Henry James*[85]

To live, for James, is to work, to *cultivate* interest in consciousness, in memory, and in the "presence of life." James remains committed to the "act of life"—"It all takes doing—& I *do*"—and he calls to his friend, from across the abyss of their shared losses, to act with him. James does not say whether they will together find sadness, joy, or the two forever intermingled. But only through cultivation, he insists, can one live as long and as well as one is able.

The Unspeakability of Trauma, the Unspeakability of Joy

With characteristic perspicuity, in 1996 the art critic Hal Foster noted the ambiguities involved in the theoretical elevation of the category of trauma:

> On the one hand, in art and theory, trauma discourse continues the poststructuralist critique of the subject by other means, for again, in a psychoanalytic register, there is no subject of trauma; the position is evacuated, and in this sense the critique of the subject is most radical here. On the other hand, in popular culture, trauma is treated as an event that guarantees the subject, and in this psychologistic register the subject, however disturbed, rushes back as witness, testifier, survivor. Here is indeed a traumatic subject, and it has absolute authority, for one cannot challenge the trauma of another: one can believe it, can identify with it, or not. *In trauma discourse, then, the subject is evacuated and elevated at once.* And in this way trauma discourse magically resolves two contradictory imperatives in culture today: deconstructive analysis and identity politics. This strange rebirth of the author, this paradoxical condition of absentee authority, is a significant turn in contemporary art, criticism, and cultural politics.[86]

The second of these two hands might seem the most self-evident and, despite persistent critique, it continues to shape politics in all of its forms. Although we know from the work of Allan Young, Ruth Leys, Didier Fassin, and Richard Rechtman, among many others, that trauma—and in particular the kinds of responses to traumatic events associated with Post-Traumatic Stress Disorder—has a history, we continue to operate with the broad ethical injunction articulated by work around the diagnosis from the 1980s and 1990s.[87]

The psychologist Judith Herman, in *Trauma and Recovery: The Aftermath of Violence—From Domestic Abuse to Political Terror* (1992), insists that the first thing one must do in response to the violence suffered by another is to *believe*.[88] To do so is to make the victim real, to make what happened to her true. Herman therefore conflates the real and the true in a way that draws out all of the promises and dangers of this position. Herman writes within a specific therapeutic and political context, but the injunction to believe operates much more broadly, from the political realm to the historical. With it comes the privileging of the survivor as the one who knows, the one who has access to the historical reality of violence in a way that demands political, ethical, and historiographical fidelity.

And this in turn leads to a tendency to read people from marginalized or under-represented groups *as* victims; increasingly, claims to epistemological privilege depend on the proximity to trauma and it is trauma, not justice, that makes ethical demands on others.[89]

There have been numerous challenges to the tenability of this stance, yet it endures. The accusations of satanic ritual abuse in the 1990s, for example, suggest just how dangerous the ethical injunction to believe might become.[90] The debates around Binjamin Wilkomirski's *Fragments: Memories of a Wartime Childhood* (1995), however, highlight the continuing dynamic of a certain will to belief.[91] When the journalist and historian Stefan Maechler demonstrates that Wilkomirski is, in fact, Bruno Dössekker (born Bruno Grosjean), Maechler does not argue that Wilkomirski made up his story of childhood trauma, that he wrote fiction, or that he lied. (For simplicity's sake, I will here simply refer to him as Wilkomirski.) Instead, Maechler argues that there was something of Wilkomirski's own putatively traumatic childhood visible in *Fragments*. Wilkomirski, Maechler argues, transmuted aspects of his own childhood into a fictional account of a child surviving the Holocaust. Maechler maintains that some aspect of Wilkomirski's story is true, some part of it real; this is the traumatic core that cannot be questioned.

Yet why does Wilkomirski tell the story of his traumatic childhood as a Holocaust story? Maechler does not answer this question, but it leads to the other side of the paradox laid out by Foster. For at the heart of the diagnosis of PTSD lies the notion that one *dissociates* or *represses* the trauma—that in some real way, one does *not* experience it. Two seemingly very different accounts of trauma and how it affects memory are embedded in the terms "dissociation" and "repression." For some, purportedly following the psychoanalyst Sigmund Freud, traumatic memories are repressed. The therapeutic claim is that through the process of free association these memories can be uncovered and reintegrated into one's conscious memory. With this reclamation, the symptoms through which the repressed made itself known are dissolved. Others return to the work of the nineteenth-century French neurologist Pierre Janet to argue that traumatic memories are not repressed, but instead that during the experience of a horrifying event a person disassociates from himself. The goal of therapy is then to allow the event not only to be remembered—according to this model, the sufferer never really forgets the trauma he has undergone—but experienced as his own. This occurs, again, through its detailed recounting. Both those indebted to Freud and those who seemingly renounce him make use of his "talking cure." (Janet himself made use of hypnosis to resolve the symptoms of hysteria and related disorders, all of which were rooted, in some way, in the experience of traumatic events.) Both claim, although in different ways, that in some important manner the victim of a traumatic event *does not experience* that event, or, perhaps better, *does not live* that experience except through the process of therapy.[92]

All of this points to the complexity of the relationship between subjectivity, memory, and trauma. Maechler's work on Wilkomirski depends on these contentious and complicated theories, even if only implicitly. The question that emerges is how one can ever adequately name one's trauma if the events that engender it so overwhelm the subject as to render him or her unable to experience them? Is there something about the testimony of the survivor that makes it simultaneously (1) inadequate to its object—and for its subject—and (2) impossible, ethically, to disbelieve?[93] Moreover, there is a tendency in the contemporary literature on trauma to assume that the more unspeakable the event, the more authoritative the witness and hence, the more inarticulate the witness, the more true that which she tries to tell us.

The historian Dominick LaCapra, in a series of important essays on the role of trauma theory and testimonial in the writing of history, points to an uncanny parallel between contemporary theoretical and historiographical discussions of trauma and what he calls "negative theology." What worries LaCapra is what he describes as "an important tendency in modern culture and thought to convert trauma into the occasion for sublimity, to transvalue it into a test of the self or of the group and an entry into the extraordinary. In the sublime, the excess of trauma becomes an uncanny source of elation or ecstasy."[94] Clearly thinking of Georges Bataille's essay "On Hiroshima," LaCapra goes on to claim that even such events as the Holocaust or the dropping of the atomic bombs on Hiroshima and Nagasaki "may become occasions of negative sublimity or displaced sacralization. They may also give rise to what may be termed founding traumas— traumas that paradoxically become the valorized or intensely cathected basis of identity for an individual or a group rather than events that pose the problematic question of identity."[95]

LaCapra recognizes the implicitly theological language that surrounds much contemporary discussion of trauma and uses it as the basis for a careful critique.

> Some of the most powerful forms of modern art and writing, as well as some
> of the most compelling forms of criticism (including deconstruction), often
> seem to be traumatic writing or post-traumatic writing in closest proximity

to trauma. They may also involve the feeling of keeping faith with trauma in a manner that leads to a compulsive preoccupation with aporia, an endlessly melancholic, impossible mourning, and a resistance to working through. I think one is involved here in more or less secularized displacements of the sacred and its paradoxes. The hiddenness, death, or absence of a radically transcendent divinity or of absolute foundations makes of existence a fundamentally traumatic scene in which anxiety threatens to color, and perhaps confuse, all relations. One's relation to every other—instead of involving a tense, at times paradoxical, interaction of proximity and distance, solidarity and criticism, trust and wariness—may be figured on the model of one's anxiety ridden "relation without relation" to a radically transcendent (now perhaps recognized as absent) divinity who is totally other.[96]

In the absence of God, LaCapra asks, has secular art and criticism—and certain forms of secular politics—made trauma sacred? Have pain and violence and anxiety become the real, to the exclusion of all else? And what does that mean for how we listen to one another? For who we determine to be worth listening to? For what we can hear from them or deem worthy of our attention?

What I want to ask, finally, is whether returning to the Middle Ages, to the discourses of cataphatic and apophatic theology as they are articulated around the life stories of saintly women and men, helps us to understand our contemporary situation and to pose another possibility—the possibility that joy might *also* be the site of an unspeakable real. At the same time, I want to ask why we believe in the realness and the truth of the traumatic—its properly *historical* truth—but seem unable to hear joy. (Henry Adams could hear joy, but he could not find a way to make it real in the present.) What if the reality of trauma does not depend, necessarily, on the historical truth of the claims made about it? (This seems to me, in fact, to be self-evidently the case. I am not nearly as credulous a reader as the opening panel of this triptych might suggest. I just ask that we pause and think about what claims we are rejecting and why.) More importantly, what if the inarticulateness of joy also marks something real? How might that change the way in which we write the history of religion and understand it in our midst? And how might it offer new ways to think about the movement from the real to the true, or the varieties of ways in which truth might manifest itself?

I am going to use an extreme example, a story I assume that very few modern readers will believe; yet it is a story that some interpret in terms of hysteria, a disorder itself rooted in some kind of unnamed, unspoken trauma.[97]

Most importantly, in many readings of this story, a woman's suffering is understood to be real, even if the events recorded about that suffering are taken as hyperbolic. I will turn, then, to the *Life of Christina the Astonishing*, written by Thomas of Cantimpré in the years shortly after her death. (She died in 1224; the life is written in 1232.)

(A note on hagiography, a term that was initially used to name holy writing—that is, scripture—but that in the nineteenth century was narrowed to refer to a particular kind of holy writing, namely, the lives of the saints. Many scholars would argue that hagiography is precisely *not* history and that the stories told within it are not meant to be read in the ways that we read historical and protohistorical documents. What matters, so it is said, is the holiness of the person in question and that holiness is one shared by all of the saints; hence you can move material from one hagiography to another without concern for misrepresentation, for all saints participate in the singular life of sanctity. Yet despite such claims, historians continue to read hagiographical sources for historical material, either about what was considered holy in a particular time and place or as telling us something about the person under discussion once we cut out all of the supernatural, generic, and typological material. This is a dubious enterprise, but one that is particular rife in the study of material on women from the high and latter Middle Ages, a time when we have hagiographies written in close proximity to the death of their subject and often with explicit claims to direct or indirect knowledge of the subject. We will see in what follows how this plays out in the *Life of Christina the Astonishing*.)[98]

It needs to be repeated: the *Life of Christina the Astonishing* reads like science fiction. It is very hard to believe that anyone ever believed it, to the point that I have at times wondered if it is not fictional—and known to be fictional by its first audiences. The author, Thomas of Cantimpré, knows people are going to find it hard to believe. He himself, moreover, does not claim to have known Christina. He tells us that he would not even have written the life if another priest, the widely known and respected James of Vitry (1160/70–1240),[99] had not already mentioned Christina (without naming her), in the prologue to his life of the beguine Marie of Oignies.

Thomas opens the *Life of Christina the Astonishing* with these lines from James's *Life of Marie of Oignies*:

> I saw another in whom God worked so wondrously that after she had lain dead for a long time—but before her body was buried in the ground—her soul

returned to her body and she lived again. She obtained from the Lord that she would endure purgatory, living in this world in her body. It was for this reason that she was afflicted for a long time by the Lord, so that sometimes she rolled herself in the fire, and sometimes in the winter she remained for lengthy periods in icy water and at other times she was driven to enter the tombs of the dead. But after she had performed penance in so many ways, she lived in peace and merited grace from the Lord and many times, rapt in the spirit, she led the souls of the dead as far as purgatory, or through purgatory as far as the kingdom of heaven, without any harm to herself.[100]

All of this might strike historians operating with the kind of naturalistic and empirical assumptions I described in the first panel of this triptych as implying a certain credulity on James's part, while at the same time being plausible as an account of what one woman and those around her believed about her experience. The very framing of the prologue to the *Life of Marie of Oignies* works to reinforce this reading, as it is addressed to Fulk, the bishop of Toulouse, to whom James describes having seen Christina and the other holy women of Liège about whom James writes. (This addressee also points to the specific religious framework within which the *Life* was written, for Fulk had been ousted from southern France by the Cathars and James writes the *Life of Marie*, at least in part, to contribute to the campaign against them.)

Thomas insists that he has not only this written testimony, but also many other eyewitness accounts of Christina's deeds and of her words.

> I have as many witnesses to most of the events I have described as there were rational persons living at the time in the town of Saint Trond. These things were not done in narrow corners but openly among the people. Nor has so much time elapsed that oblivion has swallowed up and buried these occurrences, for I wrote this *Life* not more than eight years after her death. I personally heard other things that no one could have known except Christina herself from people who swore they learned them from her own mouth.[101]

Remember, this is a story about a woman who claims to have died and come back to life. So what do we do with the care with which Thomas notes the abundance of eyewitness accounts, including that of a bishop and future member of the Roman Curia? Thomas *knows* the story is unbelievable, yet he persists in telling it and does everything he can to vouch for its authority.

Should we suspend disbelief in order to attempt to find what is real and what true in the story? Like Henry Adams's Esther Dudley, I do not believe that resurrection from the dead is likely, and increasingly I do not think it gets at what I most value. (I used to think that Christianity without the resurrection of the body was pointless. I still believe that something vital is at stake in the claim that human bodies—life itself—are of such value that we might want them to last eternally. Yet I now believe that there might be more illuminating and ethical ways to affirm that value.) More important than my disbelief, however, is that there are significant reasons *not* to assume that Thomas is making claims about historical reality and truth. First, as I mentioned before and will discuss further below, it is not at all clear that we should understand the *Life* as intended to be read historically. Secondly, as I argue in "Inside Out: Beatrice of Nazareth and Her Hagiographer," the kinds of somatic miracles found throughout the *Life of Christina* also appear in other hagiographies of medieval women (short of the resurrection), and yet there is ample evidence that women themselves, in their own writings, resisted the depiction of their sanctity in terms of bodily abjection.

Yet this is precisely the aspect of the *Life* to which some give the most credence. Historically minded readers tend to assume that Christina was in a coma from which she revived, leaving out the idea of resurrection so vital to the text. But that she suffered unspeakable pain, submitted herself to torture, and generally acted like an insane woman, this some very perspicacious readers accept.[102] Why? What problems does this particular form of credulity raise in terms of modern strategies of reading medieval texts (and those from any other place and time)? And, finally, might there be unspeakable aspects of the *Life of Christina* that modern readers are less likely to hear or to understand in the way Thomas and his contemporaries might have? We see and hear suffering, abjection, and horror, but what about joy?[103]

And yet, the *Life of Christina* begins with a death and a resurrection. Rather than working toward the miraculous, it begins with an event so wonderful as to test the credulity of the most faithful readers. The text also begins with a test of love, whose fruits it then recounts. According to Thomas, the strength of Christina's desire for God leads to her death. Yet when she dies, her beloved immediately asks for a self-sacrifice through which others might be brought to him. We know this, Thomas writes, because this is what Christina herself told those she encountered when she returned to life. Thomas gives us a version of these words, a long discourse purportedly from the mouth of the newly arisen Christina.

First Christina tells of her death and of her anguish at seeing souls in torment. She is then led to the Lord, who says to her,

> "Certainly, my dearest, you will be with me, but I now offer you two choices, either to remain with me now or to return to the body and suffer there the sufferings of an immortal soul in a mortal body without damage to it, and by these your sufferings to deliver all those souls on whom you had compassion in that place of purgatory, and by the example of your suffering and your way of life to convert living people to me and to turn aside from their sins, and after you have done all these things to return to me having accumulated for yourself a reward of such great profit."[104]

Christina's love of God leads her to acquiesce to his request. She comes back to life during her funeral service and, after floating to the rafters of the church, she begins "to do those things for which she had been sent back by the Lord." She thrusts herself into fiery ovens where bread is being baked, throws herself into roaring fires, jumps into cauldrons of boiling water, and immerses herself in the freezing waters of the local river for days at a time. All of these torments are experienced as excruciatingly painful—her howls, Thomas tells us, were terrible to hear. Yet her body remains unmarked by her self-torture. So sensitive and light that when praying she floats to the tops of trees or church steeples, unable to bear the stench of human beings and the weight of the earth, Christina's body appears to be a resurrected body.

Not surprisingly, Thomas depicts Christina's family and neighbors as distressed by her actions, thinking that she is mad. They misinterpret Christina's behavior in ways Thomas anticipates his readers' will. Her sisters and neighbors repeatedly capture and chain Christina down, attempting to curtail her self-harm; yet God takes care of her bodily needs (her virginal breasts drip sweet milk and later sweet oil to sustain her during imprisonment) and eventually restores her freedom. After having acted out her purgatorial suffering before crowds of people, she prays to God that her actions might become more moderate. They do so and she is accepted as a prophetic figure in the community.

As the historian Robert Sweetman shows, Thomas depicts Christina's prophetic and preaching mission as effected through both her words and her actions.[105] Most importantly, her dramatic bodily displays are themselves part of her preaching apostolate. Through the extremity of her suffering, Christina demonstrates to onlookers the effects of sin and the horrors of purgatorial suffering; in this way she warns them not to continue in their sins and turns them toward repentance. There is a progression in Thomas's account of Christina's life: first she must prove her sanctity through bodily suffering and only then are her prophetic (and I would add mystical) powers accepted by the community.[106] These prophetic powers first evince themselves, moreover, through her actions. Christina begs door to door for her food, yet anything she receives that had been obtained by its donor through sin is rejected by her body. Only later do we see her discussing events that occur at a distance or in the future and telling people of the fate of the dead and dying. At a time when women's words were distrusted and their ability to preach, teach, and interpret scripture severely limited,[107] Christina's bodily actions give her a religious authority otherwise unavailable to her. Only after her dramatic suffering, bodily enacted, could she teach with words.

In a rich analysis of Thomas's *Life of Christina*, the literary critic and historian Barbara Newman argues that there is good reason to understand Christina's behavior in terms of hysteria.[108] Like James of Vitry, Thomas describes Christina as engaging in a host of activities similar to those found in nineteenth- and early-twentieth-century cases of hysteria: deathlike trances, levitations, extreme asceticism, self-exorcisms, screams, tears, and bodily contortions. In grief over the damnation of sinners, Thomas writes, Christina "wept and twisted herself and bent herself backwards and bent and re-bent her arms and fingers as if they were pliable and had no bones." Another time she "cried out as if in childbirth and twisted her limbs and rolled about on the ground with great wailing."[109] There are strong parallels here with the photographs of hysterics taken at the Salpêtrière under the guidance of the nineteenth-century neurologist Jean-Martin Charcot (1825–93), photographs in which a small number of hysterical women exhibit extreme bodily contortions and spasms.[110] Hence, for Newman, it is not surprising that Christina is a figure of fear and consternation to the townspeople of St. Trond, who assume that she is mad or possessed by demons (as the Middle English version of the *Life* puts it).[111]

Sweetman argues that Thomas depicts Christina's postresurrection life as a long *exemplum* through which she instructs others and at the same time frees souls from purgatory through her suffering. She provides a theatrical depiction of purgatorial pain and of postresurrection bodily lightness and joy, thereby teaching through her deeds, as she will eventually come to preach through her words. For Newman this explanation of the *Life of Christina* remains insufficient; always mindful of the impossibility of ever fully uncovering the "real

Christina," Newman still wants to understand the person behind the text, one whose extreme actions and bodily symptoms seem pathological to modern readers. She asserts that we need to ask why "Thomas of Cantimpré took the risk of representing the village lunatic as a saint."[112]

A number of questions emerge here, the first and most obvious of which is why we should assume the historical truth or accuracy of anything Thomas tells us in the *Life*. His claim to rely on secondhand eyewitness accounts and his appeal to the authority of James of Vitry might be read not as marks of historical veracity, but instead as devices through which Thomas creates the effect of reality, a verisimilitude against which the extraordinary nature of Christina's life in death or death in life is all the more starkly apparent.[113] The extravagance of Thomas's claims may be understood as an indication of the vital theological truth on display in his story, one that for Thomas surely overrides any concern with historical veracity.

One can imagine the *Life of Christina the Astonishing* emerging out of two very different scenes. In the first, Thomas reads James of Vitry's *Life of Marie of Oignies* and becomes curious about the unnamed woman who rose from the dead described in James "prologue." He then hastens to learn everything he can about her, talking to those who knew her before her death and after her return from the dead. On this reading, the *Life of Christina* is a theologically rich rendering of the stories people told about Christina after her second death, organized and shaped by Thomas's vision of Christian perfection. Newman reads the *Life* in this way and wants, as far as she can, to get to the woman lying behind Thomas's version. But there is another possibility. (There are many possibilities, but these are the two that most interest me here.) What if Thomas read James's *Life of Marie of Oignies* and saw in the unnamed woman of James's prologue the seed of a story in which the reality of the holy women of Liège as Christ-like—even as other Christs—in their self-sacrifice, rapture, and devotion might be fully displayed? What if he expanded the story from James's prologue to make the case that this woman, now named, pointedly, Christina, a female Christ, died and rose from the dead and in her resurrected state brought others to salvation—both those she releases from purgatory through her suffering and those she frees from sin through her example? This reading becomes even more persuasive given that Thomas borrows from the lives of the desert fathers and the virgin martyrs and the tortures to which they were subjected in filling out James's story.[114] We can never know which, if either, of these reconstructions of Thomas's writing practice is right, but we need to recognize that both are possible.

Yet regardless of how we understand the historical veridicality of Thomas's story, the second question raised by Newman's argument is, what is at stake for modern historians in accepting nineteenth- and twentieth-century evaluations of Christina and other holy women as mentally ill and, in particular, as hysterical?[115] The association of medieval women's sanctity and the forms of mysticism most often found among women with hysteria runs throughout the modern literature on both phenomena. Charcot, so important in the modern medical study of hysteria for his insistence that hysteria is a disease of the nerves rather than a sign of moral degeneration, malingering, and laziness, first introduced the reading of mysticism as hysteria in *La foi qui guérit*, written shortly before his death. There he argues that Francis of Assisi and Teresa of Ávila were "undeniable hysterics" with the ability, nonetheless, to cure the ailment in others. Charcot remains puzzled by these curative skills.[116] In another text, cowritten with Paul Richer, *Les démoniaques dans l'art* (1886), Charcot and Richer retroactively diagnose demonic possession as hysteria.[117] The association of mysticism—particularly the visionary and somatic forms of mysticism most often associated with women—and hysteria was used throughout the early twentieth century (and beyond) to disparage and denigrate women's experience and writing.[118]

Simone de Beauvoir, for example, distinguishes between the mysticism of Saint Teresa, the product of "a sane, free consciousness" and that of her "lesser sisters." Beauvoir interprets the mysticism of Angela of Foligno, Jean Guyon, and others as a form of erotomania and hysteria (the two are often indistinguishable in the literature), with hysteria understood in a broadly Freudian sense. The hysteric, for Freud, is one who suffers bodily symptoms he or she does not know how to interpret. These symptoms mark the return of desires that, due to the force of repression, can appear only in veiled form (and so are not immediately legible). (They are as such also experienced traumatically.) Thus for Beauvoir, whereas Teresa controls her bodily, sexualized experiences of the divine (a claim Teresa would find surprising), the bodies of other women signify without their conscious consent and without their knowledge of the bodies' meanings (a sign of degradation for Beauvoir).[119]

Beauvoir's feminist analysis leaves room for a distinction between hysteria and mysticism even as she assimilates most examples of female mysticism to the former, degraded category. Most scholars who have wanted to understand mysticism with some sympathy have, as a result, either avoided the term "hysteria" entirely or reserved it for those figures seen as somehow marginal, excessive, or troubling. (My tendency has been to distinguish mysticism from hagiography, in which, before the fourteenth century, most of the hysterical symptoms occur and then to read the fourteenth- and fifteenth-century texts as autohagiographical. This is a start, I now think, but not sufficient.) Not surprisingly, then, the term has recently reemerged around women who display a particularly somatic mysticism, namely, Christina and Margery Kempe.[120] Although, as Newman shows, other saints' lives produced in Belgium and the Low Countries during the thirteenth century contain accounts of divine possession that differ only in degree from that ascribed to Christina, in reading all of these texts it is vital to mark that possession is ascribed to these women by male hagiographers.[121]

For the moment, let's follow Newman in her assumption that there is a woman behind Thomas's Christina about whose experience we can make at least some educated guesses. Let's assume, moreover, that her behavior was read as somehow pathological by those around her—as is clear in Thomas's text. Newman hypothesizes that Christina, having survived a unknown illness and deathlike coma, shows signs of severe mental disturbance: "antisocial behavior, violent self-mutilation, peculiar and repellent choices in food and dress."[122] The people of St. Trond, judging her to be ill, attempt to restrain her, make her a public spectacle, and have her exorcized, all to no avail. She remains an unassimilable mad woman, reduced to begging to stay alive (an act which, according to Newman, at that point would have had no religious significance for Christina or her neighbors).[123] "Into this wretched existence," Newman continues,

> came a cleric. . . . Seeing Christina's extravagant suffering, he assimilated them to the mortifications offered by women like Marie of Oignies for the benefit of souls and devised a new interpretation of her state. Christina was indeed tormented—but her torments now had meaning: she was a madwoman with a mission. . . . Under the tutelage of this priest and his circle, Christina became increasingly pious and began to model her behavior, insofar as she could control it, on the devotions of lay *mulieres sanctae*.[124]

Thus by a "stroke of pastoral genius," the bodily pathologies of a hysterical woman are transformed into a theologically coherent glimpse of the next world. Newman thus argues that the theological value of Christina's hysterical experience is read into it by a male advisor; only then does it take on religious significance and hence become something other than hysteria.

As I mentioned above, despite their extremity, Christina's actions, like those of the other woman discussed in James of Vitry's prologue, conform to thirteenth-century understandings of religious experience. As Dyan Elliott shows, thirteenth-century philosophers like Alexander of Hales (d. 1245), William of Auvergne (d. 1249), and Thomas Aquinas (d. 1274) frequently use the terms "rapture," "ecstasy," and "alienation" or "departure of the mind" (*alienatio mentis* or *excessus mentis*) "to connote the alienation from the senses that occurs during an encounter with a higher spirit."[125] Debate about the nature of such experiences focused on Paul's description of being caught up into the third heaven (2 Cor 12:2–4). Following Augustine's distinction between corporeal, spiritual, and intellectual vision, most scholars agreed that Paul describes an unmediated experience of intellectual vision, one that does not depend on images. The general belief was that such intellectual vision, and even the lesser experience of spiritual vision, depended on an alienation from the body and from the sensitive faculty of the soul (the senses), if not from the vegetative faculty (the animating principle itself). (In the thirteenth century, these monastic ideas come together with the medical discourse on the physical effects of lovesickness, as I show in "'That Glorious Slit,'" included here.) Alienation of the mind or the senses, then, gives rise to trance states and a deathlike bodily appearance. As Bernard McGinn points out, James of Vitry's *Life of Marie of Oignies* is the first text to use language traditionally associated with the heights of monastic contemplation (*separatus a corpore, a sensibilibus abstracta, in excessu rapta*) for these trance-like states. Whereas earlier monastic literature (by Gregory the Great and Bernard of Clairvaux, for example) emphasized the brevity of this moment, James depicts Marie and other women remaining in trance-like states for hours, even days, on end.[126]

In the thirteenth-century philosophical, medical, and theological literature, moreover, women's bodies were seen as particularly suited to such rapture in that they were judged to be more porous, permeable, and weak than men's. In addition, the great humidity and softness of women's bodies were taken as making them more impressionable and so more imaginative. Although often a source of problems for women, this imaginative capacity could also make them more open to spiritual vision. However, hysteria or suffocation of the womb was also known to medieval thinkers as a pathological condition almost indistinguishable from rapture or demonic possession. It was widely believed that "the absence of sex permits corrupted humours to build up so that the womb actually rises and presses against the heart," giving rise to a death-like appearance. Even Thomas of Cantimpré recognizes that death-like trances might be the sign of bodily illness rather than rapture.[127] (And for Thomas's English translator, as for many others, demonic possession becomes another possibility almost completely indistinguishable, at least externally, from divine rapture or ecstasy.) Therefore, theologians and spiritual advisors needed to be adept at interpreting the bodily and spiritual signs in order to determine if they were caused by rapture, demonic possession, or simply disease.

Newman's recuperation of the category of hysteria to discuss demonic possession and at least some examples of mystical experience—whether real, fictional, or some heady and uncanny mix of the two—raises, then, the crucial question of who is authorized to interpret bodily phenomena. One of the commentators on pseudo-Albert the Great's *De secretis mulierum* (*Women's Secrets*) shows that conflicts of interpretation were already at work in the medieval period. Women who suffer from "suffocation of the womb," he writes,

> lie down as if they were dead. Old women who have recovered from it say that it was caused by an ecstasy during which they were snatched out of their bodies and borne to heaven or to hell, but this is ridiculous. The illness happens from natural causes, however they think that they have been snatched out of their bodies because vapors rise to the brain. If these vapors are very thick and cloudy, it appears to them that they are in hell and they see black demons; if the vapors are light, it seems to them that they are in heaven and that they see God and his angels shining brightly.[128]

Here we see a case where women offer theological interpretations of their "hysteria" (note the proximity and the gap between medieval and modern usages) that are rejected by male authorities. The obvious question with regard to Newman's reading of the *Life of Christina* is why we should suppose, given the absence of any account of such a mediating influence, that Christina herself did not interpret her experience theologically—or that she was not depicted as doing so by Thomas.

But, of course, Thomas *does* depict Christina as interpreting her own experience.[129] In the first chapter of the *Life*, in fact, Thomas describes Christina giving her own account of what occurred to her, one starkly reminiscent of the kinds of reports Albert describes.

> As soon as I died, angels of God, the ministers of light, received my soul and led me into a dark and terrible spot which was filled with the souls of human beings. The torments that I saw in that place were so many and so cruel that no tongue is adequate to tell of them. There I saw many dead men whom I

had previously known in the flesh. Having not a little compassion on those wretched souls, I asked them what place this was. I thought it was hell, but my guides said to me, "This place is purgatory and it is here that repentant sinners atone for the sins they committed while they were alive." They then led me to the torments of hell and there also I recognized some people whom I had known while I was alive.

After these events, I was carried into paradise, to the throne of the Divine Majesty.[130]

So while a woman like Christina may have needed male clerical approbation to sanction her interpretation, there is no evidence within either the *Life of Marie of Oignies* or the *Life of Christina* to suggest that Christina—whether a real woman or a character in an extended theological exemplum—did not develop this interpretation of her experience on her own. (The only possible influences depicted are the nuns of St. Catherine's outside of St. Trond and the recluse Ivetta of Huy, pointing to a very different narrative about women and theological community.)

Newman's reading appears to rest on assumptions like those of Freud and Beauvoir—what is most salient about hysteria is less its symptomology than the victim's lack of consciousness with regard to the cause of her symptoms. To label Christina (and the demoniacs whom Newman also analyzes in her essay) as hysterical seems to presume that she has no available interpretative frame for her experience. When one is provided by a priest, Newman argues, hysteria takes on meaning, becomes theologized, and is transformed into a profound religious experience. Newman's hysteric, then, is one who cannot read her symptoms or, as the author of *Women's Secrets* shows, who interprets them incorrectly. Yet available evidence contradicts Newman's thesis, suggesting that women both desired and were able to interpret their own symptoms, even if at times in the face of male resistance. Perhaps Thomas, in telling Christina's story, is more true to the testimony of medieval women than Newman allows herself to be.

Beauvoir asks whether the mystic submits to bodily symptoms or controls them with a "sane, free consciousness"; for medieval women and men, however, this poses far too stark a contrast. Women like Christina presumably understood themselves as overpowered by an experience beyond their control (this is the way contemporary texts by women talk about such raptures), yet there is evidence that they struggled to maintain the authority to interpret that experience against the often competing claims of male medical and ecclesial authorities.

Most importantly for my purposes, these experiences are not only—and perhaps not even primarily—ones of suffering and pain. Newman very usefully demonstrates that the suffering and pain she associates with hysteria are not in and of themselves religiously significant; it is only when suffering is understood within a theological framework, when that suffering is understood to be salvific, that it is valorized. I make similar claims about the transmutation of mourning and trauma into theologically rich experiences of the *imitatio Christi* in my essay "Acute Melancholia." What interests me is the way in which Newman and I focus on the traumatic, mournful, and violent aspects of our sources to the exclusion of other important features. Although Newman does not render explicit the link between trauma and hysteria, the two are inevitably connected once hysteria is no longer seen as a physiological or moral disorder. Trauma either engenders hysteria (the early Freud) or is itself experienced traumatically (arguably the later Freud.) And these traumas are often losses. We can take Newman's argument a step further and hypothesize that Christina's putative hysteria is a result of her mourning the death of her parents, suffering at the hands of cruel or indifferent family members, and undergoing near death and burial. (She might also be traumatized by the guilt concomitant with religious life in much of medieval Christianity.) On this reading, what is really real in the *Life of Christina the Astonishing* is Christina's suffering and her victimization. So despite Newman's desire to underline the theological nature of the *Life*, in searching for the woman behind it she ineluctably grounds her reading in the depth and reality of Christina's suffering. (I do something very similar in my reading of Beatrice of Nazareth and Margaret Ebner in "Acute Melancholia.")

Yet in telling the story of Christina's actions and her words, Thomas of Cantimpré does not just narrate suffering, screams, and lamentation. Christina also sings, jubilantly, in Latin. At other times, Thomas depicts a more wondrous and indescribable sound emerging from Christina's body, a sounds whose source Christina and the women around her have little difficulty in naming, even if that source, like Christina's song, remains in some fundamental way ineffable.

Now she was very familiar with the nuns of St Catherine's outside the town of Saint Trond. Sometimes while she was sitting with them, she would speak of Christ and suddenly and unexpectedly she would be ravished in the spirit and her body would whirl around like a hoop in a children's game. She whirled around with such extreme violence that the individual limbs of her body could not be distinguished. When she had whirled around for a long time in this manner, it seemed as if she became weakened by the violence of the rolling and her limbs grew quiet. Then there sounded between her throat and her breast a wondrous harmony that no other mortal human being could understand, nor could it be imitated by any artificial instrument. That song of hers had only the pliancy and the tones of music. But the words of the melody, so to speak—if they could even be called words—sounded together incomprehensibly. No sound or breath came out of her mouth or nose during this time, but a harmony of the angelic voice resounded only from between her breast and throat.

While all this was happening, all her limbs were quiet and her eyes were closed as if she were sleeping. Then after a while, restored to herself somewhat, she rose up like one who was drunk—indeed she was drunk—and cried aloud, "Bring the nuns to me that together we might praise Jesus for the great liberality of his miracles." Shortly thereafter the nuns of the convent came running from all sides (for they greatly rejoiced in Christina's solace) and she began to sing the *Te Deum laudamus*. All the convent joined in as she finished her song. Afterwards, when she was fully restored to herself and learned from the others what she had done and how she had invited the community to praise Christ, she fled for shame and embarrassment, and if anyone forcibly detained her, she languished with a great sorrow and declared herself stupid and foolish.[131]

What is unspeakable here is not Christina's suffering, but her joy.

Thomas depicts sounds coming from Christina's body in a way that is rooted in the exuberance and order of song, although not reducible to it. As in John Cassian's *Conferences*—required reading for medieval monastics—the individual moves through the corporate recitation or singing of the Psalms to a wordless exaltation, and then back to the measured voices of the community.[132] Joy is engendered through practice—it is, to use Henry James's word, cultivated—and yet remains a mystery. For the medieval monk or nun, canon or beguine, there is no contradiction between these assertions.[133] Joy is both engendered through practice and given by divine grace; it is simultaneously recognizable and ineffable; it elevates Christina—she takes control of the woman around her, commanding them as only an abbess should do—and returns her to herself in all humility.

Why does Christina's joyful, ineffable song escape modern ears? If the depth of the reality of trauma is articulated through its ineffability, can the same be true of joy? Might joy be as real as trauma, or at least potentially so? Or alternatively, should a certain suspicion about joy and its source cause us to question the trust we place in those who claim to have undergone unspeakable trauma? Remember, I asked with regard to Wilkomirski's *Fragments* why a reader as critical as Maechler presumes that Wilkomirski was traumatized, even as he shows that the story Wilkomirski tells about that trauma cannot be true. What lies in the gap between what Wilkomirski experienced and the story he tells about it? How do we move from one to the other? Precisely the same question runs through Newman's reading of Thomas's *Life of Christina*, with Newman assuming that a woman like Christina could not tell a plausible and meaningful story about her own trauma. Newman suggests that it required priestly intervention to overcome the gap between Christina's trauma or hysteria and the story she tells about it. Does the priest Newman imagines intervening in Christina's life serve as an analyst or therapist, helping the traumatized, hysterical woman better to understand—or learn to live with—her symptoms?

As I have argued, there is no priest in evidence in the *Life of Christina*, suggesting either that Christina, like Wilkomirski, forged her own story about her trauma or that Thomas, in elaborating on a vignette he finds in James's *Life of Marie of Oignies*, chose to depict Christina as doing so. Newman as a reader of the *Life of Christina* and Maechler as a reader of Wilkomirski's *Fragments* share certain assumptions about the plausibility of the stories these two traumatized subjects are depicted as telling about their suffering, its source, and its meaning. For Newman, Christina's story is such a healing and powerful one that Newman doubts someone as deeply traumatized and hysterical as Christina could have articulated it on her own. The story is untrue, at least as history, but the trauma is real. Maechler even more clearly insists that the story Wilkomirski tells is a lie. Yet like Newman, Maechler insists that Wilkomirski's trauma is real. The power of the cultural narrative within which Wilkomirski places his own traumatized childhood, Maechler suggests, renders it a readily available narrative through which to interpret his own experience. From Maechler's perspective, it might seem self-evident that a woman like Christina would learn to understand her suffering through the most cultural salient narrative about trauma available in thirteenth-century Northern Europe. But again, in both cases, the reality of the trauma itself is never questioned.

The greatest divergence between the *Life of Christina* and *Fragment* lies in the absence of joy in the latter story. Wilkomirski's story is one in which jubilation has no place. It is, after all, a story about the Holocaust. But do the historical facts Wilkomirski borrows in order to understand and convey his own putatively traumatized childhood render it impossible to ever hear joy—or to ever hear it as anything other than a fantasy? Of course, the problem long precedes the particular historical events to which Wilkomirski helps himself in *Fragments*. For Henry Adams, joy seems a thing of the past. Yet he still tries to tell stories about it, at least in *Mont Saint Michel and Chartres*. In *Esther*, too, Adams's titular character finds joy in spirituality and eroticism, even as Adams depicts a Christianity—and a secularism—that constrains the excess of these dual desires, and so destroys joy itself.

A minor character in *Esther*, the painter Wharton, provides a figure for our current situation. Like Esther after her father's death, Wharton reaches a stage in his life when, untethered from human bonds of love and companionship, everything seems to him unreal. Esther turns at such a moment to the realm of the spirit, and to the bodily charms of Stephen Hazard. Wharton, much like the artists at the turn of the twenty-first century described by Hal Foster, finds the real only in suffering and death.

> Nothing seemed real. What earned me my first success was an attempt I made to paint the strange figures and fancies which possessed me. I studied nothing but the most extravagant of subjects. For a time nothing could satisfy me but to draw from models at the moments of intense suffering and at the instant of death. Models of that kind do not offer themselves and are not to be bought. I made friends with surgeons and got myself admitted to one of the great hospitals. I happened to be there one day when a woman was brought in suffering from an overdose of arsenic. This was the kind of subject I wanted. She was fierce, splendid, a priestess of the oracle! Tortured by agony and clinging to it though it were a delight! The next day I came back to look for her: she was then exhausted and half dead. She was a superb model, and I took an interest in her.[114]

The woman becomes Wharton's wife; in the wake of the destruction she wrecks in his life, he finds himself wanting to paint only "purity and repose," yet they continually elude him. Are we, like Wharton, only capable of finding the real in "intense suffering and at the instant of death"? (Can we see in Wharton a harbinger of Georges Bataille, meditating on the photographic images of a man being tortured to death? And, of course, both inherit the tradition of Christian meditation on Christ's Passion.) Are we no longer capable of telling stories in which the unspeakable is the site of jubilation rather than lamentation, of beautiful voiceless song rather than inarticulate screams, of a body spinning with delight rather than one twisted in agony?

The danger of Thomas's *Life of Christina the Astonishing* and the story it tells about joy and suffering is that the one depends on the other. Like Christ who must die before he can, through his resurrection, promise eternal life, Christina must die before she can live as Christ. She bursts forth from the casket into which her family places her, disrupting the lines between the living and the dead, yet her new life is premised on the intensity of her suffering. The *Life* suggests ways, however, in which we might disentangle, if not life and death, then perhaps joy and suffering. Or perhaps better, the *Life* suggests a way in which we might come to deploy the processes of incorporation that mark the melancholic subject to engender a richer array of living, spontaneous affects. For Thomas depicts Christina participating in monastic prayer, the recitation or singing of the Psalms in the daily round of the Divine Office. Cassian, in describing the role of the recitation of the Psalms in a life devoted to Christian perfection, explains that the goal of the practice is to become so one with the Psalmist that his words come spontaneously to one's lips. Spontaneity takes work; it is a cultivated habitus that engenders the full range of affect articulated within the Psalms themselves: fear, dread, shame, and sorrow, but also gratitude, joy, triumph, love, and ecstasy.

Through the recitation of the Psalms, Christians come to know and re-create themselves affectively in and through God. Yet the recitation of the Psalms, the movement through their seemingly endless proliferation of names for God, is the enacted site of both cataphasis and apophasis. God, self, and community are both said and unsaid through the multiplicity of the Psalms and the long tradition of Christian songs their recitation has engendered. There may be something inherently melancholic about the handing down of tradition—it always involves the internalization of a lost and idealized other, in this case the Psalmist, but also Christ as the referent and often the speaker of the Psalms, a lost other in the face of whom we will always be in some way lacking—yet tradition need not rest on the assertion that loss, suffering, and death alone are real. Christianity insists that it *not* be, but that presence, pleasure, and life are *also* real, that we live in the interplay between presence and absence, suffering and pleasure, life and death, sorrow and joy.

For too long, the injunction to critique has rested on unquestioned—uncritiqued—melancholic foundations. For Freud, the self-critical function comes into the psyche through melancholic incorporation. Today, I think, the internalized judging agency has become the sorrowing, suffering world.[135] Those of us living in privilege—and those living, often barely, without it—are unable to look away, unable to act, unable, in the fullest sense of the word, to live. Yet the energy for efficacious action comes not solely through melancholy, but also through joy, through a love of the world that, in love, demands change. What Christianity shows—what Henry James, putative bastion of the bourgeoisie, shows—is that this takes work, work on ourselves and work on the world, an unalienated labor in and through which we become who we are. Not suffering *or* joy, for we can't have the one without the other; we can't live well—we can't *live*—on sorrow and anger and rage alone.

PART I

ACUTE MELANCHOLIA

NO ONE in my family can tell a story without telling twenty-five, not just because one story inevitably leads to another, but also because any given story is embedded with endless digressions, only seemingly incidental anecdotes, all wending their way toward some grand narrative finale, which tends never quite to arrive. (As my students know, this is all too often the way I teach.) I am going to give the abbreviated, nondigressive version of the story of my paternal great-grandmother, Maria (long i) Hollywood. (It will be—for me, at least—incredibly difficult.)

My mother is the one who told me this story, one she had heard from my Grandfather Hollywood. His mother, after whom I was unwittingly named (here is the first long, omitted digression, and I promise now to stop marking each of them), my great-grandmother, starved herself to death. She lived in lower Manhattan. Her bartender husband, my great-grandfather, Patrick, died young, leaving her with those of their eight children who remained alive at the time. My grandfather, Joseph, graduated from the sixth grade just after his father died, left school, and worked to support his mother and younger brothers and sisters. First he sold newspapers; but he loved chemistry and somehow caught the eye of a chemical salesman who sold to the paper. (Not as a chemist, of course, but as a salesman. He was apparently one of those guys who could sell anything to anybody.) Eventually, he co-owned a chemical sales business. But that was later. Through his twenties he lived with his mother and one remaining sister, until, when she was sixteen, that last sister, Mary, died. And when Mary died, his mother, my great-grandmother, Maria, stopped eating, refused doctors, and she too died.

There is something awful now in thinking about my mother telling me this story when I was just a small child. But the truth is, I loved my mother's stories, even when they involved starving Irish grannies and impecunious youth, maybe in part because I never quite believed them. Now I can see all the key narrative elements—Horatio Alger meets *Newsies* meets a certain much beloved (to Irish Americans at least) strand of melodramatic Gothic.

So I loved the story—or was at least fascinated by it—and later could analyze its religious, political, ethnic, and gender implications, and the play of power, oppression, desire, and anxiety that ran through each episode (and, perhaps even more, provided the conditions of its telling). On some fundamental level, though, the older I got, the less I believed it.

But the thing is, it turned out to be true. After my father died, I opened the grey lock box that I had seen on his desk for years (and oddly, given that I had rifled through every other available object in the house, had never touched). I remember only two of the documents that were in the box: my father's flight record from World War II (it was the original flight record, now lost) and a copy, now also lost, of my great-grandmother's death certificate. Maria Smith (therein lies yet another complex story) Hollywood died at the age of fifty-five. The cause of death: acute melancholia.

I tell this story—about the power of loss literally to kill—because it serves as a cautionary backdrop for my current research. From medieval Christian mysticism to psychoanalysis and contemporary feminist philosophy—an odd array, I grant—I have learned that one way we deal with loss is through an internalization of the lost other, who then becomes part of who we are. I am interested in the bodily, psychic, spiritual, and mental practices by which we are formed and reformed; in the role of loss and incorporation in those practices; and in the ways in which they give rise to forms of subjectivity that are always and necessarily intersubjective. (And also always and necessarily, although in complex ways, sexed, gendered, sexualized, raced, and marked by the other salient differences that constitute the social worlds of which we are a part.)

It is not an accident, of course, that the relationship between mourning, melancholia, and Christian mysticism first became starkly apparent to me—it had always been, I can now see, a crucial yet undertheorized aspect of my work—the year that one of my brothers and one of my sisters were both very ill. I was, inevitably, thinking about mourning and melancholia and, less inevitably, reading Margaret Ebner's *Revelations*.[1] There it was—the complex interactions between trauma and loss, mourning and melancholy—enacted in and by Ebner's book.

Despite my own worries about reading anachronistically, I am convinced these interactions are in this text and in many others, and not just a result of me reading melancholically.

I hope to convince you of this and to suggest the foundational role of trauma and loss, mourning and melancholic incorporation in the writings by and about two medieval women. I will then turn, albeit briefly, to what these women's stories can tell us about Freud, melancholia, and what we might call the theological imagination. To get at these questions, I need first to lay out a three- or sometimes fourfold movement visible in the devotional, visionary, and mystical lives of Beatrice of Nazareth (1200–68) and Margaret Ebner (ca. 1291–1351).[2] The most striking feature of this pattern is its movement from external objects to their internalization by the devout person (the key component of melancholy for both medieval and modern theorists), and then their subsequent re-externalization in and on the body of the believer (the rendering visible of melancholic incorporation whereby the holy person becomes Christ to those around her).

BEATRICE OF NAZARETH

Beatrice of Nazareth was a Cistercian nun, the author of a short vernacular treatise, *Seven Manners of Loving*, and the subject of an extensive Latin life. I've written at length about the crucial differences between Beatrice's own text and the hagiography, presumably written by a male cleric shortly after her death. Here I will read the two documents together, however, for only then do we see the three- and fourfold pattern of female sanctity in which I am interested.[3] Most crucially, the hagiographer tells us about Beatrice's use of external objects as an aid to devotion, just as he will emphasize the external manifestations of belief on Beatrice's body. Beatrice, on the other hand, is intent on describing her experience as *internal*, and eschews discussion of external objects of devotion and of her own, externally apprehended body. Although as an historian, I remain skeptical about whether Beatrice's hagiographer gives an accurate account of her life, medieval readers decidedly were not. Hence taken together the two texts—Beatrice's treatise and her hagiography—give a picture of movement from external to internal and back again that we then find repeated in fourteenth-century texts like Margaret Ebner's *Revelations*.[4]

After briefly describing the ascetic rigors to which Beatrice subjects herself, the hagiographer writes of her devotion, particularly to the cross of Christ:

> Day and night she wore on her breast a wooden cross, about a palm in length, tightly tied with a knotted string. On it was written the Lord's passion, the horror of the last judgment, the severity of the judge and other things she wanted always to keep in mind. Besides this she also carried tied to her arm another image of the Lord's cross painted on a piece of parchment. She had a third, painted on a piece of wood, set before her when she was writing, so that wherever she went, or whatever exterior work she did, all forgetfulness would be banished, and by means of the image of the cross she would keep [firmly] impressed on her heart and memory whatever she feared to lose.[5]

Not only does the hagiographer portray Beatrice as making use of devotional objects to aid in her meditative practice, but there is a proliferation of these objects, suggesting both a desire that the cross be ever present to the believer and its tendency to slip from memory in the absence of external reminders.[6]

The wooden cross and images of the cross painted on wood and parchment ultimately, however, become unnecessary. The goal of Beatrice's meditation on Christ's cross seems to be met when she has so fully internalized the image of Christ's Passion that she is unable *not* to see it before her mind's eye:

> Thereafter for about five unbroken years she had the mental image of the Lord's passion so firmly impressed in her memory that she scarcely ever quit this sweet meditation, but clung from the bottom of her heart with wonderful devotion to everything he deigned to suffer for the salvation of the human race. (*LBN*, 92–93)

The hagiographer thus depicts Beatrice as having so successfully internalized that which is represented by the cross as no longer to require external aids for her meditative practice.[7]

Turning to Beatrice's own treatise, *Seven Manners of Loving*, we find no explicit reference to her devotion to Christ's cross, either as externally apprehended through created objects or as internally present to the mind. Yet the language Beatrice uses to describe her intense love for God can be traced to contemporary discourses on and representations of the Passion (discourses and representations closely tied to ancient and medieval medical accounts of melancholia).

In describing the violent and overwhelming experience of the fifth manner of loving, Beatrice writes that

> at times love becomes so boundless and so overflowing in the soul, when it itself is so mightily and violently moved in the heart, that it seems (*dunct*) to the soul that the heart is wounded again and again, and that these wounds increase every day in bitter pain and in fresh intensity. It seems (*dunct*) to the soul that the veins are bursting, the blood spilling, the marrow withering, the bones softening, the bosom burning, the throat parching, so that her visage and her body in its every part feels this inward (*van binnen*) heat, and this is the fever of love.[8]

The wounding of the heart by love calls to mind both Song of Songs 4:9 ("You have wounded my heart, my sister, my bride, with one of thy eyes") and the piercing of Christ's side by Longinus's spear. In sermon 61 on the Song of Songs, Bernard of Clairvaux writes that the spear, in piercing Christ's side, laid bare his heart, the very heart wounded by the glance of his beloved.[9] Beatrice's words, then, evoke the Passion in ways that may seem oblique to modern readers but would have been clear to her contemporaries. In writing of her own heartache, moreover, she not only internalizes a mental image of the Passion, but herself comes to experience internally the suffering Christ felt on the cross (a movement of identification facilitated by the Song of Songs itself, which moves between the laments of the Bridegroom and his Bride).

The conflation of language from the Song of Songs with events from the Passion narrative is further reinforced by the application of medical accounts of lovesickness and melancholia to the Song of Songs. Twelfth-century commentators on the Song wrestle with the problem of how lovesickness, which they considered to be a physical illness, "could signify spiritual love." Yet by the thirteenth century, William of Auvergne, bishop of Paris, argues that the medical language of lovesickness can be used to help describe and understand mystical rapture.[10] The soul languishing for love of God ("for I am sick with love," Song of Songs 2:5; 5:8) becomes emblematic of mystical rapture itself, and the effects of lovesickness and mystical desire are almost indistinguishable.[11] Medieval natural philosophers and theologians, moreover, closely associated lovesickness with melancholia and both, it must be added, with languor.[12] Although in the Middle Ages, melancholia is often associated with acedia and anger[13] and, much less often, with envy and avarice[14]—all sinful states—lovesickness as a species of melancholia is clearly not, or at least not always, sinful. Instead, mania, sorrow, despair, and languor (not easily assimilable categories, to modern ears) are so closely associated with melancholic lovesickness that by the twelfth century, as Mary Wack explains, "the medical *signa amoris* came to be applied to mystical love."[15] And not only, I argue, with mystical love of the soul for God, but also with the love of Christ for humanity.

When Beatrice writes that it seems to her as if her veins were bursting, her marrow withering, her bones softening, her throat parching, and, above all, her blood spilling, she borrows from late-medieval medical discourses about lovesickness and melancholia.[16] She describes herself as sick with love, not for another human being, but for God. By juxtaposing this language with that of the heart wound, moreover, she conflates the soul's love for God with God's love for the soul as demonstrated by the Son's death on the cross. For medieval medical writers within both the Christian and the Muslim traditions, lovesickness as a form of melancholia (or sometimes as a forerunner to melancholia) is a malfunctioning of judgment or the estimative faculty. Like Freud, as we will see, Avicenna and those who follow him argue that the melancholic (whether lovesick or not) overestimates his or her object.[17] Although often read within the terms of humoral theory (a complicating factor I don't have space to discuss here), Avicenna and his followers fundamentally agree with Freud that lovesickness and melancholy involve an overvaluation of the object, suffering in the face of one's own inadequacy before the beloved and the beloved's loss or absence. We can discern here why melancholic lovesickness for God or Christ cannot be sinful, for the object of love cannot be overvalued, nor the lover ever sufficiently debased before its divine beloved.[18]

The tie between Beatrice's internal experience of a lovesickness reminiscent of Christ's Passion and her meditation on the Passion of Christ becomes clearer when we see how Beatrice's hagiographer chose to translate the passage of the treatise cited above. As elsewhere in his rendering of Beatrice's words, the hagiographer externalizes what she describes as internally apprehended experiences:

> Indeed her heart, deprived of strength by this invasion, often gave off a sound like that of a shattering vessel, while she both felt the same and heard it exteriorly. Also the blood diffused through her bodily members boiled over through her open veins. Her bones contracted and the marrow disappeared; the

dryness of her chest produced hoarseness of throat. And to make a long story short, the very fervor of her holy longing and love blazed up as a fire in all her bodily members, making her perceptibly (*sensibiliter*) hot in a wondrous way. (*LBN*, 308–11)

Lest this body, with blood boiling over through its open veins, seem far from the representations of Christ's Passion on which Beatrice might have meditated, we have only to turn to an image now in Cologne, and probably produced in the Rhineland during the fourteenth century (see figure 7.2).[19]

Here we see Christ depicted as awash in blood, suggesting a visual rendition of the reading of Christ's Passion as lovesickness evoked textually by Beatrice's hagiographer. We cannot know if she ever saw images like this one. Nonetheless, it is clear that a common set of biblical and medical references enables the conflation of Christ's Passion with the love of the Bridegroom for his Bride in the Song of Songs and medieval discourses on lovesickness. Christ's Passion *is*—iconically and experientially—melancholic lovesickness. In taking on that lovesickness, internalizing and then externally enacting Christ's melancholic desire, Beatrice herself shares in and is depicted as reenacting Christ's Passion.

As I have said, the emphasis on external objects of devotion as aides to meditation and the subsequent externalization of the internalized image of Christ's suffering on the body of the saint appear only in Beatrice's hagiography, not in her own text. She quite explicitly emphasizes the internal nature of her experience, likely in an attempt to forestall thirteenth-century presumptions of the necessarily bodily nature of women's sanctity. As I argue in "Inside Out" and elsewhere, the hagiographer's translation of Beatrice's Dutch into Latin raises questions about whether the more extreme bodily experiences described in the *Life* even *happened*. (How could they have without her dying?) By the time Margaret Ebner writes her *Revelations* in the fourteenth century, however, women religious writers seem to have fully internalized the prescriptions for sanctity found in thirteenth-century hagiographies. For this reason, Kate Greenspan and Richard Kieckhefer have referred to books like the *Revelations* as autohagiographies, for they include accounts of both the internally apprehended and the externally visible lives of the holy person.[20] Something very close to the threefold pattern of internalization and externalization discerned in Beatrice's treatise and hagiography, then, appears explicitly in Ebner's *Revelations*.[21]

MARGARET EBNER

Ebner writes about her devotional practices and their seemingly miraculous fulfillment in ways that demonstrate the relationship of these practices to her intractable mourning over the loss of a beloved other. The close ties between lovesickness
and melancholia, loss and mourning, are thus starkly apparent within her book
(as also are the deep resonances between late medieval devotional and mystical
texts and psychoanalysis). Like Beatrice, moreover, Ebner comes not only to see
and hear Christ's suffering, but also to experience it herself. Again, in ways that
Freud will later theorize in psychoanalytic terms, the infinitely valued but absent
beloved is both idealized and internalized by the lovesick melancholic.[22]

Ebner lived from 1291 to 1351, spending most of her life in the Dominican
monastery of Maria Medingen near Dillingen in southern Germany.[23] Her life
was marked, according to the account she gives us in her *Revelations*, by continuous ill health and what we would now call paramystical phenomena. The illnesses
begin in 1312, but the real impetus for her special religious experiences seems to
have been the death of the nun who cared for her in her illness over a number of
years and, a year later, her meeting with the secular clergyman Henry of Nördlingen. (Henry would become Ebner's lifelong friend and supporter, making her
the center of a loose-knit group of like-minded religious people known as "The
Friends of God.") Up until this time in her life, Ebner describes only two experiences that might be taken as extraordinary signs of religious grace, a dream and
an audition.[24]

The relative aridity of Ebner's spiritual life changes drastically, however, with
the death of the caretaking nun, whom Ebner never names. Ebner's mourning is
intense: "There were times when I thought I could not be without my sister and
could not live without her" (*MW*, 92; *ME*, 13). Although she claims that this
sorrow often turned to joy, she admits that she "could not actually be conscious
of" this joy. The sister returns to Ebner in sleep, letting her know that she is in
heaven with the Virgin Mary, the humanity of the Lord, and the divine Trinity.
She promises, furthermore, that she will be there to greet Ebner when Ebner
dies. Yet despite these comforting dreams, Ebner's sorrow for her sister "was not
relieved" (*MW*, 92; *ME*, 15). Out of this grief, however, emerges the full range of
sensory experiences of both comfort and suffering that will mark the remainder
of Ebner's life. Thus in the year following the nun's death, in the midst of an
administrative conflict in the monastery about which Ebner claims not to care,

she went out to visit the convent graves (and presumably that of her beloved fellow sister). Later, she writes:

> As I went into choir a sweet fragrance surrounded me and penetrated through my heart and into all my limbs and the name *Jesus Christus* was given to me so powerfully that I could pay attention to nothing else. And it seemed to me that I was really in his presence. (*MW*, 93; *ME*, 15)

This marks the beginning of Ebner's multisensory experience of the divine presence, which will come to encapsulate not only smell, but also hearing, sight, taste, touch, and proprioception. It is also the first instance of one of the two devotional practices that will be central to her life from that time forward, the constant repetition of the name of Jesus Christ.[25]

Ebner insists that in her subsequent meeting with Henry of Nördlingen (in 1332), he spoke words of such comfort that the death of her sister was "never again as unbearable as it had been" (*MW*, 93; *ME*, 16). Yet immediately following this passage she describes the onset of "the greatest pain" in her head and teeth, a pain so great that she "could not bow [her] head for six weeks and all seemed bitter to [her] and [she] thought that [she] would rather suffer death each day" (*MW*, 93; *ME*, 16). The very intensity of this suffering, however, becomes the basis for the second great devotional practice of Ebner's life, her meditation on the person of Christ and, in particular, on his Passion (joined later by a parallel devotion to his childhood):

> Once during Lent [apparently in 1334] great desire and powerful grace were given to me to serve God more perfectly. I felt how our Lord's works of love increased powerfully in me. And I desired that my whole body would be full of the signs of love of the holy cross, as many as were possible to be on me, and that each one would be given to me with all its suffering and pain over my entire body. Still I desired that there be no member of my body not wounded with the pains of my Lord Jesus Christ. I also had great yearning to hear something about the signs of love and works of love (*minnenzaichen und werken*) because I felt an inner grace-filled attraction toward them. Eight days before Easter the Lord gave me a most severe and unceasing pain. In this agony I heard about the sufferings of our Lord as the four Passion narratives were being read. (*MW*, 95; *ME*, 19–20)

Ebner's desire for the stigmata ("the signs of love of the holy cross")[26] entails a desire not only for visible signs of Christ's suffering on her body, but also for the pain of that suffering. Her prayer is answered when she physically reenacts Christ's pain during Passion week (a pattern that will be repeated in subsequent years in a cycle that follows the liturgical calendar).

Ebner's devotion to Christ's cross not only brings about her own bodily suffering, but also leads to her extraordinary responses to auditory and visual representations of Christ's Passion. The passage cited above suggests the importance of the auditory, for Ebner first desires to hear the story of Christ's Passion, and then miraculously does hear the story read aloud.[27] She goes on to stress the role of the visual and the tactile in her devotion: "Every cross I came upon I kissed ardently and as frequently as possible. I pressed it forcibly against my heart constantly, so that I often thought I could not separate myself from it and remain alive" (*MW*, 96; *ME*, 20). This language, so strongly reminiscent of that used to discuss the dead nun who had cared for Ebner, suggests that, for Ebner, the cross and Christ on it have replaced this beloved sister in her affective life. Ebner continues:

> Such great desire and such sweet power so penetrated my heart and all of my members that I could not withdraw myself from the cross. Wherever I went I had a cross with me. In addition, I possessed a little book in which there was a picture of the Lord on the cross. I shoved it secretly against my bosom, open to that place, and wherever I went I pressed it to my heart with great joy and with measureless grace. When I wanted to sleep, I took the picture of the Crucified Lord in the little book and laid it under my face. Also, around my neck I wore a cross that hung down to my heart. In addition, I took a large cross whenever possible and laid it over my heart. I clung to it while lying down until I fell asleep in great grace. We had a large crucifix in choir. I had the greatest desire to kiss it and to press it close to my heart like the others. But it was too high up for me and was too large in size. (*MW*, 96; *ME*, 20–21)[28]

The one sister in whom Ebner confides this desire refuses to help her, fearing that the act would be too much for one as physically frail as Ebner. Yet, Ebner claims, what is not possible while awake God grants her in a dream: "It seemed as if I were standing before the cross filled with the desire that I usually had within me. As I stood before the image, my Lord Jesus Christ bent down from the cross and let me kiss His open heart and gave me to drink of the blood flowing from His heart" (*MW*, 96; *ME*, 21).[29]

The goal of Ebner's devotion to the name of Jesus Christ and to his Passion is suggested in these passages and very shortly attained. The following Lent (1335), as Ebner explains:

> The sweetest Name of Jesus Christ was given to me with such great love that by the interior divine power of God I could pray only with continuous speaking. I could not resist it. I do not know how to write about it except to say that the Name *Jesus Christus* was constantly on my lips. The speaking lasted until prime and I could do nothing else. Then I was silent. I could avoid speaking with other people, but I had no power to cease from this speaking. (*MW*, 100; *ME*, 27)[10]

Ebner has so fully internalized her devotional practice that she is now unable *not* to repeat continuously the name of Jesus Christ.

A similar pattern repeats itself on the auditory, visual, and tactile planes, although the process of meditative internalization is slower and involves three stages rather than two. (I am simplifying the often complex relationship between these stages.) First, Ebner desires to impress the cross and the Passion story onto her heart by voluntarily embracing visual images and repeatedly listening to or reading the Passion narrative. This is followed by an inability not to see Christ's suffering. In the Lent of 1340, while at matins, for example, "the greatest pain came over" Ebner's heart (like "the greatest pain" that comes over Ebner after she apparently accepted her fellow nun's death), "and also a sorrow, so bitter that it was as if I were really in the presence of my Beloved, my most heartily Beloved One, and as if I had seen his suffering with my own eyes and as if it were all happening before me at this very moment" (*MW*, 114; *ME*, 52). Following in the meditative tradition on Christ's life and death promulgated by the Cistercians, Franciscans, and Dominicans, Ebner here describes a perfect *meditatio* in which she no longer needs external aides, be they visual, tactile, or auditory, for Christ's Passion to be viscerally present to her.

With this internalizing movement, Christ's Passion is also reexternalized in and on Ebner's body. Laid out in pain in the choir and then the dormitory, Ebner becomes a visible sign of the suffering engendered by witnessing Christ's Passion and, ultimately, as we will see, of the Passion itself. Not only does she find herself unable *not* to repeat the name of Christ (the speaking), and not to hear of or see Christ's torment before her mind's ear and eye, but she also finds herself unable to hear about or see Christ's death without crying aloud (the outcry).[31]

She claims that other signs of the body's share in Christ's Passion often accompany this externalizing vocalization:

> But when I was given to loud exclamations and outcries by the gentle goodness of God (these were given to me when I heard the holy suffering spoken about), then I was pierced to the heart and this extended to all my members, and then I was bound and ever more grasped by the silence. In these cases, I sat a long time—sometimes longer, sometimes shorter. After this my heart was as if shot by a mysterious force. Its effect rose up to my head and passed on to all my members and broke them violently. Compelled by the same force I cried out loudly and exclaimed. I had no power over myself and was not able to stop the outcry until God released me from it. Sometimes it grasped me so powerfully that red blood spurted from me. (*MW*, 114; *ME*, 54)

Ebner's identification with the Passion shifts from identification with the onlookers to one with Christ himself. With blood gushing forth from her body, moreover, Ebner so fully incorporates Christ—the lost beloved other—that she now visibly represents his suffering for those around her.[32]

In a similar way, increasingly Ebner does not have to see representations of or hear about Christ's Passion to be overcome by what she calls the outcry. Rather, an "inner vision" overcomes her, and she is unable to restrain herself from crying out in pain and suffering. Again, these events occur particularly during Lent and with greatest intensity during Holy Week:

> And that happened to me frequently at the same time because of some inner vision especially during Lent, even when I did not hear or read the Passion. On that Wednesday when I had read vespers, the entire Passion came to me again with strong outcries and exclamations. On Thursday after that at matins I was again grasped by great sincere sympathy inwardly and outwardly. Then on Friday the Passion was so really present to me while reading the office that I cried out when I read one of the hours. (*MW*, 115; *ME*, 55–56)

Throughout the week, Ebner was in bed, "so wounded externally from the interior suffering" that she couldn't bear to have anyone touch her. Yet she shares not only in Christ's Passion, but also in his resurrection. On Easter Sunday the nun who cared for her found her "in great joy and in good health" (*MW*, 115; *ME*, 56).[33]

This pattern, of Lenten suffering followed by Easter renewal, which follows the liturgical calendar that structured a Dominican nun's daily life and year, will continue throughout Ebner's *Revelations*. Christ's name and the wounds of his Passion are further impressed on her heart and the "rending arrows" of the Lord shoot through her heart "with a swift shot from his spear of Love" (*MW*, 156; *ME*, 131; here, as in Beatrice's *Seven Manners of Loving*, language from the Song of Songs comes together with reflections on Longinus's spear). Perhaps Ebner's most complete moment of identification with Christ's suffering occurs through her own highly particular version of the stigmata. She receives not the visible wounds, nor simply the pain of the hands, feet, side wound, and head wounds (caused by the crown of thorns), but a wracking of the entire body reminiscent of late medieval and early modern representations of the crucifixion:[34]

> I felt an inner pain in my hands as if they were stretched out, torn, and broken through, and I supposed that they would always be useless to me thereafter. In my head I felt a wondrous pain as if I were pierced and broken through.[35] That seemed so excruciating to me that I began to tremble and shook so violently that the sisters had to hold me fast. I trembled while in their grasp and I felt this trembling for a long time after Easter whenever I prayed earnestly or read or talked, and I perceived the same painful brokenness in all my members, especially on both sides and on my back, arms, and legs, so that it seemed to me I was in the last throes and that all this suffering would continue until death, if it were the will of God. (*MW*, 157; *ME*, 132–33)

Even Easter no longer brings about Ebner's renewal. At this point, she writes, she longs for death, quoting Philippians 1:23 and 1:21: "*cupio dissolvi*" ("I desire to be destroyed")[36] and "*mihi vivere Christus et mori lucrum*" ("for me to live is Christ and to die is gain") (*MW*, 157; *ME*, 132–33).

A pattern common to a number of texts from the later Middle Ages, then, appears with stark clarity in Ebner's *Revelations*. Ebner moves through four stages: first, she actively remembers Christ's Passion, aided by the recitation and reading of scriptural texts, meditative guides, prayers, and the divine name, as well as by devotional images and artifacts; eventually she is unable *not* to cry out in the face of Christ's suffering; she then *involuntarily* remembers these events; and, finally, she fully internalizes and reenacts them in and on her body.

TRAUMA, MEMORY, AND MELANCHOLIA

I have argued elsewhere that the meditative practices of the later Middle Ages, which aimed to make vivid and inescapable the pain and suffering of Christ's life and death, are curiously similar to contemporary discussions of traumatic memory.[37] Researchers on trauma and Post-Traumatic Stress Disorder isolate particular forms of intensely sensory and bodily memories in which the survivor involuntarily and repetitiously relives traumatic events. Such memories are intrusive, intensely vivid, repetitive, and lack a narrative frame. They are not only visual, moreover, but also often involve other senses, presumably those heightened at the moment of trauma (for Ebner the sensory associations are often biblically based).

Contemporary research suggests that in situations of hyperarousal for which one is unprepared, memory is encoded in a different, more viscerally experiential manner than normal. (The scholarship is highly contentious.)[38] These memories are not assimilated to consciousness, and so impinge on it in uncontrollable and intrusive ways. Modern therapeutic accounts of bodily memory, intent on eradicating, controlling, or weakening its sensory strength, argue that this can be done through the process of narrativization. Complex therapies of speaking and reenacting traumatic events within controlled environments make it possible, so the argument goes, for bodily memories to be relived and reordered in meaningful narrative forms. The therapeutic claim is that such narrativization loosens the hold of bodily memories and alleviates suffering.[39]

Late medieval meditational practices like Ebner's, however, work in precisely the opposite direction. They attempt to inculcate traumatic or bodily memory—or something very like it—by rendering involuntary, vivid, and inescapable the central catastrophic event of Christian history so that the individual believer might relive and share in that trauma.[40] For medieval practitioners of meditation on Christ's Passion, the desire to inculcate something like traumatic memory is theologically justified by a promise: through sharing in the suffering of those who witnessed Christ's death or—as in Beatrice's *Seven Manners of Loving* and Ebner's *Revelations*—sharing Christ's own pain, one can participate in the salvific work of the cross. A crucial difference between late medieval practice and contemporary accounts of Post-Traumatic Stress Disorder, then, is that whereas the latter lacks a narrative frame, medieval practice always occurs—at least in theory—within the context of Christian salvation history. One might argue that through meditation on the life and death of Christ, the believer destroys all other narrative frameworks for his or her life and induces strong emotion that can then be redeployed toward the imaginative constitution of a new Christian narrative of suffering and redemption.[41] (Franciscan treatises emphasize guilt, although this is not theologically or affectively central for either Beatrice or Ebner.)

Ebner's text, in which her devotion to the Passion occurs amid intense physical suffering and the loss of loved ones (not only the first nun who cared for her, but also the death of her next caretaker and that of another beloved fellow nun), suggests further possible refinements in our understanding of the relationship between memory, meditation, and trauma within medieval mystical texts.[42] The central traumas of Ebner's *Revelations* appear to be physical suffering and, most crucially, mourning. Throughout Ebner's *Revelations* one finds constantly repeated scenes of intense physical suffering and loss. Early in the text, however, she makes these scenes theologically meaningful by assimilating her own mourning and pain to that of Christ's followers and of Christ himself on the cross. Traumatic repetition is here not simply an involuntary repetition of past losses, but a willed taking on of suffering that also renders it meaningful.

Some attention to Freud's conceptions of mourning and melancholy further advances this reading. Freud opens his seminal essay "Mourning and Melancholia" (1917) by making a sharp distinction between the two reactions to loss (whether of a human being or of some more abstract entity). Whereas in mourning, the bereaved is able "bit by bit" to detach herself from the beloved object, allowing other objects to replace that which is lost, in melancholia the bereaved refuses to detach from and replace the lost other.[43] What is putatively surprising to Freud is not that melancholia occurs, but that mourning is so difficult:

> Each single one of the memories and expectations in which the libido is bound to the object is brought up and hypercathected, and detachment of the libido is accomplished in respect to it. Why this compromise by which the command of reality [the loss of the object] is carried out piecemeal should be so extraordinarily painful is not at all easy to explain in terms of economics. It is remarkable that this painful unpleasure is taken as a matter of course by us. The fact is, however, that when the work of mourning is completed the ego becomes free and uninhibited again.[44]

Despite the seemingly inexplicable detour, then, ultimately the ego returns to the pleasure-seeking state in which it is "free and uninhibited," ready to attach itself to and find pleasure with new objects.

The apparent—and unanswered—puzzle in "Mourning and Melancholia" is why the normally pleasure-optimizing ego is unable immediately to relinquish its object. Yet Freud occupies himself in most of the essay with the opposite issue: why is the ego sometimes unable to mourn at all and instead becomes melancholic? Melancholia is marked, for Freud, by dejection, unremitting sadness, listlessness, and guilt, characteristics familiar from medieval accounts of melancholia and melancholic lovesickness. I won't here rehearse the various arguments Freud makes in his attempt to distinguish mourning and melancholia. What is crucial for my purposes here is Freud's contention that the melancholic, refusing to give up her object and engage in substitutions, instead identifies with the object and internalizes it.

Freud describes this double movement in a peculiar way, first claiming that the melancholic's "object-cathexis proved to have little power of resistance and was brought to an end." He goes on, however, to explain that in the case of melancholia, "the free libido was not displaced onto another object," but instead "was withdrawn into the ego. There, however, it was not employed in any unspecified way, but served to establish an *identification* of the ego with the abandoned object."[45] In other words, Freud claims both that the melancholic readily gives up her object and that the libido released by that loss turns to the ego in the form of an incorporation of the lost object. The melancholic, despite Freud's contrary claim, never gives up but merely internalizes the lost object. As Freud goes on to explain, this incorporation both extends the ego's narcissism and is the site of a "painful wound":

> Thus the shadow of the object fell upon the ego, and the latter could henceforth be judged by a special agency, as though it were an object, the forsaken object. In this way an object-loss was transformed into an ego-loss and the conflict between the ego and the loved person into a cleavage between the critical activity of the ego and the ego as altered by identification.[46]

The ambivalence felt toward an object that has seemingly deserted the ego—the simultaneous hatred and love of the lost object—is now fully internalized.

In "Mourning and Melancholia" Freud argues that melancholia is a pathological state, one to which normal mourning is the healthy counterpart. We can already see, however, that the incorporations crucial to melancholia are also foundational to the constitution of the ego and to what Freud suggests is a split between the "critical activity of the ego" and its originary repressive and narcissistic aspects. Freud argues much more explicitly for this bifurcation within the ego in "The Ego and the Id" (1923). There he argues that melancholic identifications and incorporations, which he had first viewed as primarily if not solely pathological, are crucial to the development of the superego:

> We succeeded in explaining the painful disorder of melancholia by supposing that [in those suffering from it] an object that was lost has been set up again inside the ego—that is, that an object-cathexis has been replaced by an identification. At the same time, however, we did not appreciate the full significance of this process and did not know how common and how typical it is. Since then we have come to understand that this kind of substitution has a share in determining the form taken by the ego and that it makes an essential contribution towards building up what is called its "character."[47]

For Freud, then, the very constitution of the subject as self-reflective and self-critical depends on melancholic incorporation. This takes a particularly Oedipal caste, for ultimately it is the father who is thus internalized—and most completely, according to Freud, by men. Yet Freud's account of melancholic idealization and incorporation in no way leads inevitably to his later claim, particularly in his essays concerning femininity, that the Oedipal narrative alone governs the development of "character." (Nor does the deployment of the Oedipal narrative itself demand that the internalized object be the father. For both boys and girls, it is the *mother* who is lost. Freud has to do a lot of work, much of it unconvincing, to make the father the object of melancholic identification and incorporation.)[48]

Freud argues for the pathological nature of melancholia because the melancholic's sadness, guilt, and ambivalence are so often experienced as debilitating, even suicidal. Ebner, arguably a chronic melancholic who mourns the deaths of those around her and the culturally valorized death of Christ, ends where she begins—wishing to die. Yet the theological and existential implications of that desire differ radically. No longer a lone, ill woman mourning the loss of her fellow sister and caretaker, by the end of the *Revelations* Ebner is a woman thoroughly identified with Christ's salvific suffering. She has become the center of the spiritual life of her convent and of a religious movement (The Friends of God) that sees in her the fulfillment of Christ's promises to his followers. Traumatic repetition here joins with melancholic incorporation, demonstrating the way in which incorporation can itself be a form of repetition. Beatrice and Ebner both necessarily close their texts during their lives, with no end in sight to the cycle of suffering. Yet the hope offered by the Christian narrative is that with death, the peace and joy experienced only intermittently on earth will supersede the traumatic repetitions, melancholic identifications, and incorporations brought about by illness and loss.[49]

LOSS, IDENTIFICATION, AND INCORPORATION

The logic of identification and incorporation, then, is remarkably similar in Beatrice, Ebner, and Freud. The crucial difference, of course, is that by the time of "The Ego and the Id," Freud describes this process as fundamental to the articulation of the psyche and repeatedly emphasizes throughout the 1920s and 1930s that it is the father who is the first and primary object of identification and incorporation. Beatrice, Beatrice's hagiographer, and Ebner, on the other hand, describe a process of identification and incorporation that occurs when Beatrice and Ebner are adults, through grace-given but also directed practices. For Beatrice and Ebner, the idealized object of love and loss is, of course, Christ. Through their identification with Christ and memorialization of Christ's Passion, they transform themselves into Christ. This gives us a key to understanding Freud's stake in the loss of the father, for just as Christ is the centrally valorized figure for medieval religious women—and for medieval Christian culture as a whole—the father may be said to occupy a similar site within modern Western culture. But what about our other losses? We can see clearly how Ebner conjoins her other, more fully human losses with the loss of Christ. Is Freud doing something similar when he refuses to acknowledge the loss of the mother—and other caretaking figures—in place of the father?

The psychoanalyst Melanic Klein suggests one way to broach both of the issues I raise here. In "Mourning and Its Relation to Manic-Depressive States" (1940), she argues that all mourning is melancholic and that incorporation is essential to "normal" mourning. For Klein, the internalization of the living others around us, as well as of the dead, is multiple and ongoing. The process of loss, identification, and incorporation constitutes subjectivity in childhood and continues throughout one's life. Thus Klein is able explicitly to link Freud's discussions in "Mourning and Melancholia" with those in "The Ego and the Id." According to Klein:

In normal mourning the individual reintrojects and reinstates, as well as the actual lost person, his loved parents who are felt to be "good" inner objects. His inner world, the one which he has built up from his earliest days onwards, in his phantasy was destroyed when the actual loss occurred. The rebuilding of this inner world characterizes the successful work of mourning.[50]

For Klein, we learn to deal with the absence of parents and other early caregivers through a process of idealization and internalization, generating a phantasy in which they constantly remain with us and are part of us. When we experience later losses, not only do we mourn them, but our parents and other caretakers are again lost. The internal world of good objects—as well as their place as constitutive of our subjectivities—is damaged. Successful mourning occurs when we are able, through identification with and incorporation of the newly lost object, to rebuild that damaged inner world.

Mourning, for Klein, is always melancholic, for it always involves processes of identification and incorporation grounded in a refusal fully to relinquish our lost objects. Melancholy is experienced pathologically—as ineradicable, disabling depression—when the subject has been unable as a child to establish a good inner world that will sustain her in the face of later losses. And, although Klein does not say this explicitly, melancholia also overwhelms the subject when the losses are too many, too overwhelming, for the "good" parents of her inner world to combat. (This is what I imagine happened to my great-grandmother.)

I would also suggest, on the basis of my work on Beatrice and Ebner, not only that inner worlds are created in childhood, but that they are created and re-created through bodily, psychic, spiritual, and mental practices. In other words, we can, to some degree at least, re-create or reshape ourselves in the image of newly idealized and internalized objects. The problem for Beatrice and Ebner, both of whom yearn to die, is that the idealized other they incorporate is idealized precisely in his suffering and death. Melancholia here feeds melancholia rather than allaying it—the death of the other leads to the idealization of and desire for one's own death.

I return, then, to the dangers of melancholia. I can only speculate, but I think that for my great-grandmother, the enormity of her losses overcame the creative possibilities of incorporation. The lost others were too many and destroyed the self. For Beatrice and Ebner, not only the enormity of their loss, but also the very qualities of that object, led to their continued desire for death. Given these dangers, why would I want to reinstate melancholia as constitutive of subjectivity?

Why ignore the widespread disavowal of melancholia, a disavowal made not only on psychological grounds, but also theologically, philosophically, and politically, anywhere that we talk about the resurrection as the denial of death, about successful mourning as a forsaking of the lost object, or about utopias in which all loss will be overcome? Yet as Beatrice and Ebner, Freud and Klein all make clear, to disavow the subject's melancholic constitution is to disavow the complex constellation of others who make us who and what we are. It is to disavow our losses and our grief as well as that which supports and enables our subjectivity, our agency, and, paradoxically, our responsibility. It is to deny our responsibility to the others within, and thereby to disavow that which makes possible our relations with others outside of ourselves, the very grounds of sociality from which our ethical and political projects emerge. The trick is to find ways to sustain ourselves in and through our losses, rather than in their disavowal. I'd like to close, then, with some brief reflections on the theological implications of these claims and a story—the only way I've found, so far, to gesture toward the intersubjectively articulated, immanent transcendence that is as close as I can come to an avowal and a practice of belief.

THEOLOGICAL IMAGININGS

Even those who most admire Freud generally dismiss his writings on religion as stupidly and willfully reductionistic—and, for those who know the history of nineteenth-century philosophy and theology, as wildly unoriginal.[51] Ludwig Feuerbach argues that God is a projection and reification of human capacities, values, and possibilities onto a divine other, the ideal being toward whom we as individuals and as a collectivity strive.[52] To this Freud seems only to add, "and he's your father." In other words, Freud explicitly Oedipalizes Feuerbach's account of projection and reification. And whereas Feuerbach aimed to enable a kind of philosophical therapy whereby we might come to recognize divine capacities, values, goals, and aspirations as peculiarly human, Freud's vision is more fully embedded in the guiding narratives of his psychoanalytic enterprise. When we recognize that it is the internalized figure of the father—the superego—that leads to our greatest accomplishments, to the heights of civilized behavior, artistic creativity, and scientific productivity, we will no longer require religion. (Or conversely, those with the strongest superegos are least in need of religion.)

Despite critics' repeated assertion that both Feuerbach and Freud reduce religion to human and psychic dimensions, I find myself wondering if they both don't get something right—something that, curiously, has enormous theological ramifications. Freud is certainly reductionist with regard to religion, just as he is reductionist with regard to melancholy, in his suggestion that God is the projection of a lost object and that the only loss we mourn is that of the father. Freud's texts, of course, are always more complicated—and more interesting—than this reductive reading allows. Yet even if we read Freud in this simplistic way, there is something right, I think, in his suggestion that what we know of the divine we know from others *around* and *within* ourselves. As yet, I do not know how to articulate the relationship between those two prepositions except by telling you another story.

The fact that I need to tell a story to get at the centrality of mourning and melancholia for the theological imagination raises a host of questions—about the relationship between narrative and theory; about storytelling as a mode of incorporation and the incorporations constitutive of subjectivity; about storytelling and theorizing as practices through which others are incorporated even as they are maintained in their exteriority to the subject. Beatrice and Ebner tell stories, and that is what I have done. I point to these theoretical issues as the background against which I tell yet another story. For reasons I need to figure out, this one requires fictionalization. It's not the whole truth—nothing ever is—yet it's as true as anything I know.

"THE GOODNESS OF OUR BROTHER'S HEART"

They didn't do eulogies.

The father liked to announce periodically that if any of his children attempted to eulogize him, he would haunt them remorselessly for the rest of their lives. The prospect was less frightening than intended—in the many years they survived him, all of his children longed for his presence, however ghostly. But still, when he died, they'd honored his wishes and kept their love to themselves.

Other losses followed, in what sometimes felt to the survivors like one long endless funeral reception. Grandmothers, aunts, uncles. Their mother. All rigorously uneulogized. A brother, who died so shortly before his mother that there was no time even to mourn. Two sisters and a brother remained. Not Mary, Martha, and Lazarus, but those names will do as well as any others.

To Mary and Martha, although they never admitted it aloud, and certainly not to each other, Lazarus was an extraordinary human being. It was less his beauty they loved—although they loved his beauty, even as it faded—than his goodness. Lazarus, however, wasn't only handsome and good, he was also troubled and unlucky, and it was difficult for Mary and Martha to decide whether his goodness led to trouble or if the one, like the other, was a sheer, astonishing accident. For Lazarus's goodness had no cause and no traceable source. It had nothing to do with the categorical imperative, or the cultivation of virtue, or a utilitarian determination of the greatest good for the greatest number. It couldn't be taught and it certainly wasn't hereditary. But maybe, Mary and Martha thought, it's just that he's our brother and we love him. Maybe he isn't any different than anyone else.

Despite such humbling thoughts, Mary and Martha worried about Lazarus. As they lost father, mother, and brother, they each thought quietly to themselves: please, not Lazarus.

They couldn't say why they thought this, but they did.

And then, with an inevitability that still managed to take both sisters by surprise, Lazarus became ill. All three denied it for as long as they could—not that he was sick, but that the sickness would kill him. "I'm not ready to die *yet*," he said to Martha.

Mary and Martha would have given up the no-eulogies rule for Lazarus, but after his death neither of them could speak—not coherently, at least, and not about Lazarus. Instead, they spoke through the songs and the readings of the Roman Catholic funeral mass his faith required. They chose passages about building an edifice for the Lord, about God as a mighty fortress, and about the father's house having many rooms. Lazarus was a builder and he had the greatest capacity for friendship and for love that either sister had ever seen. "No matter how you feel about the Bible," Mary said, "somewhere in there it says just about everything."

They thought about using the story from the Gospel of John about Jesus's friends Mary, Martha, and Lazarus—but under the circumstances it seemed self-serving, a public assertion of the superiority of their love for their brother over all other claimants. "More to the point," Mary announced in the kind of wonderful feat of projection at which she excelled, "we don't want to upset anyone. They'll hear the story, expect Jesus to come raise Lazarus up from the dead, and be pissed off when it doesn't happen."

So Mary and Martha stuck with the father's many-roomed mansion. They called in their selections to the priest, an old family friend who had known their parents and who had known Mary and Martha and Lazarus since they were children. The priest honored the no-eulogy rule and didn't speak directly about Lazarus. But, whether through chance or design the sisters never knew, he read from the Gospel of John. He read the story of Jesus's friends, Mary, Martha, and Lazarus, and of Mary and Martha's great grief and their great faith, and of Jesus raising Lazarus from the dead. And in his sermon, he spoke directly to the hearts of our Mary and Martha and he told them that their brother was not dead and that he would live forever.

But as Mary predicted, Jesus didn't come and he didn't raise Lazarus from the dead, on that day or on any other that the sisters lived to see. The priest saw their lack of faith and he spoke to it, but he couldn't heal it, because he couldn't bring their brother back to them. They were heartbroken and desolate and no longer sure even of Lazarus's goodness, now that they could no longer see it before them, sense it in the world around them, know that it lay readily available on the edges of their worlds. The old worry—that his goodness had been a mirage created by their love—returned, and with that doubt any possibility of a reality transcendent to the anguish in which he had died was forever, irrevocably, destroyed.

(To hear your brother cry "Help! Help!" and to have nothing to offer but the morphine that will kill him. Mary held him down—sitting at the feet of the Lord—while Martha got the nurse with the syringe—and Martha was busy with many things.)

But as long as someone survives, there is always more to tell. No one ever raised Lazarus from the dead, but on the day Lazarus was buried, an old woman and her husband told Mary and Martha a story. It was a story about their brother's goodness, a story that showed them that Lazarus wasn't only good in their eyes and in the reflection of their love (which in itself maybe should have been enough, but Mary and Martha were obsessed with "objectivity" and "truth," a result no doubt of their overly abundant philosophical educations), but he was good also in the eyes of at least one elderly couple. It was, Mary and Martha often said to each other in the long years they lived without their brother, a story about the kind of goodness that Jesus must have had, the kind of goodness that would make people tell stories about a man so good that he raised a beloved brother from the dead simply in order to staunch two sisters' grief, the kind of goodness that has no discernible source and so renders belief in transcendence not only possible, but inevitable. Even if it can't bring the dead back to life in the beauty and goodness of the flesh.

Perhaps no story can bear this weight. The woman told Mary and Martha that she too had loved their brother. He had built a house for her, the house in which she and her husband planned to live out their old age. She had dreamed of the house for years, its spaces and lights and shadows. She found the land for the house and Lazarus took her dream and drew plans. He came every week to talk over the work's progress, to ensure that her desires were met in each detail of its rendering. He gave her the house of her imagination.

As they planned and talked and gossiped, she told him about a drawer she had been lugging from house to house throughout her adult life. She'd inherited it from her mother, who had inherited it from her mother. It was full of broken and discarded religious objects. Catholic kitsch—Mary as Queen of Heaven with her crown of stars chipped, scapulars that wouldn't stick together any more, a baby Jesus whose upraised arm had broken off. Trash, but to this very pious family— grandmother, mother, aunts, maybe even a few uncles—holy and blessed objects that you didn't simply throw away. Yet how long, the woman wondered aloud to Lazarus, do you lug a drawer full of broken Marys and Josephs and Jesuses around.

The truth is, the woman's husband told the rest of the story because she, like Mary and Martha, could no longer speak. On the day the concrete was to go into the new house's foundation, Lazarus came and picked up the old woman, and he carried the drawer full of holy junk out of her apartment and put it in the flatbed of his truck. (This is the way the husband told the story.) Together Lazarus and the woman went to the building site and Lazarus helped her climb down into the pit that he and his workmen had dug for the foundation. He followed her down, carrying the drawer. Together, Lazarus and the old woman lay Mary and Joseph and Jesus and whoever or whatever else was in the drawer on the freshly turned dirt.

"He thought of that," the old woman said.

("He *did* it," Mary and Martha both thought, simultaneously, to themselves.)

The man and the woman lived out the rest of their lives in the house of their dreams. A house embedded with her family's faith. A house—in the words Mary told Martha or Martha told Mary, night after night for the rest of their lives—a house built with the labor of our brother's hands, with the goodness of our brother's heart.

⁂

Of my brother's—my brother Daniel's—heart.

PART II
History

FEMINIST STUDIES IN CHRISTIAN SPIRITUALITY

2

IN AN important essay on the study of spirituality as an academic discipline, Bernard McGinn tells a story about the inception of Paulist Press's "Classics of Western Spirituality" series:

> A Long Island commuter stands on a platform watching trains speeding past each other east and west in their rush towards what seem to be opposite goals. This particular commuter happens to be a religious editor who suddenly grasps this as an image of the mutual ignorance and lack of connection between Eastern and Western spiritual traditions. If only something could be done to get the trains to slow down, he thinks, to stop, to converse window-to-window, might they not realize that their opposition is not as great as it seems?[1]

McGinn reads the editor's moment of insight as akin to what Augustine calls intellectual vision, thereby suggesting some of the ways in which "the efforts of believing teachers and educators relate to first-order spirituality."[2] My interest in the story diverges from McGinn's, however, for the editor's insight speaks in compelling ways to a perhaps unforeseen achievement of the "Classics of Western Spirituality" series.

As McGinn notes in telling the anecdote, the series was initially planned to be one half of two parts, the whole to be called the "Classics of Eastern and Western Spirituality." Arguably, in the absence of its westbound train, the series fails to live up to its inspiring vision. Yet there is another conversation between apparent opposites in which it has, since its inception, participated. The first volume published in the series was Edmund Colledge and James Walsh's translation of the fourteenth- and early-fifteenth-century anchorite Julian of Norwich's *Showings*, in both its short and its long versions.[3] Many of the subsequent volumes published in the series included texts by women, texts from spiritual traditions within Christianity (and on its edges) in which women have played a crucial role (for example, the medieval English anchorite movement), or texts that show men and women in conversation, debate, and sometimes intense conflict (for example, Francis de Sales and Jane de Chantal). Of course, the "Classics" series has not been alone in making available in English texts by and about Christian women and their spirituality. Among a host of important publications, I will mention only the groundbreaking anthologies by Katharina Wilson and Elizabeth Alvilda Petroff, and Margot King's imprint devoted specifically to early and medieval Christian women's spiritual writing, Peregrina Publishing.[4]

There are some good reasons why a series dedicated to Christian spirituality might, from the outset, be compelled to include texts by both women and men. Before we get there, however, let's pause for a moment over the key terms of analysis. The categories "women" and "men" will seem unproblematic to many readers, yet Christian spiritual writings and practices raise questions about their adequacy to the past and to the present. For most of this essay I will use the terms "man" and "woman," "male" and "female," "masculine" and "feminine" as they are found in the sources and in contemporary scholarship. I will also point to ways in which the texts of the Christian spiritual tradition trouble the sex, gender, and sexual binaries that accompany the belief that human beings can be unproblematically categorized within them. I won't eschew the language of women entirely, however, for a feminist commitment to women—complexly understood—and others silenced within heteronormative, male-dominated societies remains vital to my work and to much of the work I discuss here.[5]

As to spirituality, scholars have rightly questioned the generality of the various conventional definitions, yet McGinn's understanding of it as the lived experience of belief or the striving after such experience remains compelling.[6] This seems to be how the term is most often used in scholarly and other contexts. More importantly, the term *experientia* is crucial to the Christian tradition and its articulation of the pursuit of the Christian life. Central figures, such as John Cassion (d. ca. 435) and Bernard of Clairvaux (d. 1153), use the term *experientia* to denote that which is worked on and transformed through Christian practice.[7] When Bernard calls on his listeners to read "the book of experience," asking whether experience and the biblical text can be brought together so that one says with the Bride of the Song of Songs, "Let him kiss me with the kiss of his mouth," he articulates the centrality of experience to the religious life.[8] As we will see, this position is vital to women's role in the history of Christian spirituality.

For as it turns out, a series in Western spirituality must be a place in which both men and women speak and in which, as I will show, issues of sexual difference, gender, and sexuality almost inevitably come to the forefront, whether explicitly or implicitly, simply through the choice of texts to be translated. Within the Christian tradition, at least, some of the most important texts dealing with the experience of religion have been written—and continue to be written—by women. This, despite the fact that, for much of the history of the Christian tradition, misogynist assumptions have precluded women from holding most church offices, from serving as preachers and teachers to mixed audiences of men and women except on very rare occasions, and from attending the elite educational institutions in which theology is taught. Loopholes, however, could always be found and women (and the men who often supported them) discovered, fairly early on in the Christian tradition, how to use them. A key issue was the presumption, supported by biblical texts, that women might receive special graces: within the early and medieval period and in modern Roman Catholicism especially (but by no means only) those women who dedicated themselves to God as virgins.[9] Throughout the history of the Christian tradition it was often believed that God chose to give women visions, to bestow prophecies on them, and to render Godself one with them in a union of the spirit or a union without distinction; God then also permitted—indeed, even called on—women to speak and write of these things. As a result, women's experience of Christian truth became one of the primary means through which they were empowered to speak, teach, and write.[10]

Yet even if women had not themselves written, any study of the spirituality of a tradition that purports to include women within it will address, in some way, women and issues of gender difference. Liturgical and prayer books, hagiographical texts, and guidebooks for the pursuit of the Christian life (or that of any other tradition) are key to the study of spirituality.[11] Almost every religious tradition known to scholars, furthermore, argues that the religious life be lived in ways that are clearly marked by gender. Hence, gender differentiation and spirituality often go hand in hand. In addition, almost all religious traditions use gender as a way to think through important spiritual issues. Thus, as Kate

Cooper shows in the case of early Christianity, femininity becomes a crucial category through which male religious identity and spirituality are thought and enacted.[12] What is remarkable about the Christian tradition is the extent to which women were able to participate in the written expression of spirituality, hence providing a rare glimpse into the ways in which men's understanding of how women should live and women's own self-conceptions and experience differ, as well as insight into how women "think with" gender in ways like or unlike men.

So as it turns out, within the history of Christianity, men and women have been talking about spirituality for a very long time.[13] These conversations take many different forms. Sometimes men view women as their guides and models, at other times they are seen as equals,[14] and—perhaps most often—men guide, command, even coerce women into particular forms of spiritual life.[15] Despite the near ubiquity of these conversations, however, the historical tendency to consign women's writings and lives to oblivion—either through the effacement of their stories and texts or through a refusal to see the connections between women and men and between women across time—renders it necessary once again to slow down the trains and to show the wealth of women's contributions to Christian spiritual traditions, as well as the central difference gender has made to the constructions of these traditions.

Feminist scholars of Christian spirituality have been pursuing the work of reclamation, commentary, and analysis for over thirty years (with important precursors in the late nineteenth and early twentieth centuries). It would be impossible to adequately summarize the wealth of resources that have been discovered or rediscovered, the subtlety of commentary and analysis, and the plethora of exciting new questions being asked of this material within the contemporary academy. What I will try to do is map out the terrain shaped by scholars in the 1980s and some of the most important questions inspired by their groundbreaking scholarship. The work of Caroline Walker Bynum must stand at the center of this discussion, for no other scholar has done more to shape feminist work on Christian spirituality. After careful attention to the main lines of Bynum's arguments about female spirituality within the Christian Middle Ages, I will turn to some of the most important questions raised about her work. Attention to these critiques, refinements, and extensions of Bynum's groundbreaking scholarship will in turn lead to discussion of new directions in the feminist study of spirituality.[16]

CAROLINE WALKER BYNUM AND THE HISTORY OF MEDIEVAL WOMEN'S SPIRITUALITY

Second-wave American feminism was from its outset tied to Christianity and had an immediate impact on Christian theology and spirituality.[17] The critique of male-dominant institutional structures and theological visions went hand in hand with attempts to reclaim aspects of the Christian tradition for women.[18] Caroline Walker Bynum, in a series of pivotal studies produced during the 1980s, both furthered feminist studies of Christian spirituality and raised central questions about the assumptions under which much feminist theology and work in religion then operated. Bynum challenged two key premises of second-wave feminist theology and thealogy. First, most early feminist scholarship on religion—and much of that produced today—presumes that the mainstream traditions of Christianity, with their male-governed institutional structures, male deities, and emphases on virginity, asceticism, chastity, and obedience as primary modes of access to leadership for women, were and are inherently disempowering for women. The second and related point of Bynum's critique questions the presumption that theological language and imagery reflect and sustain social structures, so that a male God both empowers men and reflects men's power and, as a consequence, the only way for women to achieve power is through the advent of gender neutral or feminine language for the divine.[19]

In *Jesus as Mother: Studies in the Spirituality of the High Middle Ages*,[20] Bynum engages in a detailed reading of key images and metaphors within the writings of twelfth- and thirteenth-century religious writers in order to show that there is little evidence for men's greater attraction to masculine language and symbols or women's greater attraction to feminine language and symbols. In fact, Bynum argues, the image of Jesus as mother is found in texts by both men and women, albeit deployed in different ways. Moreover, devotion to the Virgin Mary arguably plays a greater role in texts written by men (and so perhaps within their religious lives) than in those written by women.[21] In addition, Bynum shows that the particular forms of life adopted by both men and women (for example, monks versus canons or beguines versus nuns) had as much impact on the nature of an individual's spirituality as did gender. At the same time, Bynum argues that there *is* a change in female patterns of sanctity around 1200, although historical explanations of this phenomenon in terms of "some kind of inherent female 'emotionalism' or some kind of affinity between women and female imagery . . . will not do." As Bynum pointedly asks, "If women become mystics because they are intrinsically more emotional, imaginative, religious, or hysterical than men, why did it take centuries for this to emerge?"[22]

Bynum gives programmatic form to these historical insights in the introduction to a volume she coedited with Stevan Harrell and Paula Richman, *Gender and Religion: On the Complexity of Symbols*. At the same time, she more explicitly situates her work and that of the other contributors to the volume in relation to feminist critiques of Christianity and other male-dominant religions. Bynum follows feminist scholars in insisting "that all human beings are 'gendered'—that is, that there is no such thing as generic *Homo religiosus*." Yet, unlike those feminist critics of religion who presume that religious symbols "prescribe and transcribe reality," Bynum insists on the "polysemic" nature of religious symbols—on the varieties of ways in which symbols mean and in which they can be used:

> Gender-related symbols, in their full complexity, may refer to gender in ways that affirm or reverse it, support or question it; or they may, in their basic meaning, have little at all to do with male and female roles. Thus our analysis admits that gender-related symbols are sometimes "about" values other than gender. But our analysis also assumes that all people are "gendered." It therefore suggests, at another level, that not only gender-related symbols but all symbols arise out of the experience of "gendered" users. It is not possible ever to ask How does a symbol—*any* symbol—mean? without asking For whom does it mean?[23]

Bynum's argument works to untether gendered symbols from easy presumptions about their social effects and meanings. Yet at the same time, she insists on the possibility that men and women may use symbols in radically different ways.

Her contribution to the volume, "'. . . And Woman His Humanity': Female Imagery in the Religious Writing of the Later Middle Ages," together with essays by John Hawley and John Toews, makes just such a case. As Bynum summarizes their conclusions, she, Hawley, and Toews do not find that medieval Christian mystics, Hindi poets, and twentieth-century psychoanalysts operate with the same concepts of gender, but

> they do find that men and women of a single tradition—when working with the same symbols and myths, writing in the same genre, and living in the same religious or professional circumstances—display certain consistent

male/female differences in using symbols. Women's symbols and myths tend to build from social and biological experiences; men's symbols and myths tend to invert them. Women's mode of using symbols seems given to the muting of opposition, whether through paradox or through synthesis; men's mode seems characterized by emphasis on opposition, contradiction, inversion, and conversion. Women's myths and rituals tend to explore a state of being; men's tend to build elaborate and discrete stages between self and other.[24]

Thus, even as Bynum engages in the project of uncovering women's previously neglected history within Christian spirituality, she at the same time makes bold claims about the particularity of women's writings and women's spirituality.

Bynum's overriding thesis, articulated in both *Holy Feast and Holy Fast* and *Fragmentation and Redemption*, is that women's spirituality in the late Middle Ages differed in significant ways from men's.[25] Perhaps the most succinct formulation appears in an oft-cited passage from "The Female Body and Religious Practice in the Later Middle Ages":

> Thus, as many recent scholars have argued, the spiritualities of male and female mystics were different, and this difference has something to do with the body. Women were more apt to somatize religious experience and to write in intense bodily metaphors; women mystics were more likely than men to receive graphically physical visions of God; both men and women were inclined to attribute to women and encourage in them intense asceticisms and ecstasies. Moreover, the most bizarre bodily occurrences associated with women (e.g., stigmata, incorruptibility of the cadaver in death, mystical lactations and pregnancies, catatonic trances, ecstatic nosebleeds, miraculous anorexia, eating and drinking pus, visions of bleeding hosts) either first appear in the twelfth and thirteenth centuries or increase significantly in frequency at that time.[26]

Bynum's concern in this passage is to suggest that bodies—in this case women's bodies—have a history and that they "begin to behave in new ways at a particular moment in the European past."[27] Her answer to the question of why this should be so has been as influential on scholarship about medieval women's spirituality as her depiction of the change itself.

Bynum suggests a number of overlapping explanations for the distinctive nature of female piety in the high and late Middle Ages. We can broadly characterize these as (a) ecclesiastical and social, (b) psychological and biological, and

(c) ideological and theological. In the first instance, the particular constraints placed on women in the pursuit of the religious life and religious leadership render their appeal to experiences of the divine a central form of legitimation.[28] Moreover, women's relatively limited access to Latin education plays a role in their pursuit of the vernacular.[29] Bynum also shows that male religious leaders actively encouraged women's bodily forms of piety as a useful instrument in the fight against dualist heresies.[30]

In *Holy Feast and Holy Fast*, which argues for the centrality of food to medieval women's piety, Bynum points to women's roles within the larger society as formative of their religiosity. Hence in the medieval world, Bynum argues, food preparation was one of the few domains over which women had control. The regulation of food intake, the distribution of food as alms, and an emphasis on Christ's body as food thus emerge as key aspects of female spirituality in part because of the particularities of women's social situation.[31] Similarly, the broader argument about the bodily nature of women's piety made in *Fragmentation and Redemption* can be tied to social roles. As Bynum argues, "To some extent, women simply took . . . ordinary nurturing over into their most profound religious experience."[32]

Bynum is more hesitant to ascribe the differences between men's and women's spirituality to psychological and biological differences, although the move from an emphasis on women's role as nurturers in late medieval culture to one based on a claim for men's and women's different psychological development is relatively easy to make (and many readers of Bynum have presumed just such an argument). In *Holy Feast and Holy Fast*, moreover, Bynum appeals to the work of Nancy Chodorow and Carol Gilligan to suggest that women's role as nurturers and caregivers might give rise to particular psychological formations in women and men.[33] The move to biology does not necessarily follow, of course, and Bynum alludes to the possibility of biological differences between men and women as an explanation for their differing spiritualities only with great hesitation. "It is possible," she writes, "that there is a biological element in women's predisposition to certain kinds of bodily experience. The fact that, in many cultures, women seem more given to spirit possession and more apt to somatize their inner emotional and spiritual states suggests a physiological explanation."[34] (Note the tension between Bynum's argument here and her categorical rejection of similar hypotheses in *Jesus as Mother*.) At the same time, she argues, biology and culture are notoriously difficult to disentangle: "The various cultures in which women are more inclined than men to fast, to mutilate themselves, to experience the gift of tongues and to somatize spiritual states are all societies that associate the female with self-sacrifice and service."[35]

Ultimately, the decisive explanations for Bynum are ideological and theological. Hence, she shows that in the Christian Middle Ages women were associated with body, whereas men were associated with mind. Women, however, used these misogynist assumptions to their advantage by focusing on the central role that Christ's suffering flesh—intrinsic to his suffering humanity—played in redemption. By using the identification of women with the body (and hence with humanity) as a justification for their identification with Christ in his suffering human body, women were able to make their lowly social and ontological status the means of their participation in the salvific work of Christ. Seen from this perspective, women's extreme asceticism and bodily piety are not simply or even primarily expressions or outcroppings of medieval misogyny and antibody dualism. Rather, as Bynum movingly argues,

> Late medieval asceticism was an effort to plumb and to realize all the possibilities of the flesh. It was a profound expression of the doctrine of the Incarnation: the doctrine that Christ, by becoming human, saves *all* that the human being is. ... Thus Francis of Assisi telling his disciples that beatings are "perfect happiness," Beatrice of Ornacieux driving nails through her palms, Dorothy of Montau and Lukardis of Oberweimar wrenching their bodies into bizarre pantomimes of the moment of Crucifixion, and Serafina of San Gimignano, revered *because* she was paralyzed, were to their own contemporaries not depressing or horrifying, but glorious. They were not rebelling against or torturing their flesh out of guilt over its capabilities so much as using the possibilities of its full sensual and affective range to soar ever closer to God.[36]

Bynum here pinpoints what is arguably the central theological explanation for much medieval women's spirituality, perhaps best encapsulated in the words of the thirteenth-century beguine Hadewijch of Brabant: "We all indeed wish to be God with God, but God knows there are few of us who want to live as human beings with his Humanity, or want to carry the cross with him, or want to hang on the cross with him and pay humanity's debt to the full."[37] This, however, is what Hadewijch and many other devout women believed was necessary for those desirous of pursuing the heights of spiritual perfection.

QUESTIONING THE PARADIGM

I write in some detail about Bynum's work on women's spirituality because of both its importance and its enormous influence on subsequent scholarship. Bynum not only has been instrumental in introducing a new generation of readers to a body of hagiographical and mystical literature previously little known in English, but also provides a powerful paradigm through which that literature can be understood.[38] Although her most recent work does not dwell on gender, *Holy Feast and Holy Fast* and *Fragmentation and Redemption* continue to shape the study of sexual difference in Christian mysticism and medieval Christian culture (and often in ways that attention to the details of Bynum's texts unsettles). Much writing on Christian women's spirituality over the past thirty-odd years has operated within or struggled against that paradigm—and often both at the same time. At issue is whether a sharp distinction between women's and men's spirituality can be found in the medieval sources, the nature and character of these differences if they exist, and what, if such commonalities can be found, might be their causes. As I will argue in what follows, many scholars, including at times Bynum herself, challenge the assertion made in *Holy Feast and Holy Fast* and, in a more complex way, in *Fragmentation and Redemption* that sharp lines can be drawn between the theological views put forward in texts written by women and those written by men.

One of the complex issues raised by Bynum's claims concerns the use of sources. The arguments of *Holy Feast and Holy Fast* and *Fragmentation and Redemption*, in particular, are grounded in two very different types of literature. Bynum distinguishes, as the passage cited above shows, between women's and men's spirituality in three ways: with regard to women's harsh asceticism, the proliferation in their lives of paramystical bodily phenomena, and their use of bodily metaphors to describe their encounter and union with the divine.[39] Yet, until about 1300, only the last of these three claims holds for mystical texts authored by women. Before 1300, claims for women's harsh asceticism and paramystical bodily phenomena occur in the primarily male-authored hagiographies of religious women.[40]

Particularly in *Holy Feast and Holy Fast*, Bynum emphasizes the necessity for care in treating sources and she divides her presentation of the evidence within that study in terms of hagiographical and mystical writings.[41] Yet when she turns to the women mystics at the center of her analysis, in three of the four cases (Beatrice of Nazareth, Catherine of Siena, and Catherine of Genoa) she cites both their own writings and those of hagiographers (although it must be noted that this distinction can be difficult to make, particularly with regard to Catherine of Genoa). At times it is difficult to tell which is being cited without careful attention to the footnotes. Similarly, in her desire to provide a picture of the sweep of medieval women's spirituality, she does not look for or describe differences that occur over time; this covers over the relative lack of emphasis on bodily asceticism and paramystical phenomena in women's mystical writings before 1300 and the development, after 1300, of what Richard Kieckhefer and Kate Greenspan term "autohagiography."[42]

Of course, we cannot move from the absence of accounts of extreme asceticism in women's texts before 1300 to an assertion that women did not engage in these practices. Nor can we take the appellation "autohagiography" as a dismissal of later accounts as pious fictions.[43] Yet careful attention to the different ways in which men write about women and women write about themselves demonstrates that, although women often internalize and enact predominant views, they also resist them.[44] Moreover, when men's and women's religious writings are looked at together, we see that men and women engage in often intense relationships of mutual influence, debate, and appropriation. As a result, any clearly marked distinction between men's and women's spirituality almost immediately breaks down (although the tendency for men to *want* women's spirituality to take certain forms remains constant at least throughout the Middle Ages and no doubt well into the modern period). Not only are the differences between men's and women's spirituality less sharp than Bynum at times argues, but there are many more differences between female-authored texts than her work from the 1980s and early 1990s suggests.[45]

The methodological issue raised by Bynum's work is tied to larger historiographical questions about power, agency, and resistance. Thus David Aers and Kathleen Biddick, albeit in quite different ways, question what Aers refers to as Bynum's "empowerment thesis."[46] Once again, Bynum herself provides suggestions that lead to the critique itself. Aers notes that in the essay from 1989 cited previously, "The Female Body and Religious Practice in the Later Middle Ages," Bynum suggests the limitations of the idea that identification with Christ's suffering flesh and humanity empowers women. As Bynum writes,

> This argument must also recognize that the clergy themselves encouraged such female behavior both because female asceticism, eucharistic devotion and mystical trances brought women more closely under the supervision of spiritual

directors and because women's visions functioned for males, too, as means of learning the will of God. Moreover, theologians and prelates found women's experiential piety useful in the thirteenth-century fight against heresy. The increased emphasis on bodily miracles and indeed the appearance of new miracles of bodily transformation came at exactly the time of the campaign against Cathar dualism.[47]

The problem for Aers is that Bynum does not push these insights far enough, thereby missing an opportunity to explore the ways in which the feminized body of Christ and the suffering female saint or mystic "are produced within specific discursive regimes with specific technologies of power."[48] In describing a dominant ideology and arguing that it was empowering for women, Bynum does not ask whether this ideology in fact fed male power and male fantasies of femininity and whether anyone—male or female—resisted them.[49] Moreover, as Julie Miller argues, Bynum provides no standpoint from which one might question the valorization of violence found within the model of sanctity she describes.[50]

Bynum might read this as an anachronistic demand, yet there is significant evidence for women's resistance to male conceptions of female sanctity, especially before 1300. As I said, women's writings before that time show little concern for intense bodily asceticism and paramystical phenomena. This suggests, at the very least, that some women refused to describe themselves within the paradigms provided by primarily male-authored hagiography. The beginning of the fourteenth century saw the partial condemnation of semireligious women, known as beguines, as well as forms of spirituality associated with women, suggesting that the turn to autohagiography may mark women's capitulation to male-prescribed conceptions of sanctity in the face of increased scrutiny by religious leaders.[51]

Although I argue for added nuance to Bynum's account, Aers posits an antithesis between empowerment and domination that is far too simple to handle the complexity of the materials under discussion. Against Aers, I contend that Bynum is right to claim that women often received—and still today receive—religious recognition, ecstatic pleasure, and leadership opportunities on the basis of their adoption of male-prescribed modes of female sanctity. Kathleen Biddick's question—implicit also in Aers—remains: who was suppressed by these extraordinary women's accession to power?[52] Bynum's work itself then leads to further assessment of the vexed interplay of power and domination within Christian spiritual traditions.[53]

To get at the complexities of domination and empowerment, however, we need to remember that gender is not the only—and at times not the most salient—category of difference operative within the Christian Middle Ages or any other society. As the essays collected by Sharon Farmer and Carol Braun Pasternack in *Gender and Difference in the Middle Ages* show, medieval identities were shaped by shifting and intersecting differences—of gender, but also of social status, sexuality, and religion.[54] (Again, Bynum herself points in this direction in *Jesus as Mother*.) In a related essay, Farmer questions scholarly assertions that in the Middle Ages women were associated with bodiliness and physicality while men were associated with rationality. Looking at material from the thirteenth century that describes the different kinds of work appropriate to different members of Christian society, Farmer finds that "poor men, as well as poor women, were very much associated with the body."[55] Without denying that "at various points along the hierarchy of social status" we do find "that medieval clerical authors . . . make statements that drew stronger associations between women and the body than between men and the body," Farmer convincingly demonstrates that attention to the differences between servants and elites renders easy generalizations about gender difficult.[56]

Despite Bynum's arguments for the association of women with the body in the late Middle Ages, so aptly nuanced by Farmer and others, Bynum consistently argues against what she sees as a modern tendency to equate the body too quickly with sexuality.[57] Her explicit aim throughout her work on the body is to expand the meanings we ascribe to corporeality in medieval texts and practices. To be embodied means to be subject to hunger and thirst, pain and pleasure, fecundity and death; the pleasures enjoyed and pains suffered by embodied human beings take many forms and involve the fullness of the human sensorium. Especially in light of the preoccupation with regulating human life through sexuality still so prevalent both inside and outside of Christianity, Bynum's work is salutary and of continuing importance.

Yet a final strand of criticism circles around the worry that in her attempt to expand the range of issues associated with embodiment Bynum too quickly delimits "the erotic—and especially the homoerotic—potentialities of her own devotional polysemy of the medieval body."[58] Richard Rambuss's biggest concern is with Bynum's refusal to see same-sex desire as potentially sexual.[59] If Christ's body is feminized (and so becomes a point of identification for women), Bynum seems to assume that it cannot also be the object of female sexual desire (or even of a desire for the divine analogous to sexual desire). In insisting on the feminization of Christ's body on the cross, Bynum provides a locus for female identification with the divine and protects the divine-human relationship from even metaphorical sexualization. Rambuss not only takes issue with Bynum's assumption that identification and desire cannot accrue around the same object, but also questions whether, in its passivity and woundedness, Christ's body is necessarily feminine. In response to Bynum's reading of the blood from Christ's side wound as analogous to mother's milk, he cogently asks, "Are male bodies without their own orifices?"[60] So when the twelfth-century monk Rupert of Deutz describes himself climbing onto the altar, embracing and kissing Christ on the cross ("I sensed how pleasing he found this gesture of love, when in the midst of the kissing he opened his mouth, so that I could kiss him the more deeply"),[61] Rambuss suggests that we should read this passage as—at least on one level—homoerotic.[62]

As a number of scholars show, both medieval men and women did use explicitly erotic language to discuss their relationship with Christ, and they did so in ways that often challenged the prescriptive heteronormativity of the culture in which they lived.[63] The challenge occurs not only through women's feminization of Christ's body or of the divine, or through men's relationship with the male Christ, but also through the intense, hyperbolic deployment of apparently heterosexual imagery.[64] Among the beguines of Northern Europe, for example, arguably most well known for their so-called bridal mysticism (and hence, it would seem, for a resolutely heterosexual, nonqueer sexual imaginary), we find accounts of insane love and endless desire in which gender becomes so radically fluid that it is not clear what kind of sexuality—within the dichotomy between heterosexual and homosexual most readily available to many modern readers—is being metaphorically deployed to evoke the relationship between the human and the divine.

Although the three thirteenth-century mystics associated with the beguines, Hadewijch, Mechthild of Magdeburg, and Marguerite Porete, focus on an erotic relationship between the soul and God, one legitimated in part by early and medieval Christian readings of the Song of Songs, as Bynum recognized over thirty years ago the phrase "bridal mysticism" cannot encapsulate the full range of gendered positions occupied by the believer and God within their texts.[65] Sometimes the female soul meets a male deity, at other times the soul is male in relationship to a female divine, and at yet other moments both the soul and God are female. As Rambuss argues with regard to early modern male-authored religious poetry, the absence in these texts "of a polarizing system of sexual types tends to open these works in the direction of greater plasticity of erotic possibilities, possibilities not entirely containable by our own (often only suppositiously coherent) sexual dichotomies."[66] We cannot contain medieval religious eroticism within modern sexual categories. This does not desexualize medieval men's and women's texts and practices, but instead demonstrates their queerness in relation to modern conceptions of heteronormativity. Moreover, what is queer in these texts is not just sex but also gender, and it is not clear that the putative opposition between male and female or masculine and feminine can contain or name the nonnormative gender performances found within medieval mystical writing. Who are these, we might ask, what are these men and women anyway? Are the dualistic categories of sex and gender adequate to the evidence before us? Perhaps the medieval inquisitors who referred to Marguerite Porete as a pseudowoman (*pseudo-mulier*) were on to something, if for all the wrong reasons and to the most violent of ends.

NEW DIRECTIONS IN FEMINIST SCHOLARSHIP ON CHRISTIAN SPIRITUALITY

And yet despite the anarchic refusal of gender binaries found, albeit in quite different forms, in texts like those of Hadewijch or Marguerite Porete, much of the scholarship pushing Bynum's thesis in new and ever more subtle directions depends on distinguishing between male-authored and female-authored texts or between texts written within a clerical context and those written on its fringes, even in its shadows. There are good reasons for this, as I have shown, for women may not always describe their experience in the same way that male clerical elites do. Recent scholarship shows, however, that there are dangers in assuming any clear-cut distinction between male-authored and female-authored texts, and not only because we may not always be certain what it means to be a man or a woman, male or female, masculine or feminine. In a vein of argument perhaps more familiar to scholars of religion and spirituality than the critique of gender binaries, yet equally radical, scholars suggest that it is often a mistake to speak about Christian texts, particularly those from medieval manuscript culture, in terms of individual authorship. (Again, Bynum herself moves in this direction as early as *Fragmentation and Redemption*.) There are very few early Christian texts that can be ascribed to women and virtually all the medieval women's spiritual texts available to us are mediated in some way, either by scribes, editors, translators, or compilers.[67] In some cases, women who may not have been able to read or write either in Latin or in the vernacular made use of scribes to produce their texts. In others, male confessors or confidants collected and distributed women's work, translated it, or were otherwise instrumental in its dissemination. Often, we know very little with certainty about the mode of production and dissemination.[68]

At the center of many discussions of medieval religious women's authorship and authority lie texts ascribed to the late-thirteenth- and early-fourteenth-century Umbrian laywoman Angela of Foligno and to the fifteenth-century English laywoman Margery Kempe. In both instances, scholars have debated at great length the extent to which we can take their texts as their own. Jacques Dalarun takes historical skepticism to its limit, asking if Angela might not have been a fiction created by her Franciscan scribe.[69] At the other end of the spectrum, Lynn Staley argues with regard to Margery Kempe that her use of scribes does not decrease but rather increases her authorial status.[70] As Jennifer Summit puts it, by "collating Margery Kempe with an existing canon, the scribe establishes Kempe's authority by showing precisely that she is not an original creator, but rather one who upholds pre-existing models of *traditio* and *auctoritas*."[71] Because medieval views of authorship and authority differ so substantially from our own, what modern readers might take as a mark of inauthenticity becomes, according to Staley and Summit, the means of legitimating Kempe—a pious laywoman—as part of an authoritative tradition of visionary spirituality.

What interests Staley, Summit, and others is the way in which medieval and early modern women pursued their spiritual lives in the context of complex communities.[72] Women did write what we think of as original works with their own hands, but they also dictated, compiled, translated, and commissioned spiritual texts, and all of these diverse forms of writing must be attended to in any attempt to describe women's contributions to Christian spirituality and the possible contours and multiplicity of women's spirituality.[73]

Carolyn Dinshaw and David Wallace perhaps summarize the scholarly question most succinctly when they remind us that, on the one hand, "it would be naïve . . . to try and separate authentic female voices from masculine textual operations." Yet at the same time, we must remember "the tendency of masculine mediators to accentuate the importance of their own roles, or to occlude female involvement."[74] Moreover, as we have seen, men tend to read the women whose work they mediate in terms of male-prescribed forms of female sanctity. Even as we question simplistic conceptions of agency and authorship within writings by, to, and about women, we need to attend to the power dynamics that shape the communities in which these texts are formed, disseminated, and re-formed. Most importantly, we need to recognize that these textual communities were often—although not always—made up of men and women working with, for, and at times against one another.[75]

These complex patterns of textual production do not end for women with the introduction of print. In the early modern period, women's writing continues to be imagined as textual and treated in ways similar to that produced within a manuscript culture.[76] Religious teachings or visionary reports were often transcribed by others or written down on the basis of conversations with the holy woman. Well into the twentieth century, there are examples of holy women whose rapturous utterances are transcribed by those with whom they live (in the case of Gemma Galgani, without her knowledge or permission).[77] In other cases, women's writing and stories about women exist side by side. As Brenna Moore shows, the twentieth-century poet, memoirist, and theologian Raïssa Maritain presents herself very differently than does her husband, the philosopher Jacques Maritain, and the circle of devout Catholics with whom they surrounded themselves. For Raïssa, suffering is a dire trial to be undergone with regret and sorrow; for Jacques, Raïssa's suffering makes her a saint.[78] The commonalities between late medieval and modern prescriptions for female spirituality suggest that we may find standard periodizations inadequate to the history of women's (and perhaps also men's) spirituality, yet what at first sight appear to be common conceptions of spirituality must always be read against the background of changing social, political, and economic realities. And note that what is at stake is male prescriptions for women's sanctity; women's mystical theologies themselves may differ from one another more than we have yet had the patience to see.[79]

From the early Christian period through modernity, then, the story of women's textual production is always also a story about spiritual and textual communities, about the afterlife of religious writings by and about women, and about the history of manuscripts and books used by women. Attention to the dissemination, disappearance, and reappearance of manuscripts and books by, about, and for women yields important insights into changing conceptions of gender, authorship, and sanctity.[80] As Sara S. Poor shows, we learn an enormous amount about changing conceptions of religious authority when we follow the manuscript history of Mechthild of Magdeburg's *The Flowing Light of the Godhead* and see how portions of the text were included, generally anonymously, in late medieval mystical compendia.[81] In his work on the manuscripts of Hadewijch's corpus, Erik Kwakkel demonstrates that the way in which they are collected, the different hands in which they are written, and the method of binding pages together themselves tell complex stories.[82] Annotations can offer insights into the use of the manuscripts, as can signs of handling. Many compendia lay out a vision of the mystical life through the organization of material. In other cases, the juxtaposition of texts in a manuscript collection gives clues as to its use.[83] In exceptional cases, manuscripts contain both text and images, opening up yet further avenues for research on the interplay between the textual and the visual in the Christian spiritual life.[84]

Another way in which scholars are breaking down the rigid divide between male and female spirituality and exploring the multiplicity of women's writing is in recognizing women's visionary, multisensory, mystical experience as theology, often in conversation with those of male theologians. I noted above the thesis that women actively participated in the development of what Bernard McGinn and Nicholas Watson call "vernacular theology."[85] Barbara Newman has made another important proposal for breaking down the distinction between men's and women's religious texts with her introduction of the term "imaginative theology." According to Newman, "The hallmark of imaginative theology is that it 'thinks with' images, rather than propositions or scriptural texts or rarified inner experiences—although none of these need be excluded. The devices of literature—metaphor, symbolism, prosopopoeia, allegory, dialogue, and narrative— are its working tools."[86]

Both dream and waking visions are central to imaginative theology, and Newman's new category enables her to recast traditional distinctions between the two.[87] As a result, Newman reads the writings of the twelfth-century Platonists, Dante, and Christine of Pizan alongside those of visionaries like Mechthild of Magdeburg and Hadewijch, thereby breaking down any clear-cut distinction between the genres of male-authored and female-authored theologies. The category will arguably be of even more salience when turned to early modern and modern texts, in which fiction and poetry often become the domain in which theological positions are rendered.[88] Some of the most vital, daring, and life-sustaining theological thinking of the modern era occurs in imaginative writing. Newman suggests that this might also be the case, against all presumptions to the contrary, in the twelfth through fifteenth centuries.

In *Promised Bodies: Time, Language, and Corporeality in Medieval Women's Mystical Texts*, Patricia Dailey also argues for the theological nature of women's mystical texts, insisting on the interplay between male theological traditions and the writings of medieval women, in particular the thirteenth-century beguine Hadewijch, but also Hildegard of Bingen and Julian of Norwich. Noting that Augustine finds a place on Hadewijch's list of the perfect, Dailey argues for the strong influence of Augustine's conceptions of language, temporality, and eternity on Hadewijch, as well as situating Hadewijch's work carefully within the Augustinian-Cistercian textual milieu with which she was clearly familiar. William of St. Thierry is particularly important for Hadewijch, pointing to crucial interactions between male and female theological production in the Middle Ages.

The result is an analysis of Hadewijch's writing as theologically complex and also profoundly literary. For Dailey, in fact, the theological is always of necessity literary and to read theology well requires that one attend to its written—or spoken, sung, enacted, imaged—form. Dailey's rich and insightful readings work against the still-too-common assumption that Hadewijch's writings and those of other women religious writers are marked by their experiential, bodily, and immediate quality. The latter term is of particular importance, for Dailey demonstrates that experience and embodiment are themselves complexly literary and theological. The immediacy of union between the human and the divine may be desired, promised, and perhaps even achieved, but any account of it comes in mediated form, as does any theology humans can articulate while in this world (or arguably any incarnational theology whatsoever).

Dailey argues for the intertwined nature of two Pauline distinctions, between the inner human being and the outer human being (2 Cor 4:16) and between the fleshly body and the spiritual body (1 Cor 15:44); she then suggests that Augustine's understanding of the bodily and the spiritual senses rests on these two moments in Paul.[89] At issue is the question of the interplay between the bodily and the spiritual senses and, with it, the best understanding of bodily language as it is used by the mystic to engender, describe, and reenact her or his experience.[90] Drawing on work that revisits the distinction between the bodily and the spiritual senses in early and medieval Christian theology, Dailey shows that bodily images and metaphors are always theological for Hadewijch (as for others); theology happens in the body, whether understood as spiritual or fleshly, inner or outer. Throughout the book, in fact, Dailey shows the movement between and across these bodily registers as they occur in Paul, Augustine, Hildegard of Bingen, Julian of Norwich, and Hadewijch, and in each of them in importantly different ways.[91] (Her argument suggests, in contrast to Newman's work, that a distinction might exist between those for whom allegory, metaphor, and figuration operate in a specifically theological register—or, perhaps better, involve a theological transformation of the body, be it inner or outer—and those for whom they do not. More work, however, will be required to work out the complex issues involved.)[92]

For Niklaus Largier, Dailey, and others, interest in the bodily and spiritual senses comes together with recent work on affect and the emotions in the study of the Christian Middle Ages and of Christian mysticism. As Fiona Somerset notes, medieval mystical writers, male and female, were "emotion artists . . . specialists in the observation and description of emotion, and their writings provide especially rich sites for investigating the theory, practice, expression, and communication of emotional states."[93] Devotional and mystical authors not only describe but also incite emotion.[94] Early, medieval, and modern spiritual texts, moreover, seem to concur that both the bodily and the spiritual senses are closely linked to the affective life; to incite the senses is to elicit affect and the reverse is also true.[95]

This is not to downplay the role of cognition in the mystical life, for most early and medieval Christian spiritual authors argue that the affective and the cognitive lives are deeply intertwined. Love is itself both the primary affect and a form of knowing.[96] For those, like Marguerite Porete and Meister Eckhart, for whom the apophasis (the unsaying, unnaming, noughting) of names and images of God plays a vital role, the soul is enjoined to move beyond *both* affect and cognition. Already in Cassian, an emotion-artist of the highest order, the movement through the affective life of the Psalms occasionally lifts the soul *out of* the affective and cognitive realms to a space of what he calls fiery prayer.[97] One idea emerging from current research is that the sharp distinction between affective and speculative mysticism is the product of late medieval debates about the relationship between love and knowledge, affect and reason, and, most importantly, if not always explicitly, men and women. Yet the late medieval claim that women's mysticism is dangerously affective and men's is something else has never been a tenable reading of the sources. Most crucially, perhaps, the writings of many men are drenched in affect. The late medieval denigration of forms of mystical life associated with women reflects men's fear of women's spiritual authority and perhaps also of the gender nonconformity found in much spiritual writing and experience.[98]

As I wrote at the outset of this essay, it turns out that within Christian spiritual traditions men and women have been talking all along, although we now have a better sense of the ways in which feminist scholarship demands attention to the particular power dynamics of these conversations. The further question remains: do these conversations speak to us? At least some of the criticism of Bynum centers on uneasiness with what Dominick LaCapra calls her "redemptive view" of history.[99] Yet even as she attempts always to read the past empathically—in ways, some argue, that allow insufficient space for critique—Bynum also insists on our distance from the past. "We write the best history," she argues,

> when the specificity, the novelty, the awe-fulness, of what our sources render up bowls us over with its complexity and its significance. Our research is better when we move only cautiously to understanding, when the fear that we may appropriate the "other" leads us not so much to writing about ourselves and our fears as to crafting our stories with attentive, wondering care. . . . We must rear a new generation of students who will gaze in wonder at texts and artifacts, quick to puzzle over a translation, slow to project or to appropriate, quick to assume there is a significance, slow to generalize about it.[100]

Empathy, in other words, demands time, patience, and a refusal too quickly to collapse our concerns with those of the past. Yet, as Bynum repeatedly demonstrates in her own work, this does not preclude conversation between the past and the present.

The problem, of course, is how to recognize the theoretically and theologically vibrant insights offered by the past without abrogating our responsibility to history. Christian spiritual traditions—in all of their variety—speak in compelling ways to issues at the heart of the human situation and often also at the heart of specifically feminist concerns. Can we maintain sight of this fact without losing sight of the difference that history makes?[101]

Contemporary feminist investments in Christian spirituality take many forms, but let me speak here of one unlikely site of appropriation in order to get at the historiographical, theoretical, and theological issues. The putative division between men's and women's forms of spirituality arises already in the Middle Ages and is picked up in various ways by modern scholarship. The policing of mysticism was always also the policing of gender. Again, the distinction between affective and speculative mysticism does not bear careful scrutiny, yet it continues to wield tremendous power. In addition, female forms of spirituality, generally defined in terms of their greater emotionalism, affectivity, and visionary quality (as opposed to the intellectual, speculative, and abstract mysticism associated with men), are routinely denigrated both in the later Middle Ages and in modern scholarship. One of Bynum's great accomplishments is to have reversed this trend.

As I argue in *Sensible Ecstasy: Mysticism, Sexual Difference, and the Demands of History*, fascination with affective, visionary, and ecstatic forms of Christian spirituality also appears much earlier in the twentieth century, and in rather unlikely places. For certain French secular intellectuals, for example, among them Georges Bataille, Simone de Beauvoir, Jacques Lacan, and Luce Irigaray, affective, bodily, and ecstatic forms of spirituality serve as a central model for their thinking and practice.[102] At the heart of this fascination, I argue, lies a confrontation with the reality of human limitation, disease, and death. Critically following my French subjects, I contend that attention to the Christian mystical tradition can help us think about how to deal with the traumatic effects of illness, mortality, and loss.[103] At the same time, women like Angela of Foligno and Teresa of Ávila, with whom Bataille, Beauvoir, Lacan, and Irigaray are fascinated, "struggled to maintain interpretative control over [their] experience against the continual encroachment of male clerical elites." Similarly, I argue, "medieval women's texts proleptically resist" modern appropriations in that they contest the cultural roles prescribed for women in the Middle Ages.[104] More particularly, a number of thirteenth-century women mystics actively resist the association of women with the body so central to hagiographical accounts of female sanctity. Similarly, I argue, we must resist any too easy identification of women with the body (and hence with disease, limitation, and death), even as we attempt to find ways to recognize the embodied nature of all human subjectivity.

As Dailey's work shows, even as scholars question the widespread association of women with bodiliness, they also continually return to the role played by the body within Christian mystical traditions. One of the ways in which many of the twentieth- and twenty-first-century theoretical and theological projects invested in Christian spiritual writings differ most radically from their medieval sources is in the place given to prayer, ritual, and bodily and spiritual practices. Hence many historians and theologians follow colloquial uses of the term "spirituality" in assuming that pursuit of the spiritual life has little to do with the body, behavior, or action. Important recent scholarship, however, demonstrates the centrality of bodily and mental practices, ritual, and action to the development of the spiritual life in the Christian Middle Ages and beyond.[105] Jeffrey F. Hamburger, for example, shows that previously denigrated forms of devotional art made for—and at times by—medieval women were key to their meditative practice and hence central to their spirituality.[106] Margot Fassler, Claire Jones,

Bruce Holsinger, and Dailey emphasize the centrality of liturgical practice, in particular song, in the inculcation of the mystical life.[107] Attention to images, music, and practices, moreover, opens the door to investigation of the spirituality of men and women who do not write and are generally not written about—Christians who pursue the divine through their engagement with the ritual life of the church, paraliturgical events, and personal devotions often centered on song as well as devotional objects and images.

The fascination with practices comes together with intense interest in *things*—including the thing-likeness of language and song[108]—and in the role material objects play in the religious life. Reliquaries, relics, crucifixes, rosaries, statues of the saints and of Mary and of Christ as a child and as a man, representations of the *arma Christi* (the weapons used to torture Christ during the Passion) and of Christ's wounds,[109] and other, often gruesome devotional images all have become the subject of heated debate among contemporary scholars: what do all of these *things* mean and why is a putatively spiritual culture seemingly obsessed with them? (And do these things resist our attempt to gender them?) In fact, those most intent on pursuing a life of Christian perfection—monks, nuns, beguines, and members of the mendicant orders—make use of these kinds of religious objects as much, if not more, than the laity. Bynum's most recent work centers on just these topics, particularly *Material Christianity: An Essay on Religion in Late Medieval Europe*, in which she explores the use of these objects and images and argues for their centrality to late medieval incarnational theology.[110] Further work will surely uncover the ways in which Christian materiality—the things of which humans are made and that humans make—is subject to the interplay of cataphasis and apophasis (naming and unnaming, but perhaps also making and unmaking) so central to Christian spirituality.

As current scholarship attests, the attempt to uncover and understand forms of spirituality hitherto visible only indirectly within texts and artifacts opens up a host of methodological challenges. How do we read liturgies, prayer manuals, and guidebooks for religious and laity in the absence of first-person accounts of how such texts were used? How do we understand devotional images and objects, often in the absence of textual explanations of their significance? In approaching living traditions, what methodological principles will yield best access to and understanding of spiritual communities, their beliefs and practices? Careful attention to such methodological issues, drawing on the resources of historiography, anthropology, sociology, art history, performance studies, philosophy, theology, history of religion, and no doubt other fields is essential if we hope to bring new voices (and bodies) onto the train and to develop nuanced understandings of the conversations in which they are engaged.[111] Along the way we will need to allow seemingly fixed binary categories—male and female, masculine and feminine, heterosexual and homosexual, human and divine, angelic and animal, animate and inanimate—to be challenged by those whose wondrous visions, celestial songs, fiery love, resolute attachments, and fierce detachments unsettle them to the very core.

GENDER, AGENCY, AND THE DIVINE IN RELIGIOUS HISTORIOGRAPHY

ALMOST EVERY woman who produced religious writings in the Christian Middle Ages claimed to receive the authority for her teaching, and often the content of that teaching itself, directly from God. Submission of one's own will to that of the divine was the precondition for women's agency within the religious sphere, whether in the form of textual production or institutional development and reform. The late-twentieth-century reappraisal of medieval Christian women's writings, then, which began in the 1980s with the work of Caroline Walker Bynum, Peter Dronke, Elizabeth Petroff, Barbara Newman, and others, hinges on the categories of legitimization and authorization.[1] These and other scholars most often interpret the complex rhetorics and practices of femininity and submission that shape the texts of medieval religious women in terms of agency and authority.[2]

Although some medieval Christian men rested their religious authority on prophetic, visionary, or mystical claims, these were the primary modes of religious authorization available to women.[3] In addition, the complete loss of will or of the self in the divine, which legitimates almost all women's and some men's textual production and religious authority, is often explicitly gendered. Not only is the soul often (although not always) read as feminine in relationship to a male divinity, but also women's putative passivity and malleability render them particularly apt sites of divine agency on earth.[4] Medieval women make use of the very gender subordination that constrains them as the condition for and source of agency, an agency ultimately ascribed not to religious women themselves, but to God.[5]

My own work on the thirteenth-century semireligious woman Mechthild of Magdeburg follows in this broad line of interpretation. In *The Soul as Virgin Wife: Mechthild of Magdeburg, Marguerite Porete, and Meister Eckhart*, I show that Mechthild accentuates her humility, even abjection, as female in order to become the site of divine agency on earth. Worried by the disparity between her lack of learning and status and the task of teaching and prophecy assigned to her by God, Mechthild laments that God did not choose someone better suited to make his word known to humanity. To this God replies,

> "Where I gave especially my grace, there I sought ever the lowest, smallest, most secret place. The highest mountain on earth cannot receive the revelations of my grace, for the flood of my Holy Spirit flows naturally to the valley. One finds many a master wise in the scripture who in himself, in my eyes, is a fool. And I say to you still more, that it is a great honor to me before them and strengthens holy Christianity in them very much, that the unlearned mouth teaches learned tongues of my Holy Spirit."[6]

This dynamic, whereby the highest must flow into the lowest, is central to the theology of the *Flowing Light*. God as love always flows out to those below him. Hence the more humble Mechthild is—as a weak, changeable woman—the more receptive she is to God. According to this reading of the *Flowing Light*, Mechthild explicitly grounds her authority in a rhetoric of femininity that both constrains and empowers her.[7]

Despite the obvious cogency of this interpretation and its grounding in Mechthild's text, it seems to suggest that Mechthild strategically—whether consciously or unconsciously need not concern us here—uses theological language to enable and mask her own agency.[8] Yet in the *Flowing Light*, this account of Mechthild's receptivity is ascribed not to Mechthild, but to God. Does insistence on Mechthild's agency—be it conscious or unconscious—undermine the radicality of her book and its mode of production? Is there any way—or any reason—for a twenty-first-century feminist historian to take seriously Mechthild's claim that God speaks directly through her? If we do so, do we thereby undermine Mechthild's agency in ways inimical to the project of feminist historiography? Conversely, what—if anything—are we missing by moving too quickly to claims about agency, legitimation, and authorization, thereby bypassing what Mechthild's own text claims about its production?

I might respond to my own worries by deploying the distinction between description or understanding and explanation.[9] In his very influential book *Religious Experience*, Wayne Proudfoot argues that while descriptions of a person's or group's experience must be made in terms that such a person or group would themselves understand (otherwise it would not be a description of that experience), explanations are under no such constraint. The best explanation of an event or experience may or may not be one provided by or even available to the person who or group that undergoes the experience. Proudfoot thus tries to save the religionist from the charge of reductionism, arguing that while descriptive reductionism is a problem because it fails to capture that which it purports to describe, explanatory reductionism is both desirable and inevitable if we are to come to the best explanation of any given experience or event.[10]

Proudfoot recognizes that descriptions of an event or experience generally contain within them some explanation, however implicit, of that experience, thereby potentially rendering scholarly explanations in conflict with descriptions given by the person who has the experience. The aim of Proudfoot's entire argument is to demonstrate that this potential conflict is not epistemologically or morally pernicious. It just is the case, he implies, that people are sometimes wrong about the best explanation for their experience—hence, their descriptions of that experience, even arguably the experience itself, are epistemologically flawed.

This seems to be particularly the case for religious experience. Proudfoot goes to some lengths to show that experiences are defined as religious on the basis of the claim that they were brought about by some supernatural agency. Hence the very description of an experience as religious depends on an explanation of that experience as caused by God or some other supernatural being. According to Proudfoot, one of the problems with scholarly accounts of religious experience like those provided by Friedrich Schleiermacher and William James is that they have permitted religious explanations to stand without question, either accepting (Schleiermacher) or bracketing (James) claims to divine causality. Schleiermacher and James participate in what Proudfoot refers to as a "protectionist strategy," which attempts to safeguard religious experience from alternative explanations. Protectionism and the charge of reductionism, then, go hand in hand. For Proudfoot, however, supernatural explanations are never adequate to the phenomena and always require correction. Hence his carefully made distinction between descriptive reductionism (which is impermissible) and explanatory reductionism (which seems to be required in religious studies).[11]

Yet if the description itself contains an explanation, then on Proudfoot's reading the scholar of religion is perforce situated in opposition to her subject matter, for her explanation of religious experience will ultimately be at odds not only with the religious person's explicit explanation of his experience but also with the explanation of that experience embedded within the description. Unlike other kinds of experience, moreover, religious experience seems to be by definition inadequately explained. Hence the religious person's explanation of his or her experience (and note that Proudfoot continually suggests that it is a single explanation) is not even considered as one possible explanation of the experience by the scholarly researcher. (It goes without saying that the theologian is almost entirely written out of the scholarly community in Proudfoot's account.) Moreover, given the interplay of description and explanation, it seems unlikely that the scholar of religion, who presumes the primacy of naturalistic explanations, will be able to describe religious experience without recourse to categories derived from such explanations.[12] Any description provided by the human sciences will be subtly at odds with the experiences they purport to describe.

In relation to the first problem, we have my reading of Mechthild, which implicitly argues that even if Mechthild did not know it, what she was really doing in ascribing her writing to God was engaging in a project of self-authorization. Although we might legitimately understand authorization as one effect of women's experience of the divine, to render it a cause of this experience undermines medieval women's own self-understanding and practice. Yet in relation to the second problem outlined above, medieval women claim that they receive authority only insofar as what speaks through them is not their own will but that of the divine, thereby challenging predominate contemporary assumptions even about the effects of their experience. In other words, even if we understand authorization as merely an effect of that experience, we engage in a description of that experience shaped by modern naturalistic categories of thought.

This is, at least implicitly, the way that I have told Mechthild's story. The distinction between understanding and explanation does not help with my initial worry, for that distinction rests on a privileging of explanation and of naturalistic explanatory categories that make sense to me and my putative audience, rather than of those that make sense to my subject and hers. These explanatory categories, moreover, affect the ways in which experiences are described. All of this suggests that there might be good epistemological, ethical, and political reasons to question the extent to which we allow modern categories of analysis (be they geared toward description or explanation) to shape our reading of the past, particularly the religious past.[13] (And when it comes to religion, the same questions must also be asked of the present.)

Yet how are we to render the past comprehensible without recourse to the categories of understanding and explanation available to us? And can we engage in critical engagement with the past under these terms? For help with these questions I want briefly to show the ways in which an historian of South Asia, Dipesh Chakrabarty, argues that postcolonialist critiques of historicism lead to questions about divine agency and history similar to those I ask about medieval Christian women writers. For Chakrabarty, writing in the context of postcolonialism, the stakes of these questions become particularly clear—as do the possibilities and dangers of at least momentarily suspending naturalist categories of analysis and explanation.

Chakrabarty states the issue succinctly in his account of the double bind attendant on the writing of democratically minded histories of modern India. Describing the argument of Ranajit Guha's essay "The Prose of Counter-Insurgency," Chakrabarty follows Guha in asking "what it means when we both take the subaltern's views seriously—the subaltern ascribes the agency for their rebellion to some god [Guha here refers to the Santal, a tribal group in Bengal and Bihar who rebelled against the British and nonlocal Indians in 1855, ascribing their actions to supernatural agency]—and want to confer on the subaltern agency or subjecthood in their own history, a status the subaltern's statement denies?"[14] Guha, according to Chakrabarty, resists "analyses that see religion simply as a displaced manifestation of human relationships that are in themselves secular and worldly (class, power, economy, and so on)" (104). Yet Chakrabarty argues that Guha's move remains inadequate. Guha, like other historians, Chakrabarty claims, "will grant the supernatural a place in somebody's belief system or ritual practice" (104).[15] Yet Guha refuses to ascribe any real agency to the supernatural, for to do so goes "against the rules of evidence that give historical discourse procedures for settling disputes about the past" (104):[16] "The historian, as historian and unlike the Santal, cannot invoke the supernatural in explaining/describing an event" (106). (So my inability to grant that God legitimated Mechthild's book through a particular account of her femininity.)

How then does one engage in an alternative subaltern historiography, one that takes with utmost seriousness the ways in which subaltern peoples account for their own pasts (and presents)? For Chakrabarty this is an ethical and political question, but also an epistemological one, for the tenets of modern historiography crucially limit the life worlds and modes of temporality that are available to knowledge. According to Chakrabarty, "The Santal with his statement 'I did as my god told me to do' also faces us as a way of being in this world, and we could ask ourselves: Is that way of being a possibility for our own lives and for what we define as our present? Does the Santal help us to understand a principle by which we also live in certain instances?" (108). Unlike Guha, who even while he acknowledges the power the Santal's belief has over the Santal himself immediately translates that belief into categories assimilable to modern Western historiographical consciousness, Chakrabarty argues that a truly subaltern history must "stay with the heterogeneity of the moment," both the heterogeneity of the Santal's self-understanding to the historian's own and that between two different kinds of historical projects.

Chakrabarty defines the two historical projects in the following way: "One is that of historicizing the Santal in the interest of a history of social justice and democracy; and the other, that of refusing to historicize and of seeing the Santal as a figure illuminating a life possibility for the present" (108).[17] "Taken together," Chakrabarty argues, "the two gestures put us in touch with the plural ways of being that make up our own present" (108). Subaltern pasts render visible the disjunction that exists within the present by making other modes of being intelligible. (Furthermore, Chakrabarty explicitly connects subaltern pasts and medieval European pasts, claiming that both [can] demonstrate "the noncontemporaneity of the present with itself" [109].)

Modern liberatory narratives cast time as "secular, empty, and homogenous" (23).[18] Chakrabarty asks what happens to this conception of time when it encounters other modes of temporality, particularly those that posit a supernatural time and agency. Western historicist narratives cast this alterity as "medieval," hence attempting to render it other, past, and no longer intrusive on the contemporary world. Secular history, then, routinely translates supernatural agents into terms intelligible to it—hence my reading of women's claims to divine agency in terms of women's own agency, legitimization, and authorization.

Chakrabarty proposes a number of alternatives to this mode of translation. First, he looks to other modes of translation that do not pass through the universal (86). His example is the proximate translations that occur between Hindu and Muslim deities and religious conceptions in South Asia. Such translations remain embedded within the life worlds of two particular traditions, yet Chakrabarty argues that "the very obscurity of the translation process allows the incorporation of that which remains untranslatable" (86). Later in the same essay, however, Chakrabarty suggests that historians will continue to, perhaps even must, use putatively universal terms (for example, "god" or the "gods") to translate the past, but that they can do so in ways that "ask how this seemingly imperious, all-pervasive code might be deployed or thought about so that we have at least a glimpse of its own finitude, a glimpse of what might constitute an outside to it" (93).

In an earlier essay in *Provincializing Europe*, Chakrabarty suggests that we should think of history as (at least) double. He therefore differentiates between what he calls "History 1," which stands in an objectifying relationship to reality (comparable with Heidegger's account of the "present-at-hand"), and "History 2," in which an everyday, preanalytical, unobjectifying relationship to reality comes to the fore (comparable with Heidegger's "ready-to-hand" [68]). Chakrabarty's distinction is complex, and I can only point to a few of its ramifications here. Most pertinently for my purpose, the distinction renders visible different kinds of life worlds, which include different relationships to or conceptions of temporality itself. For those whose world is imbued with supernatural agents, time itself operates and is experienced differently than it is for secular, post-Enlightenment Europeans and Americans. (What to do with nonsecular post-Enlightenment Europeans and Americans—the extent to which they occupy the rift between Chakrabarty's History 1 and History 2—remains an open question.)[19]

Deriving the distinction from Karl Marx's account of the dual history of capital, Chakrabarty shows that History 1 constitutes "a past posited by capital itself as its precondition" (63), whereas History 2 is the multiple possibilities that History 1 must subjugate or destroy in order to render its logic inevitable.[20]

> Marx appears to suggest that entities as close and necessary to the function of capital as money and commodity do not necessarily belong by any natural connection to either capital's own life process or to the past posited by capital. Marx recognizes the possibility that money and commodity, as relations, could have existed in history without necessarily giving rise to capital. Since they do not necessarily look forward to capital, they make up the kind of past I have called History 2. (64)

History 2, then, has the capacity to interrupt "the totalizing thrusts of History 1" (66).

According to Chakrabarty, the triumph of capitalism renders the potentially liberatory narratives of History 1 essential to any politically engaged writing of history. Yet at the same time, he argues that History 1 is always already disrupted by the traces of History 2 and that a truly subaltern historical practice must render that interruption visible. Only in this way can the historian approach the reality and force of life worlds other than those of capitalism. Translated into the terms of my own analysis of medieval Christian women's religious writings, this suggests that the historian must both recognize the legitimating function of claims to divine authorization and take seriously claims to divine agency within these texts, a move that will inevitably disrupt History 1's accounts in as yet not fully discovered ways. Here the central force of Chakrabarty's understanding of History 1 does not necessarily entail his commitment to Marx's understanding of capitalism, although it might, but a more general commitment to secularization. The question that emerges, then, is what this "taking seriously" entails. For Chakrabarty, recognition of the power of beliefs over those who hold them is inadequate; instead the historian must be open to the possibility of the truth of those beliefs. The difficulties of this for the modern Western historian are, I think, precisely the point.

So, while one might be tempted to assimilate Chakrabarty's distinction between History 1 and History 2 to the distinction between explanation and understanding or description that underlies much modern historiography and religious studies, both the Santal and Mechthild's *Flowing Light* insistently remind us that accurate descriptions of another's experience generally include within them an explanation of what generated that experience. To presume, as modern historians and others in the human sciences like Proudfoot tend to do, the ultimate validity of naturalistic explanations immediately puts the historian in the position of History 1, in which other modes of explanation (and hence of existence) are invalidated from the outset.

If part of the project of women's history is to hear the other—in all of her alterity—we cannot unquestioningly presume that our own explanatory and descriptive categories are valid and those of our subject are invalid. Yet the dilemma—how to take seriously the agency of the other (the goal of emancipatory historiographical projects associated, by Chakrabarty, with History 1) when the other seems intent on ascribing her agency to God (the complexity of agency uncovered by alternative histories)—remains unresolved.

In her study of gender, agency, and spirit possession, Mary Keller follows Talal Asad in suggesting that one solution to such a dilemma lies in separating agency and subjectivity. According to Asad, "Contrary to the discourse of many radical historians and anthropologists, *agent* and *subject* (where the former is the principle of effectivity and the latter of consciousness) do not belong to the same theoretical universe and should not, therefore, be coupled."[21] As Keller goes on to explain, "agency does not reside in individual subjectivities; it resides in the interrelationships of bodies with systems of power such as economic systems and religious systems with the regimes of *disciplina*."[22] Decoupling agency and subjectivity offers the possibility of thinking about agency in new ways, in particular in terms of what Keller calls "instrumental agency." Keller's interest lies primarily with those forms of possession in which the possessed has no consciousness of that which occurs. These traditions speak of the possessed as "mounted, played, pounced, wielded, emptied, and entered" by the possessor.[23] The idea of instrumental agency allows Keller to ascribe agency to the possessed body without eliding the agency of the spirit or deity who possesses that body (even as she recognizes that she cannot make any epistemological claims about these entities).

The nuances of Keller's conception of instrumental agency render it a particularly apt way of thinking about possession, yet certain problems remain. First, in the case of Mechthild and most other medieval Christian women of whose experience we have some record, consciousness is not completely overcome in the way it putatively is for those about whom Keller writes. This highlights a more substantive concern with the idea of instrumental agency: To what extent does it reduce possessed persons to bodies? (Although arguably that is what the spirits or gods do in the cases cited by Keller.) Medieval women themselves wrestle with this problem in their writings, a number of women rejecting the cultural ascription of bodily sanctity to women in favor of an emphasis on the role of the will and understanding in the relationship between God and the soul.[24] This is not to deny the centrality of bodily, spiritual, and mental practices to medieval subjectivities. However, the ascription of agency to bodies, used as instruments by gods or spirits, potentially simplifies rather than highlights the complexity of these practices and the structures of power in which they are performed.

Medieval women's critiques of cultural presumptions about gender, agency, and sanctity suggest another problem with Keller's model. It is not clear that she allows any room for critical reflection—either by women and men within the cultures and societies that she describes or by scholars studying those cultures from the outside. Keller's primary contemporary examples of spirit possession involve dispossessed bodies through whom gods or spirits act in order to restore aspects of traditional culture effaced by global capitalism (women workers possessed by spirits in the high-tech factories of Malaysia) or to incite revolutionary action against colonial powers (the women possessed by ancestral spirits who preached revolution in Zimbabwe). In both cases, many readers will be sympathetic to the causes espoused by the spirits.

But what about the case of Uganda, where Alice Auma, possessed by an Italian spirit named Lakwena, helped overthrow the Ugandan president Milton Obote in 1985? The resulting government was unpopular, leading to civil war. As Frederick Smith explains, following the ethnography of Heike Behrend, Auma then "founded an army called the 'Holy Spirit Mobile Forces' (HSMF), directed by Lakwena. . . . Everyone, so the ideology went, was free to be possessed, but in general spirit possession involved the duty to kill."[25] Although Behrend imputes the devolution of spirit mediumship into an outlet for killing to the disenfranchisement of indigenous religions—the role of Christianity in the story is far too complex to outline here—the fact remains that few will feel comfortable simply accepting the agency of the spirits without critique.[26]

Similar problems arise in the case of the medieval Christian women about whom I write. Most famously, God incites Joan of Arc to lead men in warfare.[27] Moral and political problems are endemic, moreover, to any attempt to acknowledge agency as the source of women's and men's words and actions. If nothing else, the very form of these accounts often divinely sanctions gender subordination and particular constructions of gender.[28] (Arguably, the construction of gender and of the divine go hand in hand in many religious texts and practices, although this position implies precisely the kind of naturalizing explanation whose hegemony I here question.)

A desire to maintain the space for critique leads Chakrabarty to remain committed to the emancipatory narratives he believes are only made possible by what he refers to as History 1.[29] In other words, for Chakrabarty there must be a constant interplay between the emancipatory and critical categories of modern historiographical analysis and the alterity of voices, bodies, and practices rendered visible through alternative histories, histories sensitive to precisely that which does not fit within modern, secularizing, and naturalizing narratives. To dismiss these histories too quickly, Chakrabarty insists, is to miss the possibility of alternative life worlds and temporalities; to refuse to subject these life worlds and temporalities to critique, however, would be similarly pernicious.

From a somewhat different angle, Chakrabarty argues in *Habitations of Modernity* that historical investigation "must be possessed of an openness so radical" that he can only express it, he says, in Heideggerian terms: "the capacity to hear that which one does not already understand."[30] Yet this alternative history can never be written in pure form: "The language of the state, of citizenship, of wholes and totalities, the legacy of Enlightenment rationalism will always cut across it." The goal is to open ourselves to disruptive histories that will "grant our social life a constant lack of transparency with regard to any one particular way of thinking."[31] This does not require an abdication of critical capacities; rather, Chakrabarty here suggests that radical openness to the other will hone and enhance critical capacities with regard to both the past and the present, with regard both to others and to ourselves.[32]

A number of interrelated questions remain. First, if historians pursue alternative histories, taking seriously claims to divine agency within history, to what extent will the emancipatory narratives of what Chakrabarty no doubt too dichotomously refers to as History 1 be disrupted in ways that render it unrecognizable? In other words, can Chakrabarty remain committed to the goals of emancipatory historical narratives—and to the critical stance they enable with regard to issues of race, class, gender, sexuality, and religious difference—while allowing them to be disrupted by alternative histories? From the perspective of my own work, can a feminist historian allow alternative histories to disrupt emancipatory feminist histories without renaturalizing or relegitimizing the former's often deep misogyny?

By contrast, is Chakrabarty wrong in his presumption that emancipatory political possibilities are available only through what he calls History 1? Might there be emancipatory possibilities in the life worlds rendered visible through alternative histories? Perhaps even more radically, should we assume that agency, as understood within secular historiography, is the only way in which to think about politics (either in the past or in the present)?[33] If it is not, what happens to the very demand to make the other an agent of history that dominates the projects of subaltern and feminist history themselves?

And finally, are there ends other than those of emancipation to which we must attend in our desire to understand, explain, and promote the flourishing of human lives?[34] Might attention to alternative histories help us to see them? Mechthild desires freedom, but a freedom very different from that sought by modern feminisms. Perhaps only a suspension of disbelief—one that allows Mechthild's self-abjection in the face of the divine other to pierce feminist historiography's emancipatory presumptions—will enable us to glimpse this other possible freedom.[35]

READING AS SELF-ANNIHILATION

4

On Marguerite Porete's Mirror of Simple Souls

Beloved, what will beguines
and religious people say
When they hear the excellence
of your divine song?
Beguines, priests, clerks, and preachers,
Augustinians, and Carmelites,
And the Friars Minor will say that I err,
Because I write of the being
Of purified Love/the one purified by Love.
I do not work to save their Reason,
Who makes them say this to me.

—*Mirouer*, chap. 122

For Germany, the criticism of religion has been largely completed; and the
criticism of religion is the premise of all criticism.

—Karl Marx, "Contribution to the Critique of Hegel's *Philosophy of Right:*
Introduction"

CRITICAL READING

When I first read Michael Warner's proposal that scholars begin to consider the nature and importance of "uncritical reading," I immediately began to wonder what "critical reading" was and the extent to which it differed across contemporary disciplines (however fraught these boundaries, first established by Kant in *The Conflict of the Faculties*, have become). My presumption is that our conceptions of what constitutes uncritical reading depend on what we understand critical reading to be and I'm not sure that what's considered critical reading in one discipline might not occupy the site of that presumed to be uncritical within another. On the other hand, it might be that certain broad conceptions of reason as the source of criticism are so hegemonic within the academy as to render invisible other possible modes of reading (which might themselves, I'll suggest, be critical, although in not yet—or no longer—recognizable ways).

The first English uses of the words "critical" and "criticism" occur in the seventeenth and eighteenth centuries and seem primarily to refer to the evaluation of literary and artistic works.[1] This usage is related to the earlier (and ongoing) development of textual criticism—the attempt to determine the "complete" and "correct" text of a given, at first almost always classical, work through the comprehensive study of the original language and the careful collection and comparison of manuscripts (and later also of printed editions). Textual criticism is also pertinent for religious studies; the later Middle Ages and Reformation witnessed the desire to render the biblical text uniform, stable, and correct in the face of proliferating manuscript versions, both liturgical and extraliturgical, and the rise of vernacular translations.[2] Scholars increasingly applied to the Bible the methods developed by the humanists for establishing the texts of classical literature (although always with the understanding that, as the word of God, the Bible differed fundamentally from that literature).[3]

The term "criticism" takes on new nuance within religious studies in the eighteenth century, most pointedly with Hermann Samuel Reimarus (1694–1768) and G. E. Lessing (1729–81). Reimarus's work, first published in fragmentary form by Lessing, is routinely taken to be the point of origin for critical readings of the Bible.[4] "Critical" here refers to the ability (1) to see and name contradictions between and within texts (not that earlier readers didn't see these contradictions, but they always sought to explain them in light of the purported unity of scripture and had allegorical modes of interpretation available to help in this task); (2) to test the claims of scripture against those of reason (understood in various ways over the course of the next two hundred years); and (3) to think historically about the nature of the biblical text and its claims (and, of course, conceptions of history will also change).[5] The trajectory of what will become the historical-critical method of biblical study reaches a high point—or nadir, depending on your perspective—in 1835 with the publication of David Friedrich

Strauss's *The Life of Jesus,* in which Strauss undermines claims for the historicity of Jesus and for the accuracy of the accounts of Jesus's life and death found within the New Testament. Strauss's work was one of those Marx had in mind when he announced that in Germany, the criticism of religion was largely complete and the stage now nearly set for social, political, and economic critique and transformation. Yet Strauss himself made no such claims for his work. Instead, Strauss argued that the criticism of the historical picture of Jesus on which previous Protestant theologies too often depended was the necessary prelude to establishing the correct dogmatic account of Christianity. True faith, according to Strauss, does not require but is in fact hindered by a grounding in history.[6]

The quest for the historical Jesus, of course, was not rendered obsolete by Strauss's attack, but instead became the center of the historical study of the Bible (at least of the New Testament). Theologically inclined biblical scholars and biblically focused Christian theologians still argue about the extent to which the historical Jesus is required by or is an impediment to faith; yet most Christians ignore these debates and quietly assume that the historical nature of Jesus's life and mission is fundamental to Christianity. Despite mainstream biblical scholarship's ultimate rejection of Strauss's and other critics' more radical claims (few today question Jesus's existence—questioned by some followers of Strauss—or the New Testament's account of the broad outlines of his mission, and many accept a core group of New Testament texts as genuine sayings of Jesus, although which texts is still the subject of acrimonious and ultimately undecidable debate) and despite the significant advances beyond, supplements to, and refinements of the historical-critical method in terms of form and redaction criticism, comparative religious studies, and literary approaches to the Bible, the historical-critical method continues to pose a challenge to many Christians.

Although we can easily see what is being criticized within biblical scholarship—the reliability of scripture itself—the particular force of the term "critical" still remains opaque.[7] This opacity is a result, I think, of the changing conceptions of reason and history with which biblical critics operate. Reimarus was a deist and shared with men like John Locke and David Hume the conviction that all of our beliefs should be subject to reason, understood in generally empirical terms. Although some religious belief—that in a creator God, for example—might survive such a critique, much of the specificity of Christianity and other "revealed religions" does not. For most Protestants, the only basis for adhering to claims about Jesus's miracle working or his resurrection, for example, is the authority of the source from whence we know of these events—sacred scripture or the

Christian Bible. (And of course, scripture's authority is derived from the Bible, a bit of circularity not lost on Christianity's critics.) Hence Reimarus's turn to the Bible and to a criticism of the Bible grounded in his understanding of what it is rational to believe and of what we can hold as historically possible (history now itself constrained by human reason). As more sophisticated accounts of history emerge and the understanding of reason itself becomes historicized (most definitively, perhaps, with Hegel, thereby setting the stage for reason's critique of itself in Marx, Nietzsche, and Freud), the relationship between the rational and the historical becomes more complex. Yet within biblical studies the understanding of historiography as guided by reason—quite broadly defined[8]—remains firm.

Friedrich Schleiermacher, who died in 1834, the year before Strauss's *Life of Jesus* appeared, was among the first to insist on philosophical and theological grounds that the forms of criticism applied to classical texts are (or should be) the same as those applied to the Bible.[9] He also arguably responds to Strauss and other radical critics of the Bible (in the case of Strauss, before the fact). Schleiermacher claims that what is essential in the New Testament is less the historical accuracy of the picture of Jesus presented within it than the accounts provided by these texts of how Jesus's followers and early converts apprehended him. Hence Schleiermacher, at least in theory, should have no difficulty dealing with the contradictions between the four gospel accounts, ascribing them to the different modes of religious apprehension found among the four authors.[10]

With Schleiermacher, religious experience—sui generis, according to most readers of Schleiermacher, but arguably a kind of aesthetic experience—becomes a mediating term between historical criticism and theology.[11] This move is central to nineteenth- and twentieth-century mainstream liberal Protestant responses to the challenges posed by historical-critical biblical scholarship. It is also vital to the development of religious studies as an academic discipline. Although Schleiermacher, against the background and in response to the arguments of Kant's first two critiques, argues that religion is something other than either reason or morality, that it is a mode of receptivity to the divine prior to and beyond the split between subject and object necessary to rational knowledge and morality, at the same time he allows reason to be determinative of the limits within which the divine can be experienced. Seeking both to reconcile reason and faith and to safeguard faith from the critical incursions of reason, Schleiermacher remains committed to forms of critical thought dependent on reasoned accounts of what we can know and how we can and should act. What is critical in religious reading, then, or in the reading of religious texts, remains that which is guided by reason.

Although religious experience may transform human beings' apprehension of the world and the divine, it does so in ways always compatible with reason. There is little sense that religious experience might give rise to forms of understanding or consciousness on the basis of which reason itself might be judged.[12]

With Marguerite Porete, to whom I'll devote most of the rest of my discussion, we are, quite obviously, in a different world. Written in the closing years of the thirteenth and opening years of the fourteenth century, Marguerite's *The Mirror of Simple Souls* is an allegorical dialogue in which Love, Soul, Reason, and a host of less prominent interlocutors provide an account of the free, simple, and annihilated soul.[13] Love, avatar of the divine, is the primary authority, although Soul, who shifts throughout the dialogue between an encumbered and an unencumbered state, is also a source of information about the gap between the two conditions. Reason is the foil, the dimwitted audience to Love's and the Soul's high-flown dialogue who constantly asks them to please explain themselves. As I will show in what follows, ultimately Reason must die if the Soul is to apprehend and become one with divine Love. In the process, what Marguerite calls the Understanding of Divine Love emerges, an understanding that guides those now possessed of two eyes to abandon one-eyed Reason and in the process to learn to read both the Bible and Marguerite's book. Through Love, then, comes a higher mode of understanding, thereby complicating the apparent dichotomy between Reason and Love that governs the *Mirror* (and arguably this essay). I want to stay with the main lines of Marguerite's allegory here, deploying it for my own purposes, yet we should keep in mind that the relationship between reason and love (or between reason and the passions, or reason and emotion) is never quite as simple as this allegorizing mode suggests. At any rate, from the standpoint of divine Love, the Soul and Love criticize Reason, her adherents (who include what Marguerite refers to as Holy Church the Little, as opposed to Holy Church the Great), and their limitations. Reason, despite her claims to critical power (and despite Marguerite's caricature of Reason's limitations, her pretension to critical power looms both within the text and on its peripheries), is unable to afford true insight because she is always blind to the double meanings that run throughout Love's discourse (which includes, once again, the Bible and Marguerite's own book).

Despite the apparent modernity of the critical reading practices to which scholars of religion adhere, then, the debate between reason and love or between reason and faith on which accounts of critical reading rest (at least within religious studies) has a long prehistory, one in which the terms are often slightly different and their valuation radically so.[14] Behind my desire to expose the variety of competing practices of critical reading visible within and around a single medieval text lies a concern to raise questions about what we now consider critical reading to be. We often presume that to read religiously is to read *uncritically*, yet for Marguerite, the insight gained through the annihilation of reason, will, and desire gives rise to a powerful critique of reason itself. Insofar as criticism is grounded in the character Reason, it is dead. Yet at the same time, Marguerite implies that Love is a more apt site from which to read critically. She is not alone. The later Middle Ages witnessed many powerful critiques of church and society by men and women who claimed to be possessed by or unified with God. Marguerite is simply one of the most explicit in associating the institutional church with reason and in arguing for another, invisible Church (Holy Church the Great), governed by divine Love.

In *Serving the Word: Literalism in America from the Pulpit to the Bench*, the anthropologist Vincent Crapanzano refers to "our own particular chivalry toward belief and faith."[15] Yet many, if not most, intellectuals presume, like Marx, that the criticism (read here rational destruction, although again grounded in claims to critical engagement) of religion is the necessary preliminary to any political, social, or economic transformation of society. Where chivalry is evident, I think, it is due to the lack of seriousness with which religion is often taken. The Christian fundamentalists about whom Crapanzano writes seem to criticize contemporary culture from a perspective other than that of reason. As long as fundamentalist or evangelical Christians are perceived as powerless and irrational, secular Americans don't much care about their critiques. (When they are perceived as powerful, on the other hand, fundamentalist Christians inspire great fear.) Secular or liberal Christian Americans, or Americans of other faith traditions, can refuse to engage with fundamentalist Christians at least in part because the former claim that fundamentalist Christians refuse to engage rationally with the world around them. Thus Crapanzano argues that fundamentalists deny the possibility of genuine dialogue with those who disagree with them (thereby shifting his central emphasis from the issue of literalism to that of engagement. It remains an open question to what extent literalism necessitates a refusal to engage with others).

Yet I can't help wondering, prompted as you will see by Marguerite, whether there are things about which the critical, generally skeptical reason that governs much modern scholarship and intellectual life refuses to speak. Do fundamentalist Christians refuse dialogue, or are they responding to a prior refusal on the part of the world around them? At the very least, the current world situation suggests that the potentially silencing chivalry of secular intellectualism is no longer adequate. Students of religion are perhaps most inescapably confronted with the problem. As scholars, often working within the secular academy, most of us are committed to at least some conception of critical reason. Yet because we purport to read, interpret, and explain religious texts and practices, we are ultimately forced to confront the limitations of reason as a source of critique. Is it possible to remain open to both critical impulses? Or do we need, at the very least provisionally, to allow other modes of apparently uncritical reading—modes that, I'll argue, are often, in fact, themselves critical, albeit in unfamiliar ways—to challenge what we conceive critical reading to be?

READING *THE MIRROR OF SIMPLE SOULS*

The earliest witness we have to Marguerite Porete's life and book is the anonymously authored continuation of the *Chronicon* of William of Nangis, written at Saint-Denis shortly after Porete's death on June 1, 1310:

> Around the Feast of the Pentecost it happened at Paris that a certain pseudowoman [*pseudo-mulier*] from Hainault, named Marguerite called "Porete," had published a certain book in which, according to the judgment of all the theologians who diligently examined it, many errors and heresies were contained—among others, "that the soul annihilated in love of the Creator, without blame of conscience or remorse, can and ought to concede to nature whatever it seeks and desires," which manifestly rings of heresy.
>
> While she did not want to abjure this little book [*labellum*] or the errors contained in it, but rather for a year or more stubbornly had endured the sentence of excommunication that the inquisitor of heretical depravity set upon her—because she did not want to appear in his presence [although] she had been sufficiently warned—finally, hardened in her wickedness, at the Place de Grève in the presence of the clergy and the people specially assembled for this purpose, with the counsel of learned men, she was brought forth and handed over to the secular court. The provost of Paris, taking her into his power immediately, in the same place caused her to be destroyed by fire the next day. She showed, however, many signs of penitence at her end, both noble and devout, by which the hearts of many were piously and tearfully turned to compassion, as revealed by the eyes of the witnesses who beheld the scene.[16]

We know nothing about Marguerite beyond what we find in her book (that's very little), the trial documents, and contemporary chronicles. She is referred to as a beguine often enough to make that attribution convincing to most historians. Some scholars believe that she traveled throughout the Southern Low Countries and Northern France with her book, a possibility opened by the beguines' semi-religious lifestyle, in which one devoted oneself to religion without taking formal vows or submitting to strict enclosure (as did most nuns and canonesses). We cannot know this, however, with any certainty, given the scant evidence about her life.

The *Chronicon* of Nangis, the later *Grand chroniques de France*, and most importantly the trial records found among the document collections of William of Nogaret and William of Plaisans allow scholars to reconstruct the probable chronology and details of Marguerite's trial and condemnation.[17] Most important for our purposes is that, in accord with standard contemporary procedures, suspect passages were taken from the *Mirror* and submitted for evaluation by a panel of prominent theologians. The theologians did not see the book as a whole, but only these selected passages. Special care was taken with Marguerite's case, perhaps because she had submitted the book to three theologians, each of whom had approved it. One of these men, Godfrey of Fontaines, was a master of theology and would have been known to at least some of Marguerite's judges. The approbation appended to the first Latin translation of the *Mirror* claims that Godfrey said the book described divine practice, but it also reports that he warned against the dangers the book might pose to those unversed in the religious life. Working against these approbations, however, is the fact, also made known in the trial documents, that Marguerite's book (or perhaps an earlier version of it) had been condemned by Guy of Colmieu, bishop of Cambrai, sometime before 1306 (the year of his death). Guy burned the book before Marguerite and warned her that she would be judged as relapsed and handed over to secular authorities if she disseminated further the teachings contained within it. Marguerite ignored Guy of Colmieu, admitting to authorities on two occasions that she still possessed the book and that she had sent copies of the book, or one similar to it, to many people.

When the Paris inquisitor condemned Marguerite to be turned over to the secular authorities for execution, he also ordered that her book be burned with her on the Place de Grève and that all known copies of the book be handed over to the Dominican prior at Paris. For over six centuries, it was assumed that the book had been effectively destroyed in 1310 and that no copies survived. In 1946, however, Romana Guarnieri announced that she had discovered Marguerite's book in a Latin text housed at the Vatican.[18] She based her claim on the near identity between the three condemned passages cited in the trial documents and the chronicle of Nangis and portions of the *Mirror*. The attestation is largely unquestioned,[19] scholarly debate centering on how to read the *Mirror* now that it is known to be Marguerite's work. Despite the *Mirror*'s condemnation, surviving manuscript evidence shows that it was copied and translated many times during the Middle Ages. About fifteen manuscripts survive, in French,[20] Latin, Middle English, and Italian.[21] There is also evidence of a Flemish translation, although a manuscript has not been found.[22] A recent discovery shows that the *Mirror* was also included in mystical compendia of unimpeached orthodoxy. The available evidence, then, shows that the *Mirror* continued to be read, translated, and copied at least until the fifteenth century, albeit anonymously.[23]

The *Mirror* and its manuscripts offer multiple possibilities for the analysis of medieval reading practices.[24] As I've said, central for me are how Love, the Soul, and the Author who caused the book to be written (another occasional interlocutor within the dialogue) demand that the *Mirror* be read and the ways in which Marguerite prefigures, through Reason, the modes of misreading in which her critics will engage. (Although it should be noted that the *Mirror* more often speaks of auditors than of readers, pointing to the possible specificity of the interpretative communities to which it was addressed.)[25] The crucial issue for me here is what it would mean to read in the way the *Mirror* demands, what stops Marguerite's inquisitors from reading in this way, and what might hinder the modern reader. If, as I will show, Love and the Soul demand the annihilation of reason, will, and affection as the necessary prerequisite to two-eyed reading, does a space remain for critical reading as generally understood? Given Love's and the Soul's outspoken criticism of Holy Church the Little, of actives, contemplatives, clerics, and members of the religious orders, it seems instead that critical reading has been transformed—arguably even made possible—by the debates between Love, Reason, and the Soul enacted within the *Mirror*.

THE ANNIHILATION OF REASON, WILL, AND DESIRE

As I've suggested, Reason's role in the dialogue is precisely that of the one-eyed reader, unable to understand the words of Love without intensive glossing (and even then, Reason often remains unable to understand Love's and the Soul's seemingly contradictory accounts of the simple soul).²⁶ This tendency toward contradiction can be seen already in Love's first description of the free and annihilated soul, which takes the form of nine points:

> [*Love*]. For there is another life, which we call the peace of charity in the annihilated life. Of this life, says Love, we wish to speak, in asking where one could find
>   1. a soul
>   2. who is saved by faith without works
>   3. who is only in love
>   4. who does nothing for God
>   5. who leaves nothing for God to do
>   6. to whom nothing can be taught
>   7. from whom nothing can be taken
>   8. or given
>   9. and who has no will.²⁷

In the following chapters—and in a sense throughout the book as a whole— Love and the Soul, prompted by Reason, comment on this initial description. Understanding, moreover, is hierarchically graded, with different glosses required for "contemplatives and actives" (chapters 11–12) and for "ordinary people" (chapter 13). Throughout, Reason cries out in pained incomprehension ("For God's sake, Love, what can this mean?" is a continual refrain here and throughout the book), only to receive in reply further paradoxical analogies and images to which she responds with shock and horror.

So to Reason's questions about how the soul can both take nothing and have nothing taken from her, Love replies with extended dialectical discussions about the nothingness and "allness" of the soul. When the soul falls into her own nothingness, she becomes God who is all.

> *Love.*—It is fitting, says Love, that this Soul should be conformable to the deity, for she is transformed into God, says Love, through whom she has retained her true form, which is confirmed and given to her without beginning from one alone who has always loved her by his goodness.
>
> *Soul.*—Oh, Love, says this Soul, the meaning of what is said makes me nothing, and the nothingness of this alone has placed me into an abyss, below less than nothing without measure. And the knowledge of my nothingness,

says the Soul, has given me the all, and the nothingness of this all, says the Soul, has taken litany and prayer from me, so that I pray for nothing. (Chap. 51, 150)

Holy Church the Little, whose practices (particularly after the Fourth Lateran Council in 1215) center on litanies, fasting, prayers, and the sacraments, asks, "What do you then do, sweetest lady and mistress over us?" The Soul, now free and unencumbered, replies;

> I rest wholly in peace . . . alone and nothing and entirely in the graciousness of the single goodness of God, without stirring myself, not with one single wish, whatever riches he has in him. This is the end of my work, says this Soul, always to wish for nothing. For so long as I wish for nothing, says this Soul, I am alone with him without myself, and entirely set free, and when I wish for anything, she says, I am with myself, and thus I have lost my freedom. But when I wish for nothing, and I have lost everything beyond my will, then I have need of nothing; being free is my support [*maintien*]. I want nothing from no one. (Chap. 51, 151–52)[28]

There the free soul "lives and remains and was and will be without any being" (chap. 52), "where she was before she was" (chap. 81, 89, 91, 111, 134).

At the center of these oft-repeated characterizations of the simple, free soul lies a distinction between those souls who will and desire and perform, not only human things but even the things of God, and those souls who have passed beyond both external and internal works to complete freedom. The first are members of Holy Church the Little, whereas the second make up the invisible community of Holy Church the Great. Marguerite will eventually lay out a complex hierarchical scheme in which there are three deaths—to sin, to nature, and to the spirit—and seven modes of being culminating in the beatific vision available only after the death of the body. Most crucial, however, remains the move from stage four (that of the lost and bewildered souls who remain tied to the virtues, love, will, affection, and reason) to stages five and six (in which, dead to the spirit, will, and reason, the soul is completely free). This central distinction and the changing role of the virtues as the soul moves from an encumbered to an unencumbered state (later described as from stage four to stage five) appear early in the *Mirror* and are, not surprisingly, the subject of two of the three condemned passages known to us.[29]

Explaining how the free soul is saved by faith without works, the dialogue shows the Soul taking leave of the Virtues:

> Virtues, I take leave of you forever,
> I will have a heart most open and gay;
> Your service is too constant, you know well.
> One time I placed my heart in you, without any disservice,
> You know that I was entirely abandoned to you;
> I was thus a slave to you; now I am free. (Chap. 6, 24)

The Soul goes on to explain, however, that she is no longer subservient to the Virtues because they now freely serve her. She has left the dominion of Reason, the Virtues, and law to enter that of Love. Since Love is mistress of the Virtues, the Soul now has dominion over them as well.

Elucidating her purpose to a scandalized and perplexed Reason, Love explains that she wishes to free souls from their suffering servitude to works, asceticism, and the cycle of ecstasy and alienation so common among the religious women among whom Marguerite lived and worked.

> *Love.*—When Love dwells in them, the Virtues serve them without any contradiction and without the work of such souls. Oh, without doubt, Reason . . . such souls who have become free have known for many days what Dominion usually does. And to the one who would ask them what was the greatest torment that a creature could suffer, they would say that it would be to dwell in Love and to be in obedience to the Virtues. For it is necessary to give to the Virtues all that they ask, whatever the cost to Nature. For it is thus that the Virtues demand honor and goods, heart and body and life. It is to be expected that such souls leave all things, and still the Virtues say to this Soul, who has given all to them, retaining nothing to comfort Nature, that the just one is saved by great pain. And thus this exhausted Soul who still serves the Virtues says that she would be assaulted by Fear, and torn in hell until the judgment day, and after that she would be saved. (Chap. 8, 28–30)

To live in Love, subject to the absolute nature of Love's desire, and yet still to remain subservient to Reason and the Virtues is torture, for the Soul can never do all that it might for Love. The greater her love for God, the more glaring her faults and omissions; the greater her ecstasy in the divine embrace of Love, the

more unbearable Love's absence. In this frenzy, the Soul recognizes her nothingness; in recognizing she is nothing, she sacrifices herself to Love and becomes
united with her. The annihilated Soul no longer requires to give or to receive.
Hence "poverty or tribulation, masses or sermons, fasting or prayers" are all one
to her and she is free to give "to Nature all that is necessary to it without any
remorse." (These are two of the passages condemned at Paris.) This will not lead
to sin, however, for the Soul is so transformed into divine Love that everything
she requires is innocent.

These double meanings, as Love calls them—Virtue as both master and servant or the Soul as both nothing and all—are impossible for Reason to grasp.
(Marguerite here foresees the inability of her inquisitors to read her book.)
Reason, for Marguerite, apprehends the divine in terms of univocal meanings
and fixed exchanges. Marguerite is unusual in that she condemns not only "ordinary people," those who attempt to follow Christ's commands and participate
in his sacraments as promulgated by scripture and the Catholic church, but also
religious people, those nuns, monks, clerics, and beguines who have devoted
their lives to the fulfillment of the apostolic way.[30] For Marguerite, "actives and
contemplatives" also belong to Holy Church the Little, governed by Reason, as
long as they believe that they can attain salvation through their prayers, fasts,
vigils—even their extraordinary experiences of divine Love. They are, according
to Marguerite, "merchants" rather than "noble" and "free." The Soul must instead
recognize her absolute nothingness in the face of divine Love in order to become
unencumbered. (I hesitate to equate freedom with salvation, given that Marguerite insists the former takes precedence over the latter.)

Love, finally, has no desire to placate Reason (and Holy Church the Little,
which is governed by her), but seeks instead to destroy her. Reason's death is
enacted twice within the *Mirror*. After her first death, Love asks what Reason
would ask if she were alive, in order to render the book comprehensible to those
not yet annihilated in Love (chaps. 87–88). Eventually Reason returns to ask the
questions herself, demonstrating the centrality of her role within the book. The
second and more dramatic death occurs toward the end of Marguerite's book and
precipitates its close. Here the Soul engages in a process of meditation that leads
to the death of reason, will, and affection. She thereby dramatizes a moment she
wishes the reader, through a similar meditative practice, to follow.[31]

> Then in my meditation I considered how it would be if he might ask me how I
> would fare if I knew that he could be better pleased that I should love another

better than him. At this my mind failed me, and I did not know how to answer, nor what to will nor what to deny; but I answered that I would ponder it.

And then he asked me how I would fare if it could be that he could love
another better than me. And at this my mind failed me, and I knew not what
to answer, or will or deny.

Yet again, he asked me what I would do and how I would fare if it could be
that he would will that another love me better than he. And in the same way,
my mind failed, and I did not know what to answer, any more than before, but
again I said that I would ponder it.

Reason here arrives at its limits, unable even to think that which Love proposes.
The final transformation of the Soul demands the annihilation of all creatureliness, including love itself insofar as it is created and human. In confronting these
imagined demands, then, the Soul kills her reason, as seen above, and ultimately
also her will and desire.

> If I have the same as you have, with the creation that you have given me, and
> thus I am equal to you except in this, that I might be able to exchange my will
> for another—which you would not do—therefore you would will these three
> things that have been so grievous for me to bear and swear. . . . And thus, lord,
> my will is killed in saying this. And thus my will is martyred, and my love is
> martyred: you have guided them to martyrdom. To think about them leads
> to disaster. My heart formerly always thought about living by love through
> the desire of a good will. Now these two things are dead in me, I who have
> departed from my infancy. (Chap. 131, 384–88)

In this movement beyond human love and the human will, the necessity for
works, either external or spiritual, comes to an end. As the Soul loses herself in
Love, Love works in and through her.

From what we know of Marguerite's trials, her critics, like Reason, were
unable to see with two eyes and to accept the double meaning of her words. The
method of decontextualizing passages itself precludes two-eyed readings, which
depends on shifts of perspective facilitated by the movement of the text. For her
inquisitors, the virtues are the mistresses of the soul rather than the soul's servant,
and the switch in perspectives that enables Marguerite to make both claims, each
suitable to a different mode of being, escapes them. Or does it? Two issues are
crucial here. First, although Marguerite is not guilty of the antinomianism with

which she seems to have been charged—Marguerite does not hold that the free soul can give to nature anything contrary to the law, but rather that the law is so internalized that she can give to nature anything it wants and all that it wants will be licit—she does clearly argue that the free soul no longer needs the mediation of the church, its laws, and its sacraments, in order to attain innocence and freedom. Although one must move *through* the laws of the church, Reason's dictates, and the mediation of the sacraments in order to attain annihilation, the final freedom of the soul depends on surpassing them. This her inquisitors seemed to intuit, even if they were unable or unwilling to name the full force of her challenge to ecclesiastical authority.[32] They are unable to conceive of reason outside of those forms embodied by the institution of the church itself.

Second, we know that Marguerite refused to respond to the charges made against her. A younger contemporary, the Dominican preacher and scholar Eckhart, also charged with disseminating teachings dangerous to good Christians, did respond to his critics and in language that might easily have been used by Marguerite. He claims that while the statements pulled out for censure were subject to heretical readings, they were also capable of being read in an orthodox way. In other words, he asked his critics to read with two eyes and hence to see the perspective from which his words were true. The commission charged to review the list of twenty-eight articles taken from Eckhart's work finally decided that they were heretical "as stated" (*prout verba sonant*), suggesting that they could only hear with one ear. As Michael Sargent argues, Eckhart's critics were radical literalists and their reasoned criticism of his work rests on a literalist hermeneutics (or antihermeneutics, if you will) in which words simply mean what they say.[33] If it sounds dangerous, it *is* dangerous. And as good literalists, Eckhart's critics would have been much more palatable to historical-critical scholarship than Eckhart, with his wild allegorizing, for much of the force of the criticism of religion and of religious texts rests on a deeply literalist set of presumptions. If today we find the literalist interpretation of the Bible stultifying and uncritical, it is important to remember its roots in a radical and *reasoned* critique of allegory.

SILENCE AND/AS ENGAGEMENT

Marguerite's silence in the face of her inquisitors sparks radically different responses in modern readers. Some admire the firmness of her resolve, while others see her as intransigent and willfully self-sacrificing in the face of an authority that could—and would—kill her. We might assume that her refusal to speak involves an implicit claim that she has surpassed dialogue.[34] Just as with the death of Reason, the will, and affections, the *Mirror* itself must end, with the author apologizing for a prolixity engendered by an uncomprehending Reason and assuring her auditors that those who attain the state of simplicity and freedom recognize each other without words, so perhaps Marguerite believed herself to have attained annihilation and so to stand in a place from which she could no longer speak to Reason's minions. Yet despite repeated warnings and censures, Marguerite continued to disseminate her book and presumably to add to it, further attempting to explain to "ordinary people" and to "actives and contemplatives" governed by Reason the wonders of divine Love, which lay just beyond the latter's grasp, and to enact before them a process of transformation they might effectively mime.[35] To read the *Mirror* well, Marguerite suggests, is to follow the Soul depicted within it in her transformation to freedom, to give up Reason's one-eyed readings in favor of the double-words and double-perspectives of the Understanding of divine Love. Seen from this angle, Marguerite's silence speaks to her sense of her interlocutors' refusal to engage with her. Pulling decontextualized sentences out of her book so destroys its movement as to render it unrecognizable. It is her readers, then, who are incapable of dialogue.

Where does this leave me as a scholar of religion? What would it mean for me to read in the way Marguerite's text demands, to annihilate myself before the power of divine Love? How can I critically engage with a text whose critical force rests on the abdication of reason—at least according to one understanding of reason, an understanding that would certainly include the forms of historical interpretation that still pass for critical in much religious studies scholarship? Is it possible to explore, confront, even engage in a dialogue with that which is on the edges of or beyond reason?[36] Although my reading of the *Mirror* may be two-eyed compared to that of Marguerite's inquisitors, without the annihilation of reason and of the self, how adequate an understanding of the *Mirror* can I ever plausibly claim to have? Most importantly, how can I allow—and when might I claim successfully to have allowed—alternative conceptions of rationality, or conceptions of criticism not grounded in rationality, to challenge my own assumptions about critical reading? Given that my subjectivity is in part shaped by critical reading and thinking as formative practices, what level of self-annihilation would be required for me to read Marguerite well? What is challenged by Marguerite that I don't want to relinquish?

These are questions to which I only have partial and still tentative answers. What I most want to take from this allegorizing of Marguerite—itself a dangerous enterprise—is that there are situations in which what looks like another's refusal to engage with us covers over our own refusal to engage with her. In other words, when we turn to the contemporary world and those communities or individuals who seem to refuse forms of rationality premised on engagement and debate, we need to ask what is entailed by our demands for engagement and how these demands annul central premises of the other's position. One presumption I generally refuse to give up— what I hold on to in the face of Marguerite, for example—is the necessity of skeptical questioning and critical reflection. My oddly intertwined conceptions of reason, of scholarship, and of democracy depend on the high value I place on criticism as a form of engagement in which I allow my assumptions to be changed by powerful counter-arguments. Yet the one assumption I don't allow to come into question is that of the value of critical, rationally grounded engagement itself. What would it mean to give oneself over—even provisionally—to a form of life in which criticism is grounded in the divine, in tradition, authority, or community (just to name some of the obvious possibilities)? I can't begin to argue for the value of my own commitments without at least attempting to hear and understand those of my interlocutor—without assuming that she might have good grounds for her view, even if it contradicts my own.[37]

Marguerite, then, demands a different form of engagement—one in which my most unquestioned presumptions are, in fact, questioned. But Marguerite has been dead for seven hundred years and the challenge she poses is therefore both complicated (hence this essay's need for historical specificity in its account of Marguerite on Love, Reason, and reading) and attenuated by distance. The world is full of others—living others—who challenge me more immediately, and to whose challenge I must respond with a willingness to hear what is different in their beliefs, their words, and their actions, even if those differences call into question the things I most deeply hold and am. The goal is not agreement, consensus, or the discovery of common ground. The goal is to try to hear what I cannot assimilate. And yet the force of the injunction rests, paradoxically, on my own values. Marguerite's allegiance to Love leads her to annihilate Love. Perhaps my allegiance to critique demands a similar annihilation of rational criticism—even, insofar as my subjectivity is tied up with my self-conception and practice as rational, self-annihilation. Am I ready to follow Marguerite, even if not quite in the way she may have intended? Can I follow her and maintain my—critical—distance? Or might critique itself be rethought as occupying the paradoxical site of what Marguerite calls the Farnear, that which in its proximity is most distant and in its distance most proximate?

PART III
Sexuality

SEXUAL DESIRE, DIVINE DESIRE; OR, QUEERING THE BEGUINES

5

You can reduce religion to sex only if you don't especially believe in either one.

—Michael Warner, "Tongues Untied"

IN THE face of what the social historian Judith Bennett refers to as "the virtual absence of actual women from the sources of medieval lesbianisms," a number of literary and cultural scholars have recently turned to texts by or about women to uncover homoerotic possibilities within the metaphoric structures of women's writings or in the practices ascribed to women or female characters within male- and female-authored literary and religious documents.[1] Karma Lochrie, for example, looks to a number of medieval devotional texts and images in which Christ's bloody side wound becomes a locus of desire.[2] According to Lochrie, not only is Christ's body feminized through its association with women's (and particularly the Virgin Mary's) nurturing breasts, as Caroline Walker Bynum famously argues, but religious representations also "genitalize" Christ's wound, associating it both imagistically and linguistically with the vulva.[3] When women mystics write about eagerly kissing the sacred wound, then, their relationship with Christ is queered, for the body they desire and with which they identify is both male and female—and so perhaps neither.[4] For Lochrie, "neither the acts/identity distinction nor the focus on same-sex desire is adequate or desirable as a framework for queering medieval mysticism."[5] Rather, Lochrie argues, the complex interplay of gender and sexuality in medieval texts and images effectively queers simple identifications of sex, gender, and sexuality.

Bennett describes the work of Lochrie and other cultural and literary critics with care and enthusiasm, yet worries that while "as literary criticism, these readings reach plausible conclusions, . . . as guides to social history, they are considerably less convincing."[6]

> It's great fun, for example, to read Lochrie's impressive exploration of the artistic, literary, and linguistic ties between Christ's wound and female genitalia, and to speculate, therefore, that the kissing of images of Christ's wound by medieval nuns somehow parallels lesbian oral sex. Yet Lochrie very wisely does not claim that any medieval nun who contemplated Christ's wound ever, in fact, was thinking about last night's tumble in bed with a sister nun.[7]

Bennett's worries about "actual people" and "plausible behaviors" lead her to argue that queer readings like Lochrie's are "intriguing-but-not-fully-historicized." Bennett's argument depends, however, on assuming that the history of lesbianisms is or should be centrally concerned with same-sex acts or identities derived from the pursuit of such acts, precisely the categories of analysis questioned by Lochrie (and, Lochrie would argue, by at least some medieval texts and images).

Bennett herself introduces the notion of "lesbian-like" in order to broaden lesbian history beyond its focus on "certifiable same-sex genital contact." Where she differs from Lochrie is in her focus on "broadly sociological" affinities between contemporary lesbians and women in the past—"affinities related to social conduct, marital status, living arrangements, and other behaviors that might be traced in the archives of past societies."[8] The pursuit of these affinities is certainly important historical work, both for women's history and for what Bennett calls the history of lesbianisms. Yet Bennett's argument is problematic if she means to suggest that these sociological categories give access to "real women" in a way that attention to the religious imagery and desires found in texts written or used by medieval women does not. Some medieval religious women did use intensely erotic language and imagery to talk about their relationship to the divine. No matter how implausible it might seem to us to understand Christ's side wound as a bloody slit that feminizes and eroticizes his corporeality, this is in fact what some medieval women (and men) did.[9]

Lochrie and Bennett are surely right to resist an easy movement from the relationship between the woman believer and Christ to sexual relationships between women (or between men and women).[10] Yet why shouldn't the complex interplay between sex, gender, and sexuality in representations of relationships between the human and the divine have as much significance for contemporary lesbian and queer history as the marital status of late medieval women—especially when the fluidity and excess that characterize discussions of divine desire may work to undermine the seemingly unquestioned supremacy of heteronormativity within medieval Christian culture (a heteronormativity itself also often seen within devotional language and imagery)?[11] Sociological questions might seem more "real" to us in the early twenty-first century, but for many Christians in the later Middle Ages, one's relationship to Christ and the language and images through which one attempted to achieve and convey something of that relationship had equal, if not greater, reality. So while Bennett and Lochrie no doubt pursue different kinds of historical questions, I think it is important that we recognize both as historically valid and as of significance to contemporary questions about sexuality and gender.

At stake here is the question not just of what constitutes reality, but also of how we are to understand the relationship between the often highly erotic and sexual imagery used by late medieval religious writers to describe the soul's relationship to Christ and human sexuality. Bynum's magisterial work on late medieval religiosity has set the tone here, for she argues against what she sees as a modern tendency to equate the bodily too quickly with the sexual. In an attempt to refute the widespread reduction of late medieval religiosity, particularly that of women, to sex, Bynum is in danger of denying even the metaphorically sexualized nature of many women's and men's religious writings. Her explicit aim, in both *Holy Feast and Holy Fast* and the essays collected in *Fragmentation and Redemption*, is to expand the meanings that we ascribe to corporeality in late medieval texts and practices. Yet as Lochrie and Richard Rambuss show, Bynum "herself can be quick to delimit the erotic—and especially the homoerotic—potentialities of her own devotional polysemy of the medieval body."[12] When Catherine of Siena writes of "putting on the nuptial garment," Bynum explains, "the phrase means suffering" and so is "extremely unerotic." She goes on to argue that in "Catherine's repeated descriptions of climbing Christ's body from foot to side to mouth, the body is either a female body that nurses or a piece of flesh that one puts on oneself or sinks into. . . . Catherine understood union with Christ not as an erotic fusing with a male figure but as a taking in and taking on—a becoming—of Christ's flesh itself."[13] Bynum makes many contentious (and, not surprisingly, vehemently anti-Freudian) assumptions about sexuality and erotic desire—most crucially, that erotic desire can be clearly distinguished from suffering, the maternal, and identification—yet as Rambuss suggests, perhaps the most salient point of Bynum's interpretation is her refusal to see same-sex desire as potentially sexual. If Christ's body is feminized (and so becomes a point of identification for women), Bynum assumes it cannot also be the locus of female sexual desire (or even of a desire for the divine analogous to sexual desire). Her insistence on the feminization of Christ serves two functions, then, both providing a locus for female identification with the divine and protecting the divine-human relationship from even metaphorical sexualization.

What I want to show here is that some late medieval women did use explicitly erotic language to discuss their relationship with Christ and they did so, often, in ways that challenged the prescriptive heteronormativity of the culture in which they lived. The challenge occurs not only through the feminization of Christ's body, but also through an intense, hyperbolic, and often ultimately self-subverting deployment of apparently heterosexual imagery. This excess often involves a displacement of Christ as the center of the religious life and emphasis on a feminized figure of divine love. Among the beguines, semireligious women who flourished in thirteenth-century northern Europe and are best known for their so-called bridal mysticism (and hence, it would seem, for a resolutely heterosexual, nonqueer sexual imaginary), we find accounts of insane love and endless desire in which gender becomes so radically fluid that it is not clear *what* kind of sexuality—within the dichotomy between heterosexual and homosexual most readily available to modern readers—is being metaphorically deployed to evoke the relationship between humans and the divine.[14] Moreover, any clear duality between male and female or masculine and feminine and so the putative duality of sex and gender themselves are called into question. As Rambuss argues with regard to early modern male-authored religious poetry, the absence in these texts "of a polarizing system of sexual types tends to open these works in the direction of a greater plasticity of erotic possibilities, possibilities not entirely containable by our own (often only suppositiously coherent) sexual dichotomies."[15] The very inability to contain medieval divine eroticism within modern categories points to its potential queerness.[16]

Religious desire and sexual desire are not the same, as Bennett usefully reminds us. Yet, in the evocative words of Michael Warner, "religion makes available a language of ecstasy, a horizon of significance within which transgressions against the normal order of the world and the boundaries of the self *can be seen as good things.*"[17] Moreover, religious writers often use the language of eroticism to express that ecstasy, excess, and transgression. Perhaps this is because erotic language is able, in ways that devotional language both exploits and intensifies, to engender affective states that push the believer beyond the limitations of his or her own body and desires.[18] At the same time, the intensity of divine desire forces sexual language into new, unheard-of configurations. Hence the emergence in the later Middle Ages of what Lochrie aptly calls the "mystical queer." These religious representations do not reflect, or even legitimate, particular configurations of human sexual relations—they often indeed seem to involve a movement beyond sexed and gendered bodies, even that of Christ, as the locus of pleasure and desire—but they do denaturalize and destabilize normative conceptions of human gender and of human sexuality in potentially radical ways.

MYSTICAL QUEER

The centrality of the Song of Songs to medieval Christian devotional literature, images, and practices sets the stage for an intensely erotic and, at least on the surface, heterosexualized understanding of the relationship between the soul and God. Origen (ca. 185–254), the first Christian commentator on the Song of Songs whose work survives, reads the series of erotic poems as an allegory both for the relationship between Christ and the church and for that between Christ and the individual believer.[19] The latter reading provides a central source for twelfth-century mystical exegetes like Bernard of Clairvaux (1090–1153), William of St. Thierry (ca. 1080–1148), and Rupert of Deutz (1077–1120), who increasingly emphasize the intensely erotic nature of the relationship between the lover and the beloved, the bridegroom and the bride, or Christ and the soul.[20] When undertaken by male authors, these allegorical readings often involve a kind of linguistic transgendering,[21] whereby the male devotee becomes the female soul joined in loving union with the male figure of Christ.[22] When undertaken by women, on the other hand, apparently normalized sexual roles often prevail.

So, for example, in Mechthild of Magdeburg's (ca. 1260–82/94) *Flowing Light of the Godhead*, an understanding of the soul as the bride of Christ is joined with traditions derived from courtly literature.[23] In book 1, Mechthild describes the soul as a lady; she dresses herself in the virtues so as to be prepared to welcome the prince. After much waiting, in which the soul watches other holy people dance, "the young man comes and says to her: 'Young lady, my chosen ones have shown off their dancing to you. Just as artfully should you now follow their lead.'" The soul replies:

> I cannot dance, Lord, unless you lead me.
> If you want me to leap with abandon,
> You must intone the song.
> Then I shall leap into love,
> From love into knowledge,
> From knowledge into enjoyment,
> And from enjoyment beyond all human sensations.
> There I want to remain, yet want also to circle higher still.[24]

Their dance is recorded in song: The young man sings, "Through me into you / And through you from me" while the soul responds, like the alternately joyful and despondent bride of the Song of Songs, "Willingly with you / Woefully from you."[25]

Mechthild makes explicit her preference for erotic over maternal metaphors in her conception of the relationship between the soul and Christ. Weary of the dance, the soul says to the senses that they should leave her so that she might refresh herself. The senses, wanting to stay with the soul, offer a series of refreshments in which they too might take part: "the blood of martyrs," "the counsel of confessors," the bliss of the angels, and, finally, the milk of the Virgin enjoyed by the Christ Child. To this, the soul replies, "That is child's love, that one suckle and rock a baby. I am a full-grown bride. I want to go to my Lover." Although there the senses will "go completely blind," the soul asserts that her true identity is found in the nature of God:

> A fish in water does not drown.
> A bird in the air does not plummet.
> Gold in fire does not perish.
> Rather, it gets its purity and its radiant color there.
> God has created all creatures to live according to their nature.
> How, then, am I to resist my nature?
> I must go from all things to God,
> Who is my Father by nature,

> *My Brother by his humanity,*
> *My Bridegroom by love,*
> *And I his bride from all eternity.*[26]

Just as Mechthild will insist that she is God's child by both grace and nature (see 6.31), so here she claims to be daughter, sister, and bride of Christ, multiplying metaphors (all derived from the Song of Songs) without undermining the eroticism of the dance of love in which the dialogue appears.

Moreover, identification does not preclude but rather seems to follow from the intensity of desire. After asserting the commonality of her nature with that of the divine, the bride of all delights goes to the Fairest of lovers in the secret chamber of the invisible Godhead. There she finds the bed and the abode of love prepared by God in a manner beyond what is human. Our Lord speaks:

> *"Stay, Lady Soul."*
> *"What do you bid me, Lord?"*
> *"Take off your clothes."*
> *"Lord, what will happen to me then?"*
> *"Lady Soul, you are so utterly ennatured in me*
> *That not the slightest thing can be between you and me. . . . "*
> *Then a blessed stillness*
> *That both desire comes over them. He surrenders himself to her,*
> *And she surrenders herself to him.*
> *What happens to her then—she knows—*
> *And that is fine with me.*
> *But this cannot last long.*
> *When two lovers meet secretly,*
> *They must often part from one another inseparably.*[27]

As long as the soul remains within the body, the lovers can only meet fleetingly. The intensity of her desire and of her fusion with the divine both demand the use of erotic language and subvert it, for the body cannot sustain the experience of the divine embrace. (Although, as I will show below, Mechthild insists that the body will ultimately be reunited with the soul and share in its final glory.) The suffering to which God's presence and absence give rise is then itself taken up as crucial to the path of desire for and identification with Christ.[28]

The interplay of suffering and desire is also crucial to the poetry and prose of Hadewijch (fl. 1250) in ways that ultimately disrupt the heteronormativity of the relationship between the soul and the divine prevalent in Mechthild's work.[29] In a poem on the seven names of love, Hadewijch makes the spectacular claim that love, Hadewijch's favored name for the divine, is hell:

> Hell is the seventh name
> Of this Love wherein I suffer.
> For there is nothing Love does not engulf and damn,
> And no one who falls into her
> And whom she seizes comes out again,
> Because no grace exists there.
> As Hell turns everything to ruin,
> In Love nothing else is acquired
> But disquiet and torture without pity;
> Forever to be in unrest,
> Forever assault and new persecution;
> To be wholly devoured and engulfed
> In her unfathomable essence,
> To founder unceasingly in heat and cold,
> In the deep, insurmountable darkness of Love.[30]

For Hadewijch, the constant "comings and goings" of Love are a source of continual suffering, for the soul is caught between the ecstasy of the divine presence, Love's unrelenting demands for fidelity, and the constant threat of God's absence. Suffering does not preclude erotic desire, but is central to it. "Aggression, violence, masochism, and dark despair," Lochrie argues, "are as fundamental to the visions of some women mystics as the tropes of marriage and . . . languorous desire." For Lochrie, this kind of excessive, violent desire is "queer in its effects—exceeding and hyperbolizing its own conventionality and fracturing the discourses of mystical love and sex."[31]

Hadewijch, like Mechthild, argues that this suffering love itself becomes a part of the soul's identification with Christ. As she writes in a letter to fellow beguines, "We all indeed wish to be God with God, but God knows there are few of us who want to live as human beings with his Humanity, or want to carry his cross with him, or want to hang on the cross with him and pay humanity's debt to the full."[32] Yet this demand that the soul identify with Christ in his suffering humanity does not preclude a desire for the divine best expressed through the language of eroticism. Again like Mechthild, Hadewijch, particularly in her visions, makes use of imagery derived from the Song of Songs as the basis for her understanding of the union between the soul and Christ. One day while at Matins, she writes, "my heart and my veins and all my limbs trembled and quivered with eager desire and, as often occurred with me, such madness and fear beset my mind that it seemed to me I did not content my Beloved, and that my Beloved did not fulfill my desire, so that dying I must go mad, and going mad I must die."[33] This leads Hadewijch to desire that her humanity "should to the fullest extent be one in fruition" with that of Christ, so that she might then "grow up in order to be God with God."[34]

The vision that follows is the fulfillment of that desire. Looking at the altar, she first sees Christ in the form of a child of three years, holding the eucharistic bread in his right hand and the chalice in his left. The child then becomes a man and administers the sacrament to Hadewijch.

> After that he came himself to me, took me entirely in his arms, and pressed me to him; and all my members felt his in full felicity, in accordance with the desire of my heart and my humanity. So that I was outwardly satisfied and transported. Also then, for a short while, I had the strength to bear this; but soon, after a short time, I lost that manly beauty outwardly in the sight of his form. I saw him completely come to naught and so fade and all at once dissolve that I could no longer recognize or perceive him outside me, and I could no longer distinguish him within me. Then it was to me as if we were one without difference. . . . After that I remained in a passing away in my Beloved, so that I wholly melted away in him and nothing any longer remained to me of myself.[35]

Full union with Christ, expressed here through intensely erotic language, leads to a fusion and identification with profound theological implications. Although heterosexual in its imagistic operation, moreover, the melting away of the soul into the divine radically undermines any stable distinction between male and female and, more importantly for Hadewijch, between human and divine. The incarnation, in which God becomes human, is the basis for humanity's full identification with the divine.

Yet Hadewijch's work also undermines the association of masculinity with the divine and of femininity with the human, particularly in her stanzaic poems, in which the divine is represented as Love (*minne*, which is feminine), the unattainable female object of desire, and the soul occupies the position of the male lover in quest of his Lady.[36] Love cannot be clearly identified with Christ, the Holy Spirit, God the Father, or the Trinity; Hadewijch continually shifts and overlaps various divine referents. These poems again stress the cruelty of Love and the anguish to which her demand for desirous fidelity reduces the masculine lover.

> Sometimes kind, sometimes hateful,
> Sometimes far, sometimes to hand.
> To him who endures this with loyalty of love
> That is jubilation;
> How love kills and embraces
> In a single action.[37]

Those who are Love live in an endless oscillation between darkness and light, the divine presence and her absence.[38] The soul is described in knightly terms, suspended between activity, in which he lays siege to Love in desire and fidelity ("the brave," one poem advises, "should strike before Love does")[39] and recognition that his "best success" lies in the suffering he undergoes when "shot by Love's arrow."[40] Even as Hadewijch stresses the gap between the (feminine) divine and the (masculine) human being or soul, then, she both undermines rigid gender distinctions and lays the groundwork for the eventual union of the soul and the divine through the soul's "mad love" and suffering desire—a union that occurs through Christ but is often poetically imagined without reference to his human body.[41]

In the dialogues that make up Marguerite Porete's (d. 1310) *The Mirror of Simple Souls*, Marguerite similarly employs the feminine figure of Love as the most prominent representation of the divine. She goes even further than Hadewijch, moreover, in suggesting that while Christ and Christ's body play a crucial role in the path of the soul to union with love, ultimately the role of the body and of Christ will be surpassed. Instead, the female soul engages in a loving dialogue both with Lady Love and with the feminine Trinity, giving the text an intensely homoerotic valence absent in Mechthild's heteronormative account of the love between the soul and Christ—although how heteronormative is it if the erotic other is God?—and Hadewijch's transgendering of the soul, in which the female soul becomes male in order to pursue Lady Love. Marguerite's allegorical figures of Love and Soul provide a representation of those souls who have become so free of all created things, including will and desire, that they are indistinguishable from the divine. I have argued elsewhere that Marguerite's pursuit of annihilation is a result of her desire to escape the intense suffering engendered by endless desire and "mad love." Absolute union with the divine occurs through the sacrifice of love by love. Yet the resulting loss of distinction between the soul and the divine also radically subverts, even erases, gender distinctions, a move both dependent on and subversive of the text's homoeroticism. (Marguerite uses the femininity of the Soul and Love to elicit pronominal ambiguities in which the gap between them is erased.)[42] Marguerite's work, with its distrust of spiritual delights, ecstasies, and visions, stands in a critical relationship to that of her beguine predecessors. This is evident in her relationship to the imagery of erotic love. For Marguerite, like Hadewijch, Love is the primary name of the divine and she at times makes use of language and imagery derived from the Song of Songs, yet always in ways that undermine the initial gendered dichotomy between lover and beloved. This subversion seems dependent, as it is in Hadewijch, on a displacement of Christ's body.

The process can be seen most starkly in a crucial scene toward the end of the *Mirror* in which a now masculine God challenges the soul concerning the strength of her fidelity. Nicholas Watson argues that the series of hypothetical scenes recounted by the soul "are eccentric versions of the love-tests found in the tale of patient Griselda." Just as Griselda is honored for patiently submitting to the various tests of her fidelity posed by her distrustful husband, so the soul imagines a series of tests posed by God. She asks herself:

> As if He Himself were asking me, how I would fare if I knew that he could be better pleased that I should love another better than Him. At this my sense failed me, and I knew not how to answer, nor what to will, nor what to deny; but I responded that I would ponder it.
>
> And then He asked me how I would fare if it could be that He could love another better than me. And at this my sense failed me, and I know not what to answer, or will, or deny.
>
> Yet again, He asked me what I would do and how I would fare if it could be that He would will that someone other love me better than He. And again my sense failed, and I knew not what to respond, no more than before, but still I said that I would ponder it.[43]

Using the imaginative meditative practices recommended within contemporary devotional treatises as a means of participating in and identifying with Christ's passion, Marguerite here enacts a Trial of Love reminiscent of those found in secular courtly literature.

The trial leads to the death of the will and of desire (that same desire more often elicited and exploited through such meditative practices). In acquiescing to demands that go against her desire to love and be loved by God alone, the soul "martyrs" both her will and her love, thereby annihilating all creatureliness and, paradoxically, attaining a union without distinction with the divine. In Watson's evocative words, Marguerite "out-griselded Griselda," taking the test of submission to such extremes that subservience becomes the means by which the soul forces God to merge with her.[44] Marguerite takes the cultural stereotype of the patient bride, who will submit to anything in fidelity to her bridegroom, and converts it into an account of how the Soul's fall into nothingness is itself the apprehension of her full share in the divine being.[45] Like Mechthild, who insists that the soul is God's child by nature, thereby challenging late medieval versions of the doctrine of grace, Marguerite stresses throughout the *Mirror* the ways in which the soul, by emphasizing and embracing her sinfulness, abjection, and humility, can become one with God.[46] Most crucially, as Watson argues, Marguerite shows the soul achieving "mystical annihilation of her own volition, *by telling herself stories.*"[47] This particular story both depends on and subverts the hierarchically ordered gender expectations of late medieval culture.

Marguerite's use of erotic and gendered language is, like that of her fellow beguines Mechthild and, particularly, Hadewijch, remarkably complex.[48] As the example offered here suggests, however, unlike Mechthild and Hadewijch—or, perhaps better, more starkly than they—Marguerite posits the goal of the soul as the eradication of any distinction between herself and the divine. Marguerite evokes this union without distinction through the unsaying or apophasis of gender and the displacement of Christ's body as the center of religious devotion. With the overcoming of gender comes also the annihilation of desire and radical detachment from the body.[49] (Perhaps the starkest evidence of this detachment from the body lies in the fact that Marguerite never mentions the doctrine of bodily resurrection.) With the annihilation of gender, will, and desire also comes an end to the painful and ecstatic eroticism that runs throughout the texts of Mechthild and Hadewijch.

Marguerite's subversion of gender difference (grounded, needless to say, in her desire to overcome the gap between the soul and the divine) leaves no room for the vagaries of desire expressed in the closing dialogue of Mechthild's *Flowing*

Light. There we hear the words of a body and soul who refuse, finally, to renounce their ambivalent and multivalent desires:

> This is how the tormented body speaks to the lonely soul: "When shall you soar with the feathers of your yearning to the blissful heights to Jesus, your eternal Love? Thank him there for me, lady, that, feeble and unworthy though I am, he nevertheless wanted to be mine when he came into this land of exile and took our humanity on himself; and ask him to keep me innocent in his favor until I attain a holy end, when you, dearest Soul, turn away from me."
>
> The soul: "Ah, dearest prison in which I have been bound, I thank you especially for being obedient to me. Though I was often unhappy because of you, you nevertheless came to my aid. On the last day all your troubles will be taken from you."

> *Then we shall no longer complain.*
> *Then everything that God has done with us*
> *Will suit us just fine,*
> *If you will only stand fast*
> *And keep hold of sweet hope.*[50]

This promise depends on the body's self-denial, for "the less the body preserves itself, the fairer its works shine before God and before people of good will."[51] It is precisely the intense suffering of this desire and the self-denial to which it leads that give rise to Marguerite's attempt to save the soul and body through the martyrdom of the will.

Marguerite's utopian vision involves an effacement of differences—between God and soul, uncreated and created (including the body, will, and desire), and male and female—that, paradoxically, both queers heteronormative desire and sacrifices the bodies and desires from which, in their multiplicity, contemporary queer theory and practice emerge. There is clearly no straight road from medieval mystical writings to contemporary practices and politics. In the writings of the beguines, desire is a resource, an opportunity, and a problem—a problem to which Mechthild, Hadewijch, and Marguerite respond in very different ways. The divergence between them shows that although we cannot simply identify their accounts of religious experience with human sexual practices, what they write about their relationship to the divine originates in and remains tied to their experiences of themselves as embodied and desirous human beings. Most importantly, perhaps, even the most apparently heteronormative texts queer sexuality in that the object of this desire is not another human being, but (a) divine (Godman). The ecstasies of religion and those of sexuality are linked at least in part because of their shared bodiliness, intensity, and excess. In Hadewijch's texts, divine love and the love she has for the divine, themselves often difficult to distinguish, stretch and transform humanity, in body and soul, heart and mind. It is precisely the pain of this excessive, unrelenting love that leads the author of *The Mirror of Simple Souls* to the annihilation of the very love that caused the book to be written. When love is martyred, the *Mirror* is complete, rendered utterly transparent—and so completely expendable—to those free and simple souls imaged, however inadequately, within it.[52]

THE NORMAL, THE QUEER, AND THE MIDDLE AGES

6

CAROLYN DINSHAW'S *Getting Medieval: Sexualities and Communities, Pre- and Postmodern* is a book of such complexity and richness that it is only after two readings (and numerous runs through sections of particular interest to me in the context of my own research) that I'm beginning to glimpse how it all, quite wonderfully, comes together. For me, perhaps the most striking and exciting aspect of the book is its articulation of a queer desire "for partial, affective connection, for community, for even a touch across time."[1] In her assessment of the queer historian's task, Dinshaw argues persuasively that the choices "are not limited simply to mimetic identification with the past or blanket alteritism, the two mutually exclusive positions that have come to be associated with [John] Boswell and [Michel] Foucault."[2] Rather, following Jacques Derrida and Judith Butler, Dinshaw argues that there is always an "alterity within mimesis itself," a "never-perfect aspect of identification" that engenders both historical difference (and at times pleasure in that difference) and "partial connections, queer relations between" these "incommensurate lives and phenomena" (another source of possible pleasure).[3] With "the new pieces of history" that she explores in *Getting Medieval*, Dinshaw "shows that queers can make new relations, new identifications, new communities with past figures who elude resemblance to us but with whom we can be connected partially by virtue of shared marginality, queer positionality."[4]

What is specifically queer about these partial connections? Dinshaw argues that queerness is itself contingent and historical; queerness "is not a hard and fast quality that I know in advance, but is a relation to a norm, and both the norm and the particular queer lack of fit will vary according to specific instances."[5] She goes on to argue that "a queer history will be about the body because it is about sex," thereby specifying the norms in relationship to which queerness is articulated as one's dealing with sex and sexuality.[6] Her move from the language of gayness, homosexuality, and same-sex desire to that of queerness depends on this conception of the queer as that which defies the norm and the normative, although the relationship between the two sets of terms is not fully articulated. (Are gayness, homosexuality, and same-sex desires subsets of the queer? And if this is so, are the former in danger, as Leo Bersani argues, of disappearing within the latter? What about intersexed and transgender people, or genderqueers who refuse fixed distinctions between sex or gender? Might queer be capacious enough for all of those who "do" sex, gender, and sexuality otherwise without thereby losing its political force? Or should queer be capacious enough to hold an even broader category of refusals, as Dinshaw often suggests?)[7] At least one reason for the shift to the language of queerness is historical: it seemingly enables Dinshaw to bypass the vexed issue of whether there were in fact homosexuals or lesbians before the nineteenth century and the concomitantly presumed distinction between acts and identity on which this putatively Foucaultian argument rests.[8] At the same time, it allows her to include within the category of the queer a woman like Margery Kempe, whose sexual imagery remained resolutely heteronormative, even as her actions often worked against the norm.

Yet, is queerness, understood as a deviation from the norm, itself susceptible to the kind of transhistorical analysis—the enabling and uncovering of partial connections across time—in which Dinshaw engages in *Getting Medieval*? The concepts of the norm, normalcy, normality, abnormality, and normativity as we now understand them first appeared in the nineteenth century and were tied to concrete developments in statistical analysis and its application to the social sciences. Statistical modes of analysis emerged in the early modern period as a form of "political arithmetic" for the "promotion of sound, well-informed state policy" and were transferred in the early nineteenth century to the field of medicine.[9] "The application of numbers," an early medical statistician argues, can "illustrate the natural history of health and disease."[10] As Lennard Davis argues in his important book *Enforcing Normalcy: Disability, Deafness, and the Body*, the French statistician Adolphe Quetelet (1796–1847) most clearly delineated a conception of the statistical norm as an imperative (that is, as normative). As Davis explains, Quetelet

> noticed that the "law of error," used by astronomers to locate a star by plotting all the sightings and then averaging the errors, could be equally applied to

the distribution of human features such as height and weight. He then took a
further step of formulating the concept of the "l'homme moyen," or the average man. Quetelet maintained that this abstract human was the average of all
human attributes in a given country.[11]

The development of a "social physics" was dependent, Quetelet asserted, on this
conception of a physically and morally average human construct.

For Davis, the embrace of the average or the norm as "a kind of ideal, a position devoutly to be wished," marks a paradoxical shift from earlier conceptions
of the ideal as an impossible and unattainable composite of all that is best in
human beings. The eugenicist and statistician Sir Francis Galton (a cousin of
Charles Darwin) dealt with this apparent dilemma by moving from the language
of "error" to that of "normal distribution," in which the extremes on a standard
bell curve are read not as errors but as deviations. At the same time, he argued
that both extremes were not necessarily equally deviant, "substituting the idea of
ranking for the concept of averaging," at least for some categories of analysis. By
dividing the standard bell curve into four parts and reversing the gradient of the
third and fourth quartiles, he posited the highest degree of upward deviation as
a new kind of ideal (particularly with regard to features like intelligence). Yet as
Davis argues, this statistical ideal remains "unlike the classical ideal, which contains no imperative to be the ideal. The new ideal of ranked order is powered by
the imperative of the norm, and then is supplemented by the notion of progress,
human perfectibility, and the elimination of deviance, to create a dominating,
hegemonic vision of what the human body should be."[12]

The concepts of the norm, normality, and abnormality are even more deeply
marked by contradiction in the well-entrenched alliance between social and medical statistics and eugenics. As Davis argues, following Donald MacKenzie's study
from 1981, *Statistics in Britain, 1865–1930*, "There is a real connection between
figuring the statistical measure of humans and then hoping to improve humans
so that deviations from the norm diminish."[13] However, this desire to "norm" the
population is by definition impossible since "the inviolable rule of statistics is
that all phenomena will always conform to a bell curve."[14] In other words, there
will always be individuals who fall below or above the mean, despite the apparent (to eugenicists, at least) malleability and perfectibility of the human body
and moral character.[15] For Davis, even psychoanalysis, with its central (although
also constantly challenged) concepts of normality and abnormality, is touched
by this progressivist, eugenicist strand: "It is instructive to think about the ways

in which Freud is producing a eugenics of the mind—creating the concepts of normal sexuality, normal function, and then contrasting them with the perverse, abnormal, pathological, and even criminal."[16]

The terms used to designate this shift in the management of human society and social beings—"norm," "normal," "normative"—all derive from the Latin *norma*, a square used by carpenters, builders, and surveyors to obtain a right angle. The meaning of *norma* extends figuratively to refer to a rule, pattern, or precept (of practice or behavior).[17] The question for further research, then, is whether *norma* was used in relationship to sexuality or sexual behavior in the Middle Ages. Recent studies suggest that the determining term for sexuality is *natura*, with sexual activity judged according to whether it is natural or against nature.[18] (The *Oxford Latin Dictionary* gives an example in which *natura* is said to have *norma*, suggesting a link between the two terms that should be further explored.) As Joan Cadden argues with regard to Peter of Abano's early-fourteenth-century commentary on Aristotle's *Problemata*, however, the meaning (as well as value) of *natura* is not self-evident, even in the Middle Ages, for Peter distinguishes between anatomical and psychological articulations of maleness and then "blurs the distinction by reducing habit to nature."[19] Dinshaw traces a similar elision between the natural and the unnatural (or, perhaps better, a naturalizing of the unnatural) in the *Twelve Conclusions of the Lollards* and the poem appended to it.[20]

I'm not sure how much to make of this potential gap between modern conceptions of the norm and medieval understandings of *natura*, but I'd like to suggest that it may contribute to some of the complexities—and arguably the need for even greater complexity—in Dinshaw's reading of Margery Kempe. Attending to the gap between modern and medieval concepts even as we attempt to make them touch is itself, as Dinshaw shows, historically illuminating. Dinshaw at first deploys her conception of queerness around the issue of gender and sexuality, finding in Margery's distinctive clothing and, somewhat less prominently, her tears and shouts a clash with the "normative heterosexual expectations of her community in Lynn."[21] As this phrase suggests, Margery's clothing is itself a mark of her gender, but also of her sexuality, in that her white garments mark her refusal to engage in sexual activity with her husband or any other human partner. By wearing white, Margery both signals her chastity and sartorially claims a virgin status unavailable to her as a wife and mother of thirteen. Dinshaw reads the distressed responses of political and religious leaders and other observers as a response to Margery's deviation from the norm—the expected heterosexual, procreative sexuality of the emergent bourgeois society of which Margery was a member.

A passage central to Dinshaw's analysis occurs when Margery appears before the mayor of Leicester, who accuses her of being "a false strumpet, a false Lollard, and a false deceiver of the people."[22] After a series of charges and counter-charges, which may include hidden allusions to sexual misconduct or sodomy, the mayor tells Margery: "I want to know why you go about in white clothes, for I believe you have come here to lure away our wives from us, and lead them off with you."[23] Dinshaw, reading this passage in relationship to the Lollard Eleventh Conclusion, in which women who take vows of chastity are accused of engaging in female homosexual acts, sees it as evidence for a possible charge of queerness in relationship to normative heterosexuality—specified here, she suggests, as same-sex relations. Yet the passage, like the interchange between Margery and the archbishop of York, in which he accuses her of advising "my Lady Greystoke to leave her husband,"[24] seems tied as much to fears of a potentially widespread refusal of heterosexuality as to fears of possible same-sex activity. (One of the things that texts like the Lollard Eleventh Conclusion do is blur this distinction.) Kempe, in embracing chastity and claiming renewed virginal status despite her marriage and motherhood, endangers the heterosexual bond by suggesting, through her words and actions, that the "highest estate" (that is, virginity) is available to lay women, married women, and women not tied to specific religious orders or enclosed within convent walls.

Margery's pursuit of this religious ideal makes her abnormal in modern terms. But would these be terms available to or recognized by her contemporaries, for whom virginity and the refusal of human-on-human sex are posited as an ideal? In other words, can the classical and medieval notion of the ideal be refigured in terms of normality? Dinshaw recognizes the problem and argues that part of Margery's queerness lies in her inability to fit the saintly ideal to which she aspires. Here Dinshaw stretches the category of the queer beyond gender and sexuality; Margery is queer in relationship not only to heterosexual norms but also to ideals of sanctity. Dinshaw bases this claim on the responses to Margery's actions recorded in the *Book* and on the apparent overphysicality of her desire. Yet the forms of sanctity that Margery imitates, particularly those found in the lives of continental holy women from the thirteenth century, are themselves intensely physical. They are often marked, moreover, by trials and persecutions, both spiritual and bodily, which demonstrate the holy woman's commonality with Christ in his suffering exile. Margery's account of her continual persecution at the hands of those less devout than herself might easily be read as following these saintly patterns. In other words, it is not clear to me that Margery fails in the way modern readers so often insist that she does. We need to remember that Margery had supporters and was able to escape condemnation, withstand her enemies, and produce her book.

Most crucially perhaps, for Dinshaw, Margery "is not and cannot be satisfied without touching Christ, but that *is* after all something that is beyond her range."[25] Yet many medieval people, including Margery, believed that it *was* possible for human beings to touch Christ, not only through the Eucharist, which was available to all Christians, but also in extraordinary experiences of the divine presence. One of the central dilemmas in women's mystical literature and mystical hagiographies written about women in the later Middle Ages is what to do when Christ's extraordinary presence is lost, as it inevitably must be as long as one remains in the body. Some women attempted to resolve the dilemma by rejecting the centrality of the physical. But certainly not all of them did, particularly as male church leadership increasingly insisted on the visibility and physicality of women's sanctity (even as this enabled them to judge some physical phenomena as illnesses or possessions rather than as marks of the divine).

For Dinshaw, finally, "Margery's whole story is a record of her inability to will that tactile contact or accept its inaccessibility—she is unable finally to write herself out of her earthly community and into a spiritual one, just (and for the same reason) as she is unable to remake her body as virginal again."[26] Yet Margery, who is unable to understand how Mary Magdalen could bear the risen Christ's command that she not touch him, claims to be continually touching and touched by Christ. She doesn't have to accept the inaccessibility of his touch, because her life, as she tells it, is full of Christ's presence, just as his command that she wear white marks *his* remaking of her body as virginal.[27] Margery insists that she attains the ideal; if she isn't normal, it is by way of excess and idealization.

From this perspective, the "drag" on Margery's spiritual and material possibilities comes not from herself or from Christ, but rather from those who refuse to accept the genuineness of her experiences of Christ's presence and her rebirth within him. The ecclesial and political world—as well as many modern readers—interprets her body and the body of her text in a battle over sanctity and over who is sanctioned to interpret women's bodies and their claims to holiness. Margery's survival and that of her book suggest that in this battle of interpretation, she was more successful than modern readers—with their presumptions about what counts as mysticism and holiness, or simply about what is possible—might be able to see. In other words, perhaps the intensity of Kempe's certainty that she touched and was touched by the divine is precisely what makes her so abnormal, so queer to modern readers—those of us for whom the norm of naturalism still has tremendous power to pathologize those who claim to be touched and to touch the supernatural.[28]

"THAT GLORIOUS SLIT"

Irigaray and the Medieval Devotion to Christ's Side Wound

READERS OF Luce Irigaray agree that one of her philosophical projects is to valorize the female sex in service of a feminine imaginary and symbolic.[1] Just as the image of the penis serves as the basis for male claims to plenitude and mastery within a phallic imaginary and symbolic, so Irigaray argues that the vulva and vagina might become the partial basis for an imaginary register supportive of women's subjectivity (and one not dependent on problematic claims to whole-ness).[2] What is less often recognized is that one of Irigaray's first attempts to valorize the female sex occurs in a reading of Christ's side wound as vulvic and vaginal.[3] Although she will later contest her earlier reading of Christ and his woundedness, in *Speculum of the Other Woman* Irigaray finds within premodern Christian mystical and devotional traditions the beginnings of a feminine imaginary.[4]

Encountering Christ, the miming voice of *Speculum*'s "*La Mystérique*" asks: "Could it be true that not every wound need remain secret, that not every laceration was shameful? Could a sore be *holy*? Ecstasy is there in that glorious slit where she curls up in her nest, where she rests as if she had found her home—and He is also in her. She bathes in a blood that flows over her, hot and purifying."[5] As I will show, Irigaray here mimes central passages from Angela of Foligno's (c. 1248–1309) *Book*, which itself draws on a long tradition of devotion to Christ's side wound. Entry into Christ's wound, in that tradition as in Irigaray's text, marks the shattering of vision into affect, an experience of wounding laceration that is simultaneously the site of an ineffable ecstatic *jouissance*.

Irigaray, in the voice of the mystic, goes on to explain the cause of her pleasure: "If in the sight of the nails and the spear piercing the body of the Son I drink in a joy concerning which it is impossible for me to speak a single word, let no one conclude too hastily that I take pleasure in his sufferings. But that the Word thus and to this extent was made flesh, this could only be so that I might become God in my finally recognized jouissance."[6] Yet as Irigaray also notes, the mystic *does* speak, a speech and a writing enabled by her divinization. Irigaray turns to Christian devotional and mystical traditions because they are the sites "within a still theological onto-logical perspective" where

> "she" speaks—and in some cases he, if he follows "her" lead—speaks about the dazzling glare which comes from the source of light that has been logi-cally repressed, about "subject" and "Other" flowing out into an embrace of fire that mingles one term into another, about contempt for form as such, about mistrust for understanding as an obstacle along the path of jouissance and mistrust for the dry desolation of reason. Also about a "burning glass" ["*miroir ardent*"].[7]

Despite Irigaray's insistence throughout *Speculum* that every theory of the sub-ject has "always already been appropriated by the 'masculine,'"[8] the Christian mystical tradition offers a glimpse of another possibility, one that will become crucial to Irigaray's later projects.

Yet even as Irigaray's work after *Speculum* returns to and augments the claim that through a rigorous process of miming and subversion new possibilities for genuinely other forms of subjectivity are possible, she rejects *Speculum*'s reading of Christ's wound as the site of a feminine imaginary and the potential base for a feminine symbolic. As I will show, in rejecting the devotional and mystical interpretation of Christ's wound as vaginal, Irigaray explicitly rejects an under-standing of the female sex as wound-like. Also salient is Irigaray's turn from an understanding of human relations in terms of penetration and penetrability to what Judith Butler refers to as a "rigorously anti-penetrative eros of surfaces."[9] Before questioning this turn in Irigaray's thought and its potentially essentializ-ing and heterosexist connotations, however, I need first to provide an account of the interlocking scriptural, devotional, and mystical texts and images embedded within *Speculum*'s highly evocative appeal to Christ's side wound.

Irigaray's description of a glorious slit into which the mystic enters, there to be covered in "hot and purifying" blood, sounds startling—even grotesque—to modern ears. So too might the words of the Umbrian mystic Angela of Foligno, whom Irigaray mimes.[10] Two passages in her *Book*, dictated by Angela to a Fran-ciscan friar, make reference to Christ's side wound.[11] In describing the stages toward union with God, Angela writes: "In the fourteenth step, while I was standing in prayer, Christ on the cross appeared . . . to me. . . . He then called me to place my mouth to the wound on his side. It seemed to me that I saw and drank the blood, which was freshly flowing from his side. His intention was to make me understand that by this blood he would cleanse me."[12] As in Irigaray's text, the blood flowing from Christ's side is purifying. Within the theological context of the Christian Middle Ages, Christ's blood renders humans clean from sin, for his suffering and death on the cross atone for human sinfulness. Angela's words echo a host of devotional texts and images that show a human being drinking from Christ's side wound in a moment of exculpation. (See figure 7.1.) Angela is particularly adamant about the extent of her own iniquity and the necessity of Christ's saving action—and cleansing blood—to render her worthy of standing before and with him.

Later in her *Book*, Angela takes the image of the side wound to more dramatic heights, writing that "at times it seems to my soul that it enters into Christ's side, and this is a source of great joy and delight."[13] Like a host of medieval devotional texts to be discussed further below, for Angela entry into Christ's side wound serves as an image of her unification with Christ.[14] Now no longer simply cleansed, purified, and saved by Christ's blood, Angela here understands herself as united with him. A graphically physical image becomes the means of rendering vivid this moment of spiritual identification, one that will lead Angela to assert her own share in Christ's salvific role. Irigaray's words in *Speculum* bring together these two sets of images (and the many others like them in medieval devotional and mystical texts) in an even more intensely physical, eroticized, and explicitly homosexuated account of the relationship between the mystic and Christ.

In describing herself as drinking the blood flowing from Christ's side and becoming unified with him through entry into that wound, Angela encapsulates at least two of the primary themes found in the late medieval devotion to Christ's wounds. As Douglas Gray shows, within this devotional tradition, Christ's wounds are "(i) a place of refuge, (ii) openings from which the faithful can drink, and (iii) openings which reveal the way to the Sacred Heart of Christ (*arcanum cordis*)."[15] (This final meaning only attains its official form in the modern era, yet in that Angela understands Christ's side wound as a place not only of refuge, but also of union with Christ, her text anticipates the complex theology of the Sacred Heart.)[16] The meanings are not arbitrary but converge around Christ's side wound through a series of metaphorical and metonymic links between what appear to be unrelated biblical texts.

FIGURE 7.1 The Passional of Abbess Kunigunde of Bohemia. National Library of the Czech Republic, Prague. MS XIV A 17, fol. 7V.

Latin narrative accounts of Christ's suffering and death play a key role in the development of devotion to Christ's wounds. A number of scholars demonstrate the centrality of meditative practice to medieval Christian religious life, first in the monastic setting and, increasingly, in the latter Middle Ages among the mendicant orders and the laity.[17] Narrative accounts of Christ's life and death—first in Latin and later in the vernaculars—serve as tools for meditation and the imaginative re-creation of events key to salvation history. These texts were designed to evoke heightened emotional responses in the reader (or, perhaps better, practitioner), who is called on by the often hortatory authorial voice to participate actively in the events as a spectator or primary figure within them. (The line between the two is often difficult to discern. Mary is the model of compassionate suffering with Christ on whom the reader is often called to model him- or herself. Yet ultimately Mary's suffering with Christ is so great as to render her Christ-like. Hence through a series of intense identifications, the reader as compassionate spectator becomes a participant in Christ's saving actions.)[18] Meditation, as Mary Carruthers brilliantly shows with regard to medieval monastic culture, is an art of memory and imagination. Meditative practice is a type of memory work that generates affect, which in turn facilitates the act of memorialization.[19] By calling forth the events of Christ's death with compassion and identification, the person meditating both commemorates and participates in the redemptive power of that moment.

In his study of the Latin Passion narratives, Thomas Bestul demonstrates that narrative rewritings of the Passion make use of a variety of traditional texts. First, of course, are the gospels themselves. The New Testament texts are sparse in detail, yet, as Bestul explains, they "contain in rudimentary form what proves to be a very productive method for embellishing the Passion story in a way that . . . carried the highest theological sanction."[20] Each of the gospel narratives attempts to demonstrate that Jesus's suffering was a fulfillment of the messianic prophecies of the Hebrew Bible. Hence the gospel writers apply verses from these prophecies to Jesus in his suffering and death. Subsequent exegetes take this as "a justification for applying almost any verse of the Hebrew Bible to the events of Christ's life, especially those of the Passion. In this way, the Hebrew Bible offered what was taken to be a divinely authorized way of filling out the details of Christ's life where the gospels were silent."[21] Other key sources for Latin Passion narratives are (1) the liturgy, particularly the conjunction of Biblical texts used to commemorate Christ's Passion; (2) the apocryphal gospels;[22] (3) the tradition of biblical exegesis that precedes the development of the specifically Passion-centered narratives; and (4) two key high medieval texts, Peter Comestor's (d. 1179) *Historia scholastica* and Jacob of Voragine's (d. 1298) *Legenda aurea*.[23] (The former is an encyclopedic historical narrative, including Christ's life and death. The latter is a compendium of hagiographical texts, also including an account of Christ's Passion.) Writers of high and late medieval Passion narratives make use of these various sources in order to imaginatively evoke the intensity of Christ's suffering.

The liturgy for Holy Week is particularly important for the development of extended narratives of Christ's Passion. The conjunction of texts and images heard and seen within the yearly ritual plays a decisive role in high and late medieval devotional practices and images. For example, following the New Testament tradition of citing the Hebrew prophets in conjunction with the figure of Christ, passages from Isaiah play a key role in the Holy Week liturgy. As befits the tenor of Isaiah's prophetic vision, these passages emphasize Christ's role as redeemer of the just and scourge of the evil.

> Who is this that cometh from Edom, with dyed garments from Bosra, this beautiful one in his robe, walking in the greatness of his strength? I, that speak justice, and am a defender to save. Why then is thy apparel red, and thy garments like theirs that tread in the winepress? I have trodden the winepress alone, and of the Gentiles there is not a man with me: I have trampled on them in my indignation, and have trodden them down in my wrath, and their blood is sprinkled upon my garments, and I have stained all my apparel.[24]

The liturgical use of Isaiah typologically identifies the man with garments dyed red from the blood of the Gentiles with Christ, bloody with the wounds of the Passion.[25] Images of Christ literally drenched in blood may reflect this liturgical tradition; Christ's blood becomes a garment in which he is fully covered, like Isaiah's man from Edom.[26] (See figure 7.2.)

Similarly, Christian exegetes often interpret the Hebrew Bible in terms of Christ's life and death. Probably the single most important source for the cluster of images conjoined in Latin Passion narratives and then in Angela's meditation on Christ's side wound is a Passion-centered reading of Song of Songs 2:14, "My dove in the clefts of the rock, in the crannies of the wall, show me your face, let your voice sound in my ears."[27] Bernard of Clairvaux (d. 1153), in his sixty-first sermon on the Song of Songs, follows Gregory the Great (d. 604) in interpreting the clefts of the rock as Christ's wounds.[28] The clefts in the rock are then read by Bernard as a place of refuge for the soul: "And really where is there safe rest for the weak except in the Savior's wounds? There the security of my dwelling depends on the greatness of his saving power."[29] Moreover, from the wounds, Bernard writes, "I can suck honey from the rock and oil from the flinty stone—I can taste and see that the Lord is good."[30] Finally, through the clefts in Christ's body "the secret of his heart is laid open, . . . that mighty mystery of loving is laid open, laid open too the tender mercies of our God, in which the morning sun from on

FIGURE 7.2 *Vision des Heiligen Bernhard (sogenanntes Blutkruzifixus)*. Schnütgen Museum, Cologne. Inv. Nr. M340.

high has risen upon us. Surely his heart is laid open through his wounds!"[31] In Bernard, then, we see all three of the aspects of the wound image laid out by Gray.

Bernard refers to the wound gored in Christ's side by a lance (Jn 19:34) in close proximity to the claim that one can drink from Christ's wound; similarly, revelation of the secrets of Christ's heart is premised on "the iron" that "pierced his soul" (Ps 104:18, here presumably read typologically with reference to the spear with which Christ's side is pierced in Jn 19:34). Yet Bernard attends equally throughout the sermon to the clefts created by the nails in Christ's feet and hands. The singular focus on Christ's side wound appears in the work of Bernard's fellow Cistercian Aelred of Rievaulx (d. 1167) in a text probably written shortly after Bernard's death.

The Rule of Life for a Recluse, written for Aelred's sister, ends with meditations on Christ's life and death. One highly compressed passage brings together many of the themes found in Bernard's sermon 61—and later to be found throughout the more fully developed narrative accounts of Christ's Passion. Amid a visually and viscerally vibrant description of Christ's suffering and death, Aelred elaborates on the Gospel of John's account of Christ's side, pierced by a Roman soldier.

> Then one of the soldiers opened his side with a lance and there came forth blood and water. Hasten, linger not, eat the honeycomb with your honey, drink your wine with your milk. The blood is changed into wine to gladden you, the water into milk to nourish you. From the rock streams have flowed for you, wounds have been made in his limbs, holes in the wall of his body, in which, like a dove, you may hide while you kiss them one by one. Your lips, stained with his blood, will become like a scarlet ribbon and your word sweet.[32]

Here it is explicitly the side wound that is understood as the cleft in which the dove of the Song of Songs finds refuge. From hence too flow the blood and water—reminiscent of the blood and water into which wine is transubstantiated in the eucharistic sacrament—that will purify and save those who imbibe it.[33]

The Latin Passion narratives often exhort the one meditating on Christ's passion to drink from the blood pouring from Christ's side wound and to enter into that wound. The theme continues to play a crucial role in the Franciscan tradition of Passion narratives, both in Latin and in the vernacular.[34] In the *Tree of Life*, Bonaventure (d. 1274) follows Bernard and Aelred in comparing the hole in Christ's side to the dove's refuge in the Song of Songs and the reader or listener is enjoined to "draw waters out of the Savior's fountains."[35] (Here Bonaventure follows Isaiah 12:3: "haurietis aquas in gaudio de fontibus salvatoris.") Bonaventure's *The Mystical Vine* calls for even more vivid representations of Christ's suffering flesh. Central to these representations are Christ's wounds and blood. The text calls on the readers or listeners to contemplate Christ's wounds and to penetrate them, coming finally to rest in Christ's heart.[36]

Bonaventure's devotional works and others falsely attributed to him were widely disseminated throughout Europe in the later Middle Ages. Even more popular was a book of meditations attributed to the Franciscan James of Milan and known in its first English translation, prepared by the Augustinian canon and mystic Walter Hilton (d. 1396) as *The Goad of Love*. *The Goad of Love*'s central image for meditative union is the soul's immersion in Christ's wounds.[37] No longer is the side wound simply a place of refuge for sinners—although it always remains that—but entry into the wound also signifies the union between the soul and Christ. Similar language is then found throughout late medieval devotional literature. In Angela we see a devout woman enacting that to which the devotional texts enjoin her.[38]

The correlation between Christ's side wound and the vagina suggested by Irigaray becomes most apparent in devotional images produced in the later Middle Ages. Clearly related to the tradition of meditation on Christ's Passion, visual representations of Christ's side wound are startling, not only in their vulvic and vaginal resonances, but also in their iconographic starkness and intensity. Images of the side wound are generally life size (or claimed to be so).[39] David S. Areford argues compellingly, in fact, that the side wound stands in for Christ's body, a form of visual synecdoche in which the wound represents the Passion in its entirety.[40]

Two of the earliest images of Christ's side wound are found in a famous early fourteenth-century Bohemian devotional collection made by Benes, a canon, for Kunigunde, abbess of St. George's Benedictine nunnery in Prague castle. In one of these images, Christ appears as the Man of Sorrows surrounded by the instruments of his torture (the *Arma Christi*), including a life-sized wound.[41] Karma Lochrie reproduces a similar image that dates from the late fourteenth century. Here again Christ appears as the Man of Sorrows; to the left is his side wound, enlarged to life size (just above two inches).[42]

Related images are found in a miscellany now in Brussels. (See figure 7.3.) The manuscript was compiled in 1320 by nuns from the Cistercian convent of Vrouwenpark, under the supervision of the Cistercian monk John of St. Trond, who was responsible for their spiritual care. Most of the manuscript consists

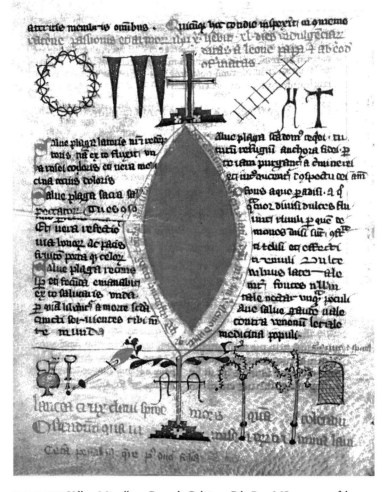

FIGURE 7.3 Villers Miscellany. Brussels, Belgium. Bib. Roy. MS 4459–70, fol. 150r.

of the lives of holy women associated with the Cistercian order.[43] Hence the miscellany is a devotional work, centered on the lives of holy women dedicated to the imitation of Christ. Included in the miscellany are drawings both of the *Arma Christi* and of Christ's side wound surrounded by the *Arma Christi*.[44]

The devotion to Christ's side wound appears in texts produced not only for nuns, but also for the laity. The earliest visual representations appear in manuscripts produced in France, also in the 1320s.[45] Among the most arresting is an image in the mid-fourteenth-century Psalter and Hours of Bonne of Luxembourg, a wealthy lay woman, later to become the mother of Charles V.[46] (See figure 7.4.) Once again, the wound appears life size, surrounded by disproportionately smaller representations of the *Arma Christi*.

Instructed in religious literature to taste, touch, suck, kiss, and enter into Christ's side wound, those who saw and held these images seem to have made them the object of intense affective response, both imaginatively and physically.[47]

FIGURE 7.4 *Psalter of Bonne of Luxembourg.* Cloisters Museum, Metropolitan Museum of New York. MS 69.86, fol. 331r.

Areford studies a woodcut from the late fifteenth century, now in the National Gallery of Art in Washington, D.C., in which what Areford describes as a "mandorla-shaped wound" stands in for Christ's body. (See figure 7.5.) To the left of the wound appears an inscription, clarifying one way in which such images were treated: "This is the length and width of Christ's wound which was pierced in his side on the Cross. Whoever kisses this wound with remorse and sorrow, also with devotion, will have as often as he does this, seven years indulgence from Pope Innocent."[48] Some manuscripts represent the wound solely with a slit in the parchment, one now so often touched, handled, and kissed as to render the manuscript itself fragile, worn, and opaque. These images and physical remnants suggest a homoerotic relationship between the female reader and a feminized representation of Christ's wound.[49]

Karma Lochrie, who reads the images of Christ's wounds as potentially homoerotic, situates her interpretation in relationship to Caroline Walker Bynum's groundbreaking work on medieval women's spirituality. As Lochrie shows, Bynum both argues against making too marked a distinction between sexuality and affectivity within mystical texts and devotional images,[50] and also insists, particularly in *Holy Feast and Holy Fast: On the Religious Significance of Food to Medieval Women* and *Fragmentation and Redemption: Essays on Gender and the Human Body in Medieval Religion*,[51] that medieval attitudes toward the body have "less to do with sexuality than with fertility and decay."[52] As Lochrie rightly notes, Bynum is motivated by what she views as an overemphasis on sex and sexuality in the reading of medieval women's writings and writings about them and a concomitant overvaluation (or, alternatively, denigration) of sexuality that ignores other salient aspects of bodily experience.[53] Bynum thereby brilliantly expands our recognition of the meanings ascribed to corporeality in late medieval texts, images, and practices. At the same time, she suggests that these other aspects of bodily existence—food, drink, fertility, disease, decay, and death—play a larger role in medieval mystical texts than sexuality.[54]

Yet Lochrie and Richard Rambuss worry that Bynum "herself can be quick to delimit the erotic—and especially the homoerotic—potentialities of her own devotional polysemy of the medieval body."[55] When Catherine of Siena (1327–80) writes of "putting on the nuptial garment," Bynum explains, "the phrase means suffering" and so is "extremely unerotic." As portrayed by her confessor and hagiographer, Raymond of Capua, Catherine, like Angela of Foligno, follows the injunctions of the meditative treatises I have described. Raymond says that Christ

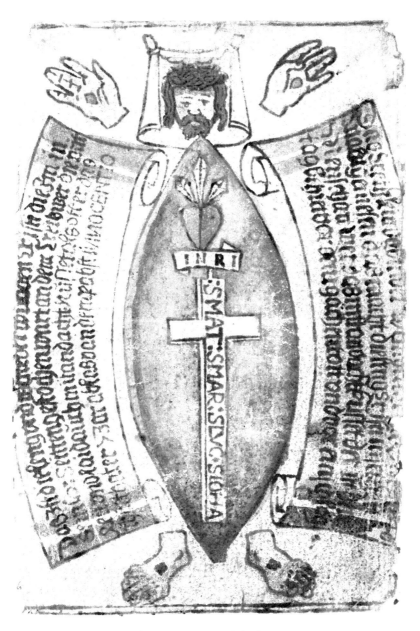

FIGURE 7.5 *The Wounds of Christ with the Symbols of the Passion.* Woodcut, c. 1490.
Courtesy of the National Gallery of Art, Washington, D.C.

put his right hand on [Catherine's] neck and drew her towards the wound on
his side. "Drink, daughter, from my side," he said, "and by that draught your
soul shall become enraptured with such delight that your very body, which for
my sake you have denied, shall be inundated with its overflowing goodness."
Drawn close in this way to the outlet of the Fountain of her Life, she fastened
her lips upon that sacred wound, and still more eagerly the mouth of her soul,
and there she slaked her thirst.[56]

Having cited this and similar passages, Bynum argues that in Catherine's
"repeated descriptions of climbing Christ's body from foot to side to mouth, the
body is either a female body that nurses or a piece of flesh that one puts on oneself
or sinks into. . . . Catherine understood union with Christ not as an erotic fusing
with a male figure but as a taking in and taking on—a becoming—of Christ's
flesh itself."[57] Bynum operates here with a number of contentious assumptions
about sexuality and erotic desire—most crucially, that erotic desire can be clearly
distinguished from suffering, the maternal, and identification. In addition, as
Rambuss and Lochrie argue, Bynum implicitly denies that same-sex desire can
be sexual.

Lochrie shows that the mystical texts Bynum discusses are full of a violent,
painful, ecstatic eroticism—one that undermines the distinction between pain,
suffering, decay, death, and sexuality Bynum is often at pains to make. As Lochrie
shows, when Bynum discusses eroticism in *Holy Feast and Holy Fast* it is always
"linked with specific images of fertility and decay." The result is that Bynum
comes very close to saying "that eroticism and sex in the religious experience of
medieval women were constructed in terms of violence, suffering, and decay."[58]
Bynum thereby usefully deromanticizes the image of bridal or nuptial mysticism
found in many accounts of medieval women's religiosity. Yet as the passage I cite
above suggests, and as Lochrie herself argues, Bynum also insists that suffering is
not erotic and so attempts to take sexuality out of the complex matrix in which
she simultaneously embeds it.

Just as Bynum separates suffering from sex and eroticism, she similarly denies
the possibility of same-sex desire. Following Rambuss's and Lochrie's arguments,
we can see that for Bynum if Christ's body is feminized (and so becomes a point
of identification for women), it cannot also be the locus of female sexual desire
(or even of a desire for the divine *analogous* to sexual desire). Bynum's insistence
on the feminization of Christ, one in which the side wound is interpreted as a
breast and the blood from that wound as life-giving milk, serves two functions,

both providing a locus for female identification with the divine and protecting the divine-human relationship from even metaphorical sexualization.

But given Bynum's own injunction that we recognize the fluidity between male and female, masculine and feminine, affective and erotic within medieval texts and images, why must we be forced to make a choice between reading the feminized Christ as maternal or erotic? As Lochrie cogently argues, "the mystical maternal body of Christ does not enact such repudiation of the sexual but 'opens a mesh of possibilities' for the queering of categories—of mystical devotion, the body of Christ, female desire, and the medieval construction of maternity."[59] Christ's wound, as we have seen, has a multiplicity of meanings within medieval texts and images, and at least some of them are explicitly erotic.

Bynum, in reading Christ's side wound as homologous to Mary's breast and hence Christ's blood as like breast milk in its nurturing and salvific nature, explicitly rejects a sexualized reading of the wound and its blood. Lochrie insists that the maternal does not exclude the sexual. Medieval medical discourses further underline the polysemy of the wound and its blood. Hence a much-commented-on treatise dealing with human reproduction and women's bodies, *Women's Secrets* (long falsely attributed to Albert the Great), argues that breast milk is created from surplus menses not released during childbirth.[60] Not only are blood and breast milk tied together within medieval medical theory, then, but that blood is explicitly menstrual blood. (Although many medical and religious texts insist on the polluting quality of menstrual blood, suggesting that its transmutation to breast milk requires a process of purification.)[61] The association of blood with Christ's side wound ties the wound both to the vagina and to the breast, thereby enabling the threefold association of wound, vagina, and breast for which Lochrie and Irigaray argue.

Medieval devotional and mystical texts and images, when brought together with salient medical and philosophical literature from the period, suggest that Lochrie and Irigaray are amply justified in associating wounds, vaginas, and breasts. Woundedness and fecundity, maternity and sexuality, masculinity and femininity—all of these categories are interlocked in complex and fungible ways within medieval Christian discourse and practice. As Irigaray demonstrates in *Speculum's* "*La Mystérique*," the Christian Middle Ages offer rich resources for thinking about sex, sexuality, and divinity in ways that radically destabilize traditional distinctions and hierarchies.

Yet Irigaray very quickly rejects *Speculum's* valorization of Christ's wounds as the site of a new feminine imaginary.[62] *Speculum* was published in 1974.

Already in 1975, an essay devoted to the psychoanalyst Jacques Lacan's account of femininity demonstrates Irigaray's growing discomfort with any image or metaphor that associates the female sex with woundedness.[63] Irigaray's later revisionary reading of Christ's wounded body and self-sacrifice, most clearly articulated in *Marine Lover of Friedrich Nietzsche*,[64] rests on this rejection of the valorization of woundedness. Irigaray argues—correctly, I think—that Lacan understands femininity as a figure for human nature in its lack, woundedness, and castration (in terms of the Christian theological tradition, one might argue, its sinfulness).[65] According to Irigaray, Lacan's move ineluctably implicates women in a rhetoric of impotence that any new feminine imaginary must challenge. "The problem," as she puts it, "is that they [Lacan and Lacanian psychoanalysts] claim to make a law of this impotence itself, and continue to subject women to it."[66]

The female sex can only be understood as a wound, Irigaray suggests, if it is read according to the logic of castration. Within psychoanalytic discourse the bleeding fissure is the site of a lack—the lack of a penis. Only within these terms does the association of sex with woundedness make sense. To read woman as emblematic of human nature in its woundedness, then, is to participate in a logic that insistently reads femininity in terms of masculinity—precisely the logic Irigaray's work unremittingly challenges. Christianity, insofar as it substitutes the bleeding body of the son for that of the mother, participates both in the association of femininity with castration, impotence, and self-sacrifice *and* in the reduction of femininity to masculinity (in the figure of the feminized man on the cross).[67]

By rejecting the association of femininity with woundedness, however, Irigaray also forecloses the possibility of a female-to-female penetrative and interpenetrative eroticism. Judith Butler's critique of Irigaray's "eros of surfaces" closely parallels, then, Lochrie's critique of Bynum on medieval devotion to Christ's wounds.[68] Already in *Speculum*, Butler argues, Irigaray's reading of Plato posits masculinity and femininity in terms of penetration and penetrability. Although Butler misses the moment—"*La Mystérique*"—in which Irigaray challenges the dominant philosophical tradition's account of sexual (in)difference, Butler is correct that throughout much of *Speculum* Irigaray is in danger of allowing that tradition to determine her own use of terms. (Butler suggests this may be an inevitable danger of Irigaray's mimetic procedure.)

As Butler argues, in Irigaray's reading of Plato, the masculine "he" is the impenetrable penetrator, and the "she" is invariably penetrated. He would not be differentiated from her were it not for this prohibition on resemblance, which establishes their positions as mutually exclusive and yet complementary. In fact, if she were to penetrate in return, or penetrate elsewhere, it is unclear whether she could remain a "she" and whether "he" could preserve his own differentially established identity. For the logic of noncontradiction that conditions the distribution of pronouns is one that establishes the "he" through this exclusive position as penetrator and the "she" through this exclusive position as penetrated. As a consequence, then, without this heterosexual *matrix*, as it were, it appears that the stability of these gendered positions would be called into question.[69]

In a telling reversal of Butler's formulation, the instability of gendered positions within medieval devotional and mystical images and practices works to unsettle precisely this heterosexual matrix. Only if it is taken as a given that penetration is masculine and penetrability feminine does the heterosexual matrix hold sway (just as it is the heterosexual matrix that renders these oppositions stable). Yet these presumptions—ones also operative within medieval medical and philosophical literature[70]—are continually undermined by the devotional texts and images Irigaray mimes in "*La Mystérique*."[71]

Both Bynum and Irigaray (at least after *Speculum*) miss the radicality of medieval devotional practices, which refuse any absolute identification between masculinity and penetration or between femininity and penetrability. The very mode of reading implied by medieval devotional texts and images, with their constantly interpenetrating biblical, extrabiblical, and liturgical citations, suggests the ubiquity of an erotics of penetration within medieval spiritual traditions.[72] The fluidity of sexual difference—of sex, gender, and sexuality—may be, at least in part, an outcome of such reading practices.

The soul in Bernard of Clairvaux's *Sermons on the Song of Songs* is described as a female beloved sucking honey from the hard rock that is Christ, even as Christ, the male Lover, is laid open to penetration through his bodily wounds. In Aelred's *The Rule of Life for a Recluse*, Christ's body is an impenetrable rock and a body full of holes—and both at the same time. Honey, wine, milk, and blood (interchangeable substances within Aelred's imaginary) stream from Christ and penetrate the body of the beloved (as food and drink, although not only as food and drink), even as the beloved hides in Christ's wounds like a dove in the cleft of a rock. Although the image of Angela with her mouth pressed to Christ's side wound evokes female-to-female sexuality, it also displaces any simplistic gender and sexual referentiality, for Christ's body is both masculine and penetrable, both rock and feminized.

Finally, medieval texts and images suggest that the analogy between the wound and the vulva and vagina operates not only to associate women with lack and castration, but also to associate men—preeminently, of course, one man—with fertility, nurturance, and healing. Christ's wounds save, heal, and solace. Their association with the breast and the vulva enables these multiple understandings. By rejecting a masculinist logic of penetration and penetrability, wholeness and lack, containment and seepage—a logic endemic to and unchallenged by the psychoanalytic tradition about and out of which Irigaray writes—Irigaray too quickly forecloses alternative imaginative possibilities available within the Christian Middle Ages. The move is related, in complex ways, to her refusal to think beyond the binary distinctions between man and woman, male and female, and masculine and feminine, a refusal that mars her otherwise often thrilling and always inventive work. Perhaps the Christ of "*La Mysterique*" is better read as refusing gender binaries than as feminized and so as refusing the distinctions Irigaray herself continues to desire, even as she calls for their radical reimagining.

PART IV
Practice

INSIDE OUT

8

Beatrice of Nazareth and Her Hagiographer

IN A discussion of ritual, the anthropologist Talal Asad argues that *The Rule of Benedict* and other medieval texts offer evidence that within medieval European Christian culture, rituals were not expressive or symbolic of some other reality, but rather were the "apt performance of what is prescribed, something that depends on intellectual and practical disciplines but does not itself require decoding."[1] According to Asad, it is a mistake of modern Western intellectualist traditions to assume that belief precedes practice; rather, following Marcel Mauss and Pierre Bourdieu, Asad argues that bodily practices inculcate belief. The body, according to this view, is the material site of enculturation. Mauss introduces the term *habitus* to designate the embodied set of dispositions, learned and internalized through bodily practices and constitutive of the subject.[2] The *habitus*, according to Bourdieu, is "history turned into nature,"[3] the site on and in which ideologies constitute subjects.[4] The result of this theoretical insight is the claim, made by Mauss and Asad, that a crisis of belief may be best understood as "a function of untaught bodies."[5]

Sarah Beckwith demonstrates the importance of the *habitus* and theories of bodily practice for materialist feminist analysis. In an important essay on the *Ancrene Wisse* and its prescriptions for female bodies and subjects, she expands the theoretical claims made by Mauss, Bourdieu, and Asad and at the same time takes issue with some contemporary feminists' idealized association of women with the body: "Although women have historically borne the burden of representing immanence for others, that does not give them privileged access to the body as a 'woman's symbol,' for women do not have particular forms of representation that are exclusively their own, but only particular relations to cultural representations and discourse."[6] In the essay, Beckwith analyzes the anchorite's relationship to her own body, through enclosure and penitential practice, and to the suffering body of Christ, through discursive and imaginary meditations. She argues that the anchorite's rule creates a particular form of interiority through the prescription and enactment of a precise set of bodily and discursive practices. Her reading offers a convincing account of the ways in which the *Ancrene Wisse* prescribes practices formative of the subjectivity of those whose lives are governed by it. She expands on the work of anthropologists and sociologists like Mauss and Asad by making use of psychoanalysis to articulate the process through which an imaginary bodily ego, experienced in a fantasmatic identification with the suffering Christ, is the interior result of bodily practices and meditations.[7]

Beckwith's work offers an important corrective to easy assimilations of women and bodiliness within medieval texts and contemporary theory, for she demonstrates the complex workings of culture and power structures in the formation of women's subjectivities and their experiences of themselves as suffering bodies.[8] I will return to this analysis below, demonstrating its usefulness in thinking about medieval women's texts. Yet an immediate problem presents itself: Beckwith's primary source for her analysis is a rule written for women by a male cleric. Although she distinguishes between "the life imagined" and that "lived in the anchorite cell," Beckwith assumes the compliance of the text's female audience.[9] I will argue here that we cannot take male-authored texts as our primary source of information for women's "relations to cultural representations and discourse," particularly when writings by women are available to us.[10] Moreover, some of these women-authored texts suggest studied resistance to the forms of female religiosity and subjectivity prescribed for them within male-authored texts. This resistance centers on the suffering body and the interplay of interiority and exteriority within religious life.

Here I will briefly follow out the logic of these theoretical arguments as they can be seen in one medieval hagiography, *The Life of Beatrice of Nazareth*. It offers a particularly apt place in which to study the relationship between exteriority and interiority in women's religious life and practice because these are the governing metaphors of the text. In addition, *The Life of Beatrice* offers an excellent opening to the question of the relationship between men's prescriptions for women and women's self-understanding, for we possess not only the *vita*, but also at least a portion of Beatrice's own vernacular writing on which the hagiographer claims to base his account. What emerges is a surprising picture of the differences between the way one medieval woman describes the life of a loving soul and the way her life and texts are read by one of her male contemporaries, a picture that calls into question many twentieth- and twenty-first-century assumptions about medieval women's religious belief and practice.[11] Genre and gender both shape these differences. Beatrice's hagiographer describes her life in ways easily assimilated to twentieth- and twenty-first-century theories of bodily practice and dispositions. Beatrice's text, however, challenges not only the picture of her life presented in *The Life of Beatrice*, but also contemporary theoretical accounts of the relationship between interiority and exteriority, soul and body, belief and practice.

* * *

Beatrice of Nazareth (1200–68) spent most of her life in one or another of the three Cistercian monasteries founded by her father; within these houses she assiduously followed *The Rule of Benedict*, copied book manuscripts, prayed, meditated, studied, and later served as prioress. She also wrote religious works in the vernacular, although only a short treatise, *Seven Manners of Loving*, survives.[12] The external events of Beatrice's life, then, were unexceptional. Yet the treatise suggests that her inner life boiled and teemed with waves of violent love and insane desire. Within the religious world of thirteenth-century Northern Europe, at least some people revered the ecstatic experiences described by Beatrice in her treatise and understood them as marks of extreme sanctity.[13] We can speculate that such a reputation for sanctity led the abbess of the monastery at Nazareth, or someone else close to Beatrice, shortly after her death, to commission a book about her life. The hagiographer had at his disposal Beatrice's own "book"; in fact, he claims that *The Life of Beatrice* is merely a translation of Beatrice's work into Latin.[14] Only for the account of Beatrice's death does he acknowledge that he must turn to the evidence of other "reliable people," including Beatrice's sister Catherine.[15] Yet despite the excellence of his primary sources, Beatrice's hagiographer found his task challenging. The problem posed by Beatrice's life (and presumably her book) was how to write a hagiographical narrative about a woman whose life and writing present little evidence of those practices marked as holy within medieval hagiographical literature—heroic or radical asceticism, extraordinary acts of charity, miracles, or healings—and only scant evidence of the visions and otherworldly journeys central to thirteenth-century mystical hagiographies.[16]

Beatrice's hagiographer never acknowledges this problem in the blunt terms in which I have posed it here. It can be deduced, however, from an examination of *The Life of Beatrice* itself, from a comparison of the *vita* with Beatrice's own writing, and from certain suggestions made by the hagiographer about the ways in which his text may pose difficulties for the reader accustomed to more traditional hagiographical works. So, simply looking at the *vita*, the reader is immediately struck that there are only sparse details about Beatrice's asceticism, no accounts of corporal miracle, and little evidence of visionary experience. The problem faced by Beatrice's hagiographer and his solution to that problem are made even more apparent, however, when we compare book 3, chapter 14, with its source text, *Seven Manners of Loving*. As I will show, whereas the hagiographer's summary of Beatrice's life is filled with bodily illness, paramystical phenomena, and ecstatic experience, *Seven Manners of Loving* is intent on the mad love of the soul and her ecstatic union with love, who is God.

Before examining these two texts in more detail, however, we should note that Beatrice's hagiographer does come close to an explicit statement of his problem late in the book:

> Others may perhaps wonder at the miracles worked by signs and acts of power so copiously and superabundantly by the saints of old. They may wonder at the demons chased out of those possessed, the corpses raised to life, and many other things like these or greater than these. The Lord said of these in the Gospel: "He that believes in me shall also do the works that I do, and greater than these shall he do." Yet, with all due reverence to the saints, I prefer Beatrice's love to many miracles and signs, of which it is said elsewhere: "Signs are given not to believers, but to unbelievers"; especially since many arrive at the kingdom of heaven without signs.[17]

And, he continues, no one will come to the kingdom of heaven without love. Although Beatrice's life may be lacking in corporal miracles such as healings, exorcisms, and resuscitations, it abounds with spiritual miracles comparable to those of the biblical prophets.[18] Under pressure from expectations for remarkable signs of Beatrice's holiness, her biographer consistently translates her internally felt experience into external, visible markings on the body of the saint. Yet Beatrice describes the spiritual life, as we will see, as occurring interiorly and with no mention of visible manifestations.

The prologue introduces the central metaphorical structure governing the *vita* as a whole and that through which the hagiographer solves his dilemma. Beatrice's life will be seen as a complex and often ambiguous interplay of exteriority and interiority, hiddenness and manifestation, darkness and light. The hagiographer uses the topos of humility to explain the seemingly hidden nature of her virtues and sanctity, while at the same time exposing them to the light for the edification of his readers. Moreover, he ascribes this double movement to Beatrice herself:

> The Lord says in the Gospel: "Take heed that you do not do your justice before men, to be seen by them," and again elsewhere: "So let your light shine before men, that they may see your good works, and glorify your Father who is in heaven." Beatrice so combined in one obedience the seeming discrepancies of these two precepts of the Lord that she foiled the strategies of the ancient enemy by first hiding her secret carefully within herself, and then bequeathing it for her neighbors' needs by bringing it forth openly in due time.[19]

Here the biographer refers to Beatrice's decision, toward the end of her life, to make known the book in which she describes the seven manners of the loving soul and, presumably, other teachings since lost. Yet he also suggests a way of understanding his externalization of the soul's experience, a movement that governs the *vita* as a whole. Throughout, he will bring forth that which Beatrice harbors and hides within. He will do this by describing Beatrice's body as bearing the marks of her interior life.

The Life of Beatrice is divided into three parts, describing Beatrice's initiation into the religious life, her progress in the virtues, and her life in perfection. The early sections of the book lend themselves well to the kind of analysis of bodily practices and their role in the formation of the subject made by Asad and Beckwith. The hagiographer's account of Beatrice's external penitential practices is stereotypical and comprises only three of the *vita*'s fifty-four chapters. Moreover, much of the description of Beatrice's ascetic practice is almost identical to that found in the life of the male Cistercian Arnulph.[20] This becomes particularly interesting, given the tendency in contemporary scholarship on medieval women to associate them with intense ascetic activity, for the hagiographer's borrowing from another text for this element of the *vita* suggests Beatrice herself did not write about ascetic practice.[21] In fact, medieval women's writing before the fourteenth century tends not to include accounts of ascetic practice.[22] As I have argued elsewhere, contemporary accounts of medieval women's ascetic practice may tell us more about how medieval men understood women's sanctity than about medieval women themselves.[23]

Much more crucial for an understanding of the way in which the *vita* depicts bodily practices as formative of the self are its detailed descriptions of Beatrice's spiritual exercises, particularly her use of devotional images and meditational practices. These exercises center on the cross, unlike Beatrice's treatise in which Christ is named explicitly on only one occasion and the cross appears only obliquely. The *vita* insists that it is the ordering of her spiritual life through meditational practice that leads Beatrice to experience the presence of God. This is apparent in the ordering of the narrative: the hagiographer first discusses the external life, then spends three chapters on the ordering and exercise of meditations, her profession into the religious life with its monastic regulation, and her friendship with Ida of Nivelles. Ida prays that Beatrice might receive special grace and has visions promising this grace to Beatrice. Only after this textual preparation, implying Beatrice's own preparation through corporal and spiritual exercises, does the hagiographer describe her first rapture. That rapture, moreover, occurs during compline: Beatrice first "quieted herself" and "with a great effort . . . raised her heart to the Lord," meditating on the text of the antiphon. She raised herself up, through meditation, to the Father's presence and only then did "she immediately leap up there, seized in an ecstasy of mind."[24] Without preparation through spiritual exercise, the hagiographer clearly implies, Beatrice would never come to experience the presence of God and absorption into divine love.

After describing this first rapture, the hagiographer returns to Beatrice's spiritual exercises, emphasizing their importance for her continued pursuit of union with God. Late in book 1, the hagiographer describes methods Beatrice uses against forgetfulness.

> Day and night she wore on her breast a wooden cross, about a palm in length, tightly tied with a knotted string. On it was written the Lord's passion, the horror of the last judgment, the severity of the judge and other things she wanted always to keep in mind. Besides this she also carried tied to her arm another image of the Lord's cross painted on a piece of parchment. She had a third, painted on a piece of wood, set before her when she was writing, so that wherever she went, or whatever exterior work she did, all forgetfulness would be banished, and by means of the image of the cross she would keep [firmly] impressed on her heart and memory whatever she feared to lose.[25]

The subsequent chapter describes Beatrice's habit of prostrating herself before "the feet of the crucified Lord, before his image,"[26] whenever troubled inwardly by harmful thoughts or misfortunes. Eventually the presence of external reminders becomes unnecessary: "Thereafter for about five unbroken years she had the mental image of the Lord's passion so firmly impressed in her memory that she scarcely ever quit this sweet meditation, but clung from the bottom of her heart with wonderful devotion to everything he deigned to suffer for the salvation of the human race."²⁷ The external practice of prostration before images and meditation on them leads to their internal appropriation and the transformation of the self. By the end of the *vita*, Beatrice no longer carries images of Christ, or even sees them continually in her mind's eye, but has herself become the image of Christ on earth for others.²⁸

Not only does the hagiographer demonstrate the ways in which exterior practices elicit internal experience, he also consistently portrays these interior experiences as marking themselves externally on Beatrice's body and in her behavior. "Therefore it frequently happened that, whether she willed it or not, her interior jubilation of mind would break out in some manifestation, and the mind's inner jubilation would betray itself outwardly either in laughing or dancing a gesture or some other sign."²⁹ Throughout the text tears, fainting spells, trancelike states, laughing, and dancing are the external manifestations of Beatrice's internal state.³⁰ She is frequently depicted as attempting to hide these external signs from her companions,³¹ or feigning illness as a mask for her inner jubilation.³² At other times, illness is itself described as a sign of her interior state.³³

Throughout the text, the hagiographer simultaneously marks and blurs the distinction between interior and exterior introduced in the prologue. He seems to require both the language of interiority and its subversion through the externalizing of Beatrice's spiritual state. It is as if he cannot adequately express the nature of her interiority without reference to her body. Once again, the hagiographer ascribes this problem to Beatrice herself: "Even if she could not explain in words what and how much spiritual delight she received, or what she sensed and tasted in this melting, it was to some extent apparent outwardly by the fainting of her bodily senses."³⁴ The claim seems plausible and yet attention to the divergences between Beatrice's treatise and the *vita*'s translation of that text raises questions about whether the hagiographer is here describing a dilemma faced by Beatrice herself, or rather one that challenged him in his attempt to fit her life and work into prevailing hagiographical and theological patterns.

The interplay between interiority and exteriority also runs through the imagery of the *vita*, particularly when describing Beatrice's meditational practice. Here the hagiographer stresses her use of traditional images of enclosure and the maintaining of boundaries between inner and outer.[35] According to her hagiographer, Beatrice compares the soul to a monastery and to an enclosed garden, emphasizing the virtues that keep guard over the boundaries between the monastery or garden and the world.[36] Just as the religious woman must guard against bad thoughts and desires entering into the soul, so the monastery is an enclosed space whose boundaries are carefully guarded. In both instances, boundaries must be maintained for holiness to be achieved.[37] Yet the language of enclosure also appears negatively, for life in the body is described as a prison (in the one spatial metaphor found in both the hagiography and Beatrice's treatise), suggesting the desire for escape from the rigid enclosures in which she lives.[38] This desire— the desire for death and the complete absorption of the soul into Love—is crucial to the seventh manner of loving and the point on which the hagiographer most starkly diverges from Beatrice's treatise.

The externalizing and somatizing movement evident throughout *The Life of Beatrice* reaches its greatest intensity in book 3, in which the hagiographer gives an account of Beatrice's life of perfection. After describing the founding of Nazareth, the hagiographer's attempt to find a narrative pattern in Beatrice's life breaks down and he devotes some miscellaneous chapters to her spiritual teachings. Although only the source for chapter 14 remains, I suspect that treatises similar to *Seven Manners of Loving* lie behind these other chapters. In each, we find suggestions of complex spiritual teachings combined with somatic and visionary phenomena. As with the *vita* as a whole, I think these passages must be read through what we learn in reading book 3, chapter 14, against its vernacular source text.

Beatrice's hagiographer, coming to the close of the book, ends with an account of the love she had for God and the love she had for her neighbor. He uses *Seven Manners of Loving* as a way of discussing Beatrice's love for God and at the same time as a way of recapitulating the narrative of her life that he has just provided for the reader. His translation, then, bears the marks of the emphases and themes that he has made central to that life—the interplay of interiority and exteriority, Beatrice's desire for a shortcut to perfection in her attempt to return to that state in which she was before she was created, the tension between the enormity of what she owes to God and her bodily ability to repay him, her desire for self-knowledge (understood as humility), and her desire for death. Comparing the *vita* and the treatise makes clear, however, the way these themes and the particular readings of them given by Beatrice's hagiographer diverge from Beatrice's own theological and mystical views.

The hagiographer immediately alters the treatise in that he assumes the soul about whom Beatrice speaks is her own.

Treatise: There are seven manners of loving, which come down from the heights and go back again far above.[39]

Vita: These then are the seven degrees or stages of love, seven in number, through which she deserved to come to her beloved, not at an even pace, but now as if walking on foot, now running swiftly, and sometimes even flying nimbly on agile wings.[40]

Beatrice writes in a removed third-person voice. Her text, while impassioned, is impersonal, distanced, and generalized in its narrative structures. The movement described is that of the soul and of the divine; at times it becomes impossible to distinguish between the soul's love for God and God as love, marking the absorption of the soul into the divine. The hagiographer personalizes and particularizes Beatrice's general description of the relationship between the divine and the loving soul.

Despite the hagiographer's translation, Beatrice's vernacular treatise does not recount degrees or stages so much as different manners of loving, manners with often scarcely apprehensible differences.[41] At issue for Beatrice is the continual movement of presence and absence between the soul and God, a movement that parallels that between the Lover and the Beloved in the Song of Songs. In learning to acquiesce to this oscillation, the soul comes to experience a deepening sense of the divine love and presence. The soul is no longer the bride or beloved, but rather the housewife of God,[42] one whose life is marked not by a dialectic of ecstasy and despair, but by a steady sense of the underlying presence of God in reality.[43] Yet this moment of quiet, which is the apparent apex of the spiritual life on earth, is only the sixth manner of loving. It too is followed by a return of mad love and the soul's desire to be fully absorbed into God, a desire that can only be fulfilled by death. In personalizing and somatizing the seven stages of loving, the hagiographer subtly alters this mystical path. Moreover, in making the madness of love a bodily experience, the desire for death becomes a movement toward death, one whose extremity causes difficulties for the hagiographer and leads to his most obvious abridgements of Beatrice's text.

The first manner of loving is an active longing, in which the soul, according to Beatrice, desires "to keep the purity and the nobility and the freedom in which it was made by its Creator, in His image and likeness."[44] The hagiographer interprets this in terms of ascetic practices, describing how through "corporal exercises" (*corporalibus exercitiis*) she sought "to obtain that liberty of spirit we mentioned."[45] For Beatrice the soul's desire is too great to be fulfilled by any creature. Again the hagiographer reads this in terms of the weakness of the flesh, hence clarifying the need for corporal exercises. Yet all of this is absent from Beatrice's text. A similar corporalizing movement occurs when the hagiographer describes Beatrice's desire for self-knowledge. For the loving soul, this entails a recognition of its essential nature as one with divine love. For the hagiographer, on the other hand, the intense self-scrutiny demanded by love leads Beatrice to "bodily languors" (perhaps better, illnesses) by which she was "so weighed down . . . that she thought death was near."[46]

The humility of the second manner of loving, which desires to serve all most faithfully, is portrayed by the hagiographer in terms of Beatrice's life of service and humility in the convent.[47] As in the first manner, then, the hagiographer attempts to read Beatrice's life itself as an enactment of the mystical journey described in her treatise. He also makes subtle shifts in Beatrice's theological arguments. According to Beatrice the soul desires to serve God for nothing, asking for no answer, no grace, and no glory. The hagiographer keeps the metaphors of Beatrice's text and yet includes a long section, not in the treatise, describing the rewards God gives her for her service. Moreover, he goes on to describe the third manner of loving as a desire to "repay, through loving service, the love which God is,"[48] whereas Beatrice's language speaks of the soul's desire to satisfy love. Fear plays a crucial role in Beatrice's actions within the *vita*; Beatrice herself insists that the loving soul knows nothing of fear and acts only out of love for love.

As in other sections of the *vita*, the personalization of Beatrice's text involves an externalization of the mystical. This becomes further apparent in the fourth manner of loving. Beatrice describes a passing away of the body, making use of a mystical commonplace to express the overwhelming nature of love's presence to the soul. The hagiographer takes this mystical commonplace and transforms it into a bodily expression.

Treatise: When the soul feels itself to be thus filled full of riches and in such fullness of heart, the spirit sinks away down into love, the body passes away, the heart melts, every faculty fails; and the soul is so utterly conquered by love that often it cannot support itself, often the limbs and the senses lose their powers. And just as a vessel filled up to the brim will run over and spill if it is touched, so at times the soul is so touched and overpowered by this great fullness of the heart that in spite of itself it spills and overflows.[49]

Vita: In this stage the holy woman's affection was so tender that she was often soaked with the flood of tears from her melted heart, and sometimes because of the excessive abundance of spiritual delight, she lay languishing and sick in bed, deprived of all her strength. . . . Just as a vessel filled with liquid spills what it contains when it is only slightly pushed, so it happened frequently that Beatrice, pushed as it were, would let spill out by many signs of holy love what she felt inside; or else she would undergo a kind of paralyzed trembling, or would be burdened with some other discomfort of languor.[50]

What Beatrice describes from the inside is transposed by the hagiographer into external and visible form, making use of the commonplaces and topoi of hagiography to facilitate his translation. Beatrice describes the passing away of the body's faculties in the soul's ecstasy; the hagiographer underlines the *signs* on the body that such an experience is occurring. The state of the soul is made manifest in and on the body, in its tears, weaknesses, and illnesses in the face of intense spiritual experience.

A similar externalization of the bodily aspects of Beatrice's text can be seen in descriptions of the fifth stage, in which her writing achieves an intensity and fervor meant to evoke the madness and violence of love. The strength of divine love is felt in both body and soul, the lines between the two becoming increasingly difficult to decipher.

Treatise: And at times love becomes so boundless and so overflowing in the soul, when it itself is so mightily and violently moved in the heart, that it seems (*dunct*) to the soul that the heart is wounded again and again, and that these wounds increase every day in bitter pain and in fresh intensity. It seems (*dunct*) to the soul that the veins are bursting, the blood spilling, the marrow withering, the bones softening, the bosom burning, the throat parching, so that her visage and her body in its every part feels this inward (*van binnen*) heat, and this is the fever of love.[51]

While Beatrice uses bodily metaphors to express the intensity of her experience, its significance, and its divine referent, the hagiographer focuses on the sensibly marked body.[52]

> *Vita*: Indeed her heart, deprived of strength by this invasion, often gave off a sound like that of a shattering vessel, while she both felt the same and heard it exteriorly. Also the blood diffused through her bodily members boiled over through her open veins. Her bones contracted and the marrow disappeared; the dryness of her chest produced hoarseness of throat. And to make a long story short, the very fervor of her holy longing and love blazed up as a fire in all her bodily members, making her perceptibly (*sensibiliter*) hot in a wondrous way.[53]

In the hagiographer's account, Beatrice possesses a divinely marked body, uncommonly like those found in the hagiographics of other medieval women. Beatrice's enlarged heart and open veins, moreover, are found elsewhere in the *vita*, suggesting the influence of the treatise's metaphors on the text as a whole.[54]

For the hagiographer, Beatrice's body is the visible site of her sanctity—it suffers, weeps, groans, grows hot, and glows, in its progression from the first aspirations toward divine love and the final achievement of union with that God who is love. Just as external practices shape the self, these internal transformations must manifest themselves externally. Throughout the *vita* the body and the soul are portrayed as mirroring each other; yet the violence of Beatrice's spiritual exercises and the manifestations of her soul's ecstasy make this reciprocity between body and soul also appear as a conflict. A struggle exists in Beatrice's own text, but in a different place and with different repercussions. The struggle of or with the body does not provide the content or enactment (perhaps more graphically, the picture) of the ascent to God. For Beatrice in the treatise, the interplay of God's presence and absence is internally experienced and described, thus providing a depiction of the soul's movement toward God. Only in the seventh manner of loving, when the soul desires death, does the body become a force with which the soul must contend, for the body now is named as a constraining prison that keeps the soul from immersion in the divine. In the earlier manners, Beatrice uses bodily language to convey her suffering; yet the hagiographer needs a more graphic, objectively apprehensible means of conveying her sanctity to the reader. He focuses attention on the *visible* body and its markings, for only through Beatrice's wounded body can the divine presence be seen.[55]

According to Beatrice, when the soul has passed through the six manners of loving, having become love itself and returned to her own nature, which is love, she laments her misery on this earth and desires to be freed from the body. Yet this very sorrow, as well as the internally experienced fissuring of the body that her desire brings about, becomes a part of the union between the soul and God. The hagiographer, although emphasizing the suffering body in his rendition of Beatrice's text, feels called on to soften her expressions of desire and their vehemence. He both literalizes and fears the audacity of Beatrice's desire to be with God.

> *Vita*: The vehemence of this desire was so excessive that she sometimes thought she would lose her mind for its grievousness, or would shorten the days of her life because of her anguish of heart and great damage to her vital bodily organs.[56]

Fearing for her health, the hagiographer tells us, Beatrice avoided thinking about heaven and her future bliss when such thoughts affected her body in this way. Again, chapter 14's recapitulation of the *vita* clarifies central issues in the text, for the hagiographer has struggled with Beatrice's desire for death since book 3, chapter 16, when the theme is first introduced. For the hagiographer, this desire is an affliction that he wishes to depict Beatrice as overcoming. Yet despite his claims to resolution the desire continually recurs.[57]

For Beatrice, the desire for death and its attendant *internally* experienced suffering are central to the movement of ascent to the divine.

> *Treatise*: So the soul refuses every consolation, often from God himself and from his creatures, for every consolation which could come to it only strengthens its love and draws it up towards a higher life; and this renews the soul's longing to live in love and to delight in love, its determination to live uncomforted in this present misery. And so there is no gift which can appease or comfort it, for the soul's one need is to be in the presence of its love.[58]

This portion of the text is not included in the *vita*, the hagiographer having lost the meaning of the treatise at this point; he writes that Beatrice's experiences "can be conceived only by [mental] experience, not by a flood of words."[59] His literalizing tendencies make it impossible, theologically and narratively, to follow Beatrice in the soul's mad desire for death. As for her contemporaries Hadewijch,

Mechthild of Magdeburg, and Marguerite Porete, for Beatrice the will is the locus of the conflict that leads to the experience of union and exile. The body is not the focus of battle, nor is it said to be externally marked by this struggle (through either ascetic practices, tears, illnesses, fevers, or paramystical phenomena), but the internal disposition of the will and affections. Thus the desire for death does not threaten death directly, as it does within the hagiography, in which internal dispositions threaten literally to tear Beatrice's body apart.

Hagiography tends to represent the internal disposition of the soul through external narrative devices. This becomes most pronounced in texts describing women's lives.[60] Various factors might contribute to the greater emphasis on the mystically marked body in hagiographies of holy women. In the Middle Ages women are identified with the body, and this identification seems to demand that their sanctification occur in and through that body.[61] Furthermore, women's access to religious authority was, in the thirteenth century, primarily (if not solely) through visionary, auditory, and other sensory spiritual and mystical experience.[62] Linked to embodiment through its ties to the imagination and often described using bodily images and metaphors, such visionary and auditory experience was also at times described in terms of its interiorly apprehended effects on the bodily experience of the holy woman. Yet the medieval hagiographer wanted externally sensible *signs* of such experience in order to verify the claims to sanctity of the woman saint. This is provided by a transposition of her accounts of internal experience to the externally visible body. The visionary woman becomes a vision, a divinely marked body, a spectacle for the viewing pleasure of her contemporaries.[63] For this reason, the internal mystical life of Beatrice is transformed into a series of bodily practices and struggles, of battles represented and enacted on the body of the holy woman.

Caroline Walker Bynum suggests a slightly different explanation for the fluidity of interiority and exteriority within medieval texts, arguing that hagiography's externalization of mystical experience is both understandable and unexceptional.

It is exactly because mystics experienced God with more than intellect, and felt comfortable using sensual language to express the experience, that they and their hagiographers sometimes differed over whether a vision was seen with the eyes of the body or the eyes of the mind. An inner, glorious, wordless moment, described in highly affective language to a sister or a confessor, easily became a vision or an apparition or a miracle as it was retold by one excited hearer after another.[64]

This argument fits well with the theoretical claims made by Mauss, Bourdieu, Asad, and Beckwith about the relationship between bodily practices and interior dispositions. For these theorists the fluidity between internal and external experience marks an implicit recognition of the role bodily practices play in the development of interiority and a refusal—on the basis of this relationship—to give priority to one over the other. Yet if distinctions between external and internal are so fluid in the medieval period, why are certain forms of exteriority so persistently highlighted within medieval texts about women? And why does Beatrice insist on the interiority of that which she sees, hears, and tastes and on the spiritual nature of her absorption into the divine? What is at stake for Beatrice in insisting on this interiority against the externalizing tendencies of hagiography, with which she was no doubt familiar?

These questions become even more pressing when we recall what is absent from Beatrice's text. Her hagiographer stresses the role of external practices in the formation of a sanctified subjectivity. Beatrice does not mention ascetic practices or spiritual exercises, such as the use of texts, images, and meditational practices so crucial to the picture of her development given in the *vita*. Her work is similar to that of other medieval women's texts, particularly her beguine contemporaries. Mechthild of Magdeburg, for example, describes her first "greeting from God" as coming unbidden and without any special preparation.[65] In part sparked by a desire to emphasize the freedom of God's gift to the soul, the refusal to discuss the "works" of the body and the soul also highlights human freedom.

Yet according to modern theories—and it would seem some medieval texts—through bodily practices dispositions are literally incorporated; in the process, bodies in practice and in contact with the world construct interiority. Contemporary psychoanalytic accounts of the construction of interiority through bodily practices and intersubjective relations may help explain the emphasis on interiority—and in particular on suffering interiority—found within Beatrice's treatise. Freud argues that the ego is first and foremost a bodily ego, an imaginary construct in which the limits and boundaries of the body are defined through its experiences of pleasure and—most crucially for Freud—pain: "Pain seems to play a part in the process, and the way in which we gain new knowledge of our organs during painful illness is perhaps a model of the way by which in general we arrive at the idea of our own body."[66] Our subjectivities are constructed by bodily practices and by the body's experience when it encounters the world, with pain taking a preeminent role in the formation of the bodily ego and hence of subjectivity. Phenomenologists also argue that we become most conscious of ourselves as embodied beings through those experiences in which corporeality intrudes itself on our attention—experiences predominantly of limitation and suffering.[67] The tendency toward the formation of subjectivity out of suffering bodily experience is heightened within medieval Christianity with its emphasis on the suffering body of Christ, often culturally associated with femaleness.[68]

Our bodily egos are formed not only through bodily practice but also through other processes of identification. For the psychoanalyst Jacques Lacan, the mirror stage describes that moment when the subject is formed through its recognition of itself in an external image (the image of a unified body in the mirror, for example, or the recognition of the child's subjectivity seen reflected in the face of the mother).[69] Lacan's theory of the mirror stage enables him to show that we always come to know ourselves as split and other than ourselves, for we always come to know ourselves through another. Because of this split in subjectivity and because of the subject's dependence on another, the subject is constituted and its existence threatened in the same moment. This can help make sense of the relationship between bodily practices and spiritual exercises centered on imagery, for the contemplation of images of divine suffering becomes internalized and then enacted in and on the bodies of those represented within these texts. In internalizing the cross of Christ, for example, her hagiographer depicts Beatrice as attempting to overcome the gap between her own subjectivity and that of the divine other through which it is constituted. Beckwith similarly argues that "just as in Lacan's mirror stage, the anchoress encounters the crucified Christ as the Other, who is at the same time the internal condition of her identity; she meets him, in Lacan's terms, in *affairement jubilatoire* and *connaissance paranoiaque*, or, in theological terms, in a perpetual oscillation between presumption and despair."[70] Beckwith thus shows how the subjectivity formed through the practice of the *Ancrene Wisse* involves the formation of an imaginary bodily ego experienced in and as a fantasmatic identification with the suffering body of Christ. It is, moreover, a subjectivity always at odds with itself, for Christ "is at once the guarantor of . . . identity and the annihilator of it."[71]

A crucial passage in *Seven Manners of Loving* suggests that Beatrice has so internalized her identification with the divine as to experience internally what was first learned in relationship to images of the cross. Throughout the treatise she has spoken of the divine as love, lord, and God; only in the seventh manner of loving does she name Christ: "Therefore the soul is filled with great longing to be set free from this misery, to be loosed from this body; and sometimes it says with sorrowing heart, as the apostle said: *Cupio dissolvi et esse cum christo,* that is 'I long to be set free and to be with Christ.' So it longs greatly and with a tormenting impatience for death to this world and for life with Christ."[72] The soul's desire for life with Christ makes this life one of unbearable torture, "a blessed martyrdom, a cruel suffering, a long torment, a murderous death and an expiring life."[73] The textual citation suggests meditational practice. Moreover, the image of Christ has been so thoroughly internalized that the soul itself is formed and constituted in that image, although it is important that Beatrice identifies this suffering only indirectly with Christ, reserving the name "life in Christ" for future bliss rather than present suffering. In following her invocation of Christ with a statement of the soul's spiritual martyrdom, however, the reader quickly identifies the soul as living the Passion of Christ on earth. Through its practice, the soul so internalizes Christ as to share in an imaginary identification with his suffering exile. On the one hand, the bodily practices have been so successful that the soul created through them feels trapped within the body and desires to burst the limits of the body itself.[74] On the other, the fissure in the self described by Lacan remains, experienced now as the alterity of the body.

Reading Beatrice's text against her hagiography suggests an important supplement to this reading, one that acknowledges Beatrice's resistance to prevalent cultural norms. As I have argued, the hagiographer insists on externalizing Beatrice's experience. Whereas she becomes absorbed in love through love, for the hagiographer Beatrice's suffering flesh—its expanding heart and bursting veins—itself becomes a sign of Christ's presence on earth. This externalization is demanded by the hagiographical genre and by cultural prescriptions about women, sanctity, and the body. Presumably, Beatrice herself was familiar with these same presuppositions; hagiographical texts were routinely read within convents and many of the thirteenth-century examples appear to have been written for this purpose.[75] In rejecting the externalizing movements of hagiography, both in relation to the road to the divine and in the account of the nature of one's identification with Christ, Beatrice implicitly rejects precisely the association of women with the body, and hence with bodily suffering, so crucial to the hagiographer. Her desire for freedom, then, can be understood as a desire to free suffering women's bodies from their literalistic identification with the suffering body of Christ. She crucially displaces typical understandings of what it means to imitate the life of Christ, arguing that imitation entails not only the suffering imprisonment of life in the body, but also life in internal and eternal rapturous identification with divine love. For Beatrice the formation of the free soul still occurs through suffering, suggesting that her displacement of identification with

Christ from suffering to ecstasy is only partial—rather than identifying with the suffering flesh, she emphasizes the interiority of her passion. It is the soul, not the body, who suffers in an internal suffering that is itself one with the ascent as long as one is on this earth. The further movement toward freedom, and the claim that the soul can be uncreated, free, and without suffering in this life, will occur in the work of Marguerite Porete and Meister Eckhart.

As Beckwith shows in her reading of the *Ancrene Wisse*, the body is not only a key site for the reproduction of material conditions and social relations, but also the site in which the social order can be reformed, reinvented, and reimagined. In her reading, the *Ancrene Wisse* represents just such a reformist moment, one in which the penitential and Christological changes of the later Middle Ages are prescribed and then, Beckwith assumes, enacted in the bodies of late medieval anchorite women. But oddly, given her feminist and materialist concerns, Beckwith conflates male-authored textual prescriptions for women's bodily practice with that practice itself. In the example I have focused on here, Beatrice's treatise shows some evidence of an imaginary bodily ego formed out of ascetic practice and identification with the suffering Christ, yet Beatrice refuses to externalize her imaginary suffering body and only indirectly acknowledges its source in images of the suffering Christ. Her reticence about bodily asceticism and meditational practices centered on the suffering of Christ suggests that she challenges even the prescriptions for the suffering self found in texts like the *Ancrene Wisse*.[76] For Beatrice, sparing the body demands breaking the fluidity between internal and external, thereby marking off interiority as the site of suffering and ecstasy.

In closing her essay, Beckwith suggests that ascesis creates an imaginary ego that incarnates the ambiguities of embodiment. Following Judith Butler, she argues that the imaginary ego generated within the *Ancrene Wisse* is an object "neither interior nor exterior to the subject, but the permanently unstable site where that spatialized distinction is permanently negotiated."[77] The imaginary ego is the very oscillation between interior and exterior, bodily and spiritual, material and imaginary. We therefore have a new way to understand the ambiguity of Beatrice's language, which uses sensual imagery to describe the movements of the soul. Yet we cannot lose sight of the fact that the hagiographer refuses ambiguity by externalizing Beatrice's experiences, whereas Beatrice refuses this ambiguity by insisting on the interiority of the soul's experience.

Beckwith argues that the aim of asceticism is to transcend ambiguity; it is, she writes, "indeed an impossible, defiant, and hopelessly blighted attempt to move beyond the subject's permeability to history and to transcience; it ends up producing the spectacle of that historically marked transcience."[78] Asceticism is the attempt to attain a redeemed and redeeming body through overcoming corporal limitations, to attain the always already lost unity of the mirror image through a denial of the split within subjectivity. According to Beckwith, this attempt is always doomed and leaves behind it a record of its failure in depictions of suffering women's bodies. Yet again, Beckwith's account rests on a conflation of women's practices and male-authored texts, for it is male clerics' descriptions of and prescriptions for female asceticism that result in depictions of fissured, bleeding, and suffering women's bodies in and through which others see the divine. Through the suffering of women's bodies, the transience, historicity, and ambiguity of the reader's subjectivity are, perhaps, provisionally overcome. Beatrice, however, does not describe bodily asceticism but, to use her language, a spiritual one. We might also think of it as a linguistic asceticism, in which Beatrice desires to regulate the ambivalence of language, firmly locating her experience within. She implicitly attempts to avoid the fate described by Beckwith; her text suggests a desire to avoid becoming a spectacle of ambiguity, transience, and bodiliness through which her contemporaries can find their wholeness (through either healing miracles, intercessory prayers, or simply the experience of reading). Beatrice hopes to transcend not only history but also the bodily asceticism that others demand precede that movement into the self. Although she may not be successful in her attempts to write the free self, it is important to acknowledge the subtle shift in her understanding of asceticism and her defiance of predominant prescriptions and norms.

All of this is, I think, tied in complex ways with modern attempts to write the histories of mysticism and of the modern subject, and the curious refusal to take account of sexual difference within these histories.[79] In *The Darkness of God: Negativity in Christian Mysticism*, Denys Turner argues that the central metaphors of interiority, ascent, lightness, and darkness signify radically different things within the early Christian and medieval contexts and nineteenth-and twentieth-century discussions of mysticism:

> Put very bluntly, the difference seems to be this: that whereas our employment
> of the metaphors of "inwardness" and "ascent" appears to be tied in with the
> achievement and cultivation of a certain kind of experience—such as those
> recommended within the practice of what is called, nowadays, "centring" or
> "contemplative" prayer—the medieval employment of them was tied in with a
> "critique" of such religious experience and practices.[80]

Turner suggests that the hypostasization of a particular kind of experience as mystical may be the product of nineteenth-century studies of mysticism rather than being drawn from apt readings of medieval texts.[81] Yet he describes what he calls the apophatic mystic as reacting against "religious experience," understood as extraordinary experience of some kind. Turner tries to explain this contradiction by arguing for a twofold use of metaphors of interiority within medieval texts. Yet the tension or conflict between apophasis and the pursuit of extraordinary experiences remains.

What Turner misses is the place of medieval women mystics and their religious experience—visionary, auditory, and sensory in response to the demands of their contemporaries for some authorizing, divine agency, yet also increasingly interiorized in an attempt to escape from the externalizing demands of male-defined female sanctity. Women's writings from the thirteenth century are both visionary and apophatic; often there is an unproblematic movement between the two, the visionary moment serving as the material that is subsequently negated in a union without distinction between the soul and the divine. Other texts, like Beatrice's *Seven Manners of Loving* and Marguerite Porete's *Mirror of Simple Souls*, eschew the visionary mode and suggest a tension between it and ecstatic and apophatic movements. Not only are external works and signs sublated, but so also is the visionary as the soul moves further inward in its experience of the divine. After the condemnations of Marguerite Porete, Eckhart, and the so-called heresy of the Free Spirit at the beginning of the fourteenth century, and with the increased persecution of the beguines following these events, this alternative movement inward is complicated by an emphasis on autohagiographical gestures within women-authored texts.[82] Yet a revised genealogy of mysticism suggests that women's mystical texts are one of the places in which the interiority of the modern subject constitutes itself.

Mauss, Bourdieu, Asad, and Beckwith want to undermine modern conceptions of the self and of belief, arguing for the bodily nature of both and thereby demonstrating the complex interaction of nature, culture, and power in the formation of human subjects. Beckwith argues that this is a necessary theoretical move if we are to understand the complexity of women's subjectivities and their relationship to structures of power. She suggests a necessary alliance between feminist politics and history and materialist analysis. The fruitfulness of her readings suggests she is right and yet her reliance on male-authored texts needs to be supplemented and revised in light of medieval women's works, like Beatrice of Nazareth's *Seven Manners of Loving*, in which the soul becomes increasingly interiorized in a desire to become increasingly free. In forging this interiority, medieval women's texts are an important source for modern conceptions of the internalized self now under attack from materialist theories like those of Bourdieu, Asad, and Beckwith. Beatrice claims the autonomy of the internal self in order to free herself from cultural demands for a visibly suffering female body. Marguerite Porete will go further, attempting to free the soul from all suffering, internal and external.[83] The female imaginary in late medieval Christian culture, then, was not always and entirely governed by male prescriptions; some women rejected prescriptions for bodily and spiritual exercises centered on identification with the suffering body of Christ. Their resistance, paradoxically, generated an early version of that interiorized, disembodied subject often identified today with masculinity. This subjectivity may well be untenable—the instability of a soul who seeks death in order to be free suggests as much—yet its existence within medieval women's texts must be acknowledged in the process of rewriting and reevaluating the history of medieval and modern subjectivities.

PERFORMATIVITY, CITATIONALITY, RITUALIZATION

9

IN *BODIES THAT MATTER*, Judith Butler responds to her critics, those for whom *Gender Trouble*'s account of performative subjectivity threatens to dissolve the gendered subject into language and marks a return of liberal humanist conceptions of a voluntarist self who freely chooses her or his identity.[1] These critiques are contradictory in ways symptomatic of central theoretical dualisms Butler continually deconstructs in her work.[2] Characteristically, her response to her critics takes the form of an interrogation of the concept of materiality to which many of them appeal and an articulation of the extremely complex relationships between the "materiality of the body" and "the performativity of gender."[3] According to Butler, neither materiality nor sex is given, but rather, "the materiality of sex is constructed through a ritualized repetition of norms."[4] She argues that performativity is a kind of "citational practice" by which sexed and gendered subjects are continuously constituted.[5] The gaps and fissures in that citational process—the ways in which repetition both repeats the same and differs and defers from it—mark the multiple sites on or in which the contestation of regulatory norms occurs. Butler grounds resistance not in bodies or materialities external to systems of regulatory discourses and norms but in the processes of resignification through which body subjects are themselves constituted.

Given some of the responses to *Bodies That Matter*, I am not sure that those who thought *Gender Trouble* dissolved the body and the subject into language have been convinced by Butler's reformulation and careful articulation of the discursive practices formative of materiality, bodies, and subjects.[6] Against these continued critiques, I would place Butler's assertion that "there is no reference to a pure body which is not at the same time a further formation of that body. In this sense, the linguistic capacity to refer to sexed bodies is not denied, but the very meaning of 'referentiality' is altered. In philosophical terms, the constative claim is always to some degree performative."[7] Yet I think that Butler's focus in the 1990s on linguistic practices (narrowly construed) and psychoanalytic accounts of subject formation might usefully be supplemented with attention to the other bodily practices through which subjects are constituted.[8] Whereas *Gender Trouble* clearly understands "words, acts, gestures, and desires" as performative, Butler's reliance on Austinean notions of performativity allows many critics to miss her crucial claim that acts signify.[9] *Bodies That Matter* makes extensive use of Lacanian psychoanalytic theory, in which language serves as the master trope for signification. As a result, Butler seems even more deeply invested in the primacy of language as formative of subjectivity. In *Excitable Speech* Butler ostensibly returns to an analysis of the constitutive role of bodily practices, particularly in her discussion of Pierre Bourdieu's account of the *habitus*. Yet the language of her text tends, as I will show, to conflate bodily practices with speech acts (themselves understood as one form of bodily practice).[10] Because Butler's primary concern in *Bodies That Matter* and *Excitable Speech* is with linguistic performativity, she does not clearly articulate how actions as well as language signify.[11]

Here I will return to and supplement Butler's account of repeated actions as performative of gender,[12] extending her analysis from gender to the subject and demonstrating that the subject is formed not only through the linguistic citation of norms,[13] but also by the bodily subject's encounters with other bodies in the world and by its practical or bodily citations (this would include ritual acts and bodily practices like those analyzed by Marcel Mauss, Pierre Bourdieu, and Talal Asad—modes of walking, standing, and sitting; sleeping and eating; giving birth; nursing; healing; and so on).[14] I will argue that these encounters, insofar as they are constitutive of subjectivity, are best characterized as sharing in certain structural features of signification; yet signification is not solely linguistic. Performative actions, like linguistic performatives, constitute that to which they refer. Attention to the details of how bodily practices and rituals signify and how they form subjects, then, may work against dematerializing readings of Butler's texts.

In order to understand why readings of Butler so easily slide from a bodily to a linguistic understanding of the performative, and, at the same time, to clarify how speech acts and ritual actions signify, I will begin with Butler's reformulation of materiality as materialization and her identification of this process with ritual.[15] Following J. L. Austin in *How to Do Things with Words* and Jacques

Derrida in "Signature, Event, Context," Butler's accounts of performativity and citationality—of the ways in which language acts—rely on an at first barely articulated analogy with ritual action (actions that signify, according to some ritual theorists).[16] Butler expands the role of ritual in her account of the performative in *Excitable Speech*, going so far as to argue that speech acts are themselves rituals, a move rendered ironic by the fact that some ritual theorists now understand rituals as speech acts.[17] Ritual serves to ballast her account of the force of the performative without itself being explicitly defined or theorized.[18] What I want to do here is explore the use of the term "ritual "within the work of Butler, Austin, and Derrida in order to demonstrate the ways in which all three lean their accounts of the force of the performative on ritual. I will ask why this is so, suggest what they mean by the term, and explore the significance of their work for the understanding of ritual. I will argue that Derrida's understanding of the structures of signification offers useful suggestions for a theory of ritualization—and, by extension, of subjectification and materialization—grounded in the performative.[19] The result will be both a better reading of Butler and a new account of ritual and bodily actions as performative.

RITUAL MATTERS

In *Bodies That Matter*, Butler describes the process of materialization, as I have said, as a "ritualized repetition of norms."[20] She goes on to claim that "as a sedimented effect of a reiterative or ritual practice, sex acquires its naturalized effect, and, yet, it is also by virtue of this reiteration that gaps and fissures are opened up as the constitutive instabilities in such constructions, as that which escapes or exceeds the norm, as that which cannot be wholly defined or fixed by the repetitive labor of that norm."[21] Here "ritual" is interchangeable with "reiterative," suggesting that the term serves only to highlight the repetitive nature of those practices and citations through which the sexed body is formed.[22] This is important for Butler because it is the temporality of citationality that allows for the slippage between norms and their instantiation; resistance occurs in the space and time interval demanded by repetition.

Later in *Bodies That Matter*, Butler introduces the notion of constraint in proximity to that of ritual, further suggesting that ritual has to do not only with repeated practices but also with power:

Performativity cannot be, understood outside of a process of iterability, a regularized and constrained repetition of norms. And this repetition is not performed *by* a subject; this repetition is what enables a subject and constitutes the temporal conditions for the subject. This iterability implies that "performance" is not a singular "act" or event, but a ritualized production, and ritual reiterated under and through constraint, under and through force of prohibition and taboo, with the threat of ostracism and even death controlling and compelling the shape of the production, but not, I will insist, determining it fully in advance.[23]

One might read ritual in this passage as again marking the repeated nature of the performance of gender (as opposed to a singular act or event); it is the reiterative nature of the practice that opens the door to resistance and ensures that the repetition of norms is not fully determinative of body subjects. Yet the passage also suggests an association between "ritualized production" and "a *regularized and constrained* repetition of norms" (my emphasis), leading us to ask about the precise relationships between ritual, constraint, and power. In other words, if the performative has the power to act, where does that power or, to use Austin's and Derrida's language, force come from? Does it come from outside the speech act? Or is it, rather, internal to that performance?

Butler takes up the question of the force of the performative in *Excitable Speech*. Here she posits a disjunction between Pierre Bourdieu's work on the performative and that of Derrida.[24] For Bourdieu, force is located within the social context, understood as outside of the utterance itself: "authority comes to language from outside."[25] Butler reads Derrida, conversely, as claiming that the force of the performative is a structural condition of language and marks the decontextualization necessary to iterability.[26] The antithesis Butler sets up between Bourdieu and Derrida (one implicitly operating in Bourdieu's text) is crucially tied to the concept of ritual. According to Butler, Derrida transforms ritual completely into linguistic iterability.[27] As a result, "the socially complex notion of ritual . . . is rendered void of all social meanings; its repetitive function is abstracted from its social operation and established as an inherent structural feature of any and all marks."[28] Bourdieu, in contrast, locates the power or force of the performative in convention or ritual and so in social institutions outside of the domain of language and thus closed to the changes made possible by iterability. By denying the temporality of performativity, Bourdieu renders it a fully determinative and determined linguistic practice.

Butler responds to this dilemma by tying the force of the performative neither to the structure of the sign nor to extralinguistic social institutions but rather to the body (of the speaker).[29] She locates the force of the performative in the chiasmatic relationship between speech and the body: "Speech is bodily, but the body exceeds the speech it occasions; and speech remains irreducible to the bodily means of its enunciation."[30] Furthermore, Butler argues that the body is itself constituted of and by speech acts. To facilitate this move, she appeals to Bourdieu's notion of the *habitus*, the set of bodily dispositions or embodied practices through which cultures maintain a sense of their own obviousness.[31] As Butler argues, the *habitus* is "formed, but it is also *formative:* it is in this sense that the bodily *habitus* constitutes a tacit form of performativity, a citational chain lived and believed at the level of the body."[32] The *habitus* is the embodied result of the reiteration of norms; it is the result of (or is itself?) a subjectivity constructed through the repetition of the discourses and practices into which we are born and called into subjectivity.[33]

To clarify the relationship between the force of the performative and the body, Butler points to the importance of the body lying behind the threat of hate speech. The language of the body itself, in fact, is part of the speech act and determines its force and how its force is read (that is, as threat, joke, citation). When asked why speech and the body should be given precedence given the fact that anonymous hate mail is potentially as hurtful as spoken utterances, Butler suggests that even if "performatives cannot always be retethered to their moment of utterance . . . they carry the mnemic trace of the body in the force that they exercise."[34] In other words, hate mail threatens insofar as it carries the trace of the addresser's body and the body of the addressee is then marked by the force of the utterance.[35] There seems to be a certain circularity to Butler's argument, however, for the force of the utterance on the body of the addressee points to the speaking body. Perhaps the materiality of hate mail and of language itself effects this movement from the body of the addressee to that of the speaker.

Butler goes on to argue that the body "is not simply the sedimentation of speech acts by which it has been constituted."[36] She points here to the chiasmatic relationship between speech and the body in which neither is fully contained by or reducible to the other. She is thus able to argue that the body both provides and resists the force of speech. Whereas, in Butler's Derridean account of signification, iteration provides the break necessary to resistance, the body protects against the overgeneralization of this break feared by Bourdieu. Yet I am not clear why, in Butler's analysis of the relationship between the body and the performative, the body is understood as produced only by *speech* acts, particularly given Bourdieu's (and as we will see Mauss's) concern for the day-to-day bodily practices that make up the *habitus*. Perhaps Butler understands those bodily practices formative of subjectivity, now interpreted as themselves signifying chains insofar as they are citational, as speech acts.[37] Yet I think it is important to distinguish meaningful action from language that acts, particularly given the need to clarify how action means and language acts and the specificity of these different operations.

Butler argues, finally, that the performative should be rethought as a social ritual, "as one of the very 'modalities of practices [that] are powerful and hard to resist precisely because they are silent and insidious, insistent and insinuating.' "[38] Of course, speech acts are not generally silent—although perhaps the conventions on which they depend are—pointing to a disanalogy between the performative and those bodily practices constitutive of the *habitus*. More important, if, as Butler argues, the performative needs to be read as "ritual practice" and "one of the influential rituals by which subjects are formed and reformulated," then we need a more clearly articulated theory of ritual to make sense of the performative and its force.[39] According to Butler, speech acts are like rituals in their bodiliness, their constraining power (derived from that bodiliness), and their iterability. Yet we derive this account of ritual from Butler's analysis of speech acts as constitutive of subjectivity. Within Butler's account, the particularity of bodily practices and rituals is quickly subsumed into that of the speech act, suggesting that ritual remains an untheorized ballast for the force of language. She uses Bourdieu's account of the *habitus* as a way to show that bodily practices shape the subject, only to identify those practices with speech acts. Although I think Butler implies that bodily practices themselves signify, this crucial point remains unarticulated.

FROM SPEECH ACTS TO RITUAL MEANING

To understand why Butler leans her conception of the performative on the relatively untheorized notion of ritual and to unpack further what ritual means in the context of these discussions, I would like to examine some of her sources. The proximity of ritual to the performative has its roots in the work of Austin, for whom certain ritual utterances served as prime examples of the performative and the infelicities that plague it.[40] In his preliminary isolation of the performative,

Austin differentiates it from what he calls "constative utterances." Constatives are statements that describe a situation or state of affairs and therefore are either true or false. Yet there are also grammatically unexceptional statements that do not describe a situation or state of affairs and so cannot be taken as true or false; many such statements, however, are not nonsense. They therefore require explanation and classification. Austin argues that such statements do something rather than say something. His examples include speech acts drawn from the realm of what, in "ordinary language," we often refer to as rituals, for example:

(Ex. *a*) "I do (sc. take this woman to be my lawful wedded wife)"—as uttered in the course of the marriage ceremony.
(Ex. *b*) "I name this ship the *Queen Elizabeth*"—as uttered when smashing the bottle against the stem.
(Ex. *c*) "I give and bequeath my watch to my brother"—as occurring in a will.
(Ex. *d*) "I bet you sixpence it will rain tomorrow."[41]

In all but the final example, Austin makes clear that the context is essential to the phrase performing an action (ultimately, it will be crucial for the final example too, as an actor making a promise during the performance of a play is not considered to have made a promise—although she is still performing).

It is in large part the social context of the performative that gives rise to the numerous possibilities for "misfiring." Austin offers a preliminary schematization of the conditions necessary for a happy or felicitous speech act performance, dividing them into three categories, A, B, and Gamma. A and B concern the procedures and conventions necessary for the adequate performance of a speech act:

(A. 1) There must exist an accepted conventional procedure having a certain conventional effect, that procedure to include the uttering of certain words by certain persons in certain circumstances, and further,
(A. 2) the particular person and circumstances in a given case must be appropriate for the invocation of the particular procedure invoked.
(B. 1) The procedure must be executed by all participants both correctly and
(B. 2) completely.

Gamma, in contrast, is concerned with the speaker and his or her relation to what is spoken:

(Γ. 1) Where, as often, the procedure is designed for use by persons having certain thoughts and feelings, or for the inauguration of certain consequential conduct on the part of any participant, then a person participating in and so invoking the procedure must in fact have those thoughts or feelings, and the participants must intend so to conduct themselves, and further

(Γ. 2) must actually so conduct themselves subsequently.[42]

These conditions are not all of the same type, for failure to meet conditions A and B leads to the misfiring of the performative (it does not, in fact, take place), while failure to meet conditions Gamma, the conditions of intentionality, constitutes an abuse of the performative, which has, nonetheless, taken place. (I have made a promise but have been insincere or made a promise and failed to live up to it.)

Only conditions A and B seem, at first sight, relevant to our exploration of the role of ritual and convention in the analysis of performative speech acts; in elaborating the failures marked by A and B, Austin makes the analogy between performatives and ritual explicit. Austin argues that because a statement must be made by the correct person, to the correct persons, and in the correct circumstances for the action to be completed, there are innumerable possibilities for failed performatives. He claims, furthermore, that this "infelicity is an ill to which *all* acts are heir which have the general character of ritual or ceremonial, all *conventional* acts."[43] This suggests that ritual, ceremonial, or conventional acts, whether linguistic or not, are marked by constraints with regard to the social context in which they occur. These constraints, moreover, are the source of the happy or unhappy performance of a speech act and, hence, by implication, of its force.[44]

The move from conditions A and B to the problem of intentionality is, arguably, one away from the understanding of the performative as tied to ritual.[45] Yet as Austin moves on in his discussion of the performative, he increasingly focuses on the issue of intentionality and the role of the assumed sovereign "I" who enacts. At a loss in his attempt to find a grammatical or semantic marker by means of which the performative can be readily distinguished from the constative, Austin argues in lecture 5 that if a certain reduction can be effected on an utterance, it is shown to have performative force. The operation involves determining whether an utterance can be rendered as an explicit performative, in which a verb (of the proper sort) appears in the first-person present indicative. (In this way, one could argue, Austin, like Butler, attempts to tether the performative to the body or to demonstrate the ways in which the performative always bears the trace of the body. Derrida, as we will see, conflates this move with claims to intentionality.) Not all statements in this form are performative, nor do all performatives appear in this form; all performatives can, however, be reduced to this form. It is the appropriate grammatical form for the performative, according to Austin, because "actions can only be performed by persons, and obviously in our cases the utterer must be the performer," and since the speech is an act, the person "must be doing something."[46] In those cases where the "I" is not explicit in the performative, moreover, she or he is always referred to either "*by his being the person who does* the uttering" or "*by his appending his signature.*"[47] There is necessarily an "I" behind the performative who somehow serves as the "utterance-*origin*" and hence as the source of the performative's force.

There is a tension, then, between Austin's claim that the conventionality of the speech act, like the conventionality of ritual, gives force to the utterance and his suggestion that the utterance-source, the speaking or signing "I," is the locus of force.[48] In "Signature, Event, Context," Derrida exploits this ambiguity in Austin's texts in order to argue for a "general theory" of the mark in which its force is tied to a conventionality not of external circumstances, but of the mark itself.[49] For Derrida, all language takes on the character of the performative and of ritual (rather than ritual being reduced to language, as Butler claims). In making this argument, Derrida associates Austin's attempt to tie the force of the performative to the speaking subject with his interest in intentionality as a condition for the correct use of the performative. Although this slide might not be entirely justified (and we might, with Felman and Butler, more usefully tie the force of the performative to the body of the speaker, and hence to that which often escapes conscious intentionality), it is suggestive of the ways in which subsequent readings of Austin's text have attempted to delimit the performative and protect against the erosion of the constative effected within it.[50]

Having cited Austin's claim that the possibilities for misfiring that haunt the performative are also endemic to all "ritual or ceremonial, all *conventional* acts," Derrida goes on to locate the specificity of Austin's claims and make his own generalization:

> Austin seems to consider only the conventionality that forms the *circumstances* of the statement, its contextual surroundings, and not a certain intrinsic conventionality of that which constitutes locution itself, that is, everything that

might quickly be summarized under the problematic heading of the "arbitrariness of the sign"; which extends, aggravates, and radicalizes the difficult. Ritual is not eventuality, but, as iterability, is a structural character of every mark.[51]

Ritual as iterability, Derrida claims, is what marks the sign as communicative and performative. Key for Derrida, as for Butler, is the iterability, or repeatability, of the sign; it is this reiterative structure, the fact that the sign is the same and yet also differs and defers (both from possible referents and from other signs), that marks its force (and its power of signification). Butler argues that for Derrida the force of the performative lies in its "decontextualization"; because the mark must be repeated in order to signify, it is always both tied to and divorced from its original context of utterance. This separation, according to Butler, provides the performative's force. Yet I think that this is to forget that iterability is always marked by similarity as well as difference. The force of the mark, on my account, is twofold. It derives from that which is the same in the mark and from that which differs; force is therefore subject to multiple deployments.

Butler argues that Derrida is interested in ritual only insofar as it serves as a useful analogy for his account of language as iteration. I would like to follow out a version of that argument here, yet ultimately, I will argue that more can be derived from Derrida's deployment of ritual than he himself may have intended. Embedded within Austin's notion of ritual is the understanding of social context and external constraints as intrinsic to the felicitous operation of its performance. Derrida reads Austin as equating context with intentionality (A and B, with Gamma).[52] It is in this light that Derrida points to the impossibility of ever fully determining context: "For a context to be exhaustively determinable, in the sense demanded by Austin, it at least would be necessary for the conscious intention to be totally present and actually transparent to itself and others, since it is a determining focal point of the context."[53] Yet arguably, this is precisely what is not required for ritual or conventional actions. Within ritual action, the intentionality of the players is often unimportant to the force of the utterance. By focusing on Austin's sovereign "I" as the focal point for contextualization rather than on the question of who is speaking to whom and in what circumstances, in arguing that a condition of the mark is the absence of an empirical addressee, and in emphasizing the structure of the mark over its semantic content, Derrida, as Butler argues, seems to "evacuate the social" from the realm of language and its utterance.[54]

Yet as Butler shows, Derrida never argues that the context is unimportant to determining the meaning and force of an utterance, only that this context can never be fully determined and thus the speaking subject cannot have full control of her meanings. Moreover, the question of force and constraint is crucial to Derrida and is intimately related to the iterative structure of signification (which, I will argue, can occur through both linguistic marks and action). He suggests that in providing a more general theory of language (as writing), a generalizing movement eschewed by Austin, he is able to show the way in which that which seems external to the operation of the performative is also internal to it (and, I think, constitutive of those very social institutions in which Bourdieu wants to locate the force of performatives and ritual). Derrida here points to Austin's exclusion of the citation from his account of performative and constative speech acts. For Austin, the performance of an utterance in a play or the recitation of a poem is a parasitic or abnormal use of language, dependent on the more primary ordinary language he wishes to analyze. (At issue here, it should be noted, is the question of intentionality, sincerity, and other aspects of the Gamma criteria.) For Derrida, citationality is iterability—rather than being a secondary parasite, it marks the structural conditions for signification itself. The risk of citationality—that the performative cannot be tied to an intending subject—is a risk endemic to signification itself. By clinging to intentionality as a necessary condition for determining the total context in which performative and constative uses of language can be distinguished, Derrida argues, Austin misses the primacy of citationality and the structural inability of any context to ever be fully determined.[55]

For Derrida, then, the force of the utterance lies within the structure of language as iteration. This force, as I have suggested, can work in multiple (possibly endless) ways. In a concise summation of much of his early work on writing and difference, Derrida suggests the duplicity of the force of signification:

Deconstruction does not consist in passing from one concept to another, but in overturning and displacing a conceptual order, as well as the nonconceptual order with which the conceptual order is articulated. For example, writing, as a classical concept, carries with it predicates which have been subordinated, excluded, or held in reserve by forces and according to necessities to be analyzed. It is these predicates (I have mentioned some) whose force of generality, generalization, and generativity find themselves liberated, grafted onto a "new" concept of writing which also corresponds to whatever always has *resisted* the former organization of forces, which always has constituted the *remainder* irreducible to the dominant force which organized the—to say it quickly—logocentric hierarchy. To leave this new concept the old name of writing is to maintain the structure of the graft, the transition and indispensable adherence to an effective *intervention* in the constituted historic field. And it is also to give their chance and their force, their power of *communication*, to everything played out in the operations of deconstruction.[56]

I cannot unpack these lines fully without an analysis of the context of their utterance. They serve my purposes here, however, simply by showing that force works for Derrida in at least two ways. On the one hand, force is the result of a tethering of the mark to the same, its repetition of that which has come before; yet on the other hand, deconstruction attempts to exploit the fact that to be repeated, the mark must always also differ and defer from that which it cites (although, as I will show, the ends toward which this break is deployed are open). Derrida's analysis of the structural conditions of the mark, as well as the deconstructive reversal of speech and writing, presence and absence, and ordinary language and citationality, marks a redeployment of the force of the mark toward new ends.[57]

Butler argues that in evacuating the social context from the performative, Derrida denies the historicity of language. Yet for Derrida, historicity is not only the repetition of the same. Derrida insists that history is never a fully recuperable presence or materiality but rather is change, rupture, and break (the *repetition* of the same, and hence always different). Paradoxically, the force of this rupture or of the break constitutive of history is what enables the fiction of a universal, disembodied, self-present subject. Derrida refigures or resignifies this break and its consequences, not in order to reinstall a new universalizing authority (as Bourdieu suggests) but rather to mark the alterity of history in and by writing. The universal subject is always a contextual one, regardless of whether that context is erased through a "false break" that attempts to make generalization a total and radical decontextualization (what Butler claims Derrida himself does). The generality of the mark makes it reiterable and generative; yet this generality always requires a context. The attempt to escape contextualization in general (to claim a universality untethered to any context) is a reification of one determined context at the expense of new ones.

The invocation of ritual, as it is outlined by Austin, suggests that constraint does not come from within the sign but is maintained by forces external to it—either convention or the conscious intention of the speaker. If, then, the apt performance of ritual, like that of speech acts, depends on who is speaking to whom and in what context, it might seem that there is something external to the ritual itself that determines this delimited context for applicability and provides the force of its action (this is what Bourdieu, in particular, will argue). Derrida claims, conversely, that Austin ultimately tries to reduce the source of performative force and the total context in which performativity can be discerned to the speaking subject. We might read Austin more generously as claiming that the force of the perlocutionary utterance (which requires the proper outcome follow from it in order to be performative) is dependent on the speaking subject and that of the illocutionary (in which the saying, in the right conditions, *is* the performance) on convention. Yet even the illocutionary always has a signatory—the one authorized to use this form of conventional speech. This leads to the question of who or what authorizes the signatory, again taking us to convention and determining contexts external to the speech act itself. Against both these moves, Derrida argues for the primacy of citationality and therefore the inability ever fully to determine context. In doing so, moreover, he suggests how the process of iteration is itself constitutive of those social conventions through which performatives derive their force. For Derrida, the outside is constituted by the inside and the inside by the outside.

I think it is important to remember that, just as Butler's aim in *Excitable Speech* is not to give a full account of the *habitus* as constitutive of the subject, in "Signature, Event, Context" Derrida is not interested in elaborating a theory of ritual, but rather in giving a general account of signification. Yet if we accept the claim that ritual is signifying action, Derrida's account of the sign has implications for ritual theory. In *Excitable Speech*, Butler is primarily interested in the linguistic character of signification and so at times seems in danger of conflating signification with language and hence reading Derrida as reducing ritual to language. This runs parallel to the error made by those ritual theorists who claim that ritual is meaningless. They assume that meaning necessitates reference (of a particular sort); when attempts to understand ritual actions as referring to some other reality break down, the claim is made that rituals do not signify.[58] In providing an account of signification not dependent on this kind of reference, Derrida offers a way to reformulate ritual as meaningful without claiming that it refers to independently existing external realities. Rather, social realities are constituted, at least in part, by ritual action. (Hence the move to say that rituals are performative—their meanings are not primarily constative but generated by the action itself.) Rather than reducing the social complexity of ritual, then, I believe that Derrida's analysis is suggestive for understanding ritual as meaningful action, particularly when brought together with Bourdieu's and Butler's attention to the body of the speaker or ritual actor. For Derrida, the signifying and constitutive force of the performative is a function of its reiterative structure (both as a repetition of the same and as the break) and its effect.[59] The very contexts in which the performative operates are themselves products of performative utterances and acts, subverting the distinction between utterance and context on which Austin's analysis (at least provisionally) depends. Ritual can be understood in the same way, for just as speech acts mean as well as do, rituals are signifying actions. For Derrida, force lies within the reiterative structure of ritual (as repetition and break) and as an effect of ritual, rather than solely outside ritual as that which enables its performance.

In *Bodies That Matter*, Butler takes up Derrida's emphasis on ritual as repetition, an iterability that is always marked by difference, yet she also suggests that ritual is a "regularized and constrained repetition of norms." At this point it is not clear whether Butler follows Derrida in placing the force of the performative or of citationality within the process of reiteration or whether she wishes to maintain an outside—a social world untouched by the constitutive force of the performative—from which these constraints emanate. The latter seems an unlikely position for Butler to hold, given her other philosophical commitments. In *Excitable Speech*, she argues that the force of the performative lies neither fully outside nor within the performative, but is tied to the body who speaks (and also perhaps to the body who is addressed). I think that this move places Butler closer to Derrida's position than she herself acknowledges, for her emphasis on the chiasmatic relationship of speech and the body functions in ways analogous to Derrida's critique of claims to full contextualization. Speech is of the body and the body speaks and is constituted, according to Butler, by speech acts, yet neither can be fully reduced to the other. Similarly, when Derrida argues against Austin that the citation is not a secondary example of the performative but the revelation of its very structure, of its force and its risk, Derrida does not simply exchange externally for internally generated constraints. Rather, he deconstructs the very opposition between external and internal as he describes the performative's constitutive force and the possibility of its failure. Materialization and subjectification are processes in which bodily subjects are constituted; the possibilities for resistance lie in the endless possibilities for misfiring that structure the performative itself (although the misfiring of particular performatives will depend in large part on the contexts—constituted by hosts of other performatives—in which they occur).

This clearly coincides with Butler's understanding of the possibilities for resistance in *Bodies That Matter*. Her account of the chiasmatic relationship between body and speech in *Excitable Speech*, however, at times leads to another reading, one that claims resistance is grounded in the body insofar as it is irreducible to speech acts. This move might suggest that Butler has come to distrust her own deconstructive impulses and wishes to reinstall "the body itself" as site of resistance. This reading is clearly in tension with Butler's account of the body as constituted through the performative repetition of norms that makes up the *habitus* (although Butler, as I have shown, is unclear about the relationship between speech acts and ritual actions in this process and tends to conflate ritual with speech acts). Butler suggests the irreducibility of the body to speech in order to create a space for resistance to the social and discursive norms through which subjects are constituted—a resistance she believes is foreclosed by Bourdieu's assertion that the formation of the body by these norms is completely effective. What should be emphasized here is not the irreducibility of the body to signification (as if we could somehow get to that pure presignifying body) but rather an account of bodily practices as themselves performative acts subject to the same misfirings and slippages Austin and Derrida locate in speech acts and signification in general.[60] Recent ritual theory similarly argues that outside and inside are indeterminable and that, as Butler argues, "social positions are themselves constructed through a more tacit operation of performativity."[61] As Derrida and Butler suggest, it is the process of ritualization that constitutes social beings, social worlds, and the constraints through which identities are maintained and differences enunciated.

FROM RITUAL TO RITUALIZATION

Ritual, understood as a specific kind of action or as action opposed to thought, is conceptually articulated within the modern Western study of religion, for which Protestant Christianity is hegemonic.[62] Talal Asad uses entries in the *Encyclopedia Britannica* to argue for a fairly recent change in the understanding of ritual. Whereas the entries from 1771 to 1852 define ritual as a book containing the script for religious ceremonies, in the new entry for 1910, ritual is universalized and attention shifts from the script to the action itself. As Asad explains,

A crucial part of every religion, ritual is now regarded as a type of routine behavior that symbolizes or expresses something and, as such, relates differentially to individual consciousness and social organization. That is to say, it is no longer a *script* for regulating practice but a type of practice that is interpretable as standing for some further *verbally definable*, but tacit, event.[63]

Key to this move is the claim that rituals as expressive serve some psychological or sociological function—they symbolize meanings that have their real field of operation within the realm of the mind or the social group. For Asad, the move is one from text to "behavior, which is itself *likened* to a text," a text to be read by the anthropologist or historian of religion.[64]

To this conception of ritual as symbolic action, Asad opposes an understanding of "rites as apt performances" and "disciplinary practices," a view he argues can be seen in medieval Christian conceptions of the monastic life.[65] Through an analysis of aspects of medieval monasticism, Asad argues that injunctions for the monastic life prescribe actions and rites "directed at forming and reforming Christian dispositions."[66] Asad's understanding of ritual as "disciplinary practice" is indebted to the work of Michel Foucault and to that of the sociologist Marcel Mauss. To undermine further the modern distinction between symbolic and technical actions, he makes use of Mauss's conception of bodily techniques. "The body is man's first and most natural instrument," Mauss argues; "Or more accurately, not to speak of instruments, man's first and most natural technical object, and at the same time technical means, is his body."[67] It is through bodily practices that subjectivities are formed, virtues inculcated, and beliefs embodied. Mauss first introduced Aristotle's notion of the *habitus* into modern sociological theory (although it is probably still best known from Bourdieu's work), using it to describe the "techniques and work of collective and individual practical reason" that shape embodied experience.[68]

Unlike Mauss, Asad wishes to assimilate ritual, at least outside of the modern Western context, with bodily practices. Mauss, on the contrary, is interested in those bodily practices that are, he argues, shaped by cultural as well as biological and psychological factors yet do not stand clearly within the realm of formalized, ritual, or ceremonial activity. His analysis begins with the problem of what to do with those miscellaneous phenomena such as gait, athletic styles, manners of sleeping and eating, clothing, birth and nursing patterns, and so forth that are marked by cultural styles yet do not seem to warrant the designation of ritual. Asad suggests that outside of the modern Western context, these kinds of regulated bodily activities are continuous with the more constrained activities of what we would call the ritual life.⁶⁹ Thus there is no clearly marked differentiation between symbolic and technical activities; the distinction is instead between those activities (or aspects of activities) in which bodies are the objects and means of transformation and those in which other tools are employed to other ends.

Asad's assumption of the continuity between bodily practices and ritual actions is congruent with Catherine Bell's argument that historians of religion and anthropologists might usefully move away from a concept of ritual to one of ritualization. Bell refuses to define ritual as a static entity:

> Ritualization is fundamentally a way of doing things to trigger the perception that these practices are special. A great deal of strategy is employed simply in the degree to which some activities are ritualized and therein differentiated from other acts. While formalization and periodization appear to be common techniques for ritualization, they are not intrinsic to "ritual" per se; some ritualized practices distinguish themselves by their deliberate informality, although usually in contrast to a known tradition or style of ritualization. Hence, ritual acts must be understood within a semantic framework whereby the significance of an action is dependent upon its place and relationship within a context of all other ways of acting: what it echoes, what it inverts, what it alludes to, what it denies.⁷⁰

Although the formalization of actions—their limitation to certain times, places, contexts, ritual agents—is one of the techniques used to mark off some practices as having a special significance within the life of the community, Bell insists that the ways in which ritualization occurs are specific to individual groups and communities; in other words, ritualization works and must be understood contextually (even if the total context can never be fully determined).

Bell also argues that ritualization, in giving special significance to certain practices, does so not because these actions refer to or symbolize meanings external to them but rather because social subjects and their relations are engendered through the bodily practices of ritual life. Against common functionalist theories of ritual, which understand it as an attempt to forge social solidarity, to resolve conflicts within the community, or to transmit shared beliefs, Bell argues that ritual involves "the production of ritualized agents, persons who have an instinctive knowledge of these schemes embedded in their bodies, in their sense of reality, and in their understanding of how to act in ways that both maintain and qualify the complex microrelations of power."[71] To questions about the relationship between ritualization and power, then, Bell argues that power and its dispositions are generated and regulated through rituals themselves, rather than lying outside them as that which constrains or otherwise marks these activities off as special.

Bell's account of ritualization, then, can be rendered consonant with the understanding of ritual we have drawn out of Derrida's reading of Austin. For both Bell and Derrida, ritual is like language not because it is a text whose symbolic meanings must be uncovered or deciphered but because rituals are actions that generate meanings in the specific context of other sets of meaningful actions and discourses. Meaning is generated through the iteration and differentiation of signs. Signs refer to other signs within the signifying chain rather than to external realities. Although linguistic signs can and do refer to extralinguistic realities as well as to other signs (a question with which Derrida is concerned in his work on names), in the realm of signifying actions (such as bodily practices and rituals), the distinction between signifying chain and external reality is more difficult to maintain. In other words, ritual actions are—not surprisingly—more like performative speech acts than like constatives. Meanings are constitutive and generate that to which they refer.[72]

Methodologically, Bell stresses the importance of the total context to understanding what counts as a ritual within a particular community, whereas Derrida emphasizes our inability to ever fully delimit the context and thereby to fix the meanings or ritualized nature of any activity. (This may give rise to the very un-Derridean tendency in Bell's work to separate the performer of an action from the action and its effects. In my Derridean account, the two are inseparable, for actions themselves constitute performers.) Through repetition, the movement whereby actions or marks are repeated in another time and place, subjectivities and relations between them are generated. The openness of Bell's understanding of ritualization might usefully be augmented by a crucial insight from Derrida, for repetition (at some level) is the one constraint on ritualization—the one bit of formalization that is constitutive of the process of ritualization itself.[73] This also suggests the aspect of ritualization that establishes continuity between bodily practices and more fully ritualized activities, for both depend on iteration and hence generate meanings and constitute realities. The meaning is the constituted reality, thereby rendering ritual actions more like illocutions (in which the doing or saying, in the right conditions, is the performance) than like perlocutions (in which the proper outcome must follow from the saying or doing for it to be counted a performative). The *habitus*, in the sense used by Bourdieu and Butler, is made up of bodily practices and rituals (and the distinction between the two is itself a fluid one).

Bell's conception of ritualization and its relationship to power is directly influenced by the work of Foucault, particularly his reconceptualization of power. This helps explain the agreement between her analysis of the ambiguities of subjectivization and that of Butler. Against those theories of ritual that see it as the field in which the power of an elite is wielded and maintained over the populace, Bell argues that ritualization involves the (often very unequal) circulation of power among all the players within the ritual field: "Ritual mastery, that sense of ritual which is at least a basic social mastery of the schemes and strategies of ritualization, means not only that ritualization is the appropriation of a social body but that the social body in turn is able to appropriate a field of action structured in great measure by others. The circulation of this phenomenon is intrinsic to it."[74] Like other discursive formations generative of subjectivity, ritual is productive of the subject and marks the possibility of that subject's resistance to the very norms and rituals through which it is constituted.[75] Against those theorists who stress the conservative nature of ritual, Bell argues that ritual mastery "experiences itself as relatively empowered, not as conditioned or molded."[76] In a similar way, Margaret Thomson Drewal argues that ritual involves repetition but always (as does all repetition) repetition with a difference (it has to occur in a different time and place for it to be repetition). The room opened for improvisation (which differs in different ritualizations) within the ritual space marks it as a site of both domination and resistance.[77]

Austin argues that the right conditions are necessary for the successful performance of an illocutionary speech act; absent those conditions, the performative misfires and does not, strictly speaking, take place. Derrida and Butler, together with ritual theorists like Asad, Bell, and Drewal, help us to think about the misfiring of the performative in new ways. In changed conditions, performatives constitute new kinds of subjects and communities. Seen in this way, misfiring looks less like a danger than a possibility, one that opens room for improvisation and resistance within the very authoritarian structures (for example, of child rearing, education, and religion) in which subjects are constituted. We do not freely choose ourselves or our communities, nor are the worlds into which we are born absolutely determinative ones in which no new meanings can be enacted. Instead, subjects and communities are created and sustained by the complex interplay of sameness and difference constitutive of repetition itself.

PRACTICE, BELIEF, AND FEMINIST PHILOSOPHY OF RELIGION

10

TWO OF the first and most important and comprehensive feminist interventions in the philosophy of religion—Pamela Sue Anderson's *A Feminist Philosophy of Religion* and Grace Jantzen's *Becoming Divine: Toward a Feminist Philosophy of Religion*[1]—follow the mainstream of analytic and continental philosophy of religion in focusing on belief.[2] Anderson arguably remains closer to that tradition than Jantzen. Rather than changing the aims of philosophy of religion, Anderson insists that gender must become a crucial analytic category within accounts of the process of the justification of belief. More centrally (and more audaciously), she argues that philosophical arguments grounded in feminist concerns must not only justify but also evaluate belief and its constitution. Jantzen, on the other hand, eschews justification, arguing that feminist philosophy of religion has different aims than its Anglo-American counterpart. For Jantzen, philosophy of religion is theological and practical; properly pursued, it will lead to the "becoming divine" of women rather than the justification of religious belief. Yet Jantzen too focuses her attention on "religious discourse and the symbolic of which it is a part." The goal of feminist philosophy of religion is less to justify or to argue for the truth or falsity of belief than to "restructur[e] that myth in ways that foster human dignity—perhaps in ways that oblige and enable us to become divine."[3] Questions of justification thereby give place to questions of moral or political adequacy. Jantzen suggests the primacy of moral or political over epistemological justification, whereas in Anderson the two exist side by side.

Jantzen, however, is finally unable to avoid the epistemological issues she wishes to displace. Ultimately she and Anderson both address the issue of the "truth" or "objectivity" of belief. Yet neither provides a satisfactory account of the ontological status of the objects of religious belief. Both Anderson and

Jantzen challenge the split between reason and desire that would render belief solely a matter of rationality and conscious cognition, yet they remain on the level of the discursive, the symbolic, or the mythic, giving little attention to the place of ritual and practice in religion.

My contention here is that these two problems are closely related. The unsatisfactory nature of current arguments about the ontological status of the objects of religious belief is tied to the neglect of practice and ritual. Put in another way, attention to the role of practice and ritual in religion will force feminist philosophers to understand religious belief and its objects in new ways. Given the more immediately bodily nature of ritual and other forms of religious practice, moreover, any philosophy of religion attendant to them will be forced to acknowledge and to theorize those differences inscribed in and on bodies (often through rituals and bodily, mental, and spiritual practices themselves). We will then be better able to understand why religion is such an important site for the inculcation of bodily differences and to analyze the relationship between religious practice, belief, and sexual—as well as other—differences (themselves objects of belief inculcated on bodies through the bodily, mental, and discursive repetition of norms).[4]

THE ONTOLOGICAL STATUS OF THE OBJECTS OF RELIGIOUS BELIEF

Anderson deals directly with the issue of the ontological status of the object of belief, asking in relationship to the work of Luce Irigaray, "To what extent, if any, can one say that the female or feminine divine exists?" Anderson begins by distinguishing between a variety of different ways in which something might be said to exist. Existence might be:

1. real or empirical;
2. ideal;
3. fictional;
4. mythical;
5. illusory; or
6. historical (which for Anderson entails something like a collectively held illusion).[5]

Anderson will be most interested in the ideal and the mythical conceptions of existence, bringing them together in a modified Kantianism by means of which she attempts to safeguard the legitimacy of religious belief and the reality of its objects without committing herself to empiricist claims about the existence or nature of the divine.[6]

Anderson begins with Kant's assertion that transcendental ideas (like that of God's existence) do not constitute knowledge, but are regulative principles that direct human understanding toward the summation and limits of what can be known. Various post-Kantian accounts of the transcendental ideas as regulative principles, she argues, provide sufficient "ground to treat myth as a regulative principle and not to equate it with constitutive knowledge of supersensible reality."[7] When we talk about God or the divine, we talk not about entities available to our senses and hence to empirical knowledge, but rather about the conditions of knowledge—both pure and practical (moral)—themselves. In stark contrast to Kant, Anderson wishes to allow an epistemological and moral role for desire. She insists, moreover, that this desire is neither psychologistic nor narcissistic, but grounded in the shared embodiment of human beings and hence susceptible to universalization. For feminist philosophy, she argues, "authentically conceived and strongly objective theistic beliefs of women would not come from psychological need alone, nor from epistemological ignorance but, significantly, from a rational passion for justice."[8] Moreover, "reason, in its substantive form of yearning, represents the human potential for justice and freedom or liberty. These potentials are Enlightenment ideals; in Kantian terms, they are regulative ideals."[9] When feminist philosophers talk about God, then, they are talking about the potential for human self-flourishing and human justice by means of which moral and political life should be regulated. In this sense, Anderson claims to maintain objectivity and ontological realism while at the same time avoiding any assertion of the empirical reality of supersensible beings at odds with the presumptions of her own Kantianism.

Anderson's inventive solution to the problem of theological realism and the ontological status of the divine depends on the close correlation of two central Kantian principles. Kant's argument about the concept of God as a regulatory principle of pure reason occurs in the *Critique of Pure Reason*, yet Anderson's larger argument is grounded in his *Critique of Practical Reason* and its complex moral argument for the justification—even necessity—of accepting the postulate of God's existence.[10] The *Critique of Practical Reason* rests on two presumptions: (1) that reason in its practical dimension demands that human beings follow the moral law given to them by reason; and (2) that rationality demands the moral law be capable of fulfillment (for Kant, it would be irrational for human beings to pursue an end they know is incapable of attainment).

Fulfillment of the moral law, however, depends on human freedom and the possibility of a perfect conjunction between virtue and happiness—the highest good, according to Kant. The latter in turn depends on the immortality of the soul and on the existence of God. Only if a being exists in which the phenomenal (the realm of happiness) and the noumenal (that of human freedom) come together can the highest end be possible. Although freedom, immortality, and God's existence cannot be known by pure reason, then, reason in its practical dimension requires that we postulate their existence. In this sense, moral ideals readily available to reason serve as the grounds for religious belief.

For Kant, we can never know God exists empirically. The very constitutive categories of understanding preclude knowledge of God, for God, as eternal and omnipresent, stands outside of these categories and thus can never become an object of knowledge. In the *Critique of Pure Reason*, Kant argues that the concept of God is a regulative ideal of pure reason, that which marks the limits of reason and the sum total of its audacious—if unfulfillable—desire. The *Critique of Practical Reason* argues that we must accept as a postulate, a necessary hypothesis, that God exists, albeit in a manner never knowable by human beings. In both the *Critique of Pure Reason* and the *Critique of Practical Reason*, moreover, these ideals—be they epistemological or moral—are ideals the *existence of which* renders pure reason or practical reason and the moral life themselves rational. In other words, despite his insistence on the limitations of reason, Kant's God must be hypothesized as existing. Kant's realism is, then, arguably more radical and far-reaching than Anderson's.

Despite crucial differences between Anderson's and Jantzen's projects, Jantzen falls back on a similar modified Kantianism when it comes to the question of the nature of divine existence. Rereading Ludwig Feuerbach's account of the divine as the projection of human ideal becoming, Jantzen argues that in speaking of the divine we "speak . . . of ideals, indeed regulatory ideals in a Kantian sense. Projections need to be those which embody our best and deepest aspirations, so that we are drawn forward to realize them."[11] Like Anderson, Jantzen brings together the concept of God's existence as an epistemological regulative ideal for pure reason with God's existence as a postulate necessary to the rationality of the moral law. Within the terms of practical reason, what is ideal is not the concept of God, but that of the moral law itself, its complete fulfillment, and its coincidence with absolute happiness (that is, the highest good). God can only be said to be an ideal of practical reason in that God's existence renders the highest good possible.

Like Anderson, Jantzen also hopes to show that attention to the communities of faith for whom religious projections are meaningful enables feminist philosophy of religion to avoid the charge of relativism, arguing cogently that "partiality of insight is not the same as absence of criteria" for adjudicating competing truth claims, or, as she prefers to put it, symbolic systems.[12] She is not interested in defending philosophical realism, however, and so saves herself from some of the worries faced by Anderson. Yet with Jantzen as with Anderson, we are left with the problem that their accounts of belief—and most crucially their accounts of the ontological nature of the objects of religious belief—do not correspond to what people most often mean when they say that they believe in God. (This, incidentally, includes Kant. Although he gives different grounds for belief than do those not directly influenced by his work, his understanding of *what* is believed comes closer, I think, to the kind of theological realism espoused by many—if not most—religious, or at least Christian, people.)

Arguably, as constructive philosophical theologians, neither Anderson nor Jantzen need be concerned by my critique. They might easily respond that their projects entail an ameliorative reconception of what is meant by religious belief. Yet the question remains open as to what kind of power these putatively regulative ideals have if we do not believe in their realist instantiations. For Kant, once again, without belief in God's existence, reason becomes self-contradictory. Reason in its practical dimension, in particular, would demand a course of action that would be irrational to pursue, given that without God's existence the moral law's ends are unfulfillable. At the same time, however, Kant argues that to know God through pure reason would itself jeopardize morality, for we would then act out of a fear or love of God rather than from duty alone. (Hence Kant's insistence that we need to postulate the existence of God not in order to make moral action desirable, but rather to render it fully rational.)[13] Jantzen takes advantage of an ambiguity within the *Critique of Practical Reason* and argues that hope in the possibility of an ideal's realizability by human nature is all that is required for either religion or morality.

Jantzen's argument depends on the conflation of Feuerbach's theory of projection with a modified Kantianism. Yet she overlooks a crucial dimension of Feuerbach's theory of religion in her appeal to the divine as a realizable projection of human ideals. For Feuerbach, reason alone is inadequate to explain religious belief; *desire* motivates projection and with it the insistence on the ontological independence of that which is projected. As Van Harvey shows, for Feuerbach pain and ecstasy fuel humanity's projection of a divine other. When one human being encounters another,

> the individual I experiences a powerful inrush of two types of feeling: on the one hand, a painful feeling of limitation and inadequacy over against the unlimitedness of the species and, on the other, an ecstatic sense of the attractiveness of the species, an attractiveness grounded in the individual's joy in the exercise of his/her own distinctive powers. But because the idea of the species is an abstraction and as such has very little emotional power, it is seized upon by the imagination and transformed into the idea of a single being. The individual, driven by his/her desire to live and his/her sense of finitude, finds in the perfection of the divine being a substitute for the true bearer of these predicates, the species, as well as an assurance of his/her worthiness and immortality as an individual.[14]

Unlike the forms of Christianity analyzed by Feuerbach, Jantzen is not interested in asserting the unlimitedness and immortality of the species. Yet ideals—however limited—remain abstract. Feuerbach suggests that to attain emotional force they require concretization in an object of belief held to be ontologically independent of the believer.[15]

Perhaps most importantly, what if we understand philosophy of religion less as an attempt to justify or redefine belief than as an attempt to account philosophically for those aspects of human existence broadly characterized as religious? Philosophy of religion understood in this way cannot move so quickly from the descriptive to the prescriptive, for it is responsible to religious phenomena as lived by practitioners and believers. From this perspective, the question of the ontological status of the objects of religious belief cannot be resolved by redefining the nature of divine existence in terms of regulative ideals (be they epistemological or moral). Nor can religion be equated solely with belief. For many religious people, practice takes precedence over belief; a philosophy of religion that does not account for the function and meaning of practice will never be adequate to its object.

As I suggested above, the issues of the ontological status of the objects of religious belief and of the centrality of practice to religion are intimately related. The early-twentieth-century French sociologist, a son-in-law and intellectual heir of Émile Durkheim, Marcel Mauss makes the argument most starkly: "I believe precisely that at the bottom of all our mystical states there are body techniques which we have not studied, but which were studied fully in China and India, even in very remote periods. This socio-biological study should be made. I think that there are necessarily biological means of entering into communion with God."[16] If mystical states are understood as God's existence made bodily and spiritually inescapable, then this leads to the possibility that skepticism about or disbelief in God's existence is itself, as Talal Asad puts it, "a function of untaught bodies."[17]

BODILY PRACTICE, THE *HABITUS*, AND PRACTICAL REASON

Asad uses Mauss's argument about the constitutive power of bodily practice in order to intervene in two related debates within contemporary anthropology, the first having to do with the supposed primacy of belief over practice and the second with the putative distinction between ritual and instrumental human actions. Both debates stem from modern Western European Protestantism's rejection of ritualism and insistence on the primacy of faith. Understanding religion primarily through the models provided by their own religious tradition (regardless of how distanced individual philosophers and proto-anthropologists may have been from that tradition), early students of religion assumed the centrality of belief to religion.[18] Ritual action, understood as a debased form of religiosity, needed to be distinguished from instrumental action; the former operates symbolically, the latter practically. In other words, rituals are understood to be actions that must be interpreted in terms of preexisting systems of belief rather than described in terms of what they do (the presumption being that they do not do anything).[19] Mauss's rejection of the clear-cut distinction between instrumental and ritual action makes it possible for Asad to contest claims to the primacy of belief within religion (a contestation increasingly demanded by students of religion on empirical grounds—even, as I will show, in the study of Protestant Christianity).

Mauss argues that "the body is man's first and most natural instrument. Or more accurately, not to speak of instruments, man's first and most natural technical object, and at the same time technical means, is his body."[20] Mauss is interested in those forms of bodily practice marked by culture (as well as by biology and psychology) yet not easily read in terms of symbolic meaning: gait, athletic styles, manners of sleeping and eating, clothing, and birth and nursing patterns. These forms of bodily practice form subjectivity, inculcate virtue, and embody belief. They constitute what Mauss calls the *habitus*:

> Please note that I use the Latin word ... *habitus*. The word translates infinitely better than "*habitude*" [habit or custom], the "*exis*" the "acquired ability" and "faculty" of Aristotle (who was a psychologist). ... These "habits" do not vary just with individuals and their imitations; they vary especially between societies, educations, proprieties, and fashions, prestiges. In them we should see the techniques and work of collective and individual practical reason rather than, in the ordinary way, merely the soul and its repetitive faculties.[21]

As Asad explains, Mauss's understanding of the *habitus* enables social scientists "to analyze the body as an assemblage of embodied attitudes, not as a medium of symbolic meanings."[22] The distinction between bodily practices in the Maussian sense and ritual thus breaks down; for Asad both are disciplinary practices through which bodies, dispositions, and subjectivities are formed and transformed.[23] Rituals, like bodily practices, do not carry symbolic meanings but instead *do things*. They create certain kinds of subjects, dispositions, moods, emotions, desires, and beliefs. Put in another way, they are like performative speech acts, for that to which they refer is constituted through the action itself.[24]

As Asad shows, Mauss provides the framework for an historicized Kantianism or "an anthropology of practical reason." Practical reason is not, as it is for Kant, a principle of universalizability by means of which ethical rules can be determined, but rather an

> historically constituted practical knowledge, which articulates an individual's learning capacities. According to Mauss, the human body was not to be viewed simply as the passive recipient of "cultural imprints," still less as the active source of "natural expressions" that are "clothed in local history and culture," as though it were a matter of an inner character expressed in a readable sign, so that the latter could be used as a means of deciphering the former. It was to be viewed as the developable means for achieving a range of human objectives, from styles of physical movement (e.g. walking), through modes of emotional being (e.g. composure), to kinds of spiritual experience (e.g. mystical states). This way of talking seems to avoid the Cartesian dualism of the mind and objects of the mind's perception.[25]

Mauss's arguments also destabilize any rigid distinction between "body sense and body learning."[26] Bodily experience is physiological and cultural; the body can—and arguably must—be taught and the various cultural lessons learned by the body shape one's experience. Physical pain, for example, is a universal physiological phenomenon, yet according to Asad anthropological and psychological research demonstrates "that the perception of pain threshold varies considerably according to traditions of bodily training—and also according to the pain history of individual bodies."[27] Pain, understood simultaneously as one of the most universal and one of the most subjective aspects of human experiences, is always also inflected by culture.[28]

Following Mauss, then, Asad embodies and historicizes practical reason and he does so by insisting on the centrality of bodily practices and rituals as forms of discipline. The body is humanity's first technical means and object because, through disciplined body practices, bodies acquire aptitudes, emotions, dispositions, and beliefs (although it should be noted that the relationship between dispositions and beliefs requires further discussion and refinement). On first sight, then, the *habitus* represents a much broader conception of practical reason than that found in Kant. One might argue that while Kant articulates reason in its practical dimension as providing a universally available means of determining the moral law (through the process of universalizability), Mauss and Asad show that practical reason also, and perhaps more fundamentally, involves learned modes of being in the body and in the world.[29] Seen from this perspective, Asad's work nicely complements that of Anderson and Jantzen, both of whom wish to expand the grounds for religious and moral reflection to include bodily affects, emotion, and desire. Asad, by insisting on the necessity of body practices and rituals to the formation of practical reason, provides the concrete grounds for this extension in a way not provided by Anderson and Jantzen.

Yet to what extent and in what ways is Asad's conception of practical reason broader than Kant's? Asad's arguments are indebted to the work of Michel Foucault as well as to that of Mauss. Foucault offers a rough typology of different modes of morality that might be helpful in elucidating the relationship between Mauss's and Asad's conception of practical reason and that of Kant. Foucault argues that the term "morality" covers three different realities. First, there are the values and rules of action that are set forth as normative for a particular group, a "prescriptive ensemble" that Foucault calls a "moral code." Morality also refers to "the real behavior of individuals in relation to the rules and values that are recommended to them," what Foucault terms "the morality of behaviors." Finally there "is the manner in which one ought to 'conduct oneself'—that is, the manner in which one ought to form oneself as an ethical subject acting in reference to the prescriptive elements that make up the code."[30] In other words, social groups not only prescribe *what* one should do, but also attempt to form subjects who will perform certain kinds of actions in preference to others. The practices or exercises through which ethical subjects are formed also shape *how* and *toward what end* these subjects will act.

Descriptions of morality can be either descriptions of "codes," of "moral behaviors," or of "'ethics' and 'ascetics,' understood as a history of the forms of moral subjectivation and of the practices of the self that are meant to ensure it."[31] A history or anthropology of ethics and ascetics, of

> the way in which individuals are urged to constitute themselves as subjects of moral conduct would be concerned with the models proposed for setting up and developing relationships with the self, for self-reflection, self-knowledge, self-examination, for the decipherment of the self by oneself, for the transformation that one seeks to accomplish with oneself as object.[32]

One is called on not only to perform certain actions or to follow certain prohibitions, but *to be* a particular kind of moral subject, and within any given culture the models, techniques, and practices (remember that in ancient Greek *askesis* means "practice" or "exercise") through which this form of subjectivity is inculcated can be uncovered by the historian or anthropologist. These practices not only form ethical subjects of a particular sort, but also promise them certain pleasures or goods. Thus Foucault argues, technologies of the self "permit individuals to affect, by their own means, a certain number of operations on their own bodies, their own souls, their own thoughts, their own conduct, and this in a manner so as to transform themselves, modify themselves, and to attain a certain state of perfection, happiness, purity, supernatural power."[33] Although certain cultures might give more weight to the "code" and others more weight to "askesis" and the formation of the self, generally both operate together within flourishing moral systems.

Seen in light of Foucault's threefold account of morality, one might be tempted to argue that Kant's moral theory is all about codes, whereas Mauss and Asad create a space for thinking about askesis. Yet Kant does not simply provide a method for determining the maxims according to which one should act, but also argues that a particular mode of being in the world is decisive for determining the moral nature of one's actions. To behave on behalf of anything other than the moral law, Kant argues, is to act heteronomously. Morality depends on autonomy, on acting out of duty to the moral law itself. Human action must be determined solely by practical reason and the demands it makes on the subject. In providing the means for determining the moral law, then, Kant provides not only a code but also an askesis through which moral subjects are created. Kant not only tells us how to determine the proper moral code, but the very same operation also forms us as subjects who act in a particular way and toward particular ends. For Kant, then, code (or at least the means for determining the code) and askesis are inseparable. The form of askesis he recommends requires detachment from the body, emotion, and desire. It entails a bodily and mental discipline by means of which the subject becomes detached from his or her body. Thus Kant's form of askesis, like the notion outlined by Foucault, broadens Mauss's conception of practice to include mental and spiritual exercises that effect the body but are not generally acknowledged themselves to be bodily practices. (It is important to recognize, moreover, that the principle of universalizability is not reducible to the principle of detachment, although there is a close relationship between the two. Moreover, there are aspects of body practice that go beyond the parameters of that with which Kant concerns himself in his writings on practical reason. The relationship between this more broadly construed conception of *habitus* and Kant's moral law requires further elucidation.) Kant generally does not acknowledge that the form of subjectivity he wishes to inculcate is a learned mode of being in the world. Instead, he argues that it is the mode of subjectivity demanded by human reason itself, rightly understood. Yet despite his insistence that morality requires a revolution in human disposition rather than its reform, Kant's deep interest in education as central to the work of enlightenment suggests that bodily and intellectual training is necessary to the successful attainment of moral subjectivity.

Mauss and Asad, in deuniversalizing the claims of practical reason, enable us to see that the moral law and moral dispositions—even those called for by Kant—are learned. An Asadian reading of Kant, then, would demand attention to his account of the practices—bodily and intellectual—through which the mind removes itself from the body, emotion, and desire in order to determine the moral law and to attain the proper disposition for its enactment. Seen from this perspective, Anderson's and Jantzen's critique of Kant is directed toward the debilitating effects of his particular account of the moral life. They both insist that the body, emotion, and desire must play a role in practical moral reasoning and in the religious life. What Mauss and Asad offer is an insistence on the role of bodily, mental, and spiritual practices and rituals in the transformation of the moral, religious, and intellectual life. Not only can we not fully understand Kant's moral philosophy and philosophy of religion without an understanding of the role of askesis within them, we also cannot hope to bring the body, emotion, and desire back into morality and religion solely through an analysis and critique of symbols and beliefs.

EMBODYING BELIEF

Asad substantiates his claims about the constitutive role of practice in the formation of moods, emotions, dispositions, and beliefs through an analysis of medieval Christian monastic practice as codified within *The Rule of Benedict*.[34] As he argues, monastic practice formed and reformed Christian dispositions, among them humility, patience, and contrition. Following the *Rule*'s prescriptions involves undertaking a set of performative actions through which will, desire, intellect, and mind are transformed and (re)constituted. In other words, one becomes a certain kind of person, responds bodily, affectively, and intellectually in certain ways, and comes to hold certain beliefs by engaging in certain prescribed behaviors. (Of course, a certain set of beliefs determines one's decision to engage in these practices in the first place, rendering the relationship between body and practice even more complex than I can here articulate.) The monk who weeps over his sinfulness will become contrite; humiliating oneself before the abbot and the community (through manual labor, acts of homage to the abbot, and public confession) generates humility. Although Asad's detailed arguments are too complex for full elaboration here, his central, well-attested point is that "emotions, which are often recognized by anthropologists as inner, contingent events, could be progressively organized by increasingly apt performances of conventional behavior."[35]

Asad's examples focus on how subjects are constituted and transformed through practice, yet he follows Mauss in suggesting the more radical claim that religious experiences constitutive of and validating belief are also constituted through practice. Substantiating evidence for this claim can be found within the texts of the Christian Middle Ages; evidence can also be found there for the ways in which bodily differences—among them sexual difference—are both inculcated and presumed by prescriptive practices. Clear indications of the role of bodily practices and rituals in the inculcation of belief can be found in medieval meditative handbooks, saint's lives, and mystical texts. I will focus here on just one example, chosen to highlight certain crucial features of meditative practice and the variable relationship between meditation and sexual difference within the later Middle Ages.

Margaret Ebner (1291–1351) was a German Dominican nun whose religious practice and experience followed closely the traditions of meditative practice and mystical experience found in the writings of thirteenth-century religious women. In her *Revelations*, however, Ebner provides more concrete descriptions of the relationship between meditative practice and mystical experience than we find in women's and men's mystical texts from the previous century. Ebner explicitly articulates the way in which her intense meditation on Christ's Passion leads to her inability *not* to see, hear, and feel Christ's Passion and ultimately to experience it in and on her own body.

The process begins with a conscious concentration of Ebner's energies on visual representations of Christ's suffering.

> Every cross I came upon I kissed ardently and as frequently as possible. I pressed it forcibly against my heart constantly, so that I often thought I could not separate myself from it and remain alive. Such great desire and such sweet power so penetrated my heart and all of my members that I could not withdraw myself from the cross. Wherever I went I had a cross with me. In addition, I possessed a little book in which there was a picture of the Lord on the cross. I shoved it secretly against my bosom, open to that place, and wherever I went I pressed it to my heart with great joy and with measureless grace. When I wanted to sleep, I took the picture of the Crucified Lord in the little book and laid it under my face. Also, around my neck I wore a cross that hung down to my heart. In addition, I took a large cross whenever possible and laid it over my heart. I clung to it while lying down until I fell asleep in great grace. We had a large crucifix in choir. I had the greatest desire to kiss it and to press it close to my heart like the others. But it was too high up for me and was too large in size.[16]

The one sister in whom Margaret confides this desire refuses to help her, fearing that the act would be too much for one as physically frail as Margaret. Yet, Margaret claims, what is not possible while awake is granted to her in a dream: "It seemed as if I were standing before the cross filled with the desire that I usually had within me. As I stood before the image, my Lord Jesus Christ bent down from the cross and let me kiss His open heart and gave me to drink of the blood flowing from His heart."[37]

The movement from actively pursued practice to unconsciously enacted experience first occurs, then, in Ebner's dream life. We see in her a feature of religious practice suggested by Asad and highlighted by Saba Mahmood in her study of the modern Islamic women's piety movement in Egypt: the goal of consciously pursued bodily practices and rituals is ultimately to render conscious training unnecessary.[38] In Ebner, this movement nears completion when Christ's Passion becomes inescapably present to her. In the Lent of 1340, while at matins, Margaret explains: "The greatest pain came over my heart and also a sorrow, so bitter that it was as if I were really in the presence of my Beloved, my most heartily Beloved One, and as if I had seen his suffering with my own eyes and as if it were all happening before me at this very moment."[39] Following in the meditative tradition on Christ's life and death promulgated by the Franciscan and Dominican orders during the later Middle Ages, Ebner seems here to have achieved a perfect *meditatio* in which external aides, be they visual or auditory, are no longer required for Christ's Passion to be viscerally present to her.

Ebner goes even further, however, claiming not only to see Christ's Passion, but to share in it. At first, she finds herself unable not to cry out when she hears of or sees (through either the physical eye or the mind's eye) Christ's Passion before her. These outcries lead to physical suffering that renders her body itself Christ-like.

> But when I was given to loud exclamations and outcries by the gentle goodness of God (these were given to me when I heard the holy suffering spoken about), then I was pierced to the heart and this extended to all my members, and then I was bound and evermore grasped by the silence. In these cases, I sit a long time—sometimes longer, sometimes shorter. After this my heart was as if shot by a mysterious force. Its effect rose up to my head and passed on to all my members and broke them violently. Compelled by the same force I cried out loudly and exclaimed. I had no power over myself and was not able to stop the outcry until God released me from it. Sometimes it grasped me so powerfully that red blood spurted from me.[40]

With blood gushing forth from her body, Margaret seems here to become a visible representation of Christ's suffering for those around her.[41] Her identification with the Passion shifts from identification with the onlookers to one with Christ himself.

Margaret claims, like Francis of Assisi a century before her, to achieve an identification with Christ's Passion in which her own body becomes a representation of Christ's suffering for those around her. This cross-gender identification occurs seemingly without question in Ebner's text, suggesting a gender fluidity that renders culturally plausible the valorization of women's suffering bodies.[42] In fact, the situation in the later Middle Ages is more complex than this sole example might suggest. Whereas women did find ways to associate their suffering bodies and souls with that of Christ, other contemporary practices and discourses suggest that at least some men mistrusted these identifications and argued that women should identify not with Christ on the cross, but with Mary at its foot.[43] Often couched in terms of concern for the danger done to women's bodies by their excessive suffering and asceticism, texts like Henry Suso's *Life of the Servant* reserve the role of Christ-like bodily and spiritual suffering for men (in this case, for Suso himself), with Suso's Christ-like body becoming itself the center of women's devotional life.

Early in his life, Suso had engaged in intense ascetic bodily practices, like Ebner rendering his body bloody in imitation of contemporary representations of Christ on the cross. In addition, he inscribed Christ's name on his chest with a stylus. In the second part of the *Life* he eschews such violent practices, particularly for his female followers, yet the sanctification of his body through these practices remains salient. So toward the end of his life we see his "holy daughter" (Elsbet Stagel, who may have in part authored the *Life of the Servant*) sewing "this same name of Jesus in red silk onto a small piece of cloth in this form, IHS, which she herself intended to wear secretly." Moreover, she makes further images of the name of Jesus for distribution:

> She repeated this countless times and brought it about that the servant put them all over his bare breast. She would send them all over, with a religious blessing to his spiritual children. She was informed by God: whoever thus wore this name and recited an Our Father daily for God's honor would be treated kindly by God, and God would give him his grace on his final journey.[44]

Although Jeffrey Hamburger suggests that the displacement of wounds from the human body to cloth badges serves simply as a critique of Henry's early asceticism, the value of the badges to Stagel and others in Suso's circle suggests that more than this is at stake. The religious value of the cloth badges depends on their contact with Suso's tortured and so sanctified flesh.[45] Suso's male saintly body replaces the female body as the site of holiness. Women's role is now the dissemination of physical objects sanctified not by their own actions or bodies, but by those of the male saint. Thus we can see the ways in which prescriptions for bodily and meditative practice can both depend on and shape gender ideologies.

My examples, like Asad's, come from the Christian Middle Ages, a period in which the centrality of liturgical and paraliturgical practices is largely unquestioned (and the role of these practices in inculcating religious experience and belief is currently the subject of intensive study). What of modern Protestantism, however, often understood as a religious tradition determined by its insistence on the centrality of faith—understood as belief—alone? My contention that Kant's conception of practical reason depends on a particular form of askesis, one partially masked by its association with a putatively universal reason, suggests that similar forms of practice can be uncovered within Protestant Christianity. Again, I only have room here for a single example, one suggestive of the intense gendering of many Christian traditions of practice as well as of the limitations of studies of religion focused primarily on belief.

Marie Griffith's *God's Daughters: Evangelical Women and the Power of Submission* studies the Women's Aglow Fellowship, an interdenominational organization of charismatic Christian women founded in 1972 (although with roots in a smaller organization started in 1967).[46] Women's Aglow meetings center on testimonials, singing, public prayer, tears, prophecy, exorcisms, and ecstatic transportation by the Holy Spirit. Griffith provides a fascinating account of the movement through analysis of the central themes articulated in oral testimonials and those printed in Women's Aglow Fellowship periodicals. She demonstrates the ways in which the Aglow women's stories of powerlessness, abuse, secrecy, and shame parallel those found in second-wave feminist literature, even as the two groups' strategies for coping with these issues fundamentally differ.[47] Her focus on narrative enables these comparisons and provides a useful locus for attempting to undermine the sharp divide between explicitly antifeminist evangelical Christian women and feminists in the United States. From the perspective of my analysis of practice, ritual, and belief, however, Griffith too readily allows the Aglow women's self-understanding of the relationship between "spontaneity" and "ritual" to shape her telling of their story.

Griffith briefly describes a regular chapter meeting's fairly uniform schedule. Usually held in hotel conference rooms or other nonreligious public spaces, meetings begin with music, followed by announcements, testimonies, an offering, a talk by a special speaker, and ending with more music and the reception of "prayers from specially trained prayer counselors or coordinators." Griffith argues that despite these formalized elements, "the women continue to value and emphasize 'spontaneity' over 'ritual,' believing the former to maintain openness to the spirit of God while the latter effectively hinders or even closes off such a possibility."[48] Hidden by this account is the way in which the formalized movement from music and prayer to testimonials and then back to music and individualized prayer works to generate the tears, prophecies, and effusions of the spirit experienced by the Aglow women. In other words, their practice might be understood as itself strengthening belief in and engendering an experience of a judging yet also munificent and forgiving God.

Attention to the constitutive power of practice might also help elucidate the seeming intractability of debates between nonfeminist evangelical women and feminists. These differences are not simply the result of conflicting propositions about the world and women's place within it, but reflect deeply embodied dispositions, emotions, and beliefs. Appeals to reason will never be able to fully overcome the divide—a divide that tends toward an absolute refusal of debate—between the two groups. Recognition of the learned nature of one's *habitus* can begin to open spaces for understanding, yet it is the very nature of the *habitus* to cover over its own learned status. Belief successfully inculcated through bodily practice renders itself "natural" and hence resistant to critique and change.[49] (Hence the insistence of the Aglow women that God engenders their experience rather than that their experience engenders God or an encounter with God.) Even if we begin to recognize the learned nature of many of our most deeply embedded dispositions and beliefs, new practices that enable a re-formation of the self will be required for their transformation. And as Feuerbach reminds us, religion appeals not only to reason, but also to the body, emotion, and desire. This marks what is arguably the most crucial divide between the Aglow women and their secular feminist critics. Although the latter are also shaped by learned dispositions and beliefs grounded in emotion and desire, the epistemological and political assumptions of liberalism refuse to recognize the embodied nature of the *habitus*. From the standpoint of the religious believer, moreover, the consolations of liberalism are weak, insufficient to the desires satisfied, at least in part, by religion.[50]

Anderson and Jantzen both argue that we need not settle for a choice between forms of political liberalism cut off from the body, emotion, and desire and a wholesale relativism in which any claims to adjudication between competing practices and beliefs are eschewed. Desire and emotion themselves are shaped both by bodily practices and by reason (now no longer so easily differentiated), making it possible that new conceptions of practical reason and of the practices that inculcate it can be articulated and enacted. Yet without attention to bodily, mental, and spiritual practices and rituals, and their powerful shaping of the *habitus*, the transformation of practical reason and of religiosity demanded by feminist philosophers like Anderson and Jantzen will necessarily fall short.

PART V

LOVE OF NEIGHBOR AND LOVE OF GOD 11

Martha and Mary in the Christian Middle Ages

AT THE close of her wonderful study *The Making of the Magdalen: Preaching and Popular Devotion in the Later Middle Ages*, Katherine Ludwig Jansen remarks on the gains and losses involved in modern historical scholarship:

> In applying the principle of historicity to the cult of the saints, we have no doubt gained in historical accuracy, and that indeed is an important contribution to knowledge and scholarship. But the gains should not obscure the losses. We must not forget that it is our own age that officially memorializes Saint Mary Magdalen as a disciple; it was the "Dark Ages" that honored her as a preacher and apostle of the apostles.[1]

In these—the final lines of her book—Jansen raises a host of complex issues crucial to feminist historiography and the study of religion. What is it, finally, that feminist scholars seek in and from the past? And what are the most intellectually, ethically, and politically legitimate means to attain that which we seek?

Certainly it is not only intellectually but also politically and ethically necessary for us to tell the stories of women's lives as accurately as possible. Yet Jansen raises the question of whether accuracy is itself sufficient. First, critiques of positivist historiography demonstrate that the questions we ask and the answers we give to those questions are always to some extent shaped by our own ethical and political agendas. Although I am convinced that we can still evaluate historical writing in terms of its fidelity to the available sources, most historians now agree that there is no one true version of the past against which all others are to be judged.[2] Secondly, and perhaps more importantly, the kinds of historiography long applied to early Christian and medieval hagiography are always in danger of effacing the practical, affective, and religious possibilities opened up by the past. Are there ways in which the past can move us—and move us in ethically, politically, and religiously efficacious ways—that may abrogate the rules of right reading and interpretation put in place by historical scholarship?

From the standpoint of modern historical scholarship, Mary Magdalen's story is a history of misreading and misunderstanding. Yet as Jansen shows, precisely these misinterpretations generate a powerful religious figure, one who provides a forceful model of human—and specifically female—agency. I will briefly trace the complex Magdalen tradition explored by Jansen before turning to an additional aspect of that story—the conflation of Mary Magdalen with the Mary of Luke 10:38–42, the Mary who, as opposed to her sister Martha, "chose the better part." Long read as an allegory for the relationship between the active (Martha) and contemplative (Mary) lives, Luke 10:38–42 plays a crucial role in the history of early and medieval Christian religious life, one in which Mary Magdalen, once again, is the indubitable star.

Yet there is an alternative tradition in the Christian Middle Ages, one that culminates in a singularly dramatic (even by medieval standards) misreading. Preaching on Luke 10:38–42, the German Dominican Meister Eckhart (d. 1328) proclaims that *Martha*, not Mary, chose the better part. Speaking directly to issues crucial to his female contemporaries, Eckhart misreads in order to bring forth a model of female (and human) religiosity in which action and contemplation are inextricably linked. The ethical and political stakes of this move will become clear, I hope, in what follows. Whether in the twenty-first century we should or can follow Eckhart in his powerful misprisons, I leave for readers to contemplate.

❈ ❈ ❈

Katherine Jansen explores the complex traditions that accrued around the figure of Mary Magdalen in late antiquity and the Middle Ages: first, her role, grounded in the New Testament, as the earliest witness of the resurrection and hence as the "apostle to the apostles"; and second, her depiction, grounded in later hagiographical traditions, as penitential contemplative and preacher. These stories, most widely disseminated in the medieval west by Jacob of Voragine's *The Golden Legend*, show Mary Magdalen as a figure in whom the active and contemplative lives come together, although generally not at the same time.[3] There is a further aspect of the medieval conceptions of Mary Magdalen left relatively unexplored by Jansen. Rooted in complex confusions, conflations, and elisions (to paraphrase Jane Schaberg) in the reading of biblical texts, the conjunction of Mary Magdalen with the Mary, sister of Martha, of Luke's Gospel gives rise to a particular understanding of the conjunction of action and contemplation in the ideal Christian life.[4]

The central story that interests me—one that played a vital role in late antique and medieval Christian conceptions of the nature of the religious life—is Luke 10:38–42, the story of Mary and Martha. The New Revised Standard Version runs as follows:

> Now as they went on their way, he entered a certain village, where a woman named Martha welcomed him into her home. She had a sister named Mary, who sat at the Lord's feet and listened to what he was saying. But Martha was distracted by her many tasks; so she came to him and asked, "Lord, do you not care that my sister has left me to do all the work by myself? Tell her then to help me." But the Lord answered her, "Martha, Martha, you are worried and distracted by many things; there is need of only one thing. Mary has chosen the better part, which will not be taken away from her.

The Vulgate version of the story, the one likely most readily available to medieval readers and listeners, differs slightly from the Greek text on which the NRSV is based. Most importantly for our purposes, Jesus says not that Mary has chosen the "better part" but "the best part" (although this is sometimes interpreted as "the good part," "the better part," or "the stronger part").[5]

Over time, the Mary of Luke 10:38–42 is identified with Mary Magdalen, an association that will become crucial to late medieval revisionary readings of the passage. The Lukan story itself does not appear elsewhere in the New Testament, but Mary and Martha, now said to be from Bethany, appear in the Gospel of John. John 11 recounts Christ's resurrection of "Lazarus of Bethany, the village of Mary and her sister Martha." This is followed by the story of a dinner, hosted at Lazarus's home in Bethany. Lazarus sits at the table with Jesus, and his sister Martha serves; then "Mary took a pound of costly perfume made of pure nard, anointed Jesus' feet, and wiped them with her hair" (Jn 12:3). While some criticize Mary's action, Jesus accepts and praises it.

This story, or one closely related to it, appears in Matthew 26:6–13 and in Mark 14:3–8, yet without naming Mary or mentioning Martha. (Both of these versions of the story set it in Bethany, but in the home of Simon the Leper.

Moreover, the unnamed woman anoints Jesus's head rather than his feet and she does not wipe the "costly ointment" off with her hair as she does in John.) All three stories—the two almost identical versions in Matthew and Mark and the rather different Johannine account that names Mary of Bethany, sister of Martha and Lazarus—are related to a story in Luke of a nameless sinner who washes Jesus's feet and wipes them with her hair, then anoints them with ointment (Lk 7:37–38). Moreover, in Luke's Gospel, as many have noted, this story is very closely followed by mention of "Mary, called Magdalen, from whom seven demons had gone out." Luke lists her along with other women "who provided for them [Jesus and the twelve] out of their resources" (Lk 8:2–3).[6]

These texts give rise to a complex set of conflations in which John's Mary of Bethany, who wipes Jesus's feet with "costly perfume" and with her hair, is associated with Luke's nameless "sinner" (note the sin is unspecified), presumably because of the similarities of the stories told about them. The textual proximity between Luke's account of the nameless sinner and his naming of Mary Magdalen as a follower of Jesus from whom he had cast out seven demons leads to an association of that nameless sinner with Mary Magdalen (an association no doubt rendered more plausible to early Christian and medieval exegetes by their assumption that John's Mary of Bethany and Luke's nameless sinner were one and the same person.) Finally, the associations circle back to Luke's own story about Mary and Martha—one in which he does not specify the town from which they come—and this Mary is now identified as Mary Magdalen. This is the Mary Jansen describes, one who through a further set of complex textual and historical conflations came to be understood as the apostle to the apostles, a contemplative (through an association with Mary the Egyptian, who putatively spent thirty years in the desert atoning for her sinfulness), and an active preacher and teacher (early medieval traditions have Mary, Martha, and Lazarus traveling to the south of France and there preaching publicly and converting the royal family to Christianity).[7]

Most Western medieval Christian exegetes, then, assume that the Mary of the Mary and Martha stories is Mary Magdalen. From at least the third century on, moreover, Christian exegetes interpret the figures of Mary and Martha allegorically.[8] Clement of Alexandria (d. ca. 215) reads Mary and Martha as allegories for the Gospel and the law (and, on a more philosophical level, as unity and multiplicity).[9] His successor as teacher of scripture at Alexandria, Origen (d. 254), understands Martha and Mary as figuring the synagogue and the church,[10] but also the distinction between practice and theory or action and contemplation.[11]

For Augustine (d. 430), the great Latin theologian, Martha is associated with Leah and with Peter, or the present church as it exists on earth. Mary, on the other hand, is associated with Rachel and with John (identified by Augustine as "the beloved disciple") and the future heavenly church.[12]

John Cassian's (d. ca. 435) reading of the Lukan story is particularly influential. The most widely used monastic rule throughout the medieval West, that of Benedict of Nursia, recommends Cassian's *Conferences* as one of a handful of books suitable for daily reading.[13] This suggests that Cassian's work would have been known by virtually every monk and nun in the Middle Ages. Cassian takes up and further articulates the distinction, first found in Origen, between action and contemplation. According to Cassian,

> Martha and Mary are very beautifully portrayed in the Gospel as examples of this attitude and manner of behavior. For although Martha was indeed devoting herself to a holy service, ministering as she was to the Lord himself and to his disciples, while Mary was intent only on spiritual teaching and was clinging to Jesus' feet, which she was kissing and anointing with the ointment of good confession, yet it was she whom the Lord preferred, because she chose the better part, and one which could not be taken from her.[14]

Cassian here associates Luke's Mary with John's, and at the same time suggests the identification of both with "the sinner" who anoints Christ's feet (as did Mary of Bethany in John's Gospel)—hence the importance to Mary of "good confession" as well as "spiritual teaching."

Both "good confession" and "spiritual teaching," however, are identified with the monastic profession and with the life of contemplation. Jesus's words to Martha are understood by Cassian as clearly demonstrating "that the Lord considered the chief good to reside in theoria alone—that is, in divine contemplation."[15] Mary's "good part," moreover, "shall not be taken from her." Cassian takes this to mean that while the reward of Martha's good works will not be taken away, the works themselves will be: "But I am saying that the action, which either bodily necessity or a requirement of the flesh or the inequity of this world calls for, will be taken away. For diligence in reading and the affliction of fasting are exercised for the sake of cleansing the heart and chastising the flesh only in the present, as long as 'the desire of the flesh is against the spirit.' "[16] Martha's activity involves not only acts of bodily care and penitence, but also good works done on behalf of others. Both of these—"works of piety and mercy"—"are necessary in this age, as long as inequity continues to dominate. . . . But this will cease in the world to come, where equity will rule and when there will no longer exist the inequity that made these things obligatory. Then everyone will pass over from this multiform or practical activity to the contemplation of divine things in perpetual purity of heart."[17] The final goal toward which monks—and ideally all Christians—tend is a share in Mary's contemplation, "the vision of God alone." Here Cassian brings together previous strands of interpretation, demonstrating how Mary as contemplation also represents the future church whereas Martha figures action and the church as it exists in the present world.

Pope Gregory the Great (d. 604) adds additional nuance to this account.[18] Following Augustine and others, Gregory sees Jacob's wives, Leah and Rachel, as types of Martha and Mary. He thereby associates the contemplative life with Rachel, who saw more but produced less (she had two sons), and the active life with Leah, who saw less but produced more (with her ten sons).[19] This paradoxical formulation depends on the Vulgate translation of Genesis 29:16. The New Revised Standard Version reads: "Now Laban had his two daughters; the name of the elder was Leah, and the name of the younger was Rachel. Leah's eyes were lovely, and Rachel was graceful and beautiful." The Hebrew word translated here as lovely, however, is of uncertain meaning. The Vulgate, like the Greek Septuagint, reads: "Leah's eyes were bleary, and Rachel was graceful and beautiful." Hence Gregory's claim that Leah, who produced many children, did so despite seeing less than Rachel, the sharp-eyed contemplative. Perhaps more importantly, Gregory stresses throughout his use of these typologies that the distinction between action and contemplation can be understood in light of the twofold command of love. Hence to be Martha or Leah is to pursue love of neighbor, whereas Mary and Rachel focus solely on the love of God.[20]

I have spent some time laying out these traditional modes of allegorization because they provide the interpretative framework within which all subsequent Western medieval discussions of Mary and Martha (as well as Rachel and Leah) must be understood. Although Giles Constable rightly notes that early Christian exegetes "taught that the two lives were connected, interactive, and successive rather than distinct or mutually exclusive,"[21] at the same time they suggest a continual tension between love of neighbor and love of God. All presume, moreover, that the latter is a higher form of love, even as life in this world demands attention to the former. Any deviation from this standard mode of interpretation signals a break with broadly shared presumptions. It is also worth noting that over time the allegorical reading *becomes* the literal. Mary, sitting at the feet of the Lord, *is* a contemplative for early and medieval readers, just as Martha, who is busy with many things, is a person focused on the life of action. This literalizing effect renders counterreadings of Mary and Martha all the more powerful. It also allows the allegorical to pass over into putatively literal interpretations of the Lukan texts; Mary and Martha continue to be read allegorically in much modern scholarship and preaching.

Despite Mary's preeminence, positive valuations of Martha over against Mary do occur, particularly from the eleventh century on. An account of the miracles of Robert of La Chaise-Dieu, written by the poet Marbod, later bishop of Rennes, on the basis of a now lost *vita* by Robert's follower Gerald of Laveine, makes the following astonishing claim: "This new saint turned the old order of sanctity around for us. . . . He had begun far from worldly and laborious tumults, rising above the clouds with his lofty head, to look only upon divine and celestial things with the tranquil vision of his mind, and finally to the work of a stonemason."[22] Marbod depicts Robert as going "against the established custom and the faith of ancient history" by first putting contemplation before action and then rejecting contemplation in favor of action: "He [Robert] placed Martha before Mary and blasphemed, if not in voice but (which is worse) in deed, [because he was] contrary to the judgment of Christ, Who said that Mary's part was the best part. . . . With regard to order, therefore, he could not prefer Martha to Mary unless he preferred Lia to Rachel." And yet, Marbod continues, "contemplatives are greatly moved to action not only rightly but also necessarily, and they do not lose any prior merit, since if the beautiful internal sterility is diminished by this, the blear-eyed external fecundity makes up for it."[23] Notice that Marbod depicts Robert as understanding and maintaining the standard valuation of contemplation over action even as he holds that necessity demands one turn to action while in this life. He therefore stays within the terms of the relationship between action and contemplation as it was articulated by Cassian and Gregory the Great.

The twelfth-century regular canon Anselm of Havelberg (d. 1158) goes further in recasting the debate between Mary and Martha, contemplation and action, love of God and love of neighbor. In a debate with Benedictine monks, he argues that Christ praised Mary out of charity in order to keep Martha from becoming too triumphant in her superiority.[24] According to Anselm, furthermore, one should imitate neither Mary nor Martha but Christ in his active life of preaching and teaching in the world.[25] Anselm's claim that Martha's way is superior to Mary's contains within it the seeds of Eckhart's claim that Martha combines action and contemplation in a Christ-like manner.

Anselm's comments on the story of Mary and Martha are made in the context of a debate about the best way to follow the apostolic life. For centuries, some form of enclosed monastic life, in which one withdrew from the world in order to devote oneself to penitence, prayer, and conformation of the human will to that of God, was the valorized path to God and to Christian perfection. Things begin to change in the eleventh and twelfth centuries, with men and women throughout Western Europe actively seeking new ways to follow Christ and the apostles (the *vita apostolica*).²⁶ Anselm, as a regular canon following the Augustinian rule, which allowed for active service in the world together with modified forms of monastic prayer and discipline, is a part of this larger movement. For him, as for others forging and following these new forms of religious life, traditional monastic interpretations of Luke 10:38–42 are no longer entirely adequate.

Twelfth- and thirteenth-century writers—monks, canons, mendicants and others—struggle with the story and its traditional allegorical interpretation. One way to attempt to recast the relationship between action and contemplation is to emphasize the identification of Mary with Mary Magdalen and hence to claim that Mary *combines* action and contemplation. For Richard of St. Victor (d. 1173), like Anselm a regular canon, Mary's penitence, her tending to Christ, and her preaching after his death all point to the ways in which she brings together in one person action and contemplation. She chose "the better part," then, because (arguably like the regular canons) she chose *both* parts.²⁷

For women seeking new forms of religious devotion, this path was significantly more difficult to pursue and to maintain than it was for men. The regular canons (like most monks at this time) were priests, called on by their office to preach and administer the sacraments. In their polemics against enclosed monastics, they argued that their role as priests demanded a life in the world, rather than one removed from it. The Dominican movement emerges within the context of new demands made on the clergy in the twelfth century (tied to the new pastoral imperatives issued by the Fourth Lateran Council in 1215, the expansion of urban centers, and, most importantly for Dominic, the spread of heresy). Francis of Assisi (like his predecessor Peter Waldo and others) desired a more complete break with monastic traditions, calling on laymen to come together in absolute poverty and devotion; devotion was enacted not by withdrawal, but through life in the sinful world, preaching and calling others to repentance. Francis and his earliest followers were not priests, nor did he wish that honor for himself or for his brothers. (This will change very quickly, even within Francis's own lifetime, but that is another story.) Despite the Fourth Lateran Council's ban on the formation of new religious orders, Francis's movement was approved by Pope Innocent III. The women who quickly followed Francis, however, and women in northern Europe who, independently of Francis, sought to live religiously in the world had a much more difficult time finding approbation for their new conceptions of the apostolic life.

The Dominican Eckhart articulates his new conception of the relation between Mary and Martha while living surrounded by and likely under the influence of the northern European women's religious movement.[28] The movement has its origins in the Southern Low Countries (present-day Belgium and the southern Netherlands) a century or more before Eckhart began preaching.[29] In the "Prologue" to his *Life of Marie of Oignies*, James of Vitry (d. 1240) reminds Archbishop Fulk of Toulouse of the wonderful things Fulk had seen on an earlier visit to the diocese of Liège. The centrality of the passage for the early history of the beguine movement warrants its full citation.

> You saw many holy virgins in the lily gardens (cf. Song 6:2) of the Lord and you rejoiced. You saw crowds of them in different places where they scorned carnal enticements for Christ, despised the riches of this world for the love of the heavenly kingdom, clung to their heavenly Bridegroom in poverty and humility and earned a sparse meal with their hands. Although their families abounded in great riches, yet they preferred to endure distress and poverty and were forgetful of their people and the home of their father rather than abounding in riches that had been wrongly acquired or remaining in danger among worldly pomps. You saw holy women serving God and you rejoiced. With what zeal did they preserve their youthful chastity, arming themselves in their honorable resolve by salutary warnings, so that their only desire was the heavenly Bridegroom. Widows served the Lord in fasts and prayers, in vigils and in manual labor, in tears and entreaties. Just as they had previously tried to please their husbands in the flesh, so now the more did they attempt to please their heavenly Bridegroom in the spirit. Frequently they recalled to memory the words of the apostle that the widow "that lives in pleasure is dead" (1 Tim 5:6) and, because holy widows "share with any of the saints who are in need," they washed the feet of the poor, "made hospitality their special care" (Rom 12:13), applied themselves to works of mercy, and promised to bear fruit sixty-fold (cf. Mt 13:23). You have seen holy women serving the Lord devoutly in marriage and you rejoiced, women teaching their sons in the fear of the Lord, keeping honorable nuptials and "an undefiled wedding bed" (Heb 13:4), giving

themselves to prayer for a time and returning afterwards together again "in fear of the Lord lest they be tempted by Satan" (1 Cor 7:5). Many abstained from licit embraces with the assent of their husbands and, leading a celibate—indeed, an angelic—life, they were so much the more worthy of the crown since they did not burn when put into the fire (cf. 1 Cor 7–9).[30]

In 1211, Fulk had marveled at the crowds of virgins, widows, and chaste matrons praying, fasting, and keeping vigils while remaining in the world, earning their sparse livings through manual labor and caring for the poor, the ill, and the dying. Although James reports that some "shameless men . . . hostile to religion" slander these women, he insists on their abstinence, virtue, and sanctity.[31]

The Liège women not only brought together contemplation and withdrawal from the world with charitable and self-sustaining action within it, but also attained rapturous states of ecstatic union with God. In a catalogue of their virtues, James again reminds Fulk that he had seen "other women who were wasting away with such an intimate and wondrous state of love in God that they were faint with desire, and for many years they could only rarely rise from their beds. There was no other cause for their sickness except him, since their souls had melted with desire (cf. Song 5:6)."[32] Others were overwhelmed with continual tears or "so rapt outside of themselves with such a spirit of inebriation that 'while the King was on his couch' (Song 1:12) and they rested in that holy silence throughout almost an entire day, they neither spoke nor were they sensible of anything external to them." Loud noises could not wake them nor bodily pains pull them away from "the peace of God."[33]

All of the primary sources pertaining to the earliest period of beguine life, like the *Life of Marie of Oignies*, are hagiographical. In addition to James's work, there are ten other *vitae* devoted to individual holy women involved with the movement from 1190 to 1250.[34] Often written shortly after their subject's death and in each case by male clerics or monks interested in promoting a cult around the holy woman, none of these women was ever canonized nor did they all maintain the beguine lifestyle throughout their lives. In fact, as Walter Simons points out, hagiographers from the period and region seemed particularly interested in women who moved from the beguinal milieu into more traditional forms of monastic life.[35] The tension between the beguine's desire to live in the world, earning their own livings, caring for the sick and poor, and educating the young, and their claims to religious sanctity are highlighted in these hagiographies most often through recourse to the images of Mary and

Martha or Rachel and Leah.[36] Hagiographers deploy the allegorical figures in two somewhat contradictory ways. On the one hand, various early beguines are described as bringing together action and contemplation in one form of life. On the other, the *vitae* often depict them as moving from a beguinal life in the world—associated with Leah and Martha—to the "better" life of contemplation denoted by Rachel and Mary.

Let me give one example. *The Life of Ivetta*, written by Hugh of Floreffe, describes how Ivetta (d. 1228), as a young widow, chose to devote herself to the care of lepers, hoping to become a leper herself. (She went so far as to drink the water in which she had bathed the afflicted.) "Nevertheless," Hugh claims,

> among these duties of industrious servitude and the bleary-eyedness of Leah, Rachel's beauties were not forgotten: but just like Moses, now taking care in the encampment of the people, now in the tabernacle of the covenant awaiting God's responses, whatever she did externally, within she always persevered, neither in the days nor in the nights being absent from divine colloquies and prayer.[37]

Hugh stresses, moreover, that the lives of Martha and Mary are not related sequentially in Ivetta's life, but occur simultaneously:

> For although she seemed to be always occupied externally with the serving of Martha, and to be troubled about many things, she was always intent internally with Mary on the contemplation of eternal truth and was distinguished from others by a beautiful variety, so that you thought her to be always Martha, if you saw her in the office of Martha, but you hardly doubted that she was anything but Mary if [you saw her in the office of] Mary.[38]

Despite these assertions of the unity of Martha and Mary in Ivetta's person and practice, Hugh describes Ivetta eventually giving up activity in the world for the contemplative life: "And having given up the ministry of Martha, she transferred herself to the part of Mary, which is better."[39]

The tension generated by the dual nature of the beguine life does not simply repeat the tension between the demands of love of neighbor and love of God seen in Cassian and throughout the monastic tradition. Nor are the problems generated by new forms of religious life the same for the beguines as they are for regular canons and mendicant men. Put simply, claims to the superiority of the contemplative life come together with late antique and medieval misogynistic views about women's susceptibility to sin—especially sexual sin—while living in the world. Beguines, living singly, with their families, or in groups, generally outside of the control of fathers, husbands, sons, and clerical or male monastic authorities, were almost immediately seen as a threat to church order, to men, and to themselves. Many men supported the early beguines, yet many of these same men, as well as other men who were enemies to the beguine movement, believed that women's claims to and attainment of sanctity depended on their strict enclosure within monastic walls.[40] So to the worries about the relative value of action and contemplation is added the concern that, without strict enclosure, women—closer to the flesh, more open and porous in their bodily and spiritual nature, and therefore more susceptible to sin (as well as to the divine)[41]—required enclosure in order to attain "the better part."[42]

Yet the early beguine *vitae*, like that of Ivetta, as well as writings from thirteenth-century beguines, suggest a very different conception of "the better part" and of the relationship between Mary and Martha. The three beguine authors known to us—Mechthild of Magdeburg (d. ca. 1282), Hadewijch (fl. ca. 1250), and Marguerite Porete (d. 1310)—each in very different and complex ways suggest that action and contemplation are one.[43] Only in the sermons of Meister Eckhart, however, do the fruits of beguine speculation on the relationship between action and contemplation lead to radically revisionary readings of Luke 10:38–42 and the figures of Mary and Martha. Likely it required the security of priesthood to make as bold and stark a claim as that found in Eckhart's sermons—and even priesthood did not save Eckhart from censor (although not on this specific point).

Two sermons known to be by Eckhart deal with the story from Luke's gospel. The first opens with a typically Eckhartian translation of Luke 10:38, one that encapsulates the new way in which Eckhart will understand the figure of Martha. Sermon 2 opens with the Latin text: "Intravit Jesus in quoddam castellum et mulier quaedam, Martha nomine, excepit illum in domum suam." ("Jesus entered into a town and a certain woman named Martha received him into her home.") As Eckhart explains, "I have begun with a few words in Latin that are written in the gospel; and in German this means: "Our Lord Jesus Christ went up into a little town, and was received by a virgin who was a wife."[44] The sermon as a whole is devoted to explaining what it means to be a Martha, a virgin who is also a wife. Unlike Richard of St. Victor, who sees action and contemplation united in the figure of Mary, Eckhart here insists that they come together in Martha—leading to his claim in sermon 86 that it is Martha, not Mary, who receives Christ's approbation.

Although we do not know for certain the context in which sermons 2 and 86 were preached, some historians believe that Eckhart's vernacular sermons were addressed to Dominican nuns, beguines, and other lay people.[45] Given the tendency in the northern Netherlands and Germany to refer to beguine superiors as "Marthas," we might speculate that these sermons were addressed specifically to beguines.[46] At the least, the identification of Martha with the virgin who is also a wife figuratively identifies Martha with the highest form of Christian life (and hence arguably with "Marthas" or beguines). Moreover, by insisting that the virgin who is also a wife is the most fruitful of all souls, Eckhart also subverts the traditional distinction between Rachel, representing a clear-eyed but relatively unfruitful contemplation, and Leah, bleary-eyed but fruitful action. For Eckhart, the more virgin the soul, paradoxically, the more fruitful (that is, the more wifely) she is—the more successful in contemplation, the richer in works (or conversely, the richer in works, the closer to God in contemplation).

Eckhart explains that for a soul to be virgin means that she (the soul is feminine and named using feminine pronouns in Eckhart's Middle High German) is "free of all alien images, as free as she was when she was not."[47] Recognizing that created beings cannot literally empty themselves of all images, Eckhart clarifies his position:

> If I were so rational that there were present in my reason all the images that all human beings had ever received, and those that are present in God himself, and if I could be without possessiveness in their regard, so that I had not seized possessively on any one of them, not in what I did or what I left undone, not looking to past or to future, but I stood in this present moment free and empty according to God's dearest will, performing it without ceasing, then truly I should be a virgin, as truly unimpeded by any images as I was when I was not.[48]

Standing without possessiveness toward all that is, the soul finds her ground in the ground of the divine, attaining unity with and in her source.

The virgin soul, united in her ground with the divine ground of the Trinity, participates in the eternal fruitfulness of the Godhead. By giving up all possessiveness, even with regard "to prayer, to fasting, to vigils and to all kinds of exterior exercises and penances," the virgin soul "produces much fruit, and she is great, neither less nor more than is God himself."[49] Eckhart here demonstrates that for him—as for his predecessor Marguerite Porete—action includes devotions often associated with the contemplative life.[50] Only through detachment from these forms of action and devotional contemplation does the soul become absolutely empty of created things and hence become the place in which God gives birth to God's self. This, for Eckhart (again as for Marguerite), is the ultimate work: "This virgin who is a wife brings this fruit and this birth about, and every day she produces fruit, a hundred or a thousand times, yes, more than can be counted, giving birth and becoming fruitful from the noblest ground of all—or, to put it better, from that same ground where the Father is bearing his eternal Word, from that ground is she fruitfully bearing him."[51] The virgin soul gives birth to the son—to Christ—in the soul, performing the one act that is necessary.

This action may seem far removed from the love of neighbor traditionally associated with Martha, yet for Eckhart, the son, Jesus Christ, is the just human being. To give birth to the son is to give birth to justice; moreover, the virgin soul is united with the son and with the ground of the son and so *is* justice. To be just, for Eckhart, is to give to each what belongs to each, and justice, so understood, takes precedence over God: "For just human beings," he proclaims in sermon 6,

> the pursuit of justice is so imperative that if God were not just, they would not give a fig for God; and they stand fast by justice, and they have gone out of themselves so completely that they have no regard for the pains of hell or the joys of heaven or for any other thing. Yes, if all the pains that those have who are in hell, humans or devils, or all the pains that have ever been or ever will be suffered on earth were to be joined on to justice, they would not give a straw for that, so fast do they stand by God and by justice. Nothing is more painful or hard for a just human being than what is contrary to justice.[52]

Every act of justice, according to Eckhart, *is* the birth of the son in and as the soul. "In this working God and I are one; he is working and I am becoming."[53]

> Justice lies in detachment and recognition of the radical equality of all things.
>
> So therefore let us pray to God that we may be free of God, and that we may apprehend and rejoice in that everlasting truth in which the highest angel and the fly and the soul are equal—there where I was established, where I wanted what I was and was what I wanted.[54]

Although I cannot here lay out the Neoplatonically inspired metaphysical foundations for Eckhart's claims,[55] their ethical import seems clear in the stark language of the German sermons.

Martha, remember, is a privileged figure for this work and for this event. Martha, as Eckhart repeats in sermon 86, is perfect in action and in contemplation—hence Jesus says her name twice in Luke 10:41.[56] Mary, sitting at Christ's feet, "was so full of longing. She longed for she knew not what, and wanted she knew not what. We harbor the suspicion that dear Mary was sitting there more for enjoyment than for spiritual profit. Therefore Martha said, 'Lord, tell her to get up,' because she feared that she would remain stuck in this pleasant feeling and would progress no further."[57] Eckhart's thought again is closely in line with Marguerite Porete's, who in her *Mirror of Simple Souls* argues that the spiritual delights given to souls by Christ can be a source of great temptation. Marguerite outlines seven stages or states of the soul, with the crucial distinction lying between the fourth and fifth stages. In the fourth, the soul is so filled with experiences of God's loving presence that she is in mortal danger of believing that she has reached the heights of divine love. Instead, Marguerite insists, the soul must annihilate her will and desire—ultimately arguably herself—in order to return to that place where she was before she was and hence to a union without distinction between herself and the divine. Then God works so fully in and through the soul that God's work and the soul's are indistinguishable.[58]

Eckhart articulates Marguerite's insight in terms of his reading of Mary and Martha. Yet even as he understands Martha as worried that Mary will become stuck in the realm of pleasure—a pleasure brought about by Christ's presence—Christ's words to Martha are reinterpreted by Eckhart as a promise that her sister will ultimately achieve the unity of action and contemplation she herself already possesses: "Then Christ answered her, 'Martha, Martha, you are careful, you are worried about many things. One thing is necessary. Mary has chosen the best part, which can never be taken from her.' Christ did not speak these words to Martha to chasten her. Rather, he responded by giving her the comforting message that it would turn out for Mary as she desired."[59] Martha "stood in lordly, well-founded virtue with a free spirit unimpeded by anything." She lived amid things, but not in things, able to perform continual acts of justice in the world even as—or, better, *because*—she stood with God in God's eternal ground. "Hence," Eckhart argues, "she wished for her sister to be put in this same state because she saw that she was not standing firmly. It was a splendid ground out of which she wished that [Mary] might be established in all that is necessary for eternal happiness."[60] Martha fears that her sister will cling to "consolation and sweetness" and hence not attain the heights where she stands;[61] hence Eckhart argues that Christ's words to Martha that Mary has chosen the best part were said "as if to say, 'Cheer up, Martha; this will leave her. The most sublime thing that can happen to a creature shall happen to her: She shall become as happy as you.' "[62]

Eckhart insists that "Martha was so grounded in her being that her activity did not hinder her. Work and activity led her to eternal happiness." Then, in a final turn of the screw of interpretation, he claims that "Mary was a Martha before she became a Mary, for when she sat at the feet of the Lord, she was not Mary."[63] Eckhart returns to Mary and encloses Martha within Mary and Mary within Martha in order to bring into play the stories about Mary Magdalen's life after Christ's death. Only then, after Christ's death, is Mary like her sister Martha and so fully a Martha and fully a Mary. "This is what I call Mary: a well-disciplined body obedient to a wise soul."[64] When the Mary of Luke begins not only to contemplate Christ's sweetness, but also to act out of the ground of her soul, there where she and God are one, then she truly becomes a Martha—and, Eckhart preaches, truly Mary, performing those actions the hagiographical tradition ascribes to Mary Magdalen.

> But afterwards, when she had learned and Christ had ascended to heaven and she received the Holy Spirit, then she really for the first time began to serve. Then she crossed the sea, preached, taught, and became the servant and washerwoman of the disciples. Thus do the saints become saints; not until then do they really begin to practice virtue. For it is then that they gather the treasure of eternal happiness. . . . We find testimony for this in Christ: From the very beginning of God's becoming human and human God, he undertook to achieve our eternal happiness, [continuing at it] to the end, when he died on the cross. There was no part of his body that did not practice its proper virtue.[65]

This Martha Mary preaches and teaches, even as she is a servant and a washerwoman. She is the lowliest of the low and the apostle to the apostles. And hence, Martha and Mary are one with each other and they are one with Christ. For Mary and Martha, as for Christ, there is no part of their bodies that does not share in the work of the divine, which is justice.

Eckhart takes the stories that have been handed down to him—the Lukan passage and its allegorical interpretations, the hagiographies of Mary

Magdalen, perhaps also the stories of the women living around him—and he receives them in a particular time and place, one in which the very act of reception ignites new meanings. He literalizes and allegorizes, makes use of grammar, figuration, and typology; he throws everything he can find at the text to pull out of it what he needs. He names the life he sees around him with the scriptural words he and the men and women to whom he preaches both inherit and transform through the very act of living. He creates a space for life and yet never allows himself or his listeners simply to settle there, for life demands both place and movement, action and contemplation, saying and unsaying. Work—God working in and through human beings—is everything. How can we possibly say, as someone once did to me, that Eckhart, praising Martha and Mary as a Martha, gets it all wrong?

NOTES

A TRIPTYCH

Many thanks to Bob Davis, Ben Dunning, Constance Furey, Mark Jordan, and Stephanie Paulsell for their help with this piece. I also benefited greatly from discussing parts of the Adams material with Carolyn Dinshaw.

1. A dynamo is an electrical generator. In *The Education of Henry Adams*, Adams describes himself as fascinated by the display of dynamos at the Great Exposition held in Paris in 1900. On the one hand, unlike the Virgin, a dynamo extracts power from natural material; on the other, the method of extraction, devised by the human mind, remains both material and mysterious. See Henry Adams, *Novels, Mount Saint Michel, The Education* (New York: Library of America, 1983); and Christopher Perricone, "The Powers of Art: Reflections on 'The Dynamo and the Virgin,'" *Journal of Speculative Philosophy* 5, no. 4 (1991): 256–75. References from *Esther, Mount Saint Michel*, and *The Education of Henry Adams* will be to this edition unless otherwise noted.

2. For more on the variety of ways in which something can be said to be true, see my essays "Acute Melancholia," "Queering the Beguines," and "Practice, Belief, and the Feminist Philosophy of Religion," all included here. For the moment, I am focused on what many if not most Christians mean when they talk about the reality of their religious engagements and the truth of Christian claims, which are ineluctably tied to historical claims. On this see my "Reading as Self-Annihilation," also collected here.

3. I discuss the issue further in the third part of this essay.

4. Gabrielle M. Spiegel has done vital work on the question of historical truth in the Middle Ages. Spiegel, *Romancing the Past: The Rise of Vernacular Prose Historiography in Thirteenth-Century France* (Berkeley: University of California Press, 1995); Spiegel, *The Past as Text: The Theory and Practice of Medieval Historiography* (Baltimore: Johns Hopkins University Press, 1999); and Spiegel, ed., *Practicing History: New Directions in Historical Writing After the Linguistic Turn* (New York: Routledge,

2005.) As medievalists well know, however, historical truth is only one kind of truth and a relatively devalued one within the Christian medieval context. For more on this issue, see Monika Otter, *Inventiones: Fiction and Referentiality in Twelfth-Century English Historical Writing* (Chapel Hill: University of North Carolina Press, 1996); Elizabeth Allen, *False Fables and Exemplary Truth in Later Middle English Literature* (New York: Palgrave, 2005); Catherine Sanok, *Her Life Historical: Exemplarity and Female Saints Lives in Late Medieval England* (Philadelphia: University of Pennsylvania Press, 2007); and Robert Bartlett, *Why Can the Dead Do Such Great Things? Saints and Worshippers from the Martyrs to the Reformation* (Princeton: Princeton University Press, 2013). For wonderful work on related issues as they emerge in the study of visual culture, see Cynthia Hahn, *Portrayed on the Heart: Narrative Effect in Pictorial Lives of Saints from the Tenth Through the Thirteenth Centuries* (Berkeley: University of California Press, 2001); and Hahn, *Strange Beauty: Issues in the Making and Meaning of Reliquaries, 400–ca. 1204* (College Station: Penn State University Press, 2013). For an early discussion of the issue of lying, see Augustine, *Lying* and *Against Lying*, both in Augustine, *Treatises on Various Subjects*, trans. Mary Sarah Muldowney and others, ed. Roy J. Deferrari (Washington, D.C.: Catholic University Press, 1952), 53–110, 125–79. See also Paul J. Griffiths, *Lying: An Augustinian Theology of Duplicity* (Grand Rapids, Mich.: Brazos Press, 2004).

5. For more on this issue, see my "Gender, Agency, and the Divine in Religious Historiography," collected here; and Hollywood, "Saint Paul and The New Man," *Critical Inquiry* 35 (2009): 865–78.

6. In "Reading as Self-Annihilation," collected here, I ask a number of questions that are always in the back of my mind when thinking about critique. Key is the issue of the potential historical contingency of Western conceptions of critique in the face of the historical claims and historical dubiety of much of the Bible. Would the term "criticism" carry such destructive resonance in the Western academy if the Hebrew and Christian Bibles had been more "reliable" documents? To what extent does this unreliability depend on the peculiarly historical claims made by these documents and the traditions that arise from them? Or is it a feature of reason to attack, such that *any* document of faith would have been found wanting?

7. On Adams's view of history see the late historiographical essays, "The Tendency of History," *A Letter to American Teachers of History*, and "The Rule of Phase Applied to History," all of which are collected in Henry Adams, *The Degradation of the Democratic Dogma*, introduction by Brooks Adams (New York: Macmillan, 1919). While many still share the first of Adams's assumptions, the second tends to fall out of sight in contemporary historical and historiographical work, although, as I will argue here, naturalism and empiricism are generally assumed by most historical work.

8. This is true, of course, not only for nineteenth-century American Catholics, but also for Protestant evangelicals and many others across the spectrum of Christianity and at its edges, in Spiritualism and related movements. Positing the childlike character of these forms of religion, as contrasted to the maturity of those ready for atheism,

an assessment often implicit in Adams, is morally, politically, and intellectually inadequate. On Catholicism and the Protestant responses to Catholicism that create the background against which Adams writes, see Jenny Franchot, *Roads to Rome: The Antebellum Protestant Encounter with Catholicism* (Berkeley: University of California Press, 1994). For the fascination with Catholicism at the turn of the last century, and for more on Adams's own complex relationship to religion, see T. J. Jackson Lears, *No Place for Grace: Antimodernism and the Transformation of American Culture, 1880–1920* (New York: Pantheon, 1981). For the varieties of religious experience in eighteenth- and nineteenth-century America, see Ann Taves, *Fits, Trances, and Visions: Experiencing Religion and Explaining Experience from Wesley to James* (Princeton: Princeton University Press, 1999).

9. See Charles Taylor, *A Secular Age* (Cambridge, Mass.: Harvard University Press, 2007). Many of Taylor's arguments in the book have been hotly contested, particularly the notion that the shift in social imaginaries he describes marks the end result of a process of disenchantment. For Taylor's rewriting of Weber's thesis, see *A Secular Age*, but also Michael Warner, Jonathan Van Antwerpen, and Craig Calhoun, eds., *Varieties of Secularism in a Secular Age* (Cambridge, Mass.: Harvard University Press, 2013); and Judith Butler, Jürgen Habermas, Charles Taylor, and Cornell West, *The Power of Religion in the Public Sphere* (New York: Columbia University Press, 2011). For a very different account of secularism, one that contests some of Taylor's fundamental claims, see Talal Asad, *Formations of the Secular: Christianity, Islam, Modernity* (Stanford: Stanford University Press, 2003); Charles Hirschkind and David Scott, *Powers of the Secular Modern: Talal Asad and His Interlocutors* (Stanford: Stanford University Press, 2006); and Talal Asad, Wendy Brown, Judith Butler, and Saba Mahmood, *Is Critique Secular? Blasphemy, Injury, and Free Speech* (New York: Fordham University Press, 2013).

10. My work here is deeply indebted to, but slightly diverges from, that of Robert Orsi. In a series of important essays Orsi argues for the necessity of an "abundant history" or "abundant empiricism" that is able to contend with the "real presence" of spirits, saints, gods, demons, and ancestors in the lives of religious people. Citing important work by the anthropologists Stanley Tambiah and Gananeth Obeyesekere and the historian Dipesh Chakrabarty, among others, Orsi points to the necessity of finding "a vocabulary for the kinds of mental *and* bodily processes that go on among humans in the company of each other and of their gods and other special beings." "But belief," Orsi insists in another essay, "has nothing to do with it." If, by belief, we mean the mere assent to a proposition, Orsi is certainly right. However, I would contend that belief means much more than this and that it is always in play in the kinds of religious experiences to which Orsi points. He goes on to explain that he is interested in thinking about how "the really real comes to be so" and in moving beyond the claim that an experience is real for the one who undergoes it to find "presence, existence, and power in space and time." This leads him to ask how these presences become "as real as guns and stones and bread, and then how the real in turns acts as an agent for itself in history." Part of what is at work here is the belief that one's experience is not

imaginary or fictional or mistaken, but rather corresponds to something ontologically independent of the one having the experience. In other words, it entails belief, although of a much more robust kind than that which Orsi eschews as the focus of religious studies. In rejecting the category of belief, I worry that Orsi renders it impossible to deal with the issues of deception and conflicting experiences that I point to in a number of the essays included here. For a similar worry, see Stephen Prothero, "Belief Unbracketed: A Case for the Religion Scholar to Reveal More of Where He or She Is Coming From," *Harvard Divinity School Bulletin* 32, no. 2 (2004); Thomas Kselman, "How Abundant Is 'Abundant History,'" *Historically Speaking* 9, no. 7 (September/October 2008): 16–18; and Elizabeth A. Pritchard, "Seriously, What Does 'Taking Religion Seriously' Mean?," *Journal of the American Academy of Religion* 78, no. 4 (2010): 1087–1111. For the first citation from Orsi, see Robert A. Orsi, "Belief," *Material Religion* 7 (2011): 15. For the second two, see Orsi, "When 2 + 2 = 5," *American Scholar* 76 (Spring 2007): 45. See also Orsi, "Is the Study of Lived Religion Irrelevant to the World We Live In?," *Journal for the Scientific Study of Religion* 42 (2003): 169–74; Orsi, *Between Heaven and Earth: The Religious Worlds People Make and the Scholars Who Study Them* (Princeton: Princeton University Press, 2004); Orsi, "Abundant Religion: Marian Apparitions as Alternative Modernity," *Historically Speaking* 9, no. 7 (2008): 12–16; Orsi, "The Problem of the Holy," in *The Cambridge Companion to Religious Studies*, ed. Robert A. Orsi (Cambridge: Cambridge University Press, 2011), 84–105; and Orsi, "I'm Starting to Think This Is Not About the Catholics," *Fides et Historia* 44, no. 2 (2012): 80–83. For a captivating attempt to think with Orsi that also moves in slightly different directions from him, see Constance M. Furey, "Troubling Presence," *Historically Speaking* 9, no. 7 (2008): 22–25. For important work on these issues from the standpoint of Santería, see Aisha M. Beliso-De Jesús, *Electric Santería: Racial and Sexual Assemblages of Transnational Religion* (New York: Columbia University Press, 2015).

11. Adams himself struggled with and against precisely this theory. See Lears, *No Place of Grace*, 262–97.

12. See also Constance M. Furey, "Relational Virtue: Anne Bradstreet, Edward Taylor, and Puritan Marriage," *Journal of Medieval and Early Modern Studies* 42 (2012): 201–24; Furey, "Body, Society, and Subjectivity in Religious Studies," *Journal of the American Academy of Religion* 80 (2012): 7–33; and Furey, "Sexuality," in *The Cambridge Companion to Christian Mysticism*, ed. Amy Hollywood and Patricia Z. Beckman (Cambridge: Cambridge University Press, 2012), 328–40.

13. Pritchard, "Seriously, What Does 'Taking Religion Seriously' Mean?" Mahmood perhaps does not appear because she offers an account of critique in the opening of her book, one to which I will return.

14. See Robert Orsi, "Snakes Alive: Resituating the Moral in the Study of Religion," in *Between Heaven and Earth*, 177–204. Unlike most of Orsi's work, this essay does not depend on his own engagements, historical and ethnographic, with religious communities, but is a critical engagement with the journalistic study of snake handling done by Dennis Covington. Orsi's larger point is a methodological and ethical one

about the study of religion and liberal attitudes toward religion endemic to the academy and press in the United States. See Dennis Covington, *Salvation on Sand Mountain: Snake Handling and Redemption in Southern Appalachia* (Reading, Mass.: Addison-Wesley, 1995). For Orsi in a more critically engaged set of interactions with those he studies, see Robert Orsi, *Thank You St. Jude: Women's Devotion to the Patron Saint of Lost Causes* (New Haven: Yale University Press, 1998).

15. For a similar defense of Orsi against the charges raised by Pritchard and Prothero, see Tyler Roberts, *Encountering Religion: Responsibility and Criticism After Secularism* (New York: Columbia University Press, 2013), 111–18.

16. For an extension of part of the discussion that took place that day, see Asad, Brown, Butler, and Mahmood, *Is Critique Secular?* As the authors note, they do not try to answer the question directly.

17. For this assumption rendered explicit, see Wendy Brown, "Introduction," in *Is Critique Secular?*; and Stathis Gourgouris, "Detranscendentalizing the Secular," *Public Culture* 20, no. 3 (2008): 445. Saba Mahmood robustly argues against Gourgouris in "Is Critique Secular?: A Symposium at UC Berkeley," *Public Culture* 20, no. 3 (2008): 450. The problem with Brown's account, which does include the possibility that the notion of the secular might itself require critique, is that it identifies critique only with the philosophical deployment of the term in the tradition running from Kant to Marx and Critical Theory. As I suggest here and in a number of the essays included here, there is more to critique than this truncated, albeit essential, history. Although many argue that Kant introduced something essentially new with his argument that everything we take to be the case can and ought to be subjected to the critical faculty of reason and hence that tradition be granted no authority, I am interested in an alternative reading of Kant in which his recourse, especially in the moral and aesthetic philosophy, to storytelling, example, and analogy is exposed and the impossibility of the kind of radical critique he demands laid bare. This does not, I very much hope, put me in with neotraditionalists like Alasdair MacIntyre, for on my Derridean reading, tradition always involves both a passing down *and* change, even revolutionary change. To pretend that we can exist without that which is handed down—at the most fundamental level, the care by which an infant is kept alive and brought into a community—is to deny the conditions of life, and while any aspect of tradition may be subject to critique, we can't live off critique alone. My thanks to R. Lanier Anderson and others at the Stanford Humanities Center for helping me articulate this point.

18. Hence in Brown's account, Kant employed critique to limit reason's claims and to ensure that a properly chastened reason, rather than religion, will be the source of authority in intellectual and moral pursuits. What this misses is that for Kant, even a properly chastened reason *needs* religion, although one that lies "within the boundaries of mere reason." For Kant, religion's authority depends on reason's claims, yet the power to activate the will in the moral life depends, in obscure ways, on aesthetic and religious impulses. Hence the vexed role of enthusiasm across Kant's corpus, a subject on which I am currently working. See Brown, "Introduction," in *Is Critique Secular?*

19. Whether this is good, bad, or simply inevitable is the subject of heated debate. The provenance of the move in very different and politically diametrically opposed thinkers, Carl Schmitt and Walter Benjamin, demonstrates this clearly. The bibliography on the topic is vast and growing, but for an introduction to some of the relevant issues, see Hent de Vries and Lawrence E. Sullivan, eds., *Political Theologies: Public Religion in a Post-Secular World* (New York: Fordham University Press, 2006). The volume has the advantage of understanding that Carl Schmitt did not invent "political theology," nor is his usage of the phrase really about theology; instead, Schmitt uses the term to describe the putatively hidden theological source of secular power.

20. For a specific and compelling example, see Constance M. Furey, "Discernment as Critique in Teresa of Avila and Erasmus of Rotterdam," *Exemplaria: Medieval, Early Modern, Theory* 26 (2014): 254–72.

21. For compelling examples of Christian and Jewish activism from the left, see Jeffrey Stout, *Blessed Are the Organized: Grassroots Democracy in America* (Princeton: Princeton University Press, 2010). For Stout, however, it is essential that anyone participating in democracy be willing and able to make explicit their positions in terms available to all those operating within that democracy. My question is, who determines what constitutes reason? Who determines the terms in which participation, reason, or explicitness are understood? See also Stout's important book, *Democracy and Tradition* (Princeton: Princeton University Press, 2004).

22. The crucial text is, of course, Augustine, *City of God*, trans. Henry Bettenson (New York: Penguin, 2003).

23. From this perspective, the robust self-confidence of religion's contemporary despisers might easily be taken for idolatrous fideism.

24. For the limits of a religious nation's knowledge about its own and other traditions, see Amy Hollywood, "On Understanding Everything: General Education, Liberal Education, and the Study of Religion," *Proceedings of the Modern Language Association* 126, no. 2 (2011): 460–66.

25. Roberts brilliantly takes on scholars as diverse—although united on the point of religion's locative nature—as Donald Wiebe, Ivan Strenski, Russell McCutcheon, and Bruce Lincoln. See Roberts, *Encountering Religion*, 36–82.

26. Ibid., 26–27. Roberts cites J. Z. Smith, "The Wobbling Pivot," in *Map Is Not Territory* (Chicago: University of Chicago Press, 1978), 100.

27. Roberts, *Encountering Religion*, 27. Roberts here cites Smith, *Map Is Not Territory*, 101.

28. Roberts, *Encountering Religion*, 30.

29. Ibid., 41.

30. See, for example, Rowan Williams, *The Wound of Knowledge*, 2nd ed. (Cambridge: Cowley, 1990); Williams, *On Christian Theology* (Oxford: Blackwell, 2000); and Williams, *Writing in the Dust* (Grand Rapids, Mich.: Eerdmans, 2002). I am not myself sure that Williams's emphasis on epistemic humility embraces excess and destabilizes order in quite the way Roberts suggests.

31. Roberts, *Encountering Religion*, 158, 161.

32. Ibid., 168.

33. A number of secularist critics of religion—some of those with the biggest audiences, like Daniel Dennett or Katha Pollitt, but also those internal to religious studies like Russell McCutcheon—want to bypass this entire historical narrative, both in terms of the history of antireligious critique within the modern West and in terms of the role of religion itself within that critique. For these critics there are scientific grounds for rejecting religious belief, and modern scientific reasoning owes nothing to Western— or any other—religion. Despite its ubiquity, this is an exceptionally hard argument to make. I cannot here demonstrate all of the difficulties involved, but merely point to the fact that for innumerable modern philosophers who argue against either fanaticism specifically or Christianity and religion more generally, Christianity plays a key role in the constitution of modern rationality.

34. Saba Mahmood, *Politics of Piety: The Islamic Revival and the Feminist Subject* (Princeton: Princeton University Press, 2005), 36–37. Michel Foucault's and Judith Butler's accounts of critique arguably lead to a position very close to Mahmood's. At their most explicit, they both define critique, like the rationalist critics of religion I describe above, as the critique of authoritative traditions and norms. What they contest is the presumption that rationally based arguments or claims to authority can escape the dynamics of power. They go on, however, to suggest that critique is a virtue in ways that bring their arguments close to that of Mahmood. See Michel Foucault, "What Is Critique?," in *The Politics of Truth*, ed. Sylvère Lotringer and Lysa Hochroth (New York: Semiotext[e], 1997); and Judith Butler, "What Is Critique? An Essay on Foucault's Virtue," in *The Political: Readings in Continental Philosophy*, ed. David Ingram (London: Basil Blackwell, 2002).

35. Roberts does include discussion of work that draws on the Christian theological tradition, including a generous reading of some of my own previous work. But when he turns toward the kind of responsive criticism in which he is interested, he names the project philosophical and rests his account on the work of de Vries (a philosopher of religion and theologian), Santner (a literary critic and theorist), and Cavell (a philosopher). The work on Santner and Cavell is compelling. My real problem with this part of the book, as I will show, is less with Roberts than with de Vries and the ways in which Roberts relies on and allows de Vries to ground his constructive philosophical project.

36. Roberts, *Encountering Religion*, 168. Roberts here cites Hent de Vries, *Philosophy and the Turn to Religion* (Baltimore: Johns Hopkins University Press, 1999), 287; and de Vries, *Religion and Violence* (Baltimore: Johns Hopkins University Press, 2002), 177, 386, 398. Also relevant to this discussion is Hent de Vries, *Minimal Theologies: Critiques of Secular Reason in Adorno and Levinas* (Baltimore: Johns Hopkins University Press, 2005).

37. For me the crucial text on tradition is Jacques Derrida, *Archive Fever: A Freudian Impression*, trans. Eric Prenowitz (Chicago: University of Chicago Press, 1996). See also Amy Hollywood, "Tribute to Derrida," in *Saintly Influences: Texts for Edith Wyschogrod*, ed. Eric Boynton and Martin Kavka (New York: Fordham University Press, 1999), 150–60.

38. My reading focuses on Jacques Derrida, "Signature Event Context," in *Margins of Philosophy*, trans. Alan Bass (Chicago: University of Chicago Press, 1984), although one could go to multiple sites in Derrida's work.

39. According to Roberts, for de Vries reading Derrida, responsibility demands a paradoxical "forgetting without forgetting," which "is a function both of the particular, unique context in which it takes place (which is thus dependent on historical chains of ideas and circumstances) *and* of a response, by this speaker or this actor here and now, to the singularizing imperative of the absolute. It is a kind of crossing or pivot between absolute origin and history, autonomy and heteronomy." Roberts, *Encountering Religion*, 167. But of course, for Derrida there is no absolute origin and what is being described are two moments of singularity, two historical moments that are both irreducible to their historicity. This does not make them sites of radical autonomy or originarity, but instead always implicated in the general movement of the particular.

40. As Andrew Louth usefully reminds us, the practice is biblical. See Andrew Louth, "Apophatic and Cataphatic Theology," in Hollywood and Beckman, *The Cambridge Companion to Christian Mysticism*, 137–46.

41. The key texts are "Différance," in *Margins of Philosophy*; "How to Avoid Speaking: Denials," "On an Apocalyptic Tone Newly Adopted in Philosophy," and "Post-Scriptum: Aporias, Ways and Voices," all collected in Harold Coward and Toby Foshay, eds., *Derrida and Negative Theology* (Albany: State University of New York Press, 1992); and "Passions" and "*Khora*," collected together with "Post-Scriptum" in *On the Name*, trans. Thomas DuToit and David Wood (Stanford: Stanford University Press, 1995).

42. For a wonderfully Derridean—and more importantly Morrisonian—take on the liveness of tradition and what renders it dead, see Toni Morrison, *The Nobel Lecture in Literature, 1993* (New York: Knopf, 1994).

43. See, for example, Beliso-De Jesús's discussion of "co-presences" in *Electric Santería*.

44. As Roberts notes, Santner also turns to what might be called Jewish theology, in particular the work of Franz Rosenzweig. See Eric Santner, *On the Psychotheology of Everyday Life* (Chicago: University of Chicago Press, 2001).

45. This is the space, then, out of which the possibility for critical engagement with systemic evil and injustice emerges. To know that we are being told lies and that the tradition (or a part of the tradition or one of the many traditions) in which we live is unjust requires a hold on the real that has also been, in some way, given to us. On my reading, this is the space in which the work of Judith Butler dwells. For my discussion of Butler, see "Perfomativity, Citationality, Ritualization," included here. See also Judith Butler, *Undoing Gender* (New York: Routledge, 2004); Butler, *Giving An Account of Oneself* (New York: Fordham University Press, 2005); and Butler, "Afterword," in *Bodily Citations: Religion and Judith Butler*, ed. Ellen Armour and Susan St. Ville (New York: Columbia University Press, 2006), 276–89.

46. Burke Wilkinson, *Uncommon Clay: The Life and Works of Augustus Saint Gaudens* (New York: Harcourt, Brace, Jovanovich, 1985), 235–36.

47.   Ibid. Yet Wilkinson refers to Michelangelo's Sistine Madonna—does he mean the Raphael Sistine Madonna?—"and the Sistine Madonna drawing her seamless toga about the Christ Child." For more on Saint Gaudens and the monument, see Lincoln Kirstein and Jerry L. Thompson, *Memorial to a Marriage: An Album on the Saint-Gaudens Memorial in Rock Creek Cemetery Commissioned by Henry Adams in Honor of His Wife, Marian Hooper Adams* (New York: Metropolitan Museum of Art, 1989); Kathryn Greenthal, *Augustus Saint-Gaudens: Master Sculpture* (New York: Metropolitan Museum of Art, 1985), esp. 133–35; Catherine Gaich and Anne Dopffer, curators, *Augustus Saint-Gaudens, 1848–1907: A Master of American Sculpture* (Toulouse: Musée des Augustins, 1999); and Henry J. Duffy and John H. Dryfhout, curators, *Augustus Saint-Gaudens: American Sculpture of the Gilded Age* (Washington, D.C.: Trust for Museum Exhibitions, 2003), esp. 78–79.

48.   Colleen McDannell, *Material Christianity: Religion and Popular Culture in America* (New Haven: Yale University Press, 1995), 123.

49.   These are the first, third, and fourth verses of the song as it appears on Timeless Truths Online Library, s.v., "Rock of Ages" by Augustus M. Toplady, http://library.timeless truths.org/music/Rock_of_Ages/.

50.   For references and a discussion of the images, see my essay " 'That Glorious Slit,' " reprinted here.

51.   McDannell, *Material Christianity*, 128. On the familially oriented form of Christianity rejected by Henry Adams, see also Lears, *No Place of Grace*.

52.   Henry had the Memorial placed there presumably because Rock Creek Park was a favorite place for Henry and Clover to ride horseback. They went every day when they were in Washington.

53.   See David F. Musto, " 'Heart's Blood': Henry Adams' *Esther* and Wife Clover," *New England Quarterly* 71, no. 2 (1998): 266–81.

54.   See Duco Van Oostrum, "Men Speaking for Women and American Literature: The Case of Henry Adams' Alias Frances Snow Compton," in *Rewriting the Dream: Reflections on the American Literary Canon* (Amsterdam: Rodopi, 1992), 75–97.

55.   It is almost as if Henry wished for his father-in-law's death and hoped it would lead Clover to turn more fully to him. Yet as I will suggest, there are also indications in the novel that Adams feared the full force of a woman's desire. For related comments, see Lears, *No Place of Grace*, 270–72.

56.   In addition to Lears, see Natalie Fuehrer Taylor, "The Flowers of Freedom; Or, the New Tyranny: Science, Art, and Religion in Henry Adams' *Esther*," in *A Political Companion to Henry Adams*, ed. Natalie Fuehrer Taylor (Lexington: Kentucky University Press, 2011), 111–25.

57.   On the novel of doubt, see R. L. Wolf, *Gains and Losses: Novels of Faith and Doubt in Victorian England* (New York: Garland, 1977); Elisabeth Jay, *The Religion of the Heart: Anglican Evangelicalism and the Nineteenth-Century Novel* (Oxford: Oxford University Press, 1979); Jay, *Faith and Doubt in Victorian Britain* (New York: Garland, 1986); and David Jasper and T. R. Wright, eds., *The Critical Spirit and the Will to Believe: Essays in Nineteenth-Century Literature and Religion* (New York: Saint

Martin's Press, 1999), especially the essays by Stephen Pricket and Rosemary Ashton. For a series of biographical studies dealing with crises of faith as represented in a variety of genres, see David Hempton, *Evangelical Disenchantment: Nine Portraits of Faith and Doubt* (New Haven: Yale University Press, 2008).

58. By the late nineteenth century, Niagara Falls was already closely associated with both the religious and the romantic sublime. Harriet Beecher Stowe describes in a letter a visit to the Falls in 1834: "Let me tell you, if I can, what is unutterable. I did not once think whether it was high or low; whether it roared or didn't roar; whether it equaled my expectations or not. My mind whirled off, it seemed to me, in a new, strange world. It seemed unearthly, like the strange, dim images in the Revelation. I thought of the great white throne; the rainbow around it; the throne in sight like unto an emerald; and oh! that beautiful water rising like moonlight, falling as the soul sinks when it dies, to rise refined, spiritualized, and pure; that rainbow, breaking out, trembling, fading, and again coming like a beautiful spirit walking the waters. Oh, it is lovelier than it is great; it is like the Mind that made it: great, but so veiled in beauty that we gaze without terror. I felt as if I could have gone over with the waters; it would be so beautiful a death; there would be no fear in it. I felt the rock tremble under me with a sort of joy. I was so maddened that I could have gone too, if it had gone." Annie Fields, ed., *The Life and Letters of Harriet Beecher Stowe* (Boston: Houghton Mifflin, 1897), 89–90; cited by Brett Grainger, "The Vital Landscape: Evangelical Religious Practice and the Culture of Nature in America, 1790–1870" (PhD diss., Harvard University, 2014), 152–53. See also Elizabeth R. McKinsey, *Niagara Falls: Icon of the American Sublime* (Cambridge: Cambridge University Press, 1985); and Patrick McGreevey, *Imagining Niagara: The Meaning and Making of Niagara Falls* (Amherst: University of Massachusetts Press, 1994).

59. Adams, *Esther*, in *Novels, Mont Saint Michel, and the Education*, 330.

60. Ibid., 331.

61. Ibid.

62. Ibid., 333.

63. Ibid.

64. Ibid. Although I don't know if Henry Adams was aware of this, the tiger is associated with Guan Yin. In one story about her, a tiger takes her to a dark realm of suffering, which she turned into a paradise with her presence. In another, Guan Yin is said not to have died, but to have been transported to heaven by a tiger. An important story about the Buddha tells of his encounter with a hungry tigress, who is about to eat her young. The Buddha offers himself to be eaten to spare the tiger cubs. For an insightful analysis of this and other *Jataka* stories that entail the Buddha's self-sacrifice, dismemberment, and death (also crucial features in the stories about Guan Yin), see Reiko Ohnuma, *Head, Eyes, Flesh, and Blood: Giving Away the Body in Indian Buddhist Literature* (New York: Columbia University Press, 2007). Christianity is not the only religious tradition that expects bloody self-sacrifice on the part of its heroes.

65. Lears, *No Place of Grace*, 271–72.

66. Adams, *Esther*, 314.

67. Ibid.

68. Ibid., 320.

69. Ibid., 321.

70. Ibid., 225.

71. Ibid., 335.

72. Lears points to a third religious possibility in the novel, one that Henry does not fully explore but that is expressed by the artist, Wharton, commissioned to create the art for a the new church where Hazard is minister. Disgusted with the merely decorative in art, Wharton wants to place a Madonna at the heart of the church. "The place has no heart," Wharton insists, "To me religion is passion. To reach Heaven you must go through hell, and carry its marks on your face and figure." This is also, it should be noted, what Wharton calls Nirvana. For Lears, religion as passion recurs in Henry's *Mont Saint-Michel and Chartres*, with the Virgin at its center. Yet although more sensual, passionate, and real, this conception of religion also threatens annihilation and so remains problematic for Adams. As I will suggest below, I think that sensual desire is also in evidence elsewhere in the novel. See Lears, *No Place of Grace*, 272, 288–97.

73. Adams, *Esther*, 262.

74. From a letter Ellen Hooper Gurney wrote to a friend describing Clover that summer. Cited in Otto Friedrich, *Clover* (New York: Simon and Schuster, 1979), 316. See also Eugenia Kaledin, *The Education of Mrs. Henry Adams* (Philadelphia: Temple University Press, 1981); and Natalie Dykstra, *Clover Adams: A Gilded and Heartbreaking Life* (New York: Houghton Mifflin Harcourt, 2012). The mystery of Clover's death has inspired much speculation, including in novelistic form.

75. Adams, *Esther*, 264.

76. Ibid., 264–65.

77. It was when untied from human connections, as Esther is after her father's death, that Wharton describes a pathological experience of unreality not unlike that which overtakes Esther. Wharton came from nothing, but his talent was discovered and money collected to send him to Europe. As he tells Esther and her friend Catherine, "It was after I had been some years at work and had got already a little reputation among Americans, that I was at my worst. Nothing seemed real. What earned me my first success was an attempt I made to paint the strange figures and fancies which possessed me. I studied nothing but the most extravagant subjects. For a time nothing would satisfy me but to draw from models at moments of intense suffering and at the instant of death." In pursuit of such subjects, he encounters a woman "suffering from an overdose of arsenic." She was a splendid model, an actress disgusted with life, who survived her own suicide attempt. Wharton marries her and she comes close to destroying his life as well as her own. Only after living through this deathlike passion does Wharton begin to "adore purity and repose," but his own experience renders it impossible for him to "get hold" of his ideal. Only innocence regained could enable it; yet only the experience of passion, destroyer of innocence, allows him to discover the ideal. See Adams, *Esther*, 251–52. I will discuss the passage further in the third part of this essay.

78. Ibid., 265.

79. Ibid.

80. Ibid., 271–72. One can't help but think here of Henry's dislike for the idea that Clover's photographs, often of intimate scenes with family and friends, be published. Following his wishes, they were not made public during either of their lifetimes.

81. Ibid., 331.

82. George Monteiro, ed., *The Correspondence of Henry James and Henry Adams, 1877–1914* (Baton Rouge: Louisiana State University Press, 1992), 78–79.

83. Cited in ibid., 32.

84. Cited in ibid., 89n2. Adams suffered a stroke in 1912 and in much of his correspondence after his recovery talks about "this queer mad world," including in a letter to James from 1913. See ibid., 87.

85. Ibid., 88–89. The letter belies James's own melancholia, although only someone so beset, I think, could write what James does here.

86. Hal Foster, *The Return of the Real* (Cambridge, Mass.: MIT Press, 1996), 168.

87. See Allen Young, *The Harmony of Illusions: Inventing Post-Traumatic Stress Disorder* (Princeton: Princeton University Press, 1995); Ruth Leys, *Trauma: A Genealogy* (Chicago: University of Chicago Press, 2000); Roger Lockhurst, *The Trauma Question* (New York: Routledge, 2008); and Didier Fassin and Richard Rechtman, *The Empire of Trauma: An Inquiry Into the Condition of Victimhood*, trans. Rachel Gomme (Princeton: Princeton University Press, 2009).

88. Judith Herman, *Trauma and Recovery* (New York: Basic Books, 1992). This position is stated briefly in Herman and becomes a central issue in the literature concerning trauma, testimony, and witness. See especially Shoshana Felman and Dori Laub, *Testimony: Crises of Witnessing in Literature, Psychoanalysis and History* (New York: Routledge, 1992); Nancy K. Miller and Jason Tougaw, eds., *Extremities: Trauma, Testimony, and Community* (Champagne-Urbana: University of Illinois Press, 2002); and Gert Buelens, Sam Durrant, and Robert Eaglestone, eds., *The Future of Trauma Theory: Contemporary Literary and Cultural Criticism* (New York: Routledge, 2014).

89. For a critique of this move, in which political and ethical claims depend increasingly on traumatic victimization, see Wendy Brown, *States of Injury: Power and Freedom in Late Modernity* (Princeton: Princeton University Press, 1995); and Ruth Leys, *From Guilt to Shame: Auschwitz and After* (Princeton: Princeton University Press, 2007).

90. For a compelling account of one case, see Lawrence Wright, *Remembering Satan: A Tragic Case of Recovered Memory* (New York: Vintage, 1995). See also Debbie Nathan and Michael Snediker, *Satan's Silence: Ritual Abuse and the Making of a Modern American Witch Hunt* (New York: Basic Books, 1995); and David Frankfurter, *Evil Incarnate: Rumors of Demonic Conspiracy and Satanic Abuse in History* (Princeton: Princeton University Press, 2008).

91. For the English translation of *Fragments* and a riveting analysis of the case, see Stefan Maechler, *The Wilkomirski Affair: A Study of Biographical Truth* (New York: Schocken, 2001). See also Amy Hungerford, *The Holocaust of Texts: Genocide, Literature, and Personification* (Chicago: University of Chicago Press, 2003), 98–121;

Anne Whitehead, *Trauma Fiction* (Edinburgh: Edinburgh University Press, 2004), 30–47; Andrew S. Gross and Michael J. Hofman, "Memory, Authority, and Identity: Holocaust Studies in Light of the Wilkomirski Debate," *Biography* 27 (2004): 25–47; Michael Bernard-Donals, *Forgetful Memory: Representation and Remembrance in the Wake of the Holocaust* (Albany: State University of New York Press, 2009), 81–98; Timothy D. Neale, "'... the credentials that would rescue me': Trauma and the Fraudulent Survivor," *Holocaust and Genocide* 24 (2010): 431–48; and Sally Miller, "Fantasy, Empathy, and Desire: Binjamin Wilkomirski's *Fragments* and Bernhard Schlink's *The Reader*," *Modernism/modernity* 20 (2013): 45–58. This is only a fraction of the work recently done on Wilkomirski's text and his "case."

92. Cathy Caruth describes trauma in terms of "unclaimed experience." Anne-Lise François offers a reading of "uncounted experience" that attempts to pull the idea away from the emphasis on trauma. Patricia Dailey writes about "unlived experience" in relationship to Christian mysticism. Like François and Dailey, I want to wrest the notion of the unspeakable and the unnamable away from its recent identification with trauma. I am less sure how to think about this in terms of experience. See Cathy Caruth, *Unclaimed Experience: Trauma, Narrative, and History* (Baltimore: Johns Hopkins University Press, 1996); Anne-Lise François, *Open Secrets: The Literature of Uncounted Experience* (Stanford: Stanford University Press, 2008); and Patricia Dailey, *Promised Bodies: Time, Language, and Corporeality in Medieval Women's Mystical Texts* (New York: Columbia University Press, 2013), esp. 79–82.

93. See also Janice Haaken, *Pillar of Salt: Gender, Memory, and the Perils of Looking Back* (New Brunswick, N.J.: Rutgers University Press, 1998).

94. Dominick LaCapra, *Writing History, Writing Trauma* (Baltimore: Johns Hopkins University Press, 2001), 23. See also Naomi Mandel, *Against the Unspeakable: Complicity, the Holocaust, and Slavery in America* (Charlottesville: University of Virginia Press, 2006); and Michael S. Roth, *Memory, Trauma, and History: Essays on Living with the Past* (New York: Columbia University Press, 2012).

95. LaCapra, *Writing History*, 23.

96. Ibid., 23–24.

97. Much of the contemporary theoretical discourse and practice surrounding trauma or, more clinically in recent years, Post-Traumatic Stress Disorder has its origins in work done during the nineteenth century on hysteria. Although in the United States hysteria disappears as a clinical phenomenon, many—although certainly not all—of its symptoms appear under the new heading of PTSD. See Herman, *Trauma and Recover*; Leys, *Trauma: A Genealogy*; and John Fletcher, *Freud and the Scene of Trauma* (New York: Fordham University Press, 2013).

98. The bibliography here is vast, but for a beginning, see Felice Lifshitz, "Beyond Positivism and Genre: 'Hagiographical' Texts as Historical Narrative," *Viator* 25 (1994): 95–113; and Thomas Head, ed., *Medieval Hagiography: A Compilation* (New York: Garland, 2000). For the idea of "living saints," see Gabriella Zarri, "Living Saints: A Typology of Female Sanctity in the Early Sixteenth Century," in *Women and Religion in Medieval and Renaissance Italy*, ed. Daniel Bornstein and Roberto Rusconi

(Chicago: University of Chicago Press, 1992). On the particular issues surrounding hagiographies about women, see my "Feminist Studies of Christian Spirituality" and "Inside Out: Beatrice of Nazareth and Her Hagiographer," both included here, and the literature I cite in those essays.

99. James of Vitry, author of the *Life of Marie of Oignies*, was an Augustinian canon from the Low Countries who went on to become bishop of Acre and a cardinal in the Roman Curia. Hence his authority had some weight for Thomas and for his audience.

100. Thomas of Cantimpré, *The Life of Christina the Astonishing*, in Thomas of Cantimpré, *The Collected Saints Lives: Christina the Astonishing, Lutgard of Aywières, Margaret of Ypres and Abbott John of Cantimpré*, ed. Barbara Newman and Margot King (Turnhout: Brepols, 2008), prologue 1, 127–28. Thomas cites James of Vitry, *The Life of Marie of Oignies*, prologue 8. An English translation is available in *Marie of Oignies: Mother of Salvation*, ed. Anneke Mulder-Bakke (Turnhout: Brepols, 2006). For the Latin of the *Life of Christina the Astonishing*, see *Acta Sanctorum*, ed. J. Bolland and others, 3rd ed. (Paris: Palmé, 1863–1925), 24 July 5:637–60. There is now a critical edition of James *Life of Marie of Oignies* and Thomas's *Supplement* to that *Life*. See James of Vitry, *Vitae Mariae Oigniacensis*, ed. R. B. E. Huygens (Turnhout: Brepols, 2012).

101. Thomas of Cantimpré, *Life of Christina*, prologue, 128. Translation slightly modified.

102. See especially Barbara Newman, "Possessed by the Spirit: Devout Women, Demoniacs, and the Apostolic Life in the Thirteenth Century," *Speculum* 73 (1998): 733–70. The long and complex article addresses numerous texts and stories about obsessed, possessed women. Only the final pages of the essay focus on Christina, esp. 763–70. As Newman recounts, early-twentieth-century readers of the *Life* tended to dismiss it as unhistorical "romancing." Yet while Newman acknowledges that we can never know the "real Christina," she goes on to offer a historical reconstruction of what she might have been like. For early-twentieth-century readings, including the charge of "romancing," see Simone Roisin, "La methode hagiographique de Thomas de Cantimpré," in *Miscellanea historica in honorem Alberti de Meyer*, vol. 1 (Louvain: Bibliothèque de l'Université, 1946), 553; and Herbert Thurston, "Christine of Saint Trond," in *Surprising Mystics*, ed. J. H. Crehan (London: Burns and Oates 1955), 149. Both cited by Newman, "Possessed by the Spirit," 764.

103. Although it does not emerge in her essay about possession, Barbara Newman shares my interest. See, for example, Barbara Newman, "The Artifice of Eternity: Speaking of Heaven in Three Medieval Poems," *Religion and Literature* 37 (2005): 1–24.

104. Ibid., 131.

105. Robert Sweetman, "Christine of Saint-Trond's Preaching Apostolate: Thomas of Cantimpré's Hagiographical Method Revisited," *Vox Benedictina* 9 (1992): 67–97. See also Robert Sweetman, "Thomas of Cantimpré: Performative Reading and Pastoral Care," in *Performance and Transformation: New Approaches to Late Medieval Spirituality*, ed. Mary Suydam and Joanna Ziegler (New York: Saint Martin's Press, 1999), 133–67. See also John Coakely, "Thomas of Cantimpré and Female Sanctity," in *History in the Comic Mode: Medieval Communities and the Matter of Person*, ed.

Rachel Fulton and Bruce W. Holsinger (New York: Columbia University Press, 2007); and Rachel Jean Dorothy Smith, "Exemplarity and its Limits in the Hagiographical Corpus of Thomas of Cantimpré (PhD diss., Harvard University, 2012).

106. For another argument about the divisions implicit in the text, see Margot King, "The Sacramental Witness of Christina *Mirabilis*: The Mystic Growth of a Fool for Christ's Sake," in *Peace Weavers*, vol. 2, *Medieval Religious Women*, ed. John A. Nichols and Lillian Thomas Shank (Kalamazoo, Mich.: Cistercian Publications, 1987), 145–64.

107. For references, see Caroline Walker Bynum, *Jesus as Mother: Studies in the Spirituality of the High Middle Ages* (Berkeley: University of California Press, 1982), 170–262; and Beverly Mayne Kienzle and Pamela Walker, eds., *Women Preachers and Prophets Through Two Millennia of Christianity* (Berkeley: University of California Press, 1998).

108. See Newman, "Possessed by the Spirit," 763–70.

109. Thomas, *Life of Christina*, nn. 26 and 37, pp. 142 and 147. Cited by Newman, "Possessed by the Spirit," 764.

110. For the photographs, see Georges Didi-Huberman, *The Invention of Hysteria: Charcot and the Photographic Iconography of Salpêtrière*, trans. Alisa Hart (Cambridge, Mass.: MIT Press, 2003).

111. Thomas, of course, does not put it that way. For the reference, see Newman, "Possessed by the Spirit," 765.

112. Ibid., 763.

113. See Roland Barthes, "The Reality Effect," in *The Rustle of Language*, trans. Richard Howard (New York: Hill and Wang, 1986), 141–49; and Amy Hollywood, *Sensible Ecstasy: Mysticism, Sexual Difference, and the Demands of History* (Chicago: University of Chicago Press, 2002), 36–59.

114. For the parallels between the *Life of Christina* and those of the desert fathers and virgin martyrs, see Newman, "Possessed by the Spirit"; and Jennifer N. Brown, *Three Women of Liège: A Critical Edition and Commentary on the Middle English Lives of Elizabeth of Spalbeek, Christina Mirabilis and Marie d'Oignies* (Turnhout: Brepols, 2008).

115. On reading the mystic or the demoniac as hysteric, see my discussions in *Sensible Ecstasy*, 244–47.

116. Jean Martin Charcot, *La foi qui guérit* (Paris: Aux Bureaux du Progrés Médical, 1897).

117. Jean Martin Charcot and Paul Richer, *Les démoniaques dans l'art* (Paris: Delahaye et Lacrosnier, 1887).

118. See for example, the debate between Oskar Pfister and Martin Grabmann with regard to Margaret Ebner. See Christina Mazzoni, *Saint Hysteria: Neurosis, Mysticism, and Gender in European Culture* (Ithaca: Cornell University Press, 1996), 20–21; and Gertrud Jaron Lewis, *By Women for Women About Women: The Sister-Books of Fourteenth-Century German* (Toronto: Pontifical Institute of Medieval Studies, 1996), 70. Nancy Partner argues for the viability of the category in explaining medieval

mysticism. See Nancy Partner, "Reading *The Book of Margery Kempe*," *Exemplaria* 3 (1991): 29–66; and Partner, "Did Mystics Have Sex?," in *Desire and Discipline: Sex and Sexuality in the Premodern West*, ed. Jacqueline Murray and Konrad Eisenbichler (Toronto: University of Toronto Press, 1996), 296–311. For a more nuanced approach, see Hope Phyllis Weissman, "Margery Kempe in Jerusalem: *Hysterica Compassio* in the Late Middle Ages," in *Acts of Interpretation: The Text in Its Contexts, 700–1600*, ed. Mary J. Carruthers and Elizabeth D. Kirk (Norman, Okla.: Pilgrim Books, 1982), 201–17.

119. Simone de Beauvoir, *The Second Sex*, trans. H. M. Parshley (New York: Knopf, 1993), 703ff. See also Hollywood, *Sensible Ecstasy*, 120–45.

120. On an alternative reading of Margery Kempe as queer, see Carolyn Dinshaw, *Getting Medieval: Sexualities and Communities, Pre- and Postmodern* (Durham: Duke University Press, 1999). I think that her queerness in part emerges from her insistence on her own interpretations of her experience, no matter how well they might accord with official scripts.

121. Female hagiographers may also have made this move as well, although the record here is scanty and complex. For discussion of the issues, see Sean L. Field, "Agnes of Harcourt, Felipa of Porcelet, and Marguerite d'Oingt: Women Writing About Women at the End of the Thirteenth Century," *Church History* 76 (2007): 298–328.

122. Newman, "Possessed by the Spirit," 766. In what follows, I borrow material from Hollywood, *Sensible Ecstasy*, 242–47.

123. For counterevidence concerning the religious importance of begging in the lives of the thirteenth-century holy women of Liège, see Amy Hollywood, *The Soul as Virgin Wife: Mechthild of Magdeburg, Marguerite Porete, and Meister Eckhart* (Notre Dame: University of Notre Dame Press, 1995).

124. Newman, "Possessed by the Spirit," 766–67.

125. Dyan Elliott, "The Physiology of Rapture and Female Spirituality," in *Medieval Theology and the Natural Body*, ed. Peter Biller and A. J. Minnis (York: York Medieval Press, 1997), 142. Elliott has pursued the work begun here further in *Fallen Bodies: Pollution, Sexuality, and Demonology in the Middle Ages* (Philadelphia: University of Pennsylvania Press, 1999); *Proving Woman: Female Spirituality and Inquisitional Culture in the Later Middle Ages* (Princeton: Princeton University Press, 2004); and *The Bride of Christ Goes to Hell* (Philadelphia: University of Pennsylvania Press, 2012). See also her entry "*Raptus*/Rapture" in Hollywood and Beckman, *The Cambridge Companion to Christian Mysticism*, 189–99.

126. Bernard McGinn, *The Flowering of Mysticism: Men and Women in the New Mysticism, 1200–1350* (New York: Crossroad, 1998), 37–38. See also Mary Wack on William of Auvergne's assimilation of the language of lovesicknesses and mystical rapture. Mary F. Wack, *Lovesickness in the Middle Ages: The "Viaticum" and Its Commentaries* (Philadelphia: University of Pennsylvania Press, 1990), 23–24.

127. Elliott, "Physiology," 159–60. Elliott cites William of Auvergne, Albert the Great, and Thomas of Cantimpré on the issue.

128. Commentator B in H. R. Lemay, *Women's Secrets: A Translation of Pseudo-Albertus Magnus's "De Secretis Mulierum" with Commentaries* (Albany: State University of New York Press, 1992), 134.

129. In one of the few cases where we have letters between a woman and her spiritual advisor or collaborator, the beguine Christina of Stommeln tends to read her experiences as demonic attacks, whereas the Dominican Peter of Dacia provides the mystical reading. See McGinn, *The Flowering of Mysticism*, 179; and John Coakley, *Women, Men, and Spiritual Power: Female Saints and Their Male Collaborators* (New York: Columbia University Press, 2006). The text, then, supports the reading Newman gives of the *Life of Christina*, although I do not think it alone can serve as a justification for the reading.

130. Thomas, *Life of Christina*, nn. 6–7, p. 131.

131. Ibid., nn. 35–36, pp. 145–46.

132. For references and a preliminary discussion, see the essays by Douglas Burton-Christie and Amy Hollywood in Hollywood and Beckman, *The Cambridge Companion to Christian Mysticism*.

133. A vital question for me now is how habitus and spontaneity, once so intimately entwined, became diametrically opposed to each other. For Cassian, monks must recite the Psalms until they come to the lips spontaneously; for most modern Protestant Christians, claims to spontaneity mark the refusal of ritual and habituation. How did this happen? How is it, in practice, continually undone? See Lori Branch, *Rituals of Spontaneity: Sentiment and Secularism from Free Prayer to Wordsworth* (Waco, Tex.: Baylor University Press, 2006); and Ted A. Smith, *The New Measures: A Theological History of Democratic Practice* (New York: Cambridge University Press, 2007).

134. Adams, *Esther*, 251.

135. Of course, in many ways it was for Freud as well. The essential text is *Totem and Taboo*, for here Freud links the incorporation of the father's prohibition in the dissolution of the Oedipus complex to the handing down of tradition from fathers to sons. Tradition is created, Freud speculates, when the sons kill the father, then recoil in a weirdly joyful grief in which they celebrate the father's death, prohibit further killing of a totem associated with the father, and create the ceremonies that will be handed down to mark the founding of the community as a community tied together by tradition.

　　Freud gives a number of different accounts of how melancholic incorporation gives rise to critique. In melancholia, the subject does not want to accept the loss of an idealized other and so internalizes her. Most simply, critique emerges as a result of our ambivalent feelings toward the lost other—love, of course, but also rage at her departure. To this Freud adds the notion that it is the Oedipal father who is lost and internalized and so with it his injunctions against the son. But I wonder if, in addition, the critical agency might be an attempt by the psyche to distinguish the living from the dead. This would help explain the relentlessness of critique, for if the psyche is constituted through the internalization of lost (and so at least symbolically dead) others, as long as I live, they live. If they die, I die. Life depends on the impossibility of ever fully distinguishing the living from the dead.

1. ACUTE MELANCHOLIA

First presented as the inaugural lecture of the Elizabeth H. Monrad Chair of Christian Studies at Harvard Divinity School, March 2, 2006. The essay originally appeared in a special issue of the *Harvard Theological Review* dedicated to the fiftieth anniversary of the acceptance of women at HDS. It appears here in a slightly revised form.

1. See note 21.

2. For new work on Beatrice of Nazareth and Margaret Ebner, both of whom figure largely here, see Jos Hus, *The Minne-Journey: Beatrice of Nazareth's* "Seven Ways of Minne": *Mystical Process and Mystagogical Implications* (Leuven: Peeters, 2013); and Barbara Koch, "Margaret Ebner," in *Medieval Holy Women in the Christian Tradition c. 1100–c. 1500*, ed. Alastair Minnis and Rosalynn Voaden (Turnhout: Brepols, 2010), 393–410. A few bibliographical additions appear in the notes.

3. For the gap between the two and its enormous importance, see Amy Hollywood, *The Soul as Virgin Wife: Mechthild of Magdeburg, Marguerite Porete, and Meister Eckhart* (Notre Dame: University of Notre Dame Press, 1995), 27–39; Hollywood, *Sensible Ecstasy: Mysticism, Sexual Difference, and the Demands of History* (Chicago: University of Chicago Press, 2001), 247–66; and Hollywood, "Inside Out: Beatrice of Nazareth and Her Hagiographer," in *Gendered Voices: Medieval Saints and Their Interpreters*, ed. Catherine Mooney (Philadelphia: University of Pennsylvania Press, 1999), 78–98, reprinted here.

4. There is no evidence that Ebner knew Beatrice's *vita* or treatise. Rather, Beatrice's *vita* and treatise and Ebner's *Revelations* provide evidence for commonly disseminated patterns of sanctity.

5. *The Life of Beatrice of Nazareth*, trans. and annotated by Roger DeGanck (Kalamazoo, Mich.: Cistercian Publications, 1991), 88–91. Hereafter cited parenthetically in the text as *LBN*.

6. Jeffrey F. Hamburger provides countless examples, particularly from late-medieval Germany, of the use of devotional images and objects. Central for Hamburger is the juxtaposition of devotional practices focused on objects and sensory, ecstatic, and unitive experiences of the divine. Yet his statements about the nature of this relationship focus on methodological and descriptive issues rather than explanatory ones and therefore require amplification, both in terms of the various ways in which medieval people themselves understood the relationship between these phenomena and in terms of how recent theoretical work on ritual, memory, and belief might help us understand medieval practices and mentalities.

   Hamburger usefully struggles with how theoretically and practically to articulate the relationship between devotional images and visions. With regard to images of the cross that give expression to the Bride's wounding love (drawing on biblical language from the Song of Songs and the tradition of Longinus), Hamburger argues: "The miniature need no more reflect a vision than Gertrude [of Helfta's] vision need rely on such a miniature. Nevertheless, the miniature's visualization of the same commonplace metaphors of mystical union is intended to stimulate and encourage the kind of experience recorded in the visions of Gertrude of Helfta." Thus while the vision might not *rely* on such visual images, the images are meant to stimulate and encourage such visions. Hamburger does not ask, however, either how images serve to stimulate and encourage visions, or how medieval people believed this occurred. Jeffrey F. Hamburger, *The Visual and the Visionary: Art and Female Spirituality in Late Medieval Germany* (New York: Zone, 1998), 127.

Elsewhere, Hamburger talks about the relationship between visions and visual images in terms of analogy: "The drawings from St. Walburg do not transcribe such visions, nor should the experience of viewing them be confused with visionary experience itself. The analogies are structural. They extend beyond straightforward parallels in imagery, the search for which reduces visionary accounts to no more than another set of textual sources or, conversely, the comparable works of art to little more than stimuli for hallucinations masquerading as authentic vatic phenomena. Instead, the wide-ranging correspondences authorized the images as instruments of meditation, just as, on occasion, works of art could authenticate visions. The analogies between works of art and visions enabled the images to inspire certain devotional experiences to which visualization and, on occasion, visionary experience were intrinsic." Hamburger's point is crucial methodologically. As he convincingly argues, the search for "sources" is inadequate and misguided: "No single passage or group of passages linked in exegesis serves as a univocal source [for an image]." Likewise, no image can serve as the univocal source for a vision or visionary account: "Instead, the devotional works that inform the drawings [from St. Walburg] stand *pars pro toto* for the spiritual readings that would have informed the nuns' response to them, just as the drawings, in turn, focused and heightened their readings of exegetical and meditational texts." See Hamburger, *Nuns as Artists: The Visual Culture of a Medieval Convent* (Berkeley: University of California Press, 1997), 130 and 168; see also 154, 164, 168–69, 214.

Although this essay does not directly touch on these issues, in future work I hope to explore the question of how visual images and texts, whether read or heard, and ascetic, paraliturgical, and liturgical practices serve as tools for meditation. I hope also to consider what meditation itself is believed to accomplish and how its effects are experienced and theologically articulated. In a figure like Margaret Ebner, moreover, these practices and experiences are not merely visual, but involve all of the senses.

On these issues, see also Sarah McNamer, *Affective Meditation and the Invention of Medieval Compassion* (Philadelphia: University of Pennsylvania Press, 2009); Margot Fassler, *The Virgin of Chartres: Making History Through Liturgy and Art* (New Haven: Yale University Press, 2010); Michelle Karnes, *Imagination, Meditation and Cognition in the Middle Ages* (Chicago: University of Chicago Press, 2011); Sara Ritchey, *Holy Matter: Changing Perceptions of the Material World in Late Medieval Christianity* (Ithaca: Cornell University Press, 2014); Thérèse de Hemptinne, Veerle Fraeters, and María Eugenia Góngora, eds., *Speaking to the Eye: Sight and*

Insight Through Text and Image, 1150–1650 (Turnhout: Brepols, 2013); Barbara New-man, "Contemplating the Trinity: Text, Image, and the Origins of the *Rothschild Canticles*," *Gesta* 52, no. 2 (2013): 133–59; June L. Mecham, *Sacred Communities, Shared Devotions: Gender, Material Culture, and Monasticism in Late Medieval Germany*, ed. Alison Beach, Constance Berman, and Lisa Bitel (Turnhout: Brepols, 2014); and Holly Flora, *"The Devout Belief of the Imagination": The Paris "Meditationes Vitae Christi" and Female Franciscan Mysticism in Trecento Italy* (Turnhout: Brepols, 2014).

7. For the tradition of meditation on the life of Christ, its goal in the internalization of Christ's Passion, and the compunction for human sinfulness that necessitates it, see Denise Despres, *Ghostly Sights: Visual Meditation in Late-Medieval Literature* (Norman, Okla.: Pilgrim Books, 1989), 19–54; Thomas Bestul, *Texts of the Passion: Latin Devotional Literature and Medieval Society* (Philadelphia: University of Pennsylvania Press, 1996), esp. 26–68; Mary Carruthers, *The Craft of Thought: Meditation, Rhetoric, and the Making of Images, 400–1200* (Cambridge: Cambridge University Press, 1998), esp. 165–83; and McNamer, *Affective Meditation*, with important correctives from Flora, *"The Devout Belief of the Imagination."* Also important on these issues is Rachel Fulton, *From Judgment to Passion: Devotion to Christ and the Virgin Mary, 800–1200* (New York: Columbia University Press, 2002).

8. Beatrice of Nazareth, *Seven Manieren van Minne*, ed. L. Reypens and J. Van Mierlo (Leuven: S. V. de Vlaamsche Boekenhalle, 1926), 19–20; Beatrice of Nazareth, "There Are of Loving," in *Medieval Women's Visionary Literature*, ed. Elizabeth Alvilda Petroff, trans. Eric Colledge (Oxford: Oxford University Press, 1986), 203. Translation modified, including that of the title. My thanks to Walter Simons for help with this difficult passage and other suggestions for reading the Dutch text.

9. Bernard of Clairvaux, sermon 61 in *On the Song of Songs III*, trans. Kilian Walsh and Irene Edmunds (Kalamazoo, Mich.: Cistercian Publications, 1979), 143–44.

10. Mary Wack, *Lovesickness in the Middle Ages: The Viaticum and Its Commentaries* (Philadelphia: University of Pennsylvania Press, 1990), 23–24.

11. As Bernard McGinn shows, James of Vitry's *Life of Marie of Oignies* (ca. 1213) is the first text to use language traditionally associated with the heights of monastic contemplation (*separatus a corpore, a sensibilibus abstracta, in excessu rapta*) for trance-like states of languor, furthering the association of lovesickness (languor) with mystical ecstasy. See McGinn, *The Flowering of Mysticism: Men and Women in the New Mysticism, 1200–1350* (New York: Crossroad, 1998), 37–38.

12. See Wack, *Lovesickness*, 6, 10, 12–13, 21, 35, 40, 56, 61, 160–62.

13. For the association between melancholia and acedia (often translated as sloth, although the term as it first appears in Cassian [d. ca. 435] and as it is used throughout the medieval period carries much more complex connotations), see in particular Morton W. Bloomfield, *The Seven Deadly Sins: An Introduction to the History of a Religious Concept, with Special Reference to Medieval English Literature* (East Lansing: Michigan State College Press, 1952), 430n61; Stanley Jackson, *Melancholia and Depression* (New Haven: Yale University Press, 1986), 66–70; Juliana Schiesari,

The Gendering of Melancholia: Feminism, Psychoanalysis, and the Gendering of Loss in Renaissance Literature (Ithaca: Cornell University Press, 1992), 154–58; and Jennifer Radden, ed., The Nature of Melancholy: From Aristotle to Kristeva (Oxford: Oxford University Press, 2000), 19–20, 69–74.

14. See Bloomfield, Seven Deadly Sins, 428n30; and Wack, Lovesickness, 12–13, 162.

15. Wack, Lovesickness, 23.

16. Ibid., 29.

17. Ibid., 56–59.

18. On Theresa and the attempt to distinguish loving desire for God from melancholia, and the reasons for this shift away from medieval Christian patterns of thought, see Radden, Nature of Melancholy, 107–17.

19. See Hamburger, Nuns as Artists, plate 1.

20. See Richard Kieckhefer, Unquiet Souls: Fourteenth-Century Saints and Their Religious Milieu (Chicago: University of Chicago Press, 1984), 6; Kate Greenspan, "The Autohagiographical Tradition in Medieval Women's Devotional Writing," A/B: Auto/Biographical Studies 6, no. 2 (1991): 157–68; and Greenspan, "Autohagiography and Medieval Women's Spiritual Autobiography," in Gender and Text in the Later Middle Ages, ed. Jane Chance (Gainesville: University Press of Florida, 1996), 216–36. How we are to read these accounts, of course, remains open to question.

21. A similar pattern can also be seen in Henry Suso's Life of the Servant, although with important differences arguably tied to gender difference. Hence Suso insists that only he can enact the physical appropriation of Christ's Passion; the women around him instead make small emblems that, when they have touched Suso's wounded body, become objects of veneration and community formation. I discuss Suso further in "Practice, Belief, and Feminist Philosophy of Religion," collected here.

22. Freud uses the terms "internalization" and "incorporation" interchangeably. See Jean Laplanche and J.-B. Pontalis, The Language of Psycho-Analysis, trans. Donald Nicholson-Smith (New York: Norton, 1973), 211–12, 226–27. Although Karl Abraham and Maria Torok argue for the necessity of distinguishing the two, I will stay with Freud's usage here.

23. For Margaret Ebner, see Philipp Strauch, ed., Margaretha Ebner und Heinrich von Nördlingen: Ein Beitrag zur Geschichte der Deutschen Mystik [ME] (Freiburg: Mohr, 1882), which contains Margaret's Revelations (1–166); and Ebner, Major Works [MW], trans. and ed. Leonard P. Hindsley (New York: Paulist Press, 1993), containing a translation of the Revelations (83–172) and a prayer attributed to Margaret, the Pater Noster (173–78). The latter volume also includes a useful introduction and bibliography. Further references will be found parenthetically as ME and MW, respectively, within the text (MW is listed first in each such reference).

24. The first is a dream in which she feels full of grace and lightness and experiences God sporting with her soul. The second is a moment in which a voice suggests the divine origin and power of her daily suffering. As Ebner explains, pain replaces active asceticism in her life, for her illness often makes her unable to participate in even the normal ascetic activities associated with her monastic rule. Suffering, however, is an

everyday occurrence. So at one moment, when her sisters believe she is at the point of death, a voice tells her, "You are not dying; indeed many of the nuns will die before you." The voice continues, "You must suffer here on earth. . . . But when you die, you will go to heaven without delay" (*MW*, 90; *ME*, 10).

25.   This practice is related, in complex ways, to the developing devotion to the name of Jesus Christ in the West and the Hesychast movement, centered on the recitation of the Jesus prayer, in Eastern Orthodox Christianity.

26.   For other examples of Ebner's desire for the stigmata, in which she explicitly invokes the famous example of Francis of Assisi, see *MW*, 110, 127; *ME*, 46, 78. For the fulfillment of this desire, in which Ebner "was given the sight of the five holy wounds" on her own body, see *MW*, 112; *ME*, 50. This probably occurred in 1339. For a more ambiguous fulfillment, in which the pain of the body wracked on the cross is invoked, see *MW*, 157; *ME*, 132–33.

27.   As is often the case in Ebner's *Revelations*, there is a natural explanation for what occurs, although Ebner also reads the event as a sign of divine grace.

28.   Again there are clear parallels here with Francis, who desires to have Christ's cross impressed on his heart.

29.   For the kiss of the heart and drinking blood from Christ's side wound, see my essay " 'That Glorious Slit': Irigaray and the Medieval Devotion to Christ's Side Wound," reprinted here, and the literature cited there.

30.   Hindsley makes the choice to capitalize three words Ebner often uses to describe her experience, thereby hypostasizing them as special states: the Silence, the Speaking, and the Outcry. Although Ebner does use the words *swige*, *rede*, and *rüefe* to name experiences in which divine agency renders her completely passive, the line between actively keeping silence or speaking the name of Jesus Christ and being unable *not* to do these things is often less clear than Hindsley's translations allow. For this reason, I find Hindsley's capitalizations misleading and so omit them here. I don't discuss silence in this essay; suffice to say that it is a state in which Ebner is literally unable to speak, her jaw often clenched together so that nothing can pass through her lips.

31.   The complicating factor here is that the outcry first emerges around visual or oral representations of Christ's Passion and then *intensifies* when Ebner finds herself unable not to see and hear of the Passion. In the latter instances, moreover, the outcry has new bodily components.

32.   Or, at least, this is how Ebner depicts herself. How historians should read Ebner's hagiographical literalizing of metaphors found in earlier women's writing (like that of Beatrice) requires much further discussion. On the salvific power of Christ's blood and the centrality of blood in representations of the Passion, see Hollywood, " 'That Glorious Slit' "; and Caroline Walker Bynum, *Wonderful Blood: Theology and Practice in Late Medieval Northern Germany and Beyond* (Philadelphia: University of Pennsylvania Press, 2006).

33.   This pattern of Lenten suffering and post-Easter renewal will increasingly be joined with a devotion to the Christ child. Focused on Advent and Christmas, the practices involved in this devotion are not unlike those tied to Ebner's devotion to the Passion,

with an emphasis on both auditory and visual meditational practice and the use of devotional objects. See, for example, *MW*, 132–34; *ME*, 87–91. Henry of Nördlingen champions devotion to the Christ child in a letter to Ebner, suggesting that he may have been the source of this devotion (which also appears in Mechthild of Magdeburg's *Flowing Light of the Godhead*, sent to Margaret by Henry). Leonard Hindsley insists that Ebner partook in this devotion independently of Henry's influence, since the first letter in which he discusses it was sent at Christmas 1341, three years before she began to write down the *Revelations*. Yet Ebner's account of the years 1332 to 1340 deals solely with devotion to Christ's Passion and therefore seems to reflect her actual *practice* before the Christ child comes to the forefront in about 1344. She seems to accept Henry's admonition that she add devotion to the Christ child to her religious life, and at the same time accurately records the absence of that devotion before 1341. See Hindsley, "Introduction," in *MW*, 53–54; and "Letter 38" in, *ME*, 233–34.

What seems further worthy of note is that Ebner clearly marks a tension between the two, even as, in the later parts of her *Revelations*, she pursues both. When Ebner first asks the Virgin Mary to allow her to experience the joys of the Christ child together with the Passion, Mary herself remarks on the apparent disparity between these two desires: "One day I wanted our Lady to help me so that the five signs of love would be impressed upon me with the same feeling as they had been impressed upon St. Francis. On that same day I asked her to help me to perceive what divine joy there would be with her dear Child. Then I was answered lovingly by her, 'You ask me for such dissimilar things that I do not know what I should do for you'" (*MW*, 127; *ME*, 78). Ebner ends her book with an attempt to resolve this dilemma through a visionary dream in which she gives symbolic form to her experience. In the dream, she sees two sisters from her monastery. They give her two apples that have fallen from the beautiful trees among which they are wandering: "One of them was sour, the other sweet. They asked me to eat them. I took the apples and bit into them. Then I felt such great grace from the apples that I said, 'No one on earth could eat both.' They said, 'If you do not like them, give them back to us.' Then I awoke still chewing, and the grace was so sweet and so strong that I could not speak a word and could not take in breath and was really without my bodily senses. That lasted a long time with me and after that I read matins without comprehending a word" (*MW*, 171; *ME*, 159). Always within the context of the monastic rule, by which her life was strictly ordered, Ebner pursues devotions to the name of Christ, to his childhood, and to his Passion. No matter how deeply at odds these various devotions may be emotionally and affectively, they come together in her belief in Christ's humanity and its salvific work. One link between the childhood of Christ and his Passion lies in Ebner's Eucharistic devotion; another link between these two moments in Christ's life, as between Ebner's devotion to Christ's Passion, his Infancy, and the Holy Name, is the feast of the Circumcision. See Irénée Noye, "Jésus (Nom de)," *Dictionaire Spiritualité* [*DS*] 8, cols. 1109–126.

34.   See James Marrow, *Passion Iconography in Northern European Art of the Late Middle Ages and Early Renaissance: A Study in the Transformation of Sacred Metaphor Into Descriptive Narrative* (Kortrijk, Belgium: Van Ghemmert, 1979).

35. This recalls the experience of those stigmatics who either exhibit visibly or feel the pain of the wounds on Christ's head made by the crown of thorns. For a brief discussion of the variety of phenomena associated with the stigmata, attempts to catalogue and classify them, and a perceptive account of the classical and modern literature, see Pierre Adnès, "Stigmate," *DS*, 14, cols. 1211–243.

36. A text also cited by Beatrice of Nazareth at a crucial moment in *Seven Manners of Loving.*

37. There are, of course, dangers in making a potentially anachronistic retroactive diagnosis. Ebner's *Revelations* have already been put "on the couch" by Oskar Pfister, who argued in 1911 that Ebner was hysterical. There are also, of course, more general objections to psychoanalytic readings of medieval texts, and the category of trauma is itself one surrounded by controversy. See Oskar Pfister, "Hysterie und Mystik bei Margaretha Ebner (1291–1351)," *Zentralblatt für Psychoanalyse* 1 (1911): 468–85. For objections to Pfister, see Martin Grabmann, "Deutsche Mystik im Kloster Engelthal," *Sammelblatt des Historischen Vereins Eichstätt* 25/26 (1910–11): 33–34; Wolfgang Beutin, "'Hysterie und Mystik': Zur Mittelalter-Rezeption der frühen Psychoanalyse: Die 'Offenbarungen' der Nonne Margaretha Ebner (ca. 1291–1351), gedeutet durch den Zürcher Pfarrer und Analytiker Oskar Pfister," in *Mittelalter-Rezeption*, vol. 4, *Medien, Politik, Ideologie, Ökonomie*, ed. Irene von Burg et al. (Goppingen: Kümmerle, 1991), 11–26; and Gertrud Jaron Lewis, *By Women, for Women, About Women: The Sister-Books of Fourteenth-Century Germany* (Toronto: Pontifical Institute of Medieval Studies, 1996), 70–71. For a prominent attack on psychoanalytic criticism from a medievalist's perspective, see Lee Patterson, "Chaucer's Pardoner on the Couch: Psyche and Clio in Medieval Literary Studies," *Speculum* 76 (2001): 638–80. Patterson argues, somewhat reductively, that Chaucer's "Pardoner's Tale" is best understood by means of historicist, religiously grounded contextualization rather than psychoanalytically inspired interpretations. But the one does not exclude the other. In fact, for the text in question, *both* are required. One problem with Patterson's critical analysis is that he lays out in detail the case against Freud as a scientific thinker, together with the case against Freud's insistence on the sexual etiology of character and disease, but offers no challenge to the forms of Lacanian-inspired criticism used by medievalists like Aranye Fradenburg and Carolyn Dinshaw (whose work Patterson most strenuously attacks). For Lacan, the central issue is language and sexuation occurs through signification. Freud's "biologism" and "scientism" were critiqued as heavily by Lacan as they have been by Freud's enemies. As a result, Patterson's essay misses its target.

38. There is a large literature. See especially Ruth Leys, *Trauma: A Genealogy* (Chicago: University of Chicago Press, 2000); and Robert McNally, *Remembering Trauma* (Cambridge, Mass.: Harvard University Press, 2003).

39. For the most often cited version of this argument, see Judith Herman, *Trauma and Recovery* (New York: Basic Books, 1992).

40. See Hollywood, *Sensible Ecstasy*, 74–97 and the literature cited there.

41. Meditative practice itself imaginatively re-creates this narrative, one given further weight and vividness by the emotions evoked through that very practice. Yet the evocation of

emotion seems to depend at least in part on an increased focus on isolated aspects of Christ's Passion—fragmented moments and bits of Christ's body and the instruments of his suffering—thereby working against the apparently seamless Christian narrative. (See, for example, the innumerable late medieval images of the instruments of Christ's suffering and death, the *arma Christi*.) This tension in the meditative tradition requires further exploration. Moreover, Ebner's constant repetition of the narrative and experience of Christ's Passion raises the question of how adequate a therapy narrativization really is. Does one simply move from repeating visceral memories to endlessly repeating the story in which those memories are supposedly rendered meaningful? Although this might alleviate suffering to an extent, it does so through displacement or sublimation, a displacement that the viscerality of Ebner's desire refuses.

42. There seems to be at least some supporting evidence in many of the fourteenth-century German convent chronicles, which focus on both group and individual responses to death. For full information about and discussion of these sources, see Lewis, *By Women, for Women*.

43. Sigmund Freud, "Mourning and Melancholia," in *The Standard Edition of the Complete Psychological Works of Sigmund Freud [SE]*, ed. and trans. James Strachey (London: Hogarth Press, 1953–74), 14:244–49.

44. *SE*, 14:245.

45. *SE*, 14:249.

46. Ibid.

47. Freud, "The Ego and the Id," in *SE*, 19:28.

48. See especially Freud, "Some Psychical Consequences of the Anatomical Distinction Between the Sexes," in *SE*, 19:243–58; Freud, "Female Sexuality," in *SE*, 21:223–43; and Freud, "Femininity," in *SE*, 22:112–35. On the complex relationship between Freud's accounts of sexual difference and religion, see Judith Van Herik, *Freud on Femininity and Faith* (Berkeley: University of California Press, 1982).

49. One is tempted, of course, to add "and by sin," assuming that to be the theological category through which Ebner understands the necessity of the Passion; and yet sin, oddly, plays a very small role in her *Revelations*. Here, finally, is another topic that will require further exploration and explanation before the full import of mourning and trauma for understanding late-medieval devotional practice can be assessed. For Ebner, at least, mourning and the traumatic repetition of suffering and loss seem to supersede sin—and at times, even the hope of redemption on which that repetition is theologically premised.

50. Melanie Klein, "Mourning and Its Relation to Manic-Depressive States," in *Love, Guilt and Reparation, and Other Works, 1921–1945* (New York: Free Press, 1975), 363.

51. Among a number of crucial texts, I will only cite here Sigmund Freud, *Totem and Taboo: Some Points of Convergence Between the Mental Lives of Savages and Neurotics* (1913), in *SE*, 13:1–161; Sigmund Freud, *The Future of an Illusion* (1927), in *SE*, 21:5–56; and Sigmund Freud, *Moses and Monotheism: Three Essays* (1939), in *SE*, 23:7–137.

52. See especially Ludwig Feuerbach, *The Essence of Christianity*, trans. George Eliot (Amherst, N.Y.: Prometheus Books, 1989).

2. FEMINIST STUDIES IN CHRISTIAN SPIRITUALITY

An earlier version of this essay appeared in *The Blackwell Companion to Christian Spirituality* (2005), edited by Arthur Holder. Given the intended audience of the *Companion*, I focused primarily on material available in English. I have updated the essay for inclusion here and am grateful to Arthur Holder, Rachel Smith, Robert Glenn Davis, and Patricia Dailey for help on the initial version and on the revisions.

1. Bernard McGinn, "The Letter and The Spirit: Spirituality as an Academic Discipline," *Cresset: A Review of Literature, the Arts, and Public Affairs* 56, no. 7b (1993): 13–22. The danger is always that the only real meeting will be a crash.

2. Ibid., 21.

3. Julian of Norwich, *Showings*, trans. E. Colledge and J. Walsh (New York: Paulist Press, 1978).

4. Katharina M. Wilson, ed., *Medieval Women Writers* (Athens: University of Georgia Press, 1984); Elizabeth Alvilda Petroff, ed., *Medieval Women's Visionary Literature* (Oxford: Oxford University, 1986). Peregrina stopped publishing in 2005, although a number of crucial titles were picked up by Brepols in their "Medieval Women: Texts and Contexts" series. For full information about Peregrina's backlist, see www.peregrina.com. An extremely useful guide to the medieval literature can be found in Alastair Minnis and Rosalynn Voaden, eds., *Medieval Holy Women in the Christian Tradition c. 1100–c. 1500* (Turnhout: Brepols, 2010).

5. For a wonderfully engaging articulation of the complexity involved in thinking gender and sexuality today, see Maggie Nelson, *The Argonauts* (Minneapolis: Graywolf, 2015). For a steadfast refusal to identify as either male or female—to identify at all—see Beatriz Preciado, *TestoJunkie: Sex, Drugs, and Biopolitics in the Pharmacopornographic Era* (New York: Feminist Press, 2013).

6. Bernard McGinn, John Meyendorff, and Jean Leclerq, eds., *Christian Spirituality: Origins to the Twelfth Century* (New York: Crossroad, 1985), xv. For one criticism, see Carlos M. N. Eire, "Major Problems in the Definition of Spirituality as an Academic Discipline," in *Modern Christian Spirituality: Methodological and Historical Essays*, ed. Bradley C. Hansen (Atlanta: Scholars Press, 1990), 53–61. Note that for McGinn, mysticism and spirituality denote much the same thing. For my own views on how best to understand mysticism, which I also read as very close to what is meant by spirituality, see Amy Hollywood, "Introduction," in *The Cambridge Companion to Christian Mysticism*, ed. Amy Hollywood and Patricia Z. Beckman (Cambridge: Cambridge University Press, 2012), 1–33.

7. See Amy Hollywood, "Song, Experience, and the Book in Benedictine Monasticism," in Hollywood and Beckman, *The Cambridge Companion to Christian Mysticism*, 59–79. I there take issue with claims made by Denys Turner, among others, that Christian mysticism and spirituality should not be discussed in terms of experience.

8. This is in the third of Bernard's sermons on the Song of Songs. See ibid., 75. On spirituality and practice, see Pierre Hadot, *Philosophy as a Way of Life: Spiritual Exercises from Socrates to Foucault*, trans. Michael Chase (Cambridge: Cambridge University

Press, 1995). On spirituality and theology, see Mark A. McIntosh, *Mystical Theology* (Oxford: Blackwell, 1998). Crucial essays on the academic study of spirituality appear in the journal *Spiritus: A Journal of Christian Spirituality* and its earlier incarnation, *Christian Spirituality Bulletin.*

9. On the ideal of virginity for women and the ways in which virginity conferred authority on those who chose it, see Kerstin Aspegren, *The Male Woman: A Feminine Ideal in the Early Church* (Uppsala, Sweden: Almqvist and Wiksell, 1990); Barbara Newman, *From Virile Woman to WomanChrist: Studies in Medieval Religion and Literature* (Philadelphia: University of Pennsylvania Press, 1995); Jane Tibbetts Schulenburg, *Forgetful of Their Sex: Female Sanctity and Society, ca. 500–1100* (Chicago: University of Chicago Press, 1998); Anke Bernau, Ruth Evans, and Sarah Salih, eds., *Medieval Virginities* (Toronto: University of Toronto Press, 2003); Sarah McNamer, *Affective Meditation and the Invention of Medieval Compassion* (Philadelphia: University of Pennsylvania Press, 2009); and Dyan Elliott, *The Bride of Christ Goes to Hell: Metaphor and Embodiment in the Lives of Pious Women, 200–1500* (Philadelphia: University of Pennsylvania Press, 2012). I think that McNamer significantly overstates the role of virginity in high and late medieval devotional texts. For a fascinating study of the interplay between virginity and marrying Christ, see the forthcoming book by Rabia Anne Geha Gregory, *Marrying Jesus in Medieval and Early Modern Northern Europe: Popular Culture and Religious Reform.*

10. There is a large body of literature on this issue, but for some of the most important general discussions, see Petroff, *Medieval Women's Visionary Literature*; Peter Dronke, *Women Writers of the Middle Ages: A Critical Study of Texts from Perpetua (d. 203) to Marguerite Porete (d. 1310)* (Cambridge: Cambridge University Press, 1984); Barbara Newman, *Sister of Wisdom: Saint Hildegard's Theology of the Feminine* (Berkeley: University of California Press, 1987); Alison Weber, *Teresa of Avila and the Rhetoric of Femininity* (Princeton: Princeton University Press, 1990); Karma Lochrie, *Margery Kempe and Translations of the Flesh* (Philadelphia: University of Pennsylvania Press, 1991); Phyllis Mack, *Visionary Women: Ecstatic Prophecy in Seventeenth-Century England* (Berkeley: University of California Press, 1992); Kimberly Ray Connor, *Conversions and Visions in the Writing of African-American Women* (Knoxville: University of Tennessee Press, 1994); Amy Hollywood, *The Soul as Virgin Wife: Mechthild of Magdeburg, Marguerite Porete, and Meister Eckhart* (Notre Dame: University of Notre Dame Press, 1995); Diane Watt, *Secretaries of God* (Cambridge: D. S. Brewer, 1997); Beverly Mayne Kienzle and Pamela J. Walker, eds., *Women Preachers and Prophets Through Two Millennia of Christianity* (Berkeley: University of California Press, 1998); Bernard McGinn, *The Flowering of Mysticism: Men and Women in the New Mysticism, 1200–1350* (New York: Crossroad, 1998); Ruth Harris, *Lourdes: Body and Spirit in the Secular Age* (New York: Viking 1999); Denis Reveney and Christiania Whitehead, eds., *Writing Religious Women: Female Spirituality and Textual Practice in Late Medieval England* (Cardiff: University of Wales Press, 2000); Rudolph M. Bell and Christina Mazzoni, *The Voices of Gemma Galgani: The Life and Afterlife of a Modern Saint* (Chicago: University

of Chicago Press, 2003); Anne Winston-Allen, *Convent Chronicles: Women Writing About Women and Reform in the Late Middle Ages* (University Park: Penn State University Press, 2004); Thérèse de Hemptinne and María Eugenia Góngora, eds., *The Voice of Silence: Women's Literacy in a Men's Church* (Turnhout: Brepols, 2004); Linda Olson and Kathryn Kerby-Fulton, eds., *Voices in Dialogue: Reading Women in the Middle Ages* (Notre Dame: University of Notre Dame Press, 2005); Anneke Mulder-Bakker and Liz Herbert McAvoy, eds., *Women and Experience in Later Medieval Writing: Reading the Book of Life* (New York: Palgrave, 2009); Jane Tylus, *Reclaiming Catherine of Siena: Literature, Literacy, and the Sign of Others* (Chicago: University of Chicago Press, 2009); Nancy Bradley Warren, *The Embodied Word: Female Spiritualities, Contested Orthodoxies, and English Religious Culture, 1350–1700* (Notre Dame: University of Notre Dame Press, 2010); John Coakley, "Women's Textual Authority and the Collaboration of Clerics," in Minnis and Voaden, *Medieval Holy Women*, 83–104; Alison Weber, "Gender," in Hollywood and Beckman, *The Cambridge Companion to Christian Mysticism*, 315–27; Yonsoo Kim, *Between Desire and Passion: Teresa de Cartagena* (Leiden: Brill, 2012); and Patricia Dailey, *Promised Bodies: Time, Language, and Corporeality in Medieval Women's Mystical Texts* (New York: Columbia University Press, 2013). The work of Caroline Walker Bynum, so central to these discussions, will be discussed and cited at length in what follows.

11.　On the importance of rules, guidebooks, and meditational texts, see Newman, *From Virile Woman to WomanChrist*, 19–45; Constant Mews, ed., *Listen, Daughter: The Speculum Virginum and the Formation of Religious Women in the Middle Ages* (New York: Palgrave, 2001); and McNamer, *Affective Meditation*. For the centrality of liturgy and liturgical and extraliturgical song, see Margot E. Fassler, "Composer and Dramatist: 'Melodious Singing and the Freshness of Remorse,'" in *Voice of the Living Light: Hildegard of Bingen and Her World*, ed. Barbara Newman (Berkeley: University of California Press, 1998), 149–75; Fassler, "Hildegard and the Dawn Song of Lauds: An Introduction to Benedictine Psalmody," in *Psalms in Community: Jewish and Christian Textual, Liturgical, and Artistic Traditions*, ed. Harold W. Attridge and Margot E. Fassler (Atlanta, Ga.: Society of Biblical Literature, 2003); Fassler, "Music for the Love Feast: Hildegard of Bingen and the Song of Songs," in *Women's Voices Across the Musical World*, ed. J. Bernstein (Boston: Northeastern University Press, 2003), 92–117; Bruce W. Holsinger, *Music, Body, and Desire in Medieval Culture: Hildegard of Bingen to Chaucer* (Stanford: Stanford University Press, 2001); Veerle Fraeters, "Handing on Wisdom and Knowledge in Hadewijch of Brabant's *Book of Visions*," in *Women and Experience in Later Medieval Writing*, ed. Mulder-Bakker and McAvoy; Dailey, *Promised Bodies*; Claire Jones, "Christian Listening and the Ethical Community of the Liturgical Text," *Literature and Theology* 27, no. 2 (2013): 227–39; and Jones, "*Hostia jubilationis*: Psalm Citation, Eucharistic Prayer, and Mystical Union in Gertrude of Helfta's *Exercitia Spiritualia*," *Speculum* 89, no. 4 (2014). On hagiography, see Sean L. Field, ed. and trans., *The Writings of Agnes of Harcourt: The Life of Isabelle of France and the Letter on Louis IX and Longchamp* (Notre Dame: University of Notre Dame Press, 2003); Field, "Agnes of Harcourt, Felipa of Porcelet, and Marguerite D'Oingt: Women Writing About Women at the End of the Thirteenth Century," *Church History* 76 (2007): 298–328; and Rachel Jean Dorothy Smith, "Exemplarity and its Limits in the Hagiographical Corpus of Thomas of Cantimpré" (PhD diss., Harvard University, 2012). For women as scribes, see Alison I. Beach, *Women as Scribes: Book Production and Monastic Reform in Twelfth-Century Bavaria* (New York: Cambridge University Press, 2004) and material cited in what follows. For material culture, see Jane Tibbetts Schulenburg, "Holy Women and the Needle Arts: Piety, Devotion, and Stitching the Sacred, ca. 500–1150," in *Negotiating Community and Difference in Medieval Europe: Gender, Power, Patronage, and the Authority of Religion in Latin Christianity,* ed. Katherine Allen Smith and Scott Wells (Leiden: Brill, 2009) and material cited below. See also my "Song, Experience, and the Book." For a multiauthored study that brings together work in a variety of media as they pertain to one woman, see Jeffrey F. Hamburger and Gabriela Signori, eds., *Catherine of Siena: The Making of a Saint* (Turnhout: Brepols, 2013).

12. Kate Cooper, *The Virgin and the Bride: Idealized Womanhood in Late Antiquity* (Cambridge, Mass.: Harvard University Press, 1996).

13. McGinn shows this in great detail in *The Flowering of Mysticism.*

14. John Coakley, "Friars as Confidants of Holy Women in Medieval Dominican Hagiography," in *Images of Sainthood in Medieval Europe,* ed. Renate Blumenfeld-Kosinski and Timea Szell (Ithaca: Cornell University Press, 1991), 222–46; Coakley, "Gender and the Authority of Friars: the Significance of Holy Women for Thirteenth-Century Franciscans and Dominicans," *Church History* 60 (1991): 445–60; Coakley, *Men, Women, and Spiritual Power: Female Saints and Their Male Collaborators* (New York: Columbia University Press, 2006); Patricia Ranft, *Women and Spiritual Equality in Christian Tradition* (New York: Palgrave, 1998); Ranft, *The Forgotten History of Women Spiritual Directors: A Woman's Way* (New York: Palgrave, 2000); and Sara S. Poor, "Women Teaching Men in the Medieval Devotional Imagination," in *Partners in Spirit: Men, Women, and Religious Life in Germany, 1100–1500,* ed. Fiona J. Griffiths and Julie Hotchen (Turnhout: Brepols, 2014), as well as the other essays collected in that volume. For the increasing complexity of these relationships in early modernity, see Jodi Bilinkoff, *The Avila of Saint Teresa: Religious Reform in a Sixteenth-Century City* (Ithaca: Cornell University Press, 1989); and Bilinkoff, *Related Lives: Confessors and Their Female Penitents, 1450–1750* (Ithaca: Cornell University Press, 2005).

15. Newman, *Sister of Wisdom*; Jeffrey F. Hamburger, *The Visual and the Visionary: Art and Female Spirituality in Late Medieval Germany* (New York: Zone, 1998), esp. 35–109, 197–232; and Rosalynn Voaden, *God's Words, Women's Voices: The Discernment of Spirits in the Writing of Late-Medieval Women's Visionaries* (Woodbridge: York Medieval Press, 1999). For arguments that in the Christian Middle Ages clerical insistence on developing rules for the discernment of spirits led to greater clerical control over women and may have contributed to the mentality and practice of the late medieval and early modern witch hunts, see Richard Kieckhefer, *Unquiet Souls: Fourteenth-Century Saints and Their Religious Milieu* (Chicago: University

of Chicago Press, 1994); Peter Dinzelbacher, *Heilige oder Hexen? Schicksale auffäl-liger Frauen in Mittelalter und Frühneuzeit* (Zurich: Artemis and Winkler, 1995); Dyan Elliott, "*Dominae* or *Dominatae*? Female Mystics and the Trauma of Textu-ality," in *Women, Marriage, and Family in Medieval Christendom: Essays in Memory of Michael M. Sheehan, CSB*, ed. Constance M. Rousseau and Joel Thomas Rosen-thal (Kalamazoo, Mich.: Medieval Institute, 1998), 47–77; Elliott, *Fallen Bodies: Pollution, Sexuality, and Demonology in the Middle Ages* (Philadelphia: University of Pennsylvania Press, 1999), 127–63, 203; Elliott, *Proving Women: Female Spiritu-ality and Inquisitorial Culture in the Later Middle Ages* (Princeton: Princeton Uni-versity Press, 2004); Nancy Caciola, "Mystics, Demoniacs, and the Physiology of Spirit Possession in Medieval Europe," *Comparative Study of Society and History* 42 (2000): 268–306; Caciola, *Discerning Spirits: Divine and Demonic Possession in the Middle Ages* (Ithaca: Cornell University Press, 2003); Jodi Bilinkoff, "Navigating the Waves (of Devotion): Toward a Gendered Analysis of Early Modern Catholicism," in *Crossing Boundaries: Attending to Early Modern Women*, ed. Jane Donawerth and Adele Seef (Newark: University of Delaware Press, 2000), 161–72; Moshe Sluhovsky, *Believe Not Every Spirit: Possession, Mysticism, and Discernment in Early Modern Catholicism* (Chicago: University of Chicago Press, 2007); and Wendy Love Ander-son, *The Discernment of Spirits: Assessing Visions and Visionaries in the Late Middle Ages* (Tübingen: Mohr Siebeck, 2011).

16. It should be noted that feminist interventions in the study of Christian spirituality also take the form of analysis of texts, writings, and images by men produced without a female or mixed audience explicitly in mind. For an early example of such work, see Marilyn Chapin Massey, *Feminine Soul: The Fate of an Ideal* (Boston: Beacon, 1985).

17. Ann Braude, ed., *Transforming the Faith of Our Fathers: Women Who Changed Amer-ican Religion* (New York: Palgrave, 2004).

18. Central figures include Valerie Saiving, Rosemary Radford Ruether, Mary Daly, Elisabeth Schüssler Fiorenza, Judith Plaskow, and Delores Williams. For this history and the ongoing work of feminist theology, see Laurel C. Schneider, *Re-Imagining the Divine: Confronting the Backlash Against Feminist Theology* (Cleveland, Ohio: Pilgrim Press, 1998); Ellen T. Armour, *Deconstruction, Feminist Theology, and the Problem of Difference: Subverting the Race/Gender Divide* (Chicago: University of Chicago Press, 1999); and Susan Frank Parsons, ed., *The Cambridge Companion to Feminist Theology* (Cambridge: Cambridge University Press, 2002). For feminist theology in the twenty-first century, see Sheila Briggs and Mary McClintock Fulk-erson, eds., *The Oxford Handbook of Feminist Theology* (Oxford: Oxford University Press, 2014).

19. For the continuing appeal of such arguments, see Luce Irigaray, *Speculum of the Other Woman*, trans. Gillian C. Gill (Ithaca: Cornell University Press, 1985); Melissa Raphael, *Introducing Thealogy: Discourse on the Goddess* (Cleveland, Ohio: Pilgrim Press, 2000); and Johanna H. Stuckey, *Women's Spirituality: Contemporary Femi-nist Approaches to Judaism, Christianity, Islam, and Goddess Worship* (Toronto: Inanna Publications and Education, 2010). For intelligent discussion of the goddess

movement in the United States and its theoretical and historical limitations, see Cynthia Eller, *Living in the Lap of the Goddess: The Feminist Spirituality Movement in America* (Boston: Beacon, 1995); and Eller, *The Myth of Patriarchal Prehistory: Why an Invented Past Won't Give Women a Future* (Boston: Beacon, 2000). For the dangerous history of earlier interest in the goddess and matriarchal culture, see Eller, *Gentlemen and Amazons: The Myth of Matriarchal Prehistory, 1861–1900* (Berkeley: University of California Press, 2010). Nuanced and historically grounded arguments for the necessity of gender parity in religious symbolism can be found in Hildegard Elisabeth Keller, *My Secret Is Mine: Studies on Religion and Eros in the German Middle Ages* (Leuven: Peters, 2000); Barbara Newman, "Did Goddesses Empower Women?: The Case of Dame Nature," in *Gendering the Master Narrative: Women and Power in the Middle Ages*, eds. Mary C. Erler and Maryanne Kowaleski (Ithaca: Cornell University Press, 2003); and Newman, *God and the Goddesses: Vision, Poetry, and Belief in the Middle Ages* (Philadelphia: University of Pennsylvania Press, 2003). For similarly insightful work by theologians, see Emily A. Holmes and Wendy Farley, eds., *Women Writing Theology: Transforming a Tradition of Exclusion* (Waco, Tex.: Baylor University Press, 2011); and Emily A. Holmes, *Flesh Made Word: Medieval Women Mystics, Writing, and the Incarnation* (Waco, Tex: Baylor University Press, 2013).

20.   Caroline Walker Bynum, *Jesus as Mother: Studies in the Spirituality of the High Middle Ages* (Berkeley: University of California Press, 1982).

21.   On feminist studies of Mariology, see Marina Warner, *Alone of All Her Sex: The Myth and Cult of the Virgin Mary* (New York: Knopf, 1976); Elizabeth A. Johnson, "Marian Devotion in the Western Church," in *Christian Spirituality: High Middle Ages and Reformation*, ed. Jill Raitt, with Bernard McGinn and John Meyendorff (New York: Crossroad, 1987), 392–414; Johnson, *Truly Our Sister: A Theology of Mary in the Communion of the Saints* (New York: Continuum, 2003); and Newman, *God and the Goddesses*, 245–90. For rich historical work and a subtle critical engagement with Warner, see Rachel Fulton, *From Judgment to Passion: Devotion to Christ and the Virgin Mary, 800–1200* (New York: Columbia University Press, 2002). See also Miri Rubin, *Mother of God: A History of the Virgin Mary* (New Haven: Yale University Press, 2009); and Rubin, *Emotion and Devotion: The Meaning of Mary in Medieval Religious Cultures* (Budapest: Central European University Press, 2009).

22.   Bynum, *Jesus as Mother*, 172–73.

23.   Caroline Walker Bynum, Stevan Harrell, Paula Richman, eds., *Gender and Religion: On the Complexity of Symbols* (Boston: Beacon, 1986), 2–3.

24.   Ibid., 13.

25.   Caroline Walker Bynum, *Holy Feast and Holy Fast: The Religious Significance of Food to Medieval Women* (Berkeley: University of California Press, 1987); and Bynum, *Fragmentation and Redemption: Essays on Gender and the Human Body in Medieval Religion* (New York: Zone, 1991).

26.   Bynum, *Fragmentation*, 194.

27.   Ibid., 195.

28. Bynum, *Jesus as Mother*; Bynum, *Holy Feast and Holy Fast*; Bynum, *Fragmentation*; Bynum, et al., *Gender and Religion*; Petroff, *Medieval Women's Visionary Literature*; Newman, *Sister of Wisdom*; McGinn, *The Flowering of Mysticism*; Mary Frohlich, "Authority," in Hollywood and Beckman, *The Cambridge Companion to Christian Mysticism*, 305–14; and Weber, "Gender," in Hollywood and Beckman, *The Cambridge Companion to Christian Mysticism*, 315–27.

29. Bynum, *Jesus as Mother*, 170–71; and Bynum, *Fragmentation*, 196. See also Grundmann, "Die Frauen und die Literatur im Mittelalter: Ein Beitrag zur Frage nach der Enstehung des Schrifttumsin der Volksprache," *Archiv für Kulturgeschichte* 26 (1936): 129–61; Renate Blumenfeld-Kosinksi, Duncan Robertson, and Nancy Warren, eds., *The Vernacular Spirit: Essays on Medieval Religious Literature* (New York: Palgrave, 2002), and the work cited there; and Elizabeth Anderson, Henrike Lahnemann, and Anne Simon, eds., *A Companion to Mysticism and Devotion in Northern Germany in the Late Middle Ages* (Leiden: Brill, 2014). Of course many women wrote in Latin and even more could read it. See David Townsend and Andrew Taylor, eds., *The Tongue of the Father: Gender and Ideology in Twelfth-Century Latin* (Philadelphia: University of Pennsylvania Press, 1998). For the interplay of Latin and vernacular literacy among women, see de Hemptinne and Góngora, *The Voice of Silence*.

30. Bynum, *Fragmentation*, 195; see also Amy Hollywood, *Sensible Ecstasy: Mysticism, Sexual Difference and the Demands of History* (Chicago: University of Chicago Press, 2002), 253–57, and the work cited there.

31. Bynum, *Holy Feast and Holy Fast*, 189–244.

32. Bynum, *Fragmentation*, 198; see also Jo Anne McNamara, "The Need to Give: Suffering and Female Sanctity in the Middle Ages," *in Images of Sainthood*, 199–221.

33. Bynum, *Holy Feast and Holy Fast*, 282–96.

34. Bynum, *Fragmentation*, 200.

35. Ibid.

36. Bynum, *Holy Feast and Holy Fast*, 294–95.

37. Hadewijch, *The Complete Works*, trans. Mother Columba Hart (New York: Paulist Press, 1980), 61. Translation modified. Bynum notes a related theological innovation made by women, Hadewijch chief among them, surrounding the resurrection of the body. Rather than envisioning a future of static peace, Hadewijch suggests that the afterlife will be one in which humanity shares in the constant movement of the Trinity. See Caroline Walker Bynum, *The Resurrection of the Body in Western Christianity, 200–1336* (New York: Columbia University Press, 1995). This restlessness is an important mark of late medieval Christianity for Bynum and one she continues to explore in her most recent work.

38. For other important scholarship that appeared around the same time as Bynum's, see Dronke, *Women Writers of the Middle Ages*; Kieckhefer, *Unquiet Souls*; Valerie M. Lagorio, "The Medieval Continental Women Mystics: An Introduction," in *An Introduction to the Medieval Mystics of Europe*, ed. Paul E. Szarmach (Albany: State University of New York Press, 1984), 161–93; Rudolph Bell, *Holy Anorexia* (Chicago: University of Chicago Press, 1985); Peter Dinzelbacher and Dieter R. Bauer, eds.,

Frauenmystic im Mittelalter (Ostfildern: Schwabenverlag, 1985); Peter Dinzelbacher and Dieter R. Bauer, eds., *Religiöse Frauenbewegung und mystische Frömmigkeit im Mittelalter* (Cologne: Böhlau, 1988); Petroff, *Medieval Women's Visionary Literature*; Newman, *Sister of Wisdom*; John A. Nichols and Thomas Shank, *Peace Weavers: Medieval Religious Women* (Kalamazoo, Mich.: Cistercian Publications, 1987); and Ursula Peters, *Religiöse Erfahrung als literarisches Faktum: Zur Vorgeschichte und Genese frauenmysticher Texte des 13 und 14 Jahrhunderts* (Tubingen: Niemeyer, 1988).

For some of the key early twentieth-century European scholarship, see Jeanne Ancelet Hustache, *Mechthilde de Magdebourg (1207–1282): Étude de psychologie religieuse* (Paris: Champion, 1926); Herbert Grundmann, *Religious Movements in the Middle Ages: The Historical Links Between Heresy, the Mendicant Orders, and the Women's Religious Movement in the Twelfth and Thirteenth Century with the Historical Foundation of German Mysticism*, trans. Steven Rowan (Notre Dame: Notre Dame University Press, 1995; originally published in 1935, revised edition in 1961); Simone Roisin, "L'efflorescence cistercienne et le courant féminin de piété au XIIIe siècle," *Revue d'Histoire Ecclésiastique* 39 (1943): 342–78; and Roisin, *L'hagiographie cistercienne dans le diocèse de Liège au XIIIe siècle* (Louvain, Belgium: Bibliothèque de l'Université, 1947); and the essays by Ann W. Astell, Bernard McGinn, and Barbara Newman on women's study of Christian spirituality in *Spiritus: A Journal of Christian Spirituality* 13, no. 1 (2013): 1–55.

For Bynum's reflections on her career, see Caroline Walker Bynum, "My Life and Works," in *Women Medievalists and the Academy*, ed. Jane Chance (Madison: University of Wisconsin Press, 2005), 995–1006; and Caroline Walker Bynum, "Why Paradox? The Contradictions of My Life as a Scholar," *Catholic Historical Review* 98, no. 3 (2012): 432–55.

39. For some very different accounts of how to read these bodily metaphors, see Elizabeth Ann Robertson, "The Corporeality of Female Sanctity in *The Life of Saint Margaret*," in *Images of Sainthood in Medieval Europe*, ed. Renate Blumenfeld-Kosinski and Timea Klara Szell (Ithaca: Cornell University Press, 1991), 268–87; Robertson, "Medieval Medical Views of Women and Female Spirituality in the *Ancrene Wisse* and Julian of Norwich's *Showings*," in *Feminist Approaches to the Body in Medieval Literature*, ed. Linda Lomperis and Sarah Stanbury (Philadelphia: University of Pennsylvania Press, 1993), 142–67; John Giles Milhaven, *Hadewijch and Her Sisters: Other Ways of Loving and Knowing* (Albany: State University of New York Press, 1993); Rosemary D. Hale, "'Taste and See for God Is Sweet': Sensory Perception and Memory in Medieval Christian Mystical Experience," in *Vox Mystica: Essays for Valerie M. Lagorio*, ed. Anne Clark Bartlett, Thomas Bestul, Janet Goebel Bestul, and William F. Pollard (Cambridge: D. S. Brewer, 1995), 3–14; Sarah Beckwith, "A Very Material Mysticism: The Medieval Mysticism of Margery Kempe," in *Medieval Literature: Criticism, Ideology, History*, ed. David Aers (Brighton: Harvester, 1986), 34–57; Beckwith, "Passionate Regulation: Enclosure, Ascesis, and the Feminist Imaginary," *South Atlantic Quarterly* 93 (1994): 803–24; Gordon Rudy, *Mystical Language of Sensation in the Later Middle Ages* (New York: Routledge, 2002); Sara

S. Poor, *Mechthild of Magdeburg and Her Book: Gender and the Making of Textual Authority* (Philadelphia: University of Pennsylvania Press, 2004); Dailey, *Promised Bodies*; and my essay "Inside Out," collected here.

40. Hollywood, *Virgin Wife*, 27–39.

41. Bynum, *Holy Feast and Holy Fast*, 6–9. Bynum's account follows Siegfried Ringler's "Die Rezeption mittelalterlicher Frauenmystik als wissenschaftliches Problem, dargestellt am Werk der Christine Ebner," in Dinzelbacher and Bauer, *Frauenmystik im Mittelater*, 178–200.

42. Kieckhefer, *Unquiet Souls*, 6; Kate Greenspan, "The Autohagiographical Tradition in Medieval Women's Devotional Writing," *A/B: Auto/Biographical Studies* 6, no. 2 (1991): 157–68; and Greenspan, "Autohagiography and Medieval Women's Spiritual Autobiography," in *Gender and Text in the Later Middle Ages*, ed. Jane Chance (Gainesville: University Press of Florida, 1996), 216–36.

43. Jeffrey F. Hamburger, "Women and the Written Word in Medieval Switzerland," in *Bibliotheken Bauen: Tradition und Vision/Building for Books: Traditions and Visions*, ed. S. Bieri and W. Fuchs (Basel: Birkhäuser, 2001), 112–63, 152.

44. This is visible in almost all of the essays in Mooney, *Gendered Voices*.

45. For the beguine influence on the thirteenth- and early-fourteenth-century Dominican Meister Eckhart, for example, which breaks down older claims that oppose women's affective spirituality to men's speculative mysticism, see Bernard McGinn, *Meister Eckhart and the Beguine Mystics: Hadewijch of Brabant, Mechthild of Magdeburg, and Marguerite Porete* (New York: Continuum, 1994); Hollywood, *Virgin Wife*; Hollywood, "Inside Out"; and Dailey, *Promised Bodies*. Nicholas Watson makes similar arguments with regard to Richard Rolle in *Richard Rolle and the Invention of Authority* (Cambridge: Cambridge University Press, 1991).

46. David Aers and Lynn Staley, *The Powers of the Holy: Religion, Politics, and Gender in Late Medieval English Culture* (University Park: Penn State University Press, 1996); Kathleen Biddick, "Genders, Bodies, Borders: Technologies of the Visible," *Speculum* 68 (1993): 389–418, reprinted in Biddick, *The Shock of Medievalism* (Durham: Duke University Press, 1999), 135–62.

47. Bynum, *Holy Feast and Holy Fast*, 195; cited by Aers and Staley, although with notable ellipses, in *Powers of the Holy*, 34.

48. Aers and Staley, *Powers of the Holy*, 34–35.

49. Ibid., 35.

50. Julie Miller, "Eroticized Violence in Medieval Women's Mystical Literature: A Call for Feminist Critique," *Journal of Feminist Studies in Religion* 15 (1999): 25–49. See also Sarah Beckwith, *Signifying God: Social Relation and Symbolic Action in the York Corpus Christi Plays* (Chicago: University of Chicago Press, 2001). Bynum herself has many interesting things to say about the violence of medieval texts and images. See especially Caroline Walker Bynum, *Wonderful Blood: Theology and Practice in Late Medieval Germany and Beyond* (Philadelphia: Pennsylvania University Press, 2007). For other broad discussions of Christianity and violence in the Middle Ages, all of which raise questions about from what perspective and in what way we can

engage critically with that violence or its representation, see Rudolph Conrad, *Violence and Daily Life: Reading, Art, and Polemics in the Citeaux Moralia in Job* (Princeton: Princeton University Press, 1997); Jody Enders, *The Medieval Theater of Cruelty: Rhetoric, Memory, and Violence* (Ithaca: Cornell University Press, 1999); Mitchell Merback, *The Thief, the Cross, and the Wheel: Pain and the Spectacle of Culture in Medieval and Renaissance Europe* (London: Reaktion Books, 1999); and Robert Mills, *Suspended Animation: Pain, Pleasure, and Punishment in Medieval Culture* (London: Reaktion Books, 2005).

Mary Carruthers's historicist work is illuminative. She shows that medieval accounts of memory work demand things, concrete images on which to hang that which is to be remembered. Certain kinds of material things, moreover, elicit memory more readily and, perhaps even more crucially, elicit affective responses that heighten memory and perform specific religious functions. Monastic and Franciscan meditative traditions seek to elicit *compuctio cordis*—compunction of the heart entailing guilt over one's sinfulness and the desire to atone for that guilt. As Carruthers shows, moreover, *compunctio* has a broad range of interrelated meanings, carrying "both the sense of piercing a surface and the emotional sense, of goading and vexing the feelings." Memory is literally pierced or wounded through "'excessive' images." The violence of many images found within monastic memory books, as well as within devotional and mystical texts and images, lends them to the work of memory because (1) the unusual is more memorable than the common, (2) violent images carry with them emotions of grief and fear that render the images even more memorable, and (3) through these emotion-laden images the believer scares, grieves, and shames him- or herself. According to Carruthers (here following Anselm of Bec), "This is literally *compunctio cordis*, wounding oneself with the *puncti* of text and picture." See Carruthers, *The Craft of Thought: Meditation, Rhetoric, and the Making of Images, 400–1200* (Cambridge: Cambridge University Press, 1998), 100 and 105.

51. See Hollywood, *Virgin Wife*; Hollywood, "Inside Out"; Elliott, *Fallen Bodies*; and Mary C. Erler and Maryanne Kowaleski, eds., *Gendering the Master Narrative: Women and Power in the Middle Ages* (Ithaca: Cornell University Press, 2003).

52. Biddick, "Genders, Bodies, Borders."

53. For a sophisticated feminist reading of Michel Foucault, Judith Butler, and Hannah Arendt on power that might aid such an enterprise, see Amy Allen, *The Power of Feminist Theory: Domination, Resistance, Solidarity* (Boulder, Colo.: Westview, 1999). For further reflection on the question of agency, see my "Gender, Agency, and the Divine in Religious Historiography," collected here.

54. Sharon Farmer and Carol Braun Pasternack, eds., *Gender and Difference in the Middle Ages* (Minneapolis: University of Minnesota Press, 2003).

55. Sharon Farmer, "The Beggar's Body: Intersections of Gender and Social Status in High Medieval Paris," in *Monks and Nuns, Outcasts and Saints: Religion in Medieval Society,* ed. Sharon Farmer and Barbara H. Rosenwein (Ithaca: Cornell University Press, 2000), 153–71, at 170. See also Farmer, *Surviving Poverty in Medieval Paris: Gender, Ideology, and the Daily Lives of the Poor* (Ithaca: Cornell University Press, 2002).

56. Farmer, "The Beggar's Body," 171.

57. See especially, Bynum, *Holy Feast and Holy Fast*; Bynum, *The Resurrection of the Body*; and Bynum, "Why All the Fuss About the Body? A Medievalist's Perspective," *Critical Inquiry* 22 (1995): 1–33. Bynum continues to do groundbreaking work on medieval materiality, most recently in Caroline Walker Bynum, *Christian Materiality: An Essay on Religion in Late Medieval Europe* (New York: Zone, 2011).

58. Richard Rambuss, *Closet Devotions* (Durham: Duke University Press, 1998), 48. See also Karma Lochrie, "Mystical Acts, Queer Tendencies," in *Constructing Medieval Sexuality*, ed. Karma Lochrie, Peggy McCracken, and James A. Schultz (Minneapolis: University of Minnesota Press, 1997), 180–200; Sarah Salih, "When Is a Bosom Not a Bosom? Problems with 'Erotic Mysticism,'" in Bernau, Evans, and Salih, *Medieval Virginities*, esp. 18–20; Constance M. Furey, "Sexuality," in Hollywood and Beckman, *The Cambridge Companion to Christian Mysticism*, 328–40; and my essays "Sexual Desire, Divine Desire: Queering the Beguines" and "'That Glorious Slit': Irigaray and the Medieval Devotion to Christ's Side Wound," both collected here.

59. Rambuss, *Closet Devotions*.

60. Ibid., 38.

61. The passage from Rupert of Deutz appears as cited in Fulton, *From Judgment to Passion*, 310.

62. Rambuss, *Closet Devotions*, 47.

63. Bruce Holsinger, "The Flesh of the Voice: Embodiment and Homoerotics of Devotion in Hildegard of Bingen (1098–1179)," *Signs* 19 (1993): 92–125; Kathy Lavezzo, "Sobs and Sighs Between Women: The Homoerotics of Compassion in *The Book of Margery Kempe*," in *Premodern Sexualities*, ed. Louise O. Fradenburg and Carla Freccero (New York: Routledge, 1996) 175–98; Lochrie, *Margery Kemp*; Carolyn Dinshaw, *Getting Medieval: Sexualities and Communities, Pre- and Postmodern* (Durham: Duke University Press, 1999); Stephen Moore, "The Song of Songs in the History of Sexuality," *Church History* 69 (2000): 328–49, reprinted in Moore, *God's Beauty Parlor and Other Queer Spaces in and Around the Bible* (Stanford: Stanford University Press, 2001); Garrett Epp, "Ecce homo," in *Queering the Middle Ages*, ed. Glenn Burger and Steven F. Kruger (Minneapolis: University of Minnesota Press, 2001), 236–51; Ulrike Wiethaus, "Female Homoerotic Discourse and Religion in Medieval Germanic Culture," in Farmer and Pasternack, *Gender and Difference in the Middle Ages*, 288–322; Lara Farina, *Erotic Discourse and Early English Religious Writing* (New York: Palgrave, 2006); Cary Howie, *Claustrophilia: The Erotics of Enclosure in Medieval Literature* (New York: Palgrave, 2007); Bill Burgwinkle and Cary Howie, *Sanctity and Pornography in Medieval Culture: On the Verge* (Manchester, UK: Manchester University Press, 2010); and Constance Furey, "Sexuality," in Hollywood and Beckman, *The Cambridge Companion to Christian Mysticism*, 328–40. Furey provides excellent examples of the continuity between medieval and modern erotic mystical devotion.

64. Lochrie, "Mystical Acts, Queer Tendencies."

65. For the limitations of the characterization of thirteenth-century women's religious writing as bridal mysticism, see Bynum, *Jesus as Mother*, 171–72; and Newman, *From Virile Woman to WomanChrist*. For a sophisticated argument about the use of bridal imagery in women's texts when it does appear, see Keller, *My Secret Is Mine*. On the complex questions surrounding Marguerite Porete and *The Mirror of Simple Souls*, see my essay "Reading as Self-Annihilation," collected here.

66. Rambuss, *Closet Devotions*, 58.

67. Elizabeth A. Clark, "Early Christian Women: Sources and Interpretations," in *That Gentle Strength: Historical Perspectives on Women in Christianity*, ed. Lynda L. Coon, Katherine J. Haldane, and Elizabeth W. Sommer (Charlottesville: University of Virginia Press, 1990), 19–35.

68. The literature here is large and includes material cited above, but for crucial discussions and bibliographies, see Peters, *Religiöse Erfahrung*; Catherine Mooney, "The Authorial Role of Brother A in the Composition of Angela of Foligno's Revelations," in *Creative Women in Medieval and Early Modern Italy: A Religious and Artistic Renaissance*, ed. E. Ann Matter and John Coakley (Philadelphia: University of Pennsylvania Press, 1994), 34–63; Kathleen Myers, "The Mystical Triad in a Colonial Mexican Nun's Discourse: Divine Author, Visionary Scribe, and Clerical Mediator," *Colonial Latin American History Review* 6 (1997): 479–524; Jennifer Summit, "Women and Authorship," in *The Cambridge Companion to Medieval Women's Writing*, ed. Carolyn Dinshaw and David Wallace (Cambridge: Cambridge University Press, 2003), 91–108; Poor, *Mechthild of Magdeburg and Her Book*; and Anke Gilleir, Alicia C. Montoya, and Suzan van Dijk, eds., *Women Writing Back/Writing Women Back: Transnational Perspectives from the Late Middle Ages to the Dawn of the Modern Era* (Leiden: Brill, 2010).

69. Jacques Dalarun, "Angèle de Foligno a-t-elle existé?," in *"Alla Signoria": Mélanges offerts à Noëlle de La Blanchardière* (Rome: École Française de Rome, 1995), 59–97. For recent assessments in English, see Catherine Mooney, "The Changing Fortunes of Angela of Foligno, Daughter, Mother, Wife," in *History in the Comic Mode: Medieval Communities and the Matter of Persons*, ed. Rachel Fulton and Bruce W. Holsinger (New York: Columbia University Press, 2007); and Cristina Mazzoni, "Angela of Foligno," in Minnis and Voaden, *Medieval Holy Women*, 581–600.

70. Lynn Staley, "The Trope of the Scribe and the Question of Literary Authority in the Works of Julian of Norwich and Margery Kempe," *Speculum* 66 (1991): 820–38; and Staley, *Margery Kempe's Dissenting Fictions* (University Park: Penn State University Press, 1994). The literature on Margery is vast, but for more recent work with useful bibliographies, see John H. Arnold and Katherine J. Lewis, eds., *A Companion to the Book of Margery Kempe* (Cambridge: D. S. Brewer, 2004); David Wallace, *Strong Women: Life, Text, and Territory, 1347–1645* (Oxford: Oxford University Press, 2010); Valentina Castagna, *Re-Reading Margery Kempe in the 21st Century* (New York: Peter Lang, 2011); and Anthony Goodman, "Margery Kempe," in Minnis and Voaden, *Medieval Holy Women*, 217–38. On the fascinating history of the Book, see Carolyn Dinshaw, *How Soon Is Now? Medieval Texts, Amateur Readers, and the*

Queerness of Time (Durham: Duke University Press, 2012); and Julie Chappell, *Perilous Passages: The Book of Margery Kempe, 1534–1934* (New York: Palgrave, 2013).

71. Summit, "Women and Authorship," 98.

72. The influential idea of "textual communities" comes from Brian Stock, *The Implications of Literacy: Written Language and Models of Interpretation in the Eleventh and Twelfth Centuries* (Princeton: Princeton University Press, 1983). For the related and highly relevant idea of "emotional communities," see Barbara Rosenwein, *Emotional Communities in the Early Middle Ages* (Ithaca: Cornell University Press, 2006).

73. On women's use of scribes, see Joan Ferrante, "Scribe Quae Vides et Audis: Hildegard, Her Language, and Her Secretaries," in David Townsend and Andrew Taylor, *The Tongue of the Fathers*, 102–135. For women as scribes, see D. L. D'Avray, *The Preaching of the Friars: Sermons Diffused from Paris Before 1300* (Oxford: Oxford University Press, 1985), 2; Lesley Smith, "Scriba, Femina: Medieval Depictions of Women Writing," in *Women and the Book: Assessing the Visual Evidence*, ed. Jane H. M. Taylor and Lesley Smith (London: British Library, 1996), 21–44; Beach, *Women as Scribes*; Cynthia Cyrus, *The Scribes for Women's Convents in Late Medieval Germany* (Toronto: University of Toronto Press, 2009); Kim Haines-Eitzen, *The Gendered Palimpsest: Women, Writing, and Representation in Early Christianity* (New York: Oxford University Press, 2012). For women as producers of books and images, see Taylor and Smith, *Women and the Book*; Jeffrey F. Hamburger, *Nuns as Artists: The Visual Culture of a Medieval Convent* (Berkeley: University of California Press, 1997); David F. Hult, "The Roman de la Rose, Christine de Pizan, and the querelle des femmes," in Dinshaw and Wallace, *The Cambridge Companion to Medieval Women's Writing*, 184–94; and Virginia Blanton, Veronica O'Mara, and Patricia Stoop, eds., *Nuns' Literacies in Medieval Europe: The Hull Dialogue* (Turnhout: Brepols, 2013). For women as readers and commissioners of spiritual works, see Susan Groag Bell, "Medieval Women Book Owners: Arbiters of Lay Piety and Ambassadors of Culture," *Signs* 7 (1982): 742–68, reprinted in Mary Erler and Maryanne Kowaleski, eds., *Women and Power in the Middle Ages* (Athens: University of Georgia Press, 1988), 149–87; Jeffrey F. Hamburger, *The Rothschild Canticles: Art and Mysticism in Flanders and the Rhineland Circa 1300* (New Haven: Yale University Press, 1990); Hamburger, "Women and the Written Word"; Elizabeth Ann Robertson, *Early English Devotional Prose and the Female Audience* (Knoxville: University of Tennessee Press, 1990); Carole M. Meale, ed., *Women and Literature in Britain, 1150–1500* (Cambridge: Cambridge University Press, 1993); Anne Clark Bartlett, *Male Authors, Female Readers: Representation and Subjectivity in Middle English Devotional Literature* (Ithaca: Cornell University Press, 1995); David N. Bell, *What Nuns Read: Books and Libraries in Medieval English Nunneries* (Kalamazoo, Mich.: Cistercian Publications, 1995); Lesley Janette Smith and Jane H. M. Taylor, eds., *Women, the Book and the Godly* (Cambridge: D. S. Brewer, 1995); June Hall McCash, *The Cultural Patronage of Medieval Women* (Athens: University of Georgia Press, 1996); Mary A. Suydam, "Beguine Textuality: Sacred Performances," in *Performance and Transformation: New Approaches to Late Medieval Spirituality*, ed. M. A. Suydam and J. Ziegler (New York: St Martin's Press,

1999), 169–210; Mary C. Erler, *Women, Reading, and Piety in Late Medieval England* (Cambridge: Cambridge University Press, 2002); D. H. Green, *Women Readers in the Middle Ages* (Cambridge: Cambridge University Press, 2007); and Cynthia Jane Brown, *The Queen's Library: Imagine-Making at the Court of Anne of Brittany, 1477–1514* (Philadelphia: University of Pennsylvania Press, 2011).

74.   Dinshaw and Wallace, "Introduction," in Dinshaw and Wallace, *Cambridge Companion to Medieval Women's Writing*, 5.

75.   For the claim that some women's textual production was relatively independent of male authority, see Gertrud Jaron Lewis, *By Women, for Women, About Women: The Sister-Books of Fourteenth-Century Germany* (Toronto: Pontifical Institute of Medieval Studies, 1996); and Rebecca L. R. Garber, *Feminine Figurae: Representations of Gender in Religious Texts by Medieval German Women Writers, 1100–1375* (New York: Routledge, 2003). For the centrality of communal life and practice in German and the Netherlands, see Winston-Allen, *Convent Chronicles*; Wybren Scheepsma, *Medieval Religious Women in the Low Countries: The Modern Devotion, the Canonesses of Windescheim, and Their Writing* (Rochester, N.Y.: Boydell and Brewer, 2004); John Van Engen, *Sisters and Brothers of the Common Life: The Devotio Moderna and the Late Middle Ages* (Philadelphia: University of Pennsylvania Press, 2008); and John Van Engen, "Communal Life," in Minnis and Voaden, *Medieval Holy Women*, 105–31. For the interplay between men and women, in addition to the literature already cited, see Felice Lifshitz and Lisa Bitel, eds., *Gender and Christianity in Medieval Europe: New Perspectives* (Philadelphia: University of Pennsylvania Press, 2008).

76.   Jennifer Summit, *Lost Property: The Woman Writer and English Literary History, 1380–1589* (Chicago: University of Chicago Press, 2000). See also Martha Driver, "By Me Elysabeth Pykerying: Women and Book Production in the Early Tudor Period," in *Manuscripts and Printed Books in Europe, 1350–1550: Packing, Presentation and Consumption*, ed. Emma Cayley and Susan Powell (Liverpool: Liverpool University Press, 2013).

77.   For example, see Bell and Mazzoni, *The Voices of Gemma Galgani*. For an earlier example of this phenomenon, see Armando Maggi, *Uttering the Word: The Mystical Performances of Maria Maddalena de' Pazzi, a Renaissance Visionary* (Albany: State University of New York Press, 1998). Part of the issue lies in the dual charge that women's religious authority be grounded in extraordinary experiences and that women, like all Christians, be humble. The dangers of self-promotion, understood as pride and vainglory, were highly theorized in the Middle Ages. For a rich discussion of the rhetorical strategies involved in evading such charges, see Weber, *Teresa of Avila and the Rhetoric of Femininity*. Bynum shows convincingly that the rhetorical move is seen more clearly in writings by semireligious women than in those by nuns, at least in the high Middle Ages. See the closing essay in Bynum, *Jesus as Mother*. The same problems are visible in some men's lives and writings, particularly for those who lack clerical authority or base their religious claims on something other than that authority. Most exemplary for the medieval period is Rupert of Deutz, for whom, see Fulton, *From Judgment to Passion*, 309–50.

78.   Brenna Moore, *Sacred Dread: Raïssa Maritain, the Allure of Suffering, and the French Catholic Revival, 1905–1945* (Notre Dame: University of Notre Dame Press, 2013).

79.   For some examples of continuities between medieval and modern spirituality, although with keen attention to the changing religious, political, and economic contexts, see David Blackbourn, *Marpingen: Apparitions of the Virgin Mary in Nineteenth-Century Germany* (New York: Knopf, 1994); William A. Christian Jr., *Visionaries: The Spanish Republic and the Reign of Christ* (Berkeley: University of California Press, 1996); Marie-Florine Bruneau, *Women Mystics Confront the Modern World: Marie de l'Incarnation (1599–1672) and Madame Guyon (1648–1717)* (Albany: State University of New York Press, 1998); Harris, *Lourdes*; Marina Caffiero, "From the Late Baroque Mystical Explosion to the Social Apostolate, 1650–1850," in *Women and Faith: Catholic Religious Life in Italy from Late Antiquity to the Present*, ed. Gabriella Zari and Lucetta Scaraffia (Cambridge, Mass.: Harvard University Press, 1999), 176–204; Ann Taves, *Fits, Trances, and Visions: Experiencing Religion and Explaining Experience from Wesley to James* (Princeton: Princeton University Press, 1999); Leigh Eric Schmidt, *Hearing Things: Religion, Illusion, and the American Enlightenment* (Cambridge, Mass.: Harvard University Press, 2000); Susan E. Dian and Debra Meyers, eds., *Women and Religion in Old and New Worlds* (New York: Routledge, 2001); Allan Greer and Jodi Bilinkoff, eds., *Colonial Saints: Discovering the Holy in the Americas* (New York: Routledge, 2003); Jodi Bilinkoff, *Related Lives*; and Moore, *Sacred Dread*.

Michel de Certeau's work has played an enormous role in the study of mysticism and the issue of historical periodization. His work is subtly but vitally important for the study of sexual difference and mysticism. For the key texts available in English, see Michel de Certeau, *Heterologies: Discourse on the Other*, trans. Brian Massumi (Minneapolis: University of Minnesota Press, 1986); de Certeau, *The Mystic Fable*, trans. Michael B. Smith (Chicago: University of Chicago Press, 1992); and de Certeau, *The Possession at Loudun*, trans. Michael B. Smith (Chicago: University of Chicago Press, 2000). For some differing views on Certeau's influence on the study of mysticism, particularly in the English-language world, see "Symposium: Michel de Certeau," *Spiritus: A Journal of Christian Spirituality* 12, no. 2 (2012): 161–216.

80.   See Rosalynn Voaden, ed., *Prophets Abroad: The Reception of Continental Holy Women in Late-Medieval England* (Cambridge: D. S. Brewer, 1996); Karen Anne Winstead, *Virgin Martyrs: Legends of Sainthood in Late Medieval England* (Ithaca: Cornell University Press, 1997); Summit, *Lost Property*; Hamburger, "Women and the Written Word"; and Poor, *Mechthild and Her Book*.

81.   Poor, *Mechthild and Her Book*.

82.   Kwakkel is able to show definitively that the poems ascribed to Hadewijch II are, in fact, by a different author than those ascribed to Hadewijch. See Erik Kwakkel, "The Middle Dutch Hadewijch Manuscripts," in *A Companion to Hadewijch*, ed. Patricia Dailey and Veerle Fraeters (Leiden: Brill, forthcoming). See also Kwakel, "Ouderdom en genese van de veertiende-eewse Hadewijch-handschriften," *Queeste: Journal of Medieval Literature in the Low Countries* 6 (1999): 23–40; and Erik Kwakel and

Herman Mulder, "Quidem sermones: Geestelijk proza van de Ferguut-kopiist (Brussels, Koninklijke Bibliotheek, hs. 3067–73)," *Tijdschrift voor Nederlandse Taal-en Letterkunde* 117 (2001): 151–65.

83. For more on the centrality of manuscript compilations to the study of medieval women's mysticism and spirituality, see Sara S. Poor, "Transmission," in Hollywood and Beckman, *The Cambridge Companion to Christian Mysticism*, 240–51; Felice Lifshitz, *Religious Women in Early Carolingian Francia: A Study of Manuscript Transmission and Monastic Culture* (New York: Fordham University Press, 2014); Holly Flora, *"The Devout Belief of the Imagination": The Paris "Meditationes Vitae Christi" and Female Franciscan Mysticism in Trecento Italy* (Turnhout: Brepols, 2014); and my comments on the study of Marguerite Porete in "Reading as Self-Annihilation," included here. For more on manuscript studies and transmission as vital components of the study of Christian mysticism, see Marleen Cré, *Vernacular Mysticism in the Charterhouse: A Study of London*, British Library, MS additional 37790 (Turnhout: Brepols, 2004); Jessica Brantley, *Reading in the Wilderness: Private Devotion and Public Performance in Late Medieval England* (Chicago: University of Chicago Press, 2007); Wybren Scheepsma, *The Limburg Sermons: Preaching in the Medieval Low Countries at the Turn of the Fourteenth Century*, trans. David F. Johnson (Leiden: Brill, 2008); and Graham D. Caie and Denis Reveney, eds., *Medieval Texts in Context* (New York: Routledge, 2008).

84. Jeffrey F. Hamburger's work is pivotal. See especially Hamburger, *The Rothschild Canticles*; Hamburger, *Nuns as Artists*; Hamburger, *The Visual and the Visionary*; Jeffrey F. Hamburger and Anne-Marie Bouché, eds., *The Mind's Eye: Art and Theological Argument in the Middle Ages* (Princeton: Princeton University Press, 2005); and Hamburger, "Mysticism and Visuality," in Hollywood and Beckman, *The Cambridge Companion to Christian Mysticism*, 277–93. For other recent and sophisticated work on the interplay between image and text in religious practice, see Barbara Newman, "What Did It Mean to Say 'I Saw'?': The Clash Between Theory and Practice in Medieval Visionary Culture," *Speculum* 80 (2005): 1–43; Newman, "Contemplating the Trinity: Text, Image, and the Origins of the Rothschild Canticles," *Gesta* 52, no. 2 (2013): 133–59; Aden Kumler, *Translating Truth: Ambitious Images and Religious Knowledge in Late Medieval France and England* (New Haven: Yale University Press, 2011); and Alexa Sand, *Vision, Devotion, and Self-Representation in Late Medieval Art* (Cambridge: Cambridge University Press, 2014).

85. McGinn, *Meister Eckhart and the Beguine Mystics*; and Nicholas Watson, "Censorship and Cultural Change in Late-Medieval England: Vernacular Theology, the Oxford Translation Debate, and Arundel's Constitutions of 1409," *Speculum* 70 (1995): 822–63. See also McGinn, *The Flowering of Mysticism*; and Fiona Somerset and Nicholas Watson, eds., *The Vulgar Tongue: Medieval and Postmedieval Vernacularity* (University Park: Penn State University Press, 2003).

86. Newman, *God and the Goddesses*, 298. See also Newman's work on the interplay between secular and religious literature, *Medieval Crossover: Reading the Secular Against the Sacred* (Notre Dame: University of Notre Dame Press, 2013).

87. Newman here intervenes in a debate, particularly heated within the German scholar-
     ship, about the relative transparency or literary quality of vision accounts. For a sum-
     mary of the debate, see Frank J. Tobin, *Mechthild of Magdeburg: A Medieval Mystic
     in Modern Eyes* (Columbia, S.C.: Camden House, 1995), 115–22.

88. For related work on the imagination and devotion, see Brantley, *Reading in the Wil-
     derness*; Jennifer Bryan, *Looking Inward: Devotional Reading and the Private Self
     in Late Medieval England* (Philadelphia: University of Pennsylvania Press, 2008);
     McNamer, *Affective Mysticism*; and Sara Ritchey, *Holy Matter: Changing Perceptions
     of the Material World in Late Medieval Christianity* (Ithaca: Cornell University
     Press, 2014). For the centrality of imagination and writing to women's theology, see
     Dailey, *Promised Bodies*.

89. See Dailey, *Promised Bodies*, 2–19 and 27–61; and also Patricia Dailey, "The Body
     and Its Senses," in Hollywood and Beckman, *The Cambridge Companion to Christian
     Mysticism*, 264–76. The argument is nuanced, complex, and important. Bringing the
     two Pauline passages together leads Dailey to write of "inner bodies" and "outer bod-
     ies"; I don't find this specific language in Augustine, yet Dailey's reading brings out
     something important in his thinking. A crucial question raised by Dailey's work is
     how Augustinian Hadewijch finally is. Central to this question is Dailey's fascinating
     deployment of the notion of "unlived experience" to name a union that can never
     quite be experienced. At issue is how Augustine and Hadewijch understand tempo-
     rality, embodiment, and the interaction between time and eternity, all vital issues for
     Dailey. For more on these issues, see also Patricia Dailey, "Time and Memory," in Hol-
     lywood and Beckman, *The Cambridge Companion to Christian Mysticism*, 341–50.

90. It might prove helpful to read Dailey in relation to an early work by Giorgio Agam-
     ben, *Stanzas*, in which he argues that medieval physicians, philosophers, theologians,
     and poets shared in a "pneumo-phantasmology" in which the realm of *pneuma*
     (spirit) and the phantasms that inhabit that realm mediate between the lower aspects
     of bodily physicality and the soul. Phantasm and phantasy or imagination are con-
     stitutive of memory and occupy a realm somewhere between the gross physicality of
     bodies and the nonmateriality of the intellect. As Agamben argues, this is the realm
     of *pneuma*, an aetherial, spiritualized, yet still physical form of reality. The phantasms
     Agamben describes are, not surprisingly, crucial to the process of falling in love. Love
     itself is pneumatic or spiritual. Although Agamben focuses on secular poetry, the
     same movement can be seen in religious writing. As I show in "Acute Melancholia,"
     for Beatrice of Nazareth and Margaret Ebner, desire moves from the eyes to the phan-
     tasy, from phantasy to memory, and from memory to the entire body, now rendered
     Christ-like in the human being's love for and identification with the object of desire.
     Agamben argues that modern scholars have misunderstood the pneumatic nature of
     love because of the tendency to project a dualism between the body and the soul "on a
     conception whose intention was precisely to mediate and overcome this opposition."
     See Giorgio Agamben, *Stanzas: Word and Phantasm in Western Culture*, trans. Ron-
     ald L. Martinez (Minneapolis: University of Minnesota Press, 1993). For more on
     lovesickness in the Middle Ages, see my "Acute Melancholia," collected here.

91. For an earlier influential account, see Karl Rahner, "The 'Spiritual Senses' Accord-
     ing to Origen," in *Theological Investigations*, vol. 16, trans. David Morland (New
     York: Seabury Press, 1979), 81–103; Rahner, "The Doctrine of the 'Spiritual Senses'
     in the Middle Ages," in *Theological Investigations*, 16:103–34. The essays originally
     appeared in 1932 and 1933, respectively. For recent work on the topic, in addition
     to Dailey, see Rudy, *Mystical Language of Sensation*; Niklaus Largier, "Inner Senses,
     Outer Senses: The Practice of Emotion in Medieval Mysticism," in *Codierungen von
     Emotionen im Mittelalter/Emotions and Sensibilities in the Middle Ages*, ed. C. Ste-
     phen Jaeger and Ingrid Kasten (Berlin: De Gruyter, 2003); Largier, "Medieval Mysti-
     cism," in *The Oxford Handbook of Religion and Emotion*, ed. John Corrigan (Oxford:
     Oxford University Press, 2008); and Paul L. Gavrilyuk and Sarah Coakley, eds., *The
     Spiritual Senses: Perceiving God in Western Christianity* (Cambridge: Cambridge
     University Press, 2012).

92. At issue is the relationship between allegoresis as a mode of interpretation, with its
     complex ties to the question of the bodily and the spiritual senses, and allegory as a
     way of writing. The body figures there too, of course, for allegory is understood as
     giving skin or covering—integumentum—to thought. For some comments on the
     question, see Hollywood, "Introduction," in Hollywood and Beckman, *The Cam-
     bridge Companion to Christian Mysticism*, 26–27.

93. Fiona Somerset, "Emotion," in Hollywood and Beckman, *The Cambridge Compan-
     ion to Christian Mysticism*, 298. Emotion is an anachronistic term when applied to
     medieval texts, but one that has been very fruitful. Curiously, the recent turn to
     "affect" surrounding the work of Gilles Deleuze, Felix Guattari, and Brian Massumi
     seems ignorant of the centrality of *affectus* in ancient and medieval Christian texts.
     A noun drawn from the passive participle of *afficio*—to do something to someone,
     to exert an influence on another body or person, to bring another into a partic-
     ular state of mind—*affectus* connotes having had something done to one, having
     had another exert an influence on your body or person, or having been brought by
     another into a particular state of mind. The terms that surround *affectus* are gener-
     ally what we would call emotion words. Hence God acts and the resultant *affectus* of
     love, fear, praise, or sorrow is the soul's response to God's action. A complex inter-
     vention by medievalists into contemporary work on affect, feeling, and emotion is
     surely in order. For *affectus*, see Hollywood, "Song, Experience, and Book." For one
     influential contemporary theorist of affect and some of the problems raised by his
     work, see Brian Massumi, "The Autonomy of Affect," *Cultural Critique* 31 (1995):
     83–109; Massumi, *Parables of the Virtual: Movement, Affect, Sensation* (Durham:
     Duke University Press, 2002); and Ruth Leys, "The Turn to Affect: A Critique,"
     Critical Inquiry 37 (2011): 434–72. For the history of the term "emotion," see Wil-
     liam Reddy, *The Navigation of Feeling: A Framework for the History of the Emotions*
     (Cambridge: Cambridge University Press, 2001); Thomas Dixon, *From Passions to
     Emotions: The Creation of a Secular Psychological Category* (Cambridge: Cambridge
     University Press, 2003); Susan J. Matt and Peter N. Stearns, *Doing Emotions His-
     tory* (Urbana: University of Illinois Press, 2014); and Jan Plamper, *The History of the*

Emotions: An Introduction (Oxford: Oxford University Press, 2015). For medieval views of the passions, affects, or emotions, see Simo Knuuttila, *Emotions in Ancient and Medieval Philosophy* (Oxford: Oxford University Press, 2004); Barbara Rosenwein, "Worrying About Emotions in History," *American Historical Review* 107 (2002): 821–45; Rosenwein, *Emotional Communities*; Jan Plamper, "The History of Emotions: An Interview with William Reddy, Barbara Rosenwein, and Peter Stearns," *History and Theory* 49 (2010): 237–65; and the special issue *Pre-Modern Emotions, Exemplaria* 26 (2014). I remain inspired by an earlier book of Rosenwein's, *Rhinoceros Bound: Cluny in the Tenth Century* (Philadelphia: University of Pennsylvania Press, 1982).

94.   See Carruthers, *The Craft of Thought*; McNamer, *Affective Meditation*; Michelle Karnes, *Imagination, Meditation, and Cognition in the Middle Ages* (Chicago: University of Chicago Press, 2011); Smith, "Exemplarity and Its Limits"; Robert Glenn Davis, "The Force of Union: Affect and Ascent in the Theology of Bonaventure" (PhD diss., Harvard University, 2012); and Jessica A. Boon, *The Mystical Science of the Soul: Medieval Cognition in Bernadino de Laredi's Recollection Method* (Toronto: University of Toronto Press, 2012).

95.   For an extremely interesting and important account of the interplay between figural language and emotion in the eighteenth-century revaluation of enthusiasm—a term closely associated with mysticism—see Shaun Irlam, *Elations: The Poetics of Enthusiasm in Eighteenth-Century Britain* (Stanford: Stanford University Press, 1999), 70–82. According to Irlam's account, eighteenth-century accounts of poetry begin with the insistence that all poetry is religious poetry and all religious language poetic precisely because both to be religious and to be poetic is to work on the emotions.

96.   See Bernard McGinn, "Love, Knowledge, and Mystical Union in Western Christianity: Twelfth to Sixteenth Centuries," *Church History* 56, no. 1 (1987): 7–24.

97.   See Douglas Burton Christie, "Early Monasticism," in Hollywood and Beckman, *The Cambridge Companion to Christian Mysticism*, 37–58.

98.   The rich historical work on theology and affect in the Middle Ages is too vast to begin to cite here, although see Bernard McGinn, *The Growth of Mysticism* (New York: Crossroad, 1994); McGinn, *The Flowering of Mysticism*; McGinn, *The Harvest of Mysticism in Medieval Germany, 1300–1500* (New York: Crossroad, 2005); and McGinn, *The Varieties of Vernacular Mysticism, 1350–1550* (New York: Crossroad, 2012). His bibliographies are extremely useful. What is most worthy of note here is that intensely affective work is produced by men and women both and that for both, at least until the fourteenth century, the affective and the cognitive are intimately tied together.

  For some suggestive comments about the role German idealism and its uptake of medieval and early modern mysticism might play in modern scholarly distinctions, see Andrew Weeks, *German Mysticism from Hildegard of Bingen to Ludwig Wittgenstein: A Literary and Intellectual History* (Albany: State University of New York Press, 1993); and Cyril O'Regan, *The Heterodox Hegel* (Albany: State University of New York Press, 1994).

99.   Dominick La Capra, *Representing the Holocaust: History, Theory, Trauma* (Ithaca: Cornell University Press, 1994), 178–83; and in a different and more sympathetic light, Nicholas Watson, "Desire for the Past," *Studies in the Age of Chaucer* 21 (1999): 59–97.

100.   Caroline Walker Bynum, *Metamorphosis and Identity* (New York: Zone, 2001), 74. See also Bynum, "Wonder," *American Historical Review* 102, no. 1 (1997): 1–26.

101.   For a compelling account of the value of women's mystical writings for contemporary feminism, see Grace M. Jantzen, *Power, Gender and Christian Mysticism* (Cambridge: Cambridge University Press, 1995). In a review of that book, however, I argue that Jantzen gives too little attention to precisely the kind of historical detail about which Bynum so rightly cares; see Hollywood, "Justice and Gender in Mysticism: Review of Grace Jantzen, *Power, Gender and Christian Mysticism*," *Christian Spirituality Bulletin* 4, no. 1 (1996): 28–29.

102.   Hollywood, *Sensible Ecstasy*; see also Christina Mazzoni, *Saint Hysteria: Neurosis, Mysticism, and Gender in European Culture* (Ithaca: Cornell University Press, 1996); Bruce Holsinger, *The Premodern Condition: Medievalism and the Making of History* (Chicago: University of Chicago Press, 2005); and Ben Morgan, *On Becoming God: Late Medieval Mysticism and the Modern Western Self* (New York: Fordham University Press, 2013).

103.   Hollywood, *Sensible Ecstasy*, 19–21, 274–78.

104.   Ibid., 6.

105.   Caroline Bynum is, as usual, at the forefront of work in the interplay between practice, bodies, and belief in the Middle Ages. See most recently Bynum, *Wonderful Blood*; and Bynum, *Material Christianity*. In a growing bibliography on practice in the Christian Middle Ages, see Denise Louise Despres, *Ghostly Sights: Visual Meditation in Late-Medieval Literature* (Norman, Okla.: Pilgrim Press, 1989); Talal Asad, *Genealogies of Religion: Disciplines and Reasons of Power in Christianity and Islam* (Baltimore: Johns Hopkins University Press, 1993); Carruthers, *The Craft of Thought*; Suydam and Ziegler, *Performance and Transformation*; Fulton, *From Judgment to Passion*; Brantley, *Reading in the Wilderness*; McNamer, *Affective Meditation*; Miri Rubin, ed., *Medieval Christianity in Practice* (Princeton: Princeton University Press, 2009); Karnes, *Imagination, Meditation and Cognition in the Middle Ages*; and Susan Boynton and Diane J. Reilly, eds., *The Practice of the Bible in the Middle Ages: Production, Reception, and Performance in Western Christianity* (New York: Columbia University Press, 2011).

   For discussion of the importance of practice in studying philosophical and religious traditions other than Christianity, among a vast literature, see Hadot, *Philosophy as a Way of Life*; Saba Mahmood, "Rehearsed Spontaneity and the Conventionality of Ritual: Disciplines of Ṣalat," *American Ethnologist* 28 (2001): 827–54; Mahmood, "Feminist Theory, Embodiment, and the Docile Subject: Some Reflections on the Egyptian Islamic Revival," *Cultural Anthropology* 16 (2001): 202–36; Mahmood, *Politics of Piety: The Islamic Revival and the Feminist Subject* (Princeton: Princeton University Press, 2005); and my essays "Performativity, Citationality, Ritualization" and "Practice, Belief, and Feminist Philosophy of Religion," both collected here.

106. Hamburger, *Rothschild*; Hamburger, *Nuns as Artists*; and Hamburger, *The Visual and the Visionary*.

107. See Fassler, "Composer and Dramatist," in Newman, *Voice of the Living Light*, 149–75; Fassler, "Hildegard and the Dawn Song of Lauds," in Attridge and Fassler, *Psalms in Community*; Fassler, "Music for the Love Feast," in Bernstein, *Women's Voices Across the Musical World*, 92–117; Holsinger, *Music, Body, and Desire in Medieval Culture*; Dailey, *Promised Bodies*; Jones, "Christian Listening and the Ethical Community of the Liturgical Text"; and Jones, "*Hostia jubilationis*."

108. Another large bibliography might be cited here, but I will refer readers to Dailey, *Promised Bodies*; and Eleanor Johnson, "Feeling Time, Will, and Words: Vernacular Devotion in *The Cloud of Unknowing*," *Journal of Medieval and Early Modern Studies* 41, no. 2 (2011): 345–68.

109. See Lisa H. Cooper and Andrea Denny-Brown, eds., *The Arma Christi in Medieval and Early Modern Culture: With a Critical Edition of "O Vernicle"* (Burlington, Vt.: Ashgate, 2014).

110. In addition to Bynum, *Material Christianity*, see also Sarah Stanbury, *The Visual Object of Desire in Late Medieval England* (Philadelphia: University of Pennsylvania Press, 2008); Stanbury, "Premodern Culture and the Material Object," *Exemplaria* 20, no. 2 (2010); Stanbury, "Premodern Flesh," *Postmedieval: A Journal of Medieval Cultural Studies* 4, no. 4 (2013); and Ritchey, *Holy Matter*. There is a large bibliography on each of these particular kinds of things.

111. Much of the new work I have cited deals with these methodological issues. For some additional help from Americanists, see David Hall, ed., *Lived Religion in America: Toward a History of Practice* (Princeton: Princeton University Press, 1997); Robert A. Orsi, *The Madonna of 115th Street: Faith and Community in Italian Harlem, 1880–1950* (New Haven: Yale University Press, 1985); Orsi, *Thank You Saint Jude: Women's Devotion to the Patron Saint of Hopeless Causes* (New Haven: Yale University Press, 1996); Orsi, *Between Heaven and Earth: The Religious Worlds People Make and the Scholars Who Study Them* (Princeton: Princeton University Press, 2006); and R. Marie Griffiths, *God's Daughters: Evangelical Women and the Power of Submission* (Berkeley: University of California Press, 2001). My one caveat is that "lived religion" is always itself theological rather than standing in opposition to theology.

3. GENDER, AGENCY, AND THE DIVINE IN RELIGIOUS HISTORIOGRAPHY

I wrote this piece for a panel on religious historiography at the Berkshire Conference on the History of Women, held at the University of Connecticut, Storrs, in 2002. In a slightly longer version, it was printed, together with other papers from the panel and responses by Susannah Heschel and Saba Mahmood, in the *Journal of Religion*. It was meant to pose questions rather than to answer them, although readers troubled by my suggestions have not taken the piece in that spirit. There is little they raise that isn't here already, so I let the piece stand. I will see what further trouble it can cause.

For updated bibliographies on the medieval material, see "Feminist Studies in Christian Spirituality," chapter 2 of this volume.

1. See Caroline Walker Bynum, *Jesus as Mother: Studies in the Spirituality of the High Middle Ages* (Berkeley: University of California Press, 1982); Bynum, *Holy Feast and Holy Fast: The Religious Significance of Food to Medieval Women* (Berkeley: University of California Press, 1987); Bynum, *Fragmentation and Redemption: Essays on Gender and the Human Body in Medieval Religion* (New York: Zone, 1991); Peter Dinzelbacher and Dieter Bauer, *Frauenmystik im Mittelalter* (Ostfildern, Germany: Schwabenverlag, 1985); Peter Dronke, *Women Writers of the Middle Ages: A Critical Study of Texts from Perpetua (d. 203) to Marguerite Porete (d. 1310)* (Cambridge: Cambridge University Press, 1984); Barbara Newman, *Sister of Wisdom: Saint Hildegard's Theology of the Feminine* (Berkeley: University of California Press, 1987); and Elizabeth Alvilda Petroff, ed., *Medieval Women's Visionary Literature* (Oxford: Oxford University Press, 1986).

2. For the phrase "rhetoric of femininity," see Alison Weber, *Teresa of Avila and the Rhetoric of Femininity* (Princeton: Princeton University Press, 1990).

3. See, for example, the visionary exegesis of Rupert of Deutz (ca. 1070–1135) and Joachim of Fiore (d. 1202). For the two monks, as for their contemporary Hildegard of Bingen (1098–1179), visions provided direct insight into the interpretation of scripture. Bernard McGinn, "Apocalyptic Traditions and Spiritual Identity in Thirteenth-Century Religious Life," in *The Roots of the Modern Christian Tradition*, ed. E. Rozanne Elder (Kalamazoo, Mich.: Cistercian, 1984), 1–26; McGinn, *The Growth of Mysticism: Gregory the Great Through the 12th Century* (New York: Crossroad, 1994), 325–41; and Rachel Fulton, *From Judgment to Passion: Devotion to Christ and the Virgin Mary, 800–1200* (New York: Columbia University Press, 2002), 309–50.

4. Elizabeth Robertson, "The Corporeality of Female Sanctity in *The Life of Saint Margaret*," in *Images of Sainthood in Medieval Europe*, ed. Renate Blumenfeld-Kosinski and Timea Szell (Ithaca: Cornell University Press), 268–87; Robertson, "Medieval Medical Views of Women and Female Spirituality in the *Ancrene Wisse* and Julian of Norwich's *Showings*," in *Feminist Approaches to the Body in Medieval Literature*, ed. Linda Lomperis and Sarah Stanbury (Philadelphia: University of Pennsylvania Press, 1993), 142–67; Dyan Elliott, "The Physiology of Rapture and Female Spirituality," in *Medieval Theology and the Natural Body*, ed. Peter Biller and A. J. Minnis (Woodbridge, Suffolk: York Medieval, 1997), 141–73; and Nancy Caciola, "Mystics, Demoniacs, and the Physiology of Spirit Possession in Medieval Europe," *Comparative Study of Society and History* 42, no. 2 (2000): 268–306.

5. The ubiquity—as well as the cogency—of this paradigm for both the medieval and early modern periods is signaled by Diane Watt's *Secretaries of God*, the title of which is derived from a phrase found in the *Book* of the fifteenth-century English laywoman Margery Kempe. Diane Watt, *Secretaries of God* (Cambridge: Brewer, 1997). The extent to which women make explicit the need for special legitimation because of their sex differs, both between women and within writings by the same woman. Bynum, *Jesus as Mother*, 170–262; and Amy Hollywood, *The Soul as Virgin Wife: Mechthild of Magdeburg, Marguerite Porete, and Meister Eckhart* (Notre Dame: Notre Dame University Press, 1995), esp. 61.

6. Hans Neumann, ed., *Mechthild von Magdeburg, "Das fliessende Licht der Gottheit":* *Nach der Einsiedler Handschrift in kritischem Vergleich mit der gesamten Überlief-* *erung,* 2 vols. (Munich: Artemis, 1990), vol. 2, bk. 2, chap. 26, p. 69. For an excellent English translation of the text, see Mechthild of Magdeburg, *The Flowing Light of the Godhead,* trans. Frank Tobin (Mahwah, N.J.: Paulist, 1998).

7. Judith Butler shows that the split between agency and determination or victimiza-tion so often deployed in feminist studies is deeply problematic, for the very condi-tions that bring about subordination are themselves the source of subjectivity and hence of agency—however limited or constrained that agency might be in particular situations of subordination. As Amy Allen explains, subjectivity for Butler is taken on through a complex series of performative citations of the norms that constitute subjects within a given society: "However, the very fact that it is *necessary* for norms to be reiterated or cited by individuals in order for them to maintain their efficacy indicates that we are never completely determined by them. . . . If we were completely determined by gender norms, there would be no need for us to continually cite and reiterate them; that we are continually compelled to do so gives us good reason for thinking that we are not so determined." For Butler, our very ability to act in mean-ingful ways depends on our becoming (at least marginally) recognizable subjects (to at least some social group or subgroup). See Amy Allen, *The Power of Feminist Theory: Domination, Resistance, Solidarity* (Boulder, Colo.: Westview, 1999), 73; Judith Butler, *Gender Trouble: Feminism and the Subversion of Identity* (New York: Routledge, 1990); Butler, *Bodies That Matter: On the Discursive Limits of "Sex"* (New York: Routledge, 1993); and Butler, *Excitable Speech: A Politics of the Performative* (New York: Routledge, 1997).

8. For parallel accounts of—and potential problems with—particularly social-scientific accounts of spirit possession, see I. M. Lewis, *Ecstatic Religion,* 2nd ed. (New York: Routledge, 1989); and Mary Keller, *The Hammer and the Flute: Women, Power and Spirit Possession* (Baltimore: Johns Hopkins University Press, 2002), esp. 50–53.

9. For a review of the debate in philosophy of science and the social sciences, see Karl-Otto Apel, *Understanding and Explanation: A Transcendental-Pragmatic Perspective,* trans. Georgia Warnke (Cambridge, Mass.: MIT Press, 1984).

10. Wayne Proudfoot, *Religious Experience* (Berkeley: University of California Press, 1985). See also Robert Segal, *Explaining and Interpreting Religion: Essays on the Issue* (New York: Peter Lang, 1992); David Ray Griffin, "Religious Experience, Nat-uralism, and the Social Scientific Study of Religion"; J. Samuel Preus, "Explaining Griffin"; and Robert Segal, "In Defense of Social Scientific Naturalism: A Response to David Ray Griffin," all in *Journal of the American Academy of Religion* 68, no. 1 (2000): 99–125, 127–32, and 133–41.

11. Proudfoot never explicitly denies the possibility of supernatural explanations being warranted, but the entire tenor of his argument works against such a possibility and in fact seems to be premised on its denial.

12. In one of many possible examples, the early modernist Brad Gregory argues for the importance of understanding over explanation, insisting that to understand early

modern Christian martyrdom, one must take with utmost seriousness the power of religious beliefs over those who hold them. (Unlike Gregory, I find it very rare for historians of religion *not* to take seriously the power of religious belief. The problem, as I will show, lies deeper.) Gregory thereby attempts to avoid what he sees as the reductionist tendencies of historical explanations, which often rest on presumptions foreign to the texts, documents, and artifacts under analysis. Despite arguing strenuously for the centrality of understanding over explanation and the inadmissibility of modern social-scientific, philosophical, and literary categories of analysis within historical work, however, Gregory goes on almost immediately to discuss the shift between early Christian martyrdom and monasticism's heroic asceticism in terms of sublimation. Brad S. Gregory, *Salvation at Stake: Christian Martyrdom in Early Modern Europe* (Cambridge, Mass.: Harvard University Press, 1999), 8–15, 50. The term "sublimation" itself serves as a useful reminder of the historical transmutation of terms. According to the Oxford English Dictionary, "sublimation" first names a chemical process (fourteenth-century) and is then extended by analogy to the social (fifteenth-century), religious (seventeenth-century), geological (nineteenth-century), and finally psychoanalytic (twentieth-century) registers. Gregory would no doubt argue that he is using the term in its seventeenth-century sense—one never, of course, completely lost. Yet the psychoanalytic overtones are very hard not to hear. Similarly, although Mechthild herself clearly worries about authority, thereby rendering it an important descriptive term, it is very hard not to hear twentieth- and twenty-first-century feminist resonances (and putative explanatory categories) in its deployment within recent scholarship.

13. For the claim that at least one mode of modern history writing is grounded in the desire for just such emancipatory accounts of the past and emancipation of the voices of the past, see Carolyn Steedman on Jules Michelet in her *Dust: The Archive and Cultural History* (New Brunswick, N.J.: Rutgers University Press, 2002). Steedman's is just one of a number of recent reevaluations of Michelet, grounded in the work of Roland Barthes and Michel Foucault. Although one might argue that the conception of history derived from Michelet, Barthes, Foucault, Michel de Certeau, Jacques Rancière, and others engages with the other in a mode like that which I seek here, an analysis of the supernatural in their work would be required in order to solidify the claim.

14. Dipesh Chakrabarty, *Provincializing Europe: Postcolonial Thought and Historical Difference* (Princeton: Princeton University Press, 2000), 103. Further citations to this work are cited parenthetically in the text. See also Chakrabarty, *Habitations of Modernity: Essays in the Wake of Subaltern Studies* (Chicago: University of Chicago Press, 2002), esp. chaps. 1–3.

15. Gregory claims that in using social-scientific modes of analysis, historians refuse to acknowledge the power of religious beliefs over those who hold them. This is rarely the case, however, as Chakrabarty shows with regard to Guha. Similarly, it is very clear that historians of medieval women both acknowledge the religious beliefs of their subjects and also read their work in terms of agency, authorization, and legitimization.

16.   In her study of gender and possession, Keller argues in a similar manner that atten-
      tion to the beliefs of the other is inadequate, for within the social-scientific literature
      on possession these beliefs are always presumed to be false. Keller suggests, in fact,
      that the category of religious belief emerges as a way of isolating the false beliefs of
      those putatively other than the social-scientific investigator: "On the one hand, the
      possession is described as a *real belief,* but on the other hand it is *not* the belief of the
      scholar, who then presents an alternative interpretation of the *real* process at hand."
      Keller, *The Hammer and the Flute*, 29.

17.   Historicization here seems to imply the reading of the Santal in terms of political
      agency (that is, in terms of categories meaningful to modern Marxian and liberal
      historiography). This again works to homogenize the past with the present, a central
      project of historicism according to Chakrabarty. Although Foucault and others argue
      for a view of history as disruption, not unlike Chakrabarty's second description, again
      I believe that further work would be required to see the extent to which they allow the
      putatively supernatural to disrupt history in the first mode described here. This may
      be the point on which otherness ultimately collapses. (Arguably this is not true for
      Georges Bataille, hence the difficulty of assimilating his work within modern accounts
      of history. See Amy Hollywood, *Sensible Ecstasy: Mysticism, Sexual Difference, and the
      Demands of History* [Chicago: University of Chicago Press, 2002], esp. 60–87.)

18.   Chakrabarty borrows this characterization from the work of Walter Benjamin,
      another important source for alternative conceptions of history.

19.   On this issue, see Leigh Eric Schmidt, *Hearing Things: Religion, Illusion, and the
      American Enlightenment* (Cambridge, Mass.: Harvard University Press, 2000).

20.   Although derived from Chakrabarty's engagement with Marxist historiography, I
      think that the distinction has salience beyond that context. Insofar as history engages
      in the work of explanation, it tends to posit some set of antecedent events as the cause
      of that which follows. Hence there will always be the shadow of that which does not
      fit within this causal narrative.

21.   Talal Asad, *Genealogies of Religion: Discipline and Reasons of Power in Christianity
      and Islam* (Baltimore: Johns Hopkins University Press, 1993), 16, cited in Keller, *The
      Hammer and the Flute*, 63–64. Foucault's and Butler's accounts of subjectivity, of
      course, radically undermine the identification of subjectivity with consciousness,
      hence potentially rendering the distinction Keller finds in Asad moot.

22.   Keller, *The Hammer and the Flute*, 73. Again, this account of agency fits well with
      Butler's recharacterization of subjectivity.

23.   Ibid., 74.

24.   See Amy Hollywood, "Inside Out: Beatrice of Nazareth and Her Hagiographer,"
      collected here.

25.   Frederick M. Smith, "The Current State of Possession Studies as a Cross-Disciplin-
      ary Project," *Religious Studies Review* 27, no. 3 (2001): 210. Smith refers to Heike
      Behrend, "Power to Heal, Power to Kill: Spirit Possession and War in Northern
      Uganda (1986–1994)," in *Spirit Possession: Modernity and Power in Africa*, ed. Heike
      Behrend and Ute Luig (Madison: University of Wisconsin Press, 1999), 1–35.

26. See Behrend, "Power to Heal," 31.

27. The incitement of others to kill can also be discerned in many medieval religious women's approval of the Crusade against the Cathar heretics and similar events.

28. The tendency in feminist history to valorize agency has rendered it difficult to discuss—or even to recognize—those moments in which women have been agents of evil, violence, or oppression. As Susannah Heschel has put it to me in conversation, much feminist historiography still remains caught in a hagiographical mode in which women are seen either as victims or as passive—and hence not fully responsible—agents.

29. See also Chakrabarty, *Habitations of Modernity*, 20–37.

30. Ibid., 36. Chakrabarty calls for something like what Bynum recently pleads for with regard to medieval religious historiography. "We write the best history," she argues, "when the specificity, the novelty, the awe-fulness, of what our sources render up bowls us over with its complexity and its significance. Our research is better when we move only cautiously to understanding, when the fear that we may appropriate the 'other' leads us not so much to writing about ourselves and our fears as to crafting our stories with attentive, wondering care. . . . We must rear a new generation of students who will gaze in wonder at texts and artifacts, quick to puzzle over a translation, slow to project or to appropriate, quick to assume there is a significance, slow to generalize about it." The difference is Bynum's anxiety about the interpenetration of past and present, exactly that toward which Chakrabarty points the historian. See Caroline Walker Bynum, *Metamorphosis and Identity* (New York: Zone, 2001), 74.

31. Chakrabarty, *Habitations of Modernity*, 36–37.

32. On the centrality of radical openness to moral inquiry within religious studies, see Robert A. Orsi, "Snakes Alive: Resituating the Moral in the Study of Religion," in *Women, Gender, Religion: A Reader*, ed. Elizabeth A. Castelli (New York: Palgrave, 2001), 98–118.

33. Although arguably working fully within the terms of History 1, Amanda Anderson makes an important argument for the necessity of distinguishing between historical agency and critical reflection. Looking at recent historical work on Victorian women, Anderson argues that Nancy Armstrong, Mary Poovey, and other scholars "position women as continuous with modern discipline or regulation" and thereby "create not exactly an empowered but rather simply a powered subject." Most women are presented as "passive agents," enacting changing cultural scripts with little or no critical detachment or self-reflection on their role as agents of social, cultural, and political change. The central importance of critical detachment to emancipatory agency hence remains untheorized. In other words, Anderson suggests, agency itself is an inadequate category for emancipatory political projects, a position perhaps inevitable after Foucault and Butler. See Amanda Anderson, "The Temptations of Aggrandized Agency: Feminist Histories and the Horizon of Modernity," *Victorian Studies* 43 (2000): 57; and Anderson, *The Powers of Distance: Cosmopolitanism and the Cultivation of Difference* (Princeton: Princeton University Press, 2001).

34. On the limits of emancipatory conceptions of the self for analytic feminism, see Saba Mahmood, "Feminist Theory, Embodiment, and the Docile Agent: Some Reflections on the Egyptian Islamic Revival," *Cultural Anthropology* 16 (2001): 202–36.

35. And of course, women—even feminists—desire many things in addition to freedom.

4. READING AS SELF-ANNIHILATION: ON MARGUERITE PORETE'S *MIRROR OF SIMPLE SOULS*

In 2002, Michael Warner very generously invited me to speak at the English Institute on the theme of uncritical reading. The English Institute is a yearly gathering of literary scholars and theorists; I presumed, perhaps ungratefully, that I was there as a scholar of religion to represent uncritical reading itself. What follows is the final form of my rebellion against that likely imaginary scenario, a rebellion mitigated by the fact that the English Institute kindly published the piece in *Polemics*, edited by Jane Gallop.

The material on Marguerite has been updated, with the help of Sean Fields, whose work sets the standard in the field and to whom I am extremely grateful for saving me from mistakes.

1. "Critical" and "Criticism," *Oxford English Dictionary* (Oxford: Oxford University Press, 1971).

2. Why and when multiple versions become seen as a problem is a pertinent question. Earlier theologians, preachers, and ecclesiasts certainly recognized the diversity.

3. Reformation scholars are generally credited with the return to the original languages of scripture, but the impetus, if not the ability, was there long before Luther and Melancthon. The Council of Vienne in 1311 called for chairs of Greek and Hebrew at the major universities. The lack of qualified teachers was presumably responsible for the failure to implement the plan. See Beryl Smalley, "The Bible in the Medieval Schools," in *The Cambridge History of the Bible: The West from the Fathers to the Reformation*, ed. G. W. H. Lampe (Cambridge: Cambridge University Press, 1969): 218–19.

4. See Hermann Samuel Reimarus, *Reimarus: Fragments*, ed. Charles H. Talbert, trans. Ralf S. Fraser (Philadelphia: Fortress Press, 1970). For one influential account by an important Protestant theologian, see Hans W. Frei, *The Eclipse of Biblical Narrative: A Study in Eighteenth and Nineteenth Century Hermeneutics* (New Haven: Yale University Press, 1974), 113–16. For a more recent summary account, this time by biblical scholars, see Robert Morgan with John Barton, *Biblical Interpretation* (Oxford: Oxford University Press, 1988), 52–57.

5. On divergent conceptions of history within early modern exegesis, see Debora Kuller Shuger, *The Renaissance Bible: Scholarship, Sacrifice, and Subjectivity* (Berkeley: University of California Press, 1994), esp. 11–53.

6. See David Friedrich Strauss, *The Life of Jesus Critically Examined*, trans. George Eliot (Philadelphia: Fortress Press, 1972); Frei, *Eclipse*, 233–44; and Morgan with Barton, *Biblical Interpretation*, 44–52.

7.   A number of questions arise at this point about the historical contingency of Western conceptions of critique in the face of the historical claims and historical dubiety of much of the Bible. Would the term "criticism" carry such destructive resonance in the Western academy if the Hebrew and Christian Bibles had been more "reliable" documents? To what extent does this "unreliability" depend on the peculiarly historical claims made by these documents and the traditions that arise from them? Or is it a feature of reason to attack, such that *any* document of faith would have been found wanting? And might it be that criticism, understood as *engagement*, necessarily comes into conflict with religious texts, understood as providing an all-encompassing, unsurpassable, and central outlook on existence? This is the account of religion recently provided by Paul Griffiths in his sometimes perceptive—albeit highly polemical—account of religious reading, one many scholars of religion and religious people would dispute. See Paul Griffiths, *Religious Reading: The Place of Reading in the Practice of Religion* (Oxford: Oxford University Press, 1999).

8.   I take this broad definition of rational discourses to include those that (1) follow the rules of logic and correct argumentation (informal logic), (2) adhere to developing rules of evidence, and (3) have a plausibility grounded, for most historians and biblical scholars, in a kind of rough empiricism.

9.   See, for example, Friedrich Schleiermacher, *Hermeneutics and Criticism, and Other Writings*, trans. and ed. Andrew Bowie (Cambridge: Cambridge University Press, 1998).

10. See Friedrich Schleiermacher, *The Life of Jesus*, ed. and intro. Jack C. Verheyden, trans. S. Maclean Gilmour (Philadelphia: Fortress Press, 1975). Despite these claims, Schleiermacher's *The Life of Jesus* argues that one of these accounts—that of John— marks a superior apprehension of Christ. Of course, if all we can apprehend of the object of religious experience comes through our own experience or the accounts of others, it is not clear on what basis Schleiermacher judges one account superior to another. Is it closer to his own? This seems a mere personal preference. Does it more fully capture what is only alluded to in other accounts, but crucial to them? But on what basis does one determine which features are primary and secondary, given that no one account can be taken as more objectively true than another? These questions raise the issue of what kind of judgments religious judgments are. They seem closer, perhaps, to aesthetic judgments than to historical or epistemological ones, yet what does this imply about aesthetic judgments?

11. For this argument, see Morgan with Barton, *Biblical Interpretation*.

12. See especially Friedrich Schleiermacher, *On Religion: Speeches to Its Cultured Despisers*, trans. Richard Crouter (Cambridge: Cambridge University Press, 1988), esp. 96–140. For the centrality of Schleiermacher's account of experience to the modern study of religion, see Wayne Proudfoot, *Religious Experience* (Berkeley: University of California Press, 1985), esp. 1–40.

13. For debates about the title of Marguerite's book, see Luisa Muraro, "Le mirour des simples ames de Marguerite Porete: Les avatars d'un titre," *Ons geestelijk erf* 70 (1996): 3–9; and Robert E. Lerner, "New Light on the Mirror of Simple Souls," *Speculum* 85 (2010): 101–2.

14.   Biblical scholars, it should perhaps be noted, find antecedents to their practices only in those early Christian and medieval interpreters who eschew allegory—two-eyed reading in Marguerite's terms—for literal and historical interpretation. Most famous among these are the fourth- and fifth-century Antiochenes and the twelfth-century Augustinian canons of St. Victor in Paris, in particular the great scholar of Hebrew Andrew of St. Victor. See Beryl Smalley, *The Study of the Bible in the Middle Ages* (Notre Dame: University of Notre Dame Press, 1964), esp. 83–195.

15.   Vincent Crapanzano, *Serving the Word: Literalism in America from the Pulpit to the Bench* (New York: New Press, 2000), 329. For a nuanced reading of fundamentalist modes of interpretation and speech, see Susan Friend Harding, *The Book of Jerry Falwell: Fundamentalist Language and Politics* (Princeton: Princeton University Press, 2000).

16.   Sean L. Field, *The Beguine, the Angel, and the Inquisitor: The Trials of Marguerite Porete and Guiard de Cressonessart* (Notre Dame: University of Notre Dame Press, 2012), 234. Until recently, scholars relied on the edition of the trial documents and other contemporary sources by Paul Verdeyen, "Le procès d'Inquisition contre Marguerite Porete et Guiard de Cressonessart (1309–1310)," *Revue d'histoire ecclésiastique* 81 (1986): 47–94. We now are fortunate to have a translation of these materials by Sean Field, based on the Verdeyen edition but with corrections drawn from an analysis of the original documents. See Field, *The Beguine*, 209–38. Although it has problems, also useful is Elizabeth A. R. Brown, "Marguerite Porete, John of Baconthorpe, and the Chroniclers of Saint-Denis," *Medieval Studies* 27 (2013): 307–44. For an excellent online bibliography devoted to Marguerite, maintained by Zan Kocher, see http://margueriteporete.net.

17.   For a brilliant reconstruction, based on a new reading of all of the sources in manuscript, see Field, *The Beguine*. See also Henry Ansfar Kelly, "Inquisitorial Deviations and Cover-Ups: The Prosecution of Marguerite Porete and Guiard of Cressonessart, 1308–1310," *Speculum* 89 (2014).

18.   The announcement was first made in the *Osservatore Romano*, June 16, 1946. The article is reprinted in Romana Guarnieri, "Il movimento del Libero Spirito," *Archivio Italiano per Ia storia della pietà* 4 (1965): 661–63. In 1946, Guarnieri had not yet located a French version of the text. On the discovery, see Sean L. Field, Robert E. Lerner, and Sylvain Piron, "Marguerite Porete et son Miroir: Perspectives Historique," in *Marguerite Porete et le Miroir des simples âmes: perspectives historique, philosophique et littéraires*, ed. Sean L. Field, Robert E. Lerner, and Sylvain Piron (Paris: Vrin, 2013).

19.   For literature confirming Guarnieri's discovery, see Robert E. Lerner, *The Heresy of the Free Spirit in the Later Middle Ages* (Notre Dame: University of Notre Dame Press, 1972), 73. Elizabeth A. R. Brown and Lydia Wegener have raised recently raised questions about the certainty of the assertion. See Brown, "Marguerite Porete"; and Lydia Wegener, "Freiheitsdiskurs und Beginenverfolgung um 1308: Der Fall der Marguerite Porete," in *1308: Eine Topographie historischer Gleichzeitigkeit*, ed. Andreas Speer and David Wirmer (Berlin: Walter de Gruyter, 2010), 199–236.

20. Until very recently, reports were of three French manuscripts believed to have survived into modern times, only one of which is available for scholarly study (the
Chantilly manuscript, Musee Conde MS F.xiv.26). Of the other two, one disap-
peared on route between the municipal library of Bourges and the Bibliothèque
Nationale in Paris. The other was reported to be in the possession of a French-speaking
community outside of France, who would not grant access to scholars. Most now
consider the claim to a third manuscript to be a hoax. A recently discovered manuscript in the Bibliothèque Municipal of Valenciennes, however, contains several
chapters of the *Mirror*. Geneviève Hasenohr, who made the discovery, argues that
the fragments are based on a fourteenth-century version and thus represent an
early form of the text. The Chantilly manuscript is likely from the fifteenth century, both in its production and in its language, suggesting it is a translation from
Marguerite's thirteenth-century French dialect (presumably Picard, the dialectic
of the French-speaking Southern Low Countries). For the likely fallacious claims
about a third manuscript, see Michael G. Sargent, "The Annihilation of Marguerite Porete," *Viator* 28 (1997): 260. For the discovery of a third French manuscript
containing parts of the *Mirror*, see Geneviève Hasenohr, "La tradition du Miroir
des simples âmes au XVe siècle: Du Marguerite Porete (d. 1310) à Marguerite de
Navarre," *Compte rendus des séances de l'Académie des inscriptions et belles-lettres*
4 (1999): 1347–66. For medieval reports of other manuscripts of the *Mirror*, see
Fields, *The Beguine*, 204–7.

21. The *Mirror* was translated into Latin probably in the fourteenth century (five complete manuscripts and a number of fragments survive), at least twice into Italian (one
survives in a single manuscript, the other in three), and once into English in the early
fifteenth century (three manuscripts survive, all associated during the fifteenth century with the Carthusian houses around London). The English translator (M. N.)
added a preface and fifteen explanatory glosses. This English translation was then
translated into Latin at the end of the fifteenth century by Richard Methley of Mount
Grace Charterhouse, who added his own glosses to the text. The 1984 *Corpus Christianorum* edition brings together Guarnieri's version of the Chantilly manuscript
with Paul Verdeyen's critical edition of the first Latin translation. Marilyn Dorion
has edited the Middle English *Mirror*, whose glosses have been edited and translated
by Edmund Colledge and Romana Guarnieri. There is now also a new edition of the
Methley translation. See Romana Guarnieri and Paul Verdeyen, eds., *Le Mirouer des
simples ames anienties et qui seulement demourent en vouloir et desir d'amour*, in *Corpus Christiano rum: Continuatio Mediaevalis*, vol. 69 (Turnhout, Belgium: Brepols,
1986); Marilyn Dorion, ed., "The Mirror of Simple Souls: A Middle English Translation," *Archivio Italiano per la Storia della Pièta* 5 (1968): 242–355; Edmund Colledge
and Romana Guarnieri, "The Glosses of 'M. N.' and Richard Methley to 'The Mirror
of Simple Souls,'" *Archivio Italiano per la storia della pietà* 5 (1968): 357–82; and John
Clark, ed., *Speculum animarum simplicium: A Glossed Latin Version of "The Mirror of
Simple Souls*," 2 vols. (Salzburg: Institut für Anglistik und Amerikanistik, Universität
Salzburg, 2010).

22. Walter Simons and Sean Fields provide evidence that there may also have been a Flemish translation of the *Mirror*, although no manuscripts are known to survive. See Walter Simons, *Cities of Ladies: Beguine Communities in the Medieval Low Countries, 1200–1565* (Philadelphia: University of Pennsylvania Press, 2001), 137; and Fields, *The Beguine*, 207. See also John Van Engen, "Marguerite (Porete) of Hainaut and the Medieval Low Countries," in Field, Lerner, and Piron, *Marguerite Porete*.

23. As Hasenohr's discovery shows, the *Mirror* was excerpted in the mystical compendia that begin to appear in the fifteenth and sixteenth centuries. For the importance of such discoveries and our understanding of medieval mystical texts, see Hasenohr, "La tradition"; Field, *The Beguine*, 204–7; Sara S. Poor, *Mechthild of Magdeburg and Her Book: Gender and the Making of Textual Authority* (Philadelphia: University of Pennsylvania Press, 2004); Sara S. Poor, "Transmission," in *The Cambridge Companion to Christian Mysticism*, ed. Amy Hollywood and Patricia Z. Beckman (Cambridge: Cambridge University Press, 2012), 240–51; and Zan Kocher, "The Apothecary's *Mirror of Simple Souls*: Circulation and Reception of Marguerite Porete's Book in Fifteenth-Century France," *Modern Philology* 111, no. 1 (2013): 23–47.

24. For work in English on the centrality of understanding medieval textual, reading, and hearing practices within the context of a manuscript culture, and the methodological implications of this understanding, see John Dagenais, *The Ethics of Reading in Manuscript Culture: Glossing the "Libro de buen amor"* (Princeton: Princeton University Press, 1994); and Andrew Taylor, *Textual Situations: Three Medieval Manuscripts and Their Readers* (Philadelphia: University of Pennsylvania Press, 2002). This work is an extension of earlier work on reading, writing, and manuscript culture, important among them Brian Stock's call for an understanding of medieval reading communities. See Brian Stock, *The Implications of Literacy: Written Language and Models of Interpretation in the Eleventh and Twelfth Centuries* (Princeton: Princeton University Press, 1983).

Although I'll only be able to focus on two interpretative levels, let me outline the multiple ways in which the manuscript traditions might be approached in order to suggest the complexity attendant on the study of medieval reading practices. First, *The Mirror of Simple Souls* engages in textual and biblical interpretation, from the prologue (which recasts a story from the medieval Alexander legend) through the final chapters (devoted to biblical texts). Second, the central interlocutors within the *Mirror's* allegorical dialogue—Love, Soul, and Reason—repeatedly offer instructions or provide models for how the text itself should be read. Third, the first Latin translation includes an approbation of the text by three theologians. Although brief, the text is suggestive for the ways in which learned men both condoned and warned against the dangers of the *Mirror*. Fourth, the trial documents record, at least partially, the way in which the *Mirror* was read by those who condemned the book. Fifth, the translations themselves all warrant careful study in order to understand the dynamics of medieval translation as a mode of reading. Sixth, two of these translations include glosses by the translators (included in all of the surviving manuscripts of these translations). Although the Chantilly manuscript, the three manuscripts that contain the Middle English translation, and Richard Methley's Latin have been extensively described and studied, all the available manuscripts should be reconsidered in light of contemporary interest in manuscripts and their transmission. With what other texts was the *Mirror* bound? Are there other readerly markings that can be uncovered? What, if anything, can we discern about the owners and readers of the manuscript? Finally, there is testimony from at least one other early reader. Marguerite of Navarre's poem from 1547, "Prisons," includes over a hundred lines praising the *Mirror* and its author (who Marguerite knew to be a woman although we cannot know if she knew her to be Marguerite Porete). On the Middle English translator and compiler, in addition to material cited above, see Marleen Cré, "*The Mirror of Simple Souls* in Middle English Revisited: The Translator and the Compiler," in Field, Lerner, and Piron, *Marguerite Porete*. On Marguerite Porete and Marguerite of Navarre, see Jean Dagens, "Le 'Miroir des simples ames' et Marguerite des Navarre," *La Mystique Rhénane, Colloque de Strasbourg, 16–19 mai 1961* (Paris: Universitaires de France, 1963); and Suzanne Kocher, "Marguerite de Navarre's Portrait of Marguerite Porete: A Renaissance Queen Constructs a Medieval Woman Mystic," *Medieval Feminist Newsletter* 26, no. 1 (1998): 17–23.

25. My suspicion is that Marguerite wrote the book in pieces, piling on analogies, images, textual readings, and paradoxes in ever-new efforts to get across her understanding of the free and simple soul.

26. The *Mirror* continually refers to those who will hear it being read, suggesting a performance context or reading out loud within religious communities.

27. Guarnieri and Verdeyen, *Mirouer*, chap. 5, pp. 18–20. Further references will be parenthetical within the text. All translations are my own unless otherwise noted.

28. For this reading of *maintien*, see Margaret Porette [sic], *The Mirror of Simple Souls*, trans. Edmund Colledge, J. C. Marler, and Judith Grant (Notre Dame: University of Notre Dame Press, 1999), 71n2.

29. These are the claims that "a soul annihilated in the love of the Creator could, and should, grant to nature all that it desires" and that "the soul neither desires nor despises poverty, tribulation, masses, sermons, fasts, or prayers and gives to nature, without remorse, all that it ask." Paul Fredericq, *Corpus documentorum inquisitionis haereticae pravitatis Neerlandicae*, vol. 1 (Ghent: Vuylsteke, 1889), 76–77. For the condemnation seen within the context of the fourth Lateran Council (1215), see Kent Emery Jr., "Foreword: Margaret Porette [sic] and Her Book," in Colledge, Marler, and Grant, trans., *Mirror*, xvii–xviii.

30. On Marguerite's seemingly unremitting elitism, see Joanne Maguire Robinson, *Nobility and Annihilation in Marguerite Porete's "Mirror of Simple Souls"* (Albany: State University of New York Press, 2001). For the complexity of her deployment of allegory and its importance for how she thinks about social relationship and relationships between human beings and God, see Suzanne Kocher, *Allegories of Love in Marguerite Porete's "Mirror of Simple Souls"* (Turnhout: Brepols, 2009).

31. Marguerite draws here, as elsewhere in the text, on meditative traditions within late medieval Christian spirituality. Whereas most meditations on Christ's love are meant

to provoke and augment the affections and desire, however, Marguerite uses these techniques against themselves in order to destroy reason, will, and affection. For some reflections on these meditative traditions and their relationship to contemporary theory and practice, see Amy Hollywood, *Sensible Ecstasy: Mysticism, Sexual Difference, and the Demands of History* (Chicago: University of Chicago Press, 2002), 69–79.

32. As Caroline Walker Bynum, Dyan Elliott, Walter Simons, and others show, in the thirteenth century the clergy's sole control over the sacraments and the centrality of the sacraments to Christian life are relatively new. See Caroline Walker Bynum, *Jesus as Mother: Studies in the Spirituality of the High Middle Ages* (Berkeley: University of California Press, 1982), 247–62; and Dyan Elliott, *Fallen Bodies: Pollution, Sexuality, and Demonology in the Middle Ages* (Philadelphia: University of Pennsylvania Press, 1999). For splits among the clergy on these issues, particularly with regard to lay and women's piety, see Simons, *Cities of Ladies*, 118–37; and Hollywood, *Sensible Ecstasy*, 241–57.

33. It is perhaps worthy of note that modern critical reading of the Bible begins with an emphasis on the literal and historical meaning of the text not unlike that embraced today by many fundamentalist Christians.

34. As I suggested above, I think that this is the real issue for Crapanzano in his engagement with the literalism of Christian fundamentalists. He suggests that literalism may lead to particular problems with engagement, although without fully endorsing the claim. Marguerite's case can be used both for and against that thesis.

35. Marguerite's conceptions of reading and hearing might usefully be explored within the larger context of medieval conceptions of reading. Very suggestive in this light, although dealing with a different historical moment, is Adrian Johns's account of the physiology of reading in the seventeenth century. See Johns, *The Nature of the Book: Print and Knowledge in the Making* (Chicago: University of Chicago Press, 1998), 380–443.

36. My thanks to Jonathan Crewe for helping me articulate and refine these questions.

37. Saba Mahmood helped me articulate this point, one in line with much of her own work on the anthropology of religion and gender in contemporary Islam. See Saba Mahmood, "Feminist Theory, Embodiment, and the Docile Agent: Some Reflections on the Egyptian Islamic Revival," *Cultural Anthropology* 16 (2001): 202–36; Mahmood, "Rehearsed Spontaneity and the Conventionality of Ritual: Disciplines of Ṣalāt," *American Ethnologist* 28 (2001): 827–53; and Saba Mahmood and Charles Hirschkind, "Feminism, the Taliban, and Politics of Counter-Insurgency," *Anthropological Quarterly* 75 (Spring 2002): 339–54.

5. SEXUAL DESIRE, DIVINE DESIRE; OR, QUEERING THE BEGUINES

The essay was commissioned for *Queer Theology: New Perspectives on Sex and Gender* (2006), edited by Gerald Loughlin. It appeared that same year in *Theology and Eros: Transfiguring Passion at the Limits of the Discipline*, edited by Virginia Burrus and Catherine Keller. The goal of the Loughlin volume was to draw on resources within the Christian tradition in imagining a contemporary queer theology. Given the audience for the essay, I used available translations and tried to avoid overly detailed historical and textual knots. The emphasis is on the way in which historically distant material speaks to and challenges contemporary religious practice.

1. Judith Bennett, "'Lesbian-Like' and the Social History of Lesbianisms," *Journal of the History of Sexuality* 9 (2000): 7. See also the essays collected in Francesca Canadé Sautman and Pamela Sheingorn, ed., *Same Sex Love and Desire Among Women in the Middle Ages* (New York: Palgrave, 2001). For groundbreaking theoretical and historical work on the early modern period, see Valerie Traub, *The Renaissance of Lesbianism in Early Modern England* (Cambridge: Cambridge University Press, 2002). For materials directed toward specifically religious texts, see Jeffrey Jerome Cohen, *Medieval Identity Machines* (Minneapolis: University of Minnesota Press, 2003), esp. 154–87; Ulrike Wiethaus, "Female Homoerotic Discourse and Religion in Medieval Germanic Culture," in *Gender and Difference in the Middle Ages*, ed. Sharon Farmer and Carol Braun Pasternack (Minneapolis: University of Minnesota Press, 2003), 288–321; Carolyn Dinshaw, *Getting Medieval: Sexualities and Communities, Pre- and Postmodern* (Durham: Duke University Press, 1999), esp. 143–82; Karma Lochrie, "Mystical Acts, Queer Tendencies," in *Constructing Medieval Sexuality*, ed. Karma Lochrie, Peggy McCracken, and James A. Schultz (Minneapolis: University of Minnesota Press, 1997), 180–200; Bruce Holsinger, "The Flesh of the Voice: Embodiment and the Homoerotics of Devotion in the Music of Hildegard of Bingen (1098–1179)," *Signs* 19 (1993): 92–125; Mary Anne Campbell, "Redefining Holy Maidenhead: Virginity and Lesbianism in Late Medieval England," *Medieval Feminist Newsletter* 13 (1992): 14–15; and Kathy Lavezzo, "Sobs and Sighs Between Women: The Homoerotics of Compassion in *The Book of Margery Kempe*," in *Premodern Sexualities*, ed. Louise O. Fradenburg and Carla Freccero (New York: Routledge, 1996), 175–98.

2. Lochrie does not provide a full history of the image. An early, intensely erotic and eucharistic example can be found in Aelred of Rievaulx, "Rule of Life for a Recluse," a general guide to the religious life written, perhaps not surprisingly, for women. In meditating on Christ's body, Aelred encourages the reader: "Hasten, linger not, eat the honeycomb with your honey, drink your wine with your milk. The blood is changed into wine to gladden you, the water into milk to nourish you. From the rock streams have flowed for you, wounds have been made in his limbs, holes in the wall of his body, in which, like a dove, you may hide while you kiss them one by one. Your lips, stained with his blood, will become like a scarlet ribbon and your word sweet." Aelred of Rievaulx, *Treatises and the Pastoral Prayer*, trans. Theodore Berkeley, Mary Paul Macpherson, and R. Penelope Lawson (Kalamazoo, Mich.: Cistercian Publications, 1971), 90–91, cited by Thomas Bestul, *Texts of the Passion: Latin Devotional Literature and Medieval Society* (Philadelphia: University of Pennsylvania Press, 1996), 39. As Bestul points out, the passage brings together language from the Psalms and the Song of Songs. Although this kind of highly erotic devotion to Christ's wounds becomes characteristic of late medieval meditational

practice, the example from Aelred shows that it has roots in mid-twelfth-century texts and practices. For further examples from fourteenth- and fifteenth-century devotional texts, see Bestul, *Texts of the Passion*, 56–57, 59, and 62; Douglas Gray, "The Five Wounds of Our Lord," *Notes and Queries* 10 (1963): 50–51, 82–89, 127–34, 163–68; Lewis Flora, "The Wound in Christ's Side and the Instruments of the Passion: Gendered Experience and Response," in *Women and the Book: Assessing the Physical Evidence*, ed. Lesley Smith and Jane H. M. Taylor (Toronto: University of Toronto Press, 1996), 204–29; David S. Areford, "The Passion Measured: A Late Medieval Diagram of the Body of Christ," in *The Body Broken: Passion Devotion in Late-Medieval Culture*, ed. A. A. MacDonald, H. N. B. Ridderbos, and R. M. Schlusemann (Groningen, Netherlands: Egbert Forsten, 1998), 211–38; and Amy Hollywood, " 'That Glorious Slit,' " collected here. See also Michael Camille, "The Image and the Self: Unwriting Late Medieval Bodies," in *Framing Medieval Bodies*, ed. Sarah Kay and Miri Rubin (Manchester: Manchester University Press, 1994), 77.

3.   Both Bynum and Lochrie cite Raymond of Capua's *Life* of Catherine of Siena (1327–80): "With that, he tenderly placed his right hand on her neck and drew her towards the wound on his side. 'Drink, daughter, from my side,' he said, 'and by that draught your soul shall become enraptured with such delight that your very body, which for my sake you have denied, shall be inundated with its overflowing goodness.' Drawn close in this way to the outlet of the Fountain of Life, she fastened her lips upon that sacred wound, and still more eagerly the mouth of her soul, and there she slaked her thirst." Cited by Caroline Walker Bynum, *Holy Feast and Holy Fast: The Religious Significance of Food to Medieval Women* (Berkeley: University of California Press, 1987), 172; and Lochrie, "Mystical Acts," 188.

Bynum, in reading the side wound as a breast and Christ's blood as milk, explicitly rejects a sexualized reading, whereas Lochrie insists that the maternal does not exclude the sexual. In the Middle Ages, it was believed that breast milk was created from surplus menses not released in childbirth. The association of the blood with Christ's side wound, then, ties it both to the vagina *and* to breast milk, thereby enabling the threefold association of wound, vulva, and breast. On these associations, see Charles Wood, "The Doctor's Dilemma: Sin, Salvation, and the Menstrual Cycle in Medieval Thought," *Speculum* 56 (1981): 710–27. For the highly suggestive and erotic visual images, see Lochrie, "Mystical Acts"; Lewis, "Wound"; and Hollywood, " 'That Glorious Slit.' " On the linguistic association of the Latin for wound and for vulva, see Lochrie, "Mystical Acts," 189, 198n26; and Wolfgang Riehle, *The Middle English Mystics*, trans. Bernard Standring (London: Routledge and Kegan Paul, 1981), esp. 46. One wonders about the relationship between these vulvic wound images and the blood-drenched Christ discussed by Jeffrey F. Hamburger, *Nuns as Artists: The Visual Culture of a Medieval Convent* (Berkeley: University of California Press, 1997), plate 1. For a warning against the dangers of assuming all penetrable sites are feminine, see Richard Rambuss, *Closet Devotions* (Durham: Duke University Press, 1998), 19–32.

4. This queering can also be seen in a text that Lochrie mentions but does not cite, Angela of Foligno's (c. 1248–1309) *Book*, particularly the *Memorial*, dictated by Angela to a friar. In two places she discusses the wound in Christ's side: "In the fourteenth step, while I was standing in prayer, Christ on the cross appeared . . . to me. . . . He then called me to place my mouth to the wound on his side. It seemed to me that I saw and drank the blood, which was freshly flowing from his side. His intention was to make me understand that by this blood he would cleanse me." And later, she writes, "At times it seems to my soul that it enters into Christ's side, and this is a source of great joy and delight." Angela of Foligno, *The Complete Works*, trans. Paul Lachance (New York: Paulist Press, 1993), 128 and 176 (see also 246).

   These two passages are compressed in a highly erotic and homosexuated or queered reading by Luce Irigaray: "Could it be true that not every wound need remain secret, that not every laceration was shameful? Could a sore be *holy*? Ecstasy is there in that glorious slit where she curls up as if in her nest, where she rests as if she had found her home—and He is also in her. She bathes in a blood that flows over her, hot and purifying." Luce Irigaray, *Speculum of the Other Woman*, trans. Gillian C. Gill (Ithaca: Cornell University Press, 1985), 200. For other examples of "possibly queer female desire for Christ's wounds," see Lochrie, "Mystical Acts," 199n34. For more on Irigaray and mysticism, see Amy Hollywood, *Sensible Ecstasy: Mysticism, Sexual Difference, and the Demands of History* (Chicago: University of Chicago Press, 2002), esp. 187–210; and Hollywood, " 'That Glorious Slit.' "

5. Lochrie, "Mystical Acts," 195.

6. Bennett, " 'Lesbian-Like,' " 8.

7. Ibid., 8–9.

8. Ibid., 14–15. For related work, see Judith Bennett and Amy Froide, eds., *Single Women in the European Past, 1250–1800* (Philadelphia: University of Pennsylvania Press, 1999).

9. I realize that this is not quite where Bennett places the implausibility—for her it is the purported jump between religious representations and actual sexual practices between women that is implausible. But I think that behind her sense that religious representation tells us little about "actual people" lies the irreality of medieval religious beliefs for many modern readers.

10. Judith C. Brown's descriptions of the trial records concerning Sister Benedetta Carlini (1590–1661) suggest that one *might* in fact lead to the other. In this case, Benedetta Carlini's visions, in which she speaks as Christ and as a male angel, serve as the basis for her sexual relationship with another nun assigned to care for her. As Brown explains, Benedetta's "male identity consequently allowed her to have sexual and emotional relations that she could not conceive between women." In addition, the requests she made as the angel Splenditello did not differ substantially from erotic mystical language. See Judith C. Brown, *Immodest Acts: The Life of a Lesbian Nun in Renaissance Italy* (New York: Oxford University Press, 1986), 127.

11.   On the potential problems with using modern notions of normativity to understand medieval materials, see Amy Hollywood, "The Normal, the Queer, and the Middle Ages," collected here.

12.   Rambuss, *Closet Devotions*, 48. Rambuss points to similar problems with Leo Steinberg's theological readings of Christ's penis as it appears in Renaissance art. See Leo Steinberg, *The Sexuality of Christ in Renaissance Art and in Modern Oblivion*, 2nd ed. (Chicago: University of Chicago Press, 1996). For a related argument about the body of Christ in the York cycle, see Garrett J. Epp, "Ecce Homo," in *Queering the Middle Ages*, ed. Glenn Burger and Steven F. Kruger (Minneapolis: University of Minnesota Press, 2001), 236–51.

13.   Bynum, *Holy Feast and Holy Fast*, 178. For many, this would be an apt description of intense sexual desire.

14.   The beguines did not marry, but lived singly or in groups. They often supported themselves through manual labor and sometimes refused or attempted to escape from the strict jurisdiction of male ecclesial or monastic hierarchies. They were thus "lesbian-like" in the terms discussed by Bennett. Their modes of religious imagery, however, as I will argue in what follows, were queer in varying degrees.

15.   Rambuss, *Closet Devotions*, 58.

16.   At least from the standpoint of the contemporary reader. Whether these idealized conceptions of divine-human relations would have been similarly queer for medieval readers is not yet clear to me. See again Hollywood, "The Normal, the Queer, and the Middle Ages."

17.   Michael Warner, "Tongues Untied: Memoirs of a Pentecostal Boyhood," in *The Material Queer: A LesBiGay Cultural Studies Reader*, ed. Donald Morton (Boulder, Colo.: Westview, 1996), 43.

18.   See Rambuss, *Closet Devotions*, esp. 11–71; Georges Bataille, *Eroticism: Death and Sensuality*, trans. Mary Dalwood (San Francisco: City Lights, 1986); Hollywood, *Sensible Ecstasy*, 36–119.

19.   For a useful introduction to Origen and his interpretation of the Song of Songs, see Bernard McGinn, *The Foundations of Mysticism: Origins to the Fifth Century* (New York: Crossroad, 1992), 108–30. On the queering of the Song of Songs in the Christian tradition, see Stephen D. Moore, "The Song of Songs in the History of Sexuality," *Church History* 69 (2000): 328–49. The "individual believer" is a potentially gender-neutral category, yet in many male-authored texts on the Song of Songs the presumption of *reversal* in calling oneself a bride depends on the marking of that believer as male.

20.   See Bernard McGinn, *The Growth of Mysticism: Gregory the Great Through the 12th Century* (New York: Crossroad, 1994), 158–224, 225–74, and 328–33; and Shawn M. Krahmer, "The Virile Bride of Bernard of Clairvaux," *Church History* 69 (2000): 304–27.

21.   Enormously complex questions emerge here. Within medieval conceptions, is sex at stake? Gender? Or what medieval allegorizers would refer to as the integumentum— the skin or clothing with which the soul is covered whenever it is spoken or written about in personified form? This, without even getting into the complexity of

contemporary debates internal to transgender communities about how best to name their extremely varied experience.

22. For the intensity of such gender crossings (and recrossings) in seventeenth-century English devotional poetry, and the ways in which they destabilize sex, gender, and sexual categories, see Rambuss, *Closet Devotions*. The texts of a number of medieval male authors might usefully be subjected to a similar analysis, most particularly, Rupert of Deutz, Bernard of Clairvaux, Richard of St. Victor, and Henry Suso.

23. For an overview of Mechthild's life and work, see Amy Hollywood, "A Vision of Flowing Light," in *The New History of German Literature*, ed. David E. Wellbery (Cambridge, Mass.: Harvard University Press, 2005), 161–31; Hollywood, *The Soul as Virgin Wife: Mechthild of Magdeburg, Marguerite Porete, and Meister Eckhart* (Notre Dame: Notre Dame University Press, 1995), 1–86; Bernard McGinn, *The Flowering of Mysticism: Men and Women in the New Mysticism—1200–1350* (New York: Crossroad, 1998), 222–44; and Sara S. Poor, *Mechthild of Magdeburg and Her Book: Gender and the Making of Textual Authority* (Philadelphia: University of Pennsylvania Press, 2004).

24. Mechthild of Magdeburg, *The Flowing Light of the Godhead*, trans. Frank Tobin (New York: Paulist Press, 1998), 1.44, 59.

25. Ibid.

26. Ibid., 61.

27. Ibid., 62.

28. This leads in the latter books of the *Flowing Light* to Mechthild's claim that the "well-ordered" soul becomes the "housewife" of God. See *Flowing Light*, 7.3, 277; and Hollywood, *Virgin Wife*, 78–86.

29. For a general overview, see McGinn, *The Flowering of Mysticism*, 199–222. On the homoeroticism of her poems and letters, see E. Ann Matter, "My Sister, My Spouse: Woman Identified Women in Medieval Christianity," in *Weaving the Visions: New Patterns in Feminist Spirituality*, ed. Judith Plaskow and Carol P. Christ (San Francisco: Harper, 1989), 54–55. On the queering effect of the intensity of her desire, see Lochrie, "Mystical Acts," 184. For a more normalizing reading of Hadewijch's language, in relationship to late medieval theology, see Saskia Murk-Jansen, "The Use of Gender and Gender-Related Imagery in Hadewijch," in *Gender and Text in the Later Middle Ages*, ed. Jane Chance (Gainesville: University Press of Florida, 1996), 52–68.

30. Hadewijch, *Complete Works*, trans. Mother Columba Hart (New York: Paulist Press, 1980), 356.

31. Lochrie, "Mystical Acts," 184.

32. Hadewijch, *Complete Works*, 61.

33. Ibid., 280.

34. Ibid.

35. Ibid., 281–82.

36. For Hadewijch's debts to secular courtly love lyric, see Saskia Murk-Jansen, "The Mystic Theology of the Thirteenth-Century Mystic, Hadewijch, and Its Literary

Expression," *Medieval Mystical Tradition in England* 5 (1992): 117–28; Murk-Jansen, "The Use of Gender," 54–55, and the literature cited there. According to Bynum, medieval religious men used gender reversal (the soul as the Bride of Christ) to stress their humility in the face of the divinity. Murk-Jansen carries this argument to Hadewijch's poems, arguing that, since "within the conventions of the courtly love lyric it is the lady who has all the power" and "the man who is represented as of lower status," Hadewijch too uses gender reversal as a form of renunciation. This is certainly right, at least in part. However, as I will argue here, Hadewijch's knight is not simply passive in face of the unattainable Love but actively seeks her, through pain, passion, and desire. In this he combines activity and passivity (as does the bride in the Song of Songs, who goes into the streets looking for her beloved).

37. Cited and translated in Murk-Jansen, "Use of Gender," 58.

38. On the one hand, Hadewijch stresses that this is the case as long as the soul is in the body or on earth, holding forth the promise of the continual union and coming to fruition of the soul and the divine after death. Yet at other times the doubleness and cruelty of desire and its passionate, painful ecstasy seem literally endless.

39. Murk-Jansen, "Use of Gender," 58. This is reminiscent of *The Rothschild Canticles*'s representation of Song of Song's 4:9 ("You have wounded my heart, my sister, my spouse.") in which the bride holds the lance with which Christ's side is wounded on the verso side, and Christ on a stylized cross displays his side wound on the recto. *Rothschild Canticles*, New Haven, Beinecke Rare Book and Manuscript Library, MS 404, fols. 18v-19r. For the image, see Jeffrey F. Hamburger, *The Rothschild Canticles: Art and Mysticism in Flanders and the Rhineland Circa 1300* (New Haven: Yale University Press, 1991).

40. Hadewijch, *Complete Works*, 162.

41. According to Murk-Jansen, "Use of Gender," 66: "The fluid movement between masculine and feminine imagery emphasizes the basic similarity of male and female before God," leaving any account of Hadewijch's own understanding of "womanhood" "necessarily speculative." Yet doesn't the fluidity of human gender before God tell us *something* about how Hadewijch experienced gender, at least on the level of her relationship to the divine (itself central to her life)?

42. See Michael Sells, *Mystical Languages of Unsaying* (Chicago: University of Chicago Press, 1994), 180–217; and Hollywood, *Virgin Wife*, 87–119, 180–93. The version of the *Mirror* to which I refer here is from the fifteenth century, however, and so the ambiguity might not reflect the late-thirteenth- and early-fourteenth-century original. An earlier version of a few of the chapters of the *Mirror* has been discovered and would require analysis to get at this question. Regardless, the version in the critical edition circulated and so the point stands with regard to the reception of Marguerite's book, if not with certainty to the original.

43. Marguerite Porete, *The Mirror of Simple Souls*, trans. Ellen Babinsky (New York: Paulist Press, 1993), chap. 131, 213–14.

44. Nicholas Watson, "'Yf wommen be double naturelly': Remaking 'Woman' in Julian of Norwich's Revelation of Love," *Exemplaria* 8 (1996): 3.

45. For the "fall into nothingness" and the dialectic of All and Nothing in Porete, see Marguerite Porete, *Mirror*, chap. 118, 192–93.

46. The term "grace" rarely appears in the *Mirror*, and then to refer to the very lowest stages of the soul, which are clearly subordinated to the life of the spirit and that of the annihilated soul. See, for example, Marguerite Porete, *Mirror*, chap. 60, 137–38.

47. Watson, "'Yf wommen be double naturelly,'" 6.

48. The *Mirror* deploys gendered language in a number of different ways. God as Love or the Trinity, for example, often depend for their linguistic operation on the fact that these terms are feminine and so take feminine pronouns. The resultant pronominal ambiguity elides the gap between the soul and the divine. There may also be echoes in the *Mirror* of the uniting of male and female characteristics in Christ's body through the bloody side wound. In general, Marguerite focuses attention on Christ in the third and fourth realms. Yet she calls the divine in the higher realms the "Farnear," thereby evoking both courtly and biblical allusions to the beloved. This male beloved, moreover, in the sixth stage (the highest the soul can achieve in this life), opens an "aperture" to the soul in which she sees her own eternal glory. Marguerite Porete, *Mirror*, chap. 61, 138. For more on this and other uses of gendered language in the *Mirror*, see Hollywood, *Virgin Wife*, 100–101, 108–9; and Sells, *Languages of Unsaying*, 180–217.

49. Although Marguerite retains the orthodox position that full union between the soul and the divine can only occur after death, she clearly holds that the soul, while on earth, can annihilate its will and desire. In doing so, the soul overcomes the need for corporeal aids to salvation and is able to "give to nature what it wills." But it is able to do so only because the body is fully subservient to the virtues and so asks nothing contrary to God's will. See Hollywood, *Virgin Wife*, 109–12.

50. Mechthild of Magdeburg, *Flowing Light*, 335–36.

51. Ibid., 336.

52. For a related argument about the self-subverting nature of sexual desire, see Leo Bersani, "Is the Rectum a Grave?," in *AIDS: Cultural Analysis, Cultural Activism*, ed. Douglas Crimp (Cambridge, Mass.: MIT Press, 1988), 197–222; republished in *Is the Rectum a Grave, and Other Essays* (Chicago: University of Chicago Press, 2009), 3–30.

6. THE NORMAL, THE QUEER, AND THE MIDDLE AGES

This short piece was written for a panel on Carolyn Dinshaw's *Getting Medieval: Sexualities and Communities, Pre- and Postmodern*. It was presented at the American Academy of Religion Annual Conference in 2000 and published, together with the other panel papers and a response by Dinshaw, in the *Journal of the History of*

Sexuality in 2001. I include it here because it usefully troubles my own deployment of the always somewhat ineffable category of the queer.

I've read *Getting Medieval* countless times now and it just gets better with age. I also love and am inspired by Dinshaw's *How Soon Is Now? Medieval Texts, Amateur Readers, and the Queerness of Time* (2012).

1. Carolyn Dinshaw, *Getting Medieval: Sexualities and Communities, Pre- and Post-modern* (Durham: Duke University Press, 1999), 21.

2. Ibid., 34.

3. Ibid., 35.

4. Ibid., 39.

5. Ibid.

6. Ibid. On the complex relationship between the terms "sex," "sexuality," and "gender," see Eve Kosofsky Sedgwick, *Epistemology of the Closet* (Berkeley: University of California Press, 1990), 27–35. The issues are only becoming more complex and more interesting with time.

7. See Leo Bersani, *Homos* (Cambridge, Mass.: Harvard University Press, 1995).

8. On the specific problems that emerge for medievalists in writing the history of lesbianism, see Judith Bennett, "'Lesbian-Like' and the Social History of Lesbianisms," *Journal of the History of Sexuality* 9 (2000): 1–24.

9. Theodore M. Porter, *The Rise of Statistical Thinking, 1820–1900* (Princeton: Princeton University Press, 1986), 18, cited in Lennard J. Davis, *Enforcing Normalcy: Disability, Deafness, and the Body* (London: Verso, 1995), 26. See also Ian Hacking, *The Emergence of Probability: A Philosophical Study of Early Ideas About Probability, Induction and Statistical Inference* (Cambridge: Cambridge University Press, 1975).

10. Francis Bisset Hawkins, *Elements of Medical Statistics* (London: Longman, Rees, Orme, Brown, and Green, 1829), cited by Davis, *Enforcing Normalcy*, 26.

11. Davis, *Enforcing Normalcy*, 26.

12. Ibid., 35.

13. Ibid., 30; see also Donald MacKenzie, *Statistics in Britain, 1865–1930* (Edinburgh: Edinburgh University Press, 1981).

14. Davis, *Enforcing Normalcy*, 30.

15. Although, as Sedgwick reminds us, the ties between conceptions of normality and eugenics shouldn't cause us to lose sight of the sometimes profoundly efficacious political and social power of claims to normality on the part of gay men and women. See Sedgwick, *Epistemology*, 58.

16. Davis, *Enforcing Normalcy*, 39.

17. This would seem to be the basis of the French and English use of the term "normal" to mean "certified" or "approved," hence normal schools are institutions for training teachers. Michael Warner suggests, following Georges Canguilhem, that contemporary uses of the term "normal" rest on a confusion between statistical norms and evaluative norms. I think this is right, but Davis's point, with which I also agree, is that this confusion, which creates intractable contradictions, as Warner points out, is endemic to the concept of normativity itself. Note that the term "normalize"

only arises after the rise of statistics and with reference to that science. See Michael Warner, *The Trouble with Normal: Sex, Politics, and the Ethics of Queer Life* (Cambridge, Mass.: Harvard University Press, 1999), 56.

18. The central reference is to Paul's Letter to the Romans. See John Boswell, *Christianity, Social Tolerance, and Homosexuality* (Chicago: University of Chicago Press, 1980); Mark Jordan, *The Invention of Sodomy in Christian Theology* (Chicago: University of Chicago Press, 1997); and Joan Cadden, *The Meaning of Sex Difference in the Middle Ages* (Cambridge: Cambridge University Press, 1993).

19. Joan Cadden, "Sciences/Silences: The Natures and Languages of 'Sodomy' in Peter of Abano's Problemata Commentary," in *Constructing Medieval Sexuality*, ed. Karma Lochrie, Peggy McCracken, and James A. Schultz (Minneapolis: University of Minnesota Press, 1997), 52.

20. Dinshaw, *Getting Medieval*, 55–87. For a similar slide between the natural and the unnatural, see Sedgwick's discussion of Billy Budd: " 'A depravity according to nature,' like 'natural depravity,' might denote something that is depraved when measured against the external standard of nature—that is, something whose depravity is unnatural. Either of the same two phrases might also denote, however, something whose proper nature is to be depraved—that is, something whose depravity is natural." Sedgwick, *Epistemology*, 95.

21. Dinshaw, *Getting Medieval*, 147.

22. Margery Kempe, *The Book of Margery Kempe*, ed. Sanford Meech Brown and Hope Emily Allen (1940; Oxford: Oxford University Press, 1982), 112, cited in Dinshaw, *Getting Medieval*, 153. Dinshaw cites Margery's Middle English, which I have here modernized. Elsewhere, she cites both the Middle English and the modern English translation in B. A. Windeatt, *The Book of Margery Kempe* (Harmondsworth, UK: Penguin, 1985).

23. Kempe, *Book*, 116, Windeatt, 153, cited in Dinshaw, *Getting Medieval*, 155.

24. Kempe, *Book*, 133, Windeatt, 172, cited in Dinshaw, *Getting Medieval*, 156.

25. Dinshaw, *Getting Medieval*, 163.

26. Ibid., 163–64.

27. The issue for some of Margery's contemporaries, as for Dinshaw, may be that Margery claims too much. Perhaps the excess of her desire and her claims to achievement of the ideal make her queer in relationship to her contemporaries. Yet women's religious writings of the thirteenth and fourteenth centuries are full of such excesses. Whether these women and their texts were positively received by their contemporaries seems dependent on something other and more complex than the relative excess of their experience.

28. See Sedgwick, *Epistemology*, 8–9, where she remarks on the narrowing of what counts as salient about sexuality in the modern period. Perhaps this focus on sexual-object choice is related to the need to make sexual norms available to statistical analysis. Seen from this perspective, there might be a relationship between Margery's desire to have God as a sexual partner and a certain modern inability to see that as a viable, whether normal or abnormal, form of sexuality.

7. "THAT GLORIOUS SLIT": IRIGARAY AND THE MEDIEVAL DEVOTION TO CHRIST'S SIDE WOUND

I wrote this for *Luce Irigaray and the Premodern: Thresholds of History* (2005), edited by Elizabeth D. Harvey and Theresa Krier. Harvey and Krier generously allowed me to follow out my fascination with the medieval devotion to Christ's side wound and offered extraordinarily useful comments that helped me see just how and in what way "that glorious slit" was important for understanding Irigaray.

The literature by and about Irigaray is vast and grows daily. For important recent work and bibliographies, see Alison Stone, *Luce Irigaray and the Philosophy of Sexual Difference* (Cambridge: Cambridge University Press, 2009); Rachel Jones, *Irigaray* (Cambridge: Polity, 2011); Lucy Bolt, *Film and Female Consciousness: Irigaray, Cinema and Thinking Women* (New York: Palgrave, 2011); Mary C. Rawlinson, Sabrina L. Hom, and Serene J. Khader, eds., *Thinking with Irigaray* (Albany: State University of New York Press, 2011); Lenart Skof and Emily A. Holmes, eds., *Breathing with Luce Irigaray* (London: Bloomsbury, 2013); and Hanneke Canters and Grace Jantzen, *Forever Fluid: A Reading of Luce Irigaray's Elemental Passions* (Manchester: Manchester University Press, 2014). For more recent literature on the medieval material, see my "Feminist Studies in Christian Spirituality." For Caroline Walker Bynum's response to the reading of Christ's side wound offered here and by Karma Lochrie, see her *Christian Materiality: An Essay on Religion in Late Medieval Europe* (New York: Zone, 2011).

1. This is not, of course, to posit a so-called essentialist reading of Irigaray, for Irigaray posits imaginary and symbolic configurations of the female sex as sites of potential philosophical and cultural meaning rather than valorizing the female sex in and of itself. For Irigaray's explicit critique of biological (and psychological or cultural) essentialism, see Luce Irigaray, *Marine Lover of Friedrich Nietzsche*, trans. Gillian C. Gill (New York: Columbia University Press, 1991), 86, originally published as *Amante marin: De Friedrich Nietzsche* (Paris: Minuit, 1980).

2. Ewa Ziarek argues that Irigaray insists on "the discontinuous temporality of the body" and so "theorizes the interminable becoming of women's bodies" in ways that work against phallic claims to mastery and totality—and arguably also against the kinds of representative claims Irigaray appears to make in *Speculum* (although I believe that the two issues can be separated). Patricia Huntington also argues for a temporal dimension to Irigaray's conception of the imaginary, the symbolic, and their relationship. At the same time, Huntington maintains that Irigaray's conception of woman is not as empty as some of her commentators claim. (Drucilla Cornell, to whom Huntington refers, also discusses the problematic nature of Irigaray's insistence on the primacy of sexual difference.) Although I agree with Ziarek's reading of Irigaray, Irigaray's continued dependence on sexual difference as the privileged site of futural difference (however impossible that future difference may be) works to efface other conceptions of difference in deeply problematic ways. See Ziarek, "Toward a Radical Female Imaginary: Temporality

and Embodiment in Irigaray's Ethics," *Diacritics* 28 (1998): 64; 72; Patricia J. Huntington, *Ecstatic Subjects, Utopia, and Recognition: Kristeva, Heidegger, Irigaray* (Albany: State University of New York Press, 1998), 134–40, 246; Drucilla Cornell, *Beyond Accommodation: Ethical Feminism, Deconstruction and the Law* (New York: Routledge, 1991), 77–78, 166; and Judith Butler and Drucilla Cornell with Pheng Cheah and E. A. Grosz, "The Future of Sexual Difference: An Interview with Butler and Cornell," *Diacritics* 28 (1998): 19–42. For a reading of Irigaray's later work that builds on Ziarek's insight, see Penelope Deutscher, *A Politics of the Impossible Difference: The Later Works of Luce Irigaray* (New York: Routledge, 2002).

3. Thomas Bestul notes Irigaray's eroticized and sexualized reading of Christ's side wound, without rendering explicit the latter's vulvic and vaginal quality. Karma Lochrie highlights the vulvic and vaginal quality of the wound without reference to Irigaray. I am deeply indebted to both studies in the work presented here. See Thomas Bestul, *Texts of Passion: Latin Devotional Literature and Medieval Society* (Philadelphia: University of Pennsylvania Press, 1996), 231n71; and Karma Lochrie, "Mystical Acts, Queer Tendencies," in *Constructing Medieval Sexuality*, ed. Karma Lochrie, Peggy McCracken, and James A. Schultz (Minneapolis: University of Minnesota Press, 1997), 180–200.

4. See especially Irigaray, *Marine Lover*, 164–90; Irigaray, *Sexes and Genealogies*, trans. Gillian C. Gill (New York: Columbia University Press, 1993), 75–88, originally published as *Sexes et parentés* (Paris: Minuit, 1987); and Amy Hollywood, *Sensible Ecstasy: Mysticism, Sexual Difference, and the Demands of History* (Chicago: University of Chicago Press, 2002), 203–6.

5. Already in 1949 Simone de Beauvoir makes a similar claim, although to very different ends. Foreshadowing arguments more recently (and, it goes without saying, much more extensively) made by the historian of medieval spirituality Caroline Walker Bynum, Beauvoir suggests that Christ's suffering flesh is, as suffering, feminized. See Beauvoir, *The Second Sex*, trans. H. M. Parshley (New York: Vintage, 1952), 751: "In the humiliation of God she [the mystic] sees with wonder the dethronement of Man; inert, passive, covered with wounds, the Crucified is the reversed image of the white, bloodstained martyr exposed to wild beasts, to daggers, to males, with whom the little girl has so often identified herself; she is overwhelmed to see that Man, Man-God, has assumed her role. She it is who is hanging on the Tree, promised the splendor of the Resurrection." For Beauvoir, Christ's miming of suffering feminine flesh is not redemptive for women but, in its emphasis on suffering, abjection, and the body, demonstrates the inadequacy of religion and mysticism as sites of women's agency; see Hollywood, *Sensible Ecstasy*, 120–45.

6. Irigaray, *Speculum of the Other Woman*, trans. Gillian C. Gill (Ithaca: Cornell University Press, 1985), 200, translation modified, originally published *Speculum de l'autre femme* (Paris: Minuit, 1974).

7. Irigaray, *Speculum*, 191.

8. Ibid., 133.

9. Judith Butler, *Bodies That Matter: On the Discursive Limits of "Sex"* (New York: Routledge, 1993), 45.

10. In making this assertion I make no definitive claim with regard to Irigaray's sources. As I will show, the language of devotion to Christ's blood and side wound and of entering into Christ's side runs throughout late medieval piety. Irigaray does explicitly cite Angela's *Book*, rendering it a possible source for the language of *"La mystérique,"* but definitive attribution is both impossible and unnecessary. On Irigaray's miming technique and its philosophical implications, see Butler, *Bodies That Matter*, 36–49.

11. The transmission history of Angela's book is tremendously complex and has given rise to intense debates over the extent to which we can understand Angela as its author. According to the scribe who wrote the book, Angela dictated to him in her native dialect and he simultaneously translated into Latin and wrote down her words. At one point, when he reads a passage back to her, she claims to be unable to recognize it. Yet at the same time, she accepts his rendition and continues to work with him on the book. See Catherine M. Mooney, "The Authorial Role of Brother A. in the Composition of Angela of Foligno's 'Revelations,'" in *Creative Women in Medieval and Early Modern Italy: A Religious and Artistic Renaissance*, ed. E. Anne Matter and John W. Coakley (Philadelphia: University of Pennsylvania Press, 1994), 34–63; and Jacques Dalarun, "Angèle de Foligno a-t-elle existé?," in *"Alla Signoria": Mélanges offerts à Noëlle de La Blanchardière* (Rome: École Française de Rome, 1995), 59–97. For an argument about the collaborative nature of women's work with scribes, see Lynn Staley, *Margery Kempe's Dissenting Fictions* (University Park: Penn State University Press, 1994), 36; and Jennifer Summit, "Women and Authorship," in *The Cambridge Companion to Medieval Women's Writing*, ed. Carolyn Dinshaw and David Wallace (Cambridge: Cambridge University Press, 2003), 91–108. On the subject of women's use of scribes, see also Joan Ferrante, "'Scribe Quae Vides et Audis': Hildegard, Her Language and Her Secretaries," in *The Tongue of the Fathers: Gender and Ideology in Twelfth-Century Latin*, ed. David Townsend and Andrew Taylor (Philadelphia: University of Pennsylvania Press, 1998), 102–35.

12. "Quartodecimo, dum starem ad orationem, Christus ostendit se mihi . . . Et tunc vocavit me et dixit mihi quod ego ponerem os meum in plagam lateris sui, et videbatur mihi quod ego viderem et biberem sanguinem eius fluentem recenter ex latere suo, et dabatur mihi intelligere quod in isto mundaret me." Angela of Foligno, *The Complete Works*, trans. Paul Lachance (New York: Paulist Press, 1993), 128; Latin in *Il Libro della Beata Angela da Foligno*, ed. Ludger Thier and Abele Calufetti (Grottaferrata: Editiones Collegi S. Bonaventurae ad Claras Quas, 1985), 142–44.

13. "Et aliquando videtur animae quod tanta laetitia et delectatione intret intus in illud latus Christi." Angela of Foligno, *Book*, 176; *Libro*, 278. See also later in the text, where Angela is recorded exhorting others to enter into the wound in Christ's side. Angela of Foligno, *Book*, 246. For other examples of "possibly queer female desire for Christ's wounds" within the medieval period, see Lochrie, "Mystical Acts, Queer Tendencies," 199n34.

14. I will focus here on a complex nexus of texts and images that emerge within the Latin tradition of Passion narratives. Meditation on Christ's side wound and devotion to the heart of Jesus also figure prominently in Latin hagiographies of holy women, particularly among the Cistercians and early beguines, and in the many texts, in both Latin and the vernaculars, written by religious and semireligious women in the later Middle Ages. Perhaps most important for the development of the devotion to Christ's side wound are Thomas of Cantimpre's *Life of Lutgard of Aywières* and the writings by and about Gertrude the Great (1256–1301). For these and a host of other relevant texts, see Bernard McGinn, *The Flowering of Mysticism: Men and Women in the New Mysticism, 1200–1350* (New York: Crossroad, 1998), 60–61, 100–101, 118, 128, 141, 165, 172, 181, 189, 206, 230, 236, 274–81, 304–7, 312–16.

15. Douglas Gray, "The Five Wounds of Our Lord," *Notes and Queries* 208 (1963): 86.

16. See Raymond Jonas, *France and the Cult of the Sacred Heart* (Berkeley: University of California Press, 2000).

17. Denise Despres, *Ghostly Sights: Visual Meditation in Late Medieval Literature* (Norman: Pilgrim Books, 1989); Bestul, *Texts of Passion*; Mary Carruthers *The Craft of Thought: Meditation, Rhetoric, and the Making of Images, 400–1200* (Cambridge: Cambridge University Press, 1998); Jeffrey F. Hamburger, *The Rothschild Canticles: Art and Mysticism in Flanders and the Rhineland Circa 1300* (New Haven: Yale University Press, 1990); Hamburger, *Nuns as Artists: The Visual Culture of a Medieval Convent* (Berkeley: University of California Press, 1997); Hamburger, *The Visual and the Visionary: Art and Female Spirituality in Late Medieval Germany* (New York: Zone, 1998); and Rachel Fulton, *From Judgment to Passion: Devotion to Christ and the Virgin Mary, 800–1200* (New York: Columbia University Press, 2002).

18. Fulton, *Judgment to Passion*.

19. Carruthers, *Craft of Thought*.

20. Bestul, *Texts of Passion*, 27.

21. Ibid.

22. The most salient use of the apocryphal gospels with regard to the images discussed here is the *Gospel of Nicodemus*'s identification of the Roman centurion who pierced Christ's side with a lance as Longinus. References to Longinus and his spear, then, are directly tied to devotion to Christ's side wound, for Longinus's action rendered that wound. Subsequent traditions will associate this action with Song of Songs 4:9: "vulnerasti cor meum soror mea sponsa vulnerasti cor meum in uno oculorum tuorum" ("You have wounded my heart, my sister, my spouse. You have wounded my heart with one of your eyes"). An image from a fourteenth-century florilegium discussed at length by Jeffrey Hamburger shows a woman (presumably the soul as bride of the Song) holding the lance with which Christ's side is wounded. Christ, on a stylized cross, displays his side wound as he looks lovingly on the lance-bearer; see Hamburger, *The Rothschild Canticles*.

23. Bestul, *Texts of Passion*, 26–33.

24. "Quis est iste, qui venit de Edom, tinctis vestibus de Bosra? iste formosus in stola sua, gradiens in multitudine fortitudinis suae. Ego qui loquor justitiam, et propugnator

sum ad salvandum. Quare ergo rubrum est indumentum tuum, et vestimenta tua sicut calcantium in torculari? Torcular calcavi solus, et de gentibus non est vir mecum; calcavi eos in furore meo, et conculcavi eos in ira mea; est aspersus est sanguis eorum super vestimenta mea, et omnia indumenta mea inquinavi." Isaiah 63: 1–3, cited and translated in ibid., 29.

25. The passage has further iconographical ramifications, as is shown in James Marrow, *Passion Iconography in Northern European Art of the Late Middle Ages and Early Renaissance: A Study of the Transformation of Sacred Metaphor Into Descriptive Narrative* (Kortrijk, Belgium: Van Ghemmmert, 1979), 76–94. Images of Christ suffering under the beam of a winepress thus serve as pictorial allegories for the Passion.

26. The image might also be related to Byzantine crucifixes, in which Christ wears a robe, and is also clearly tied to late medieval traditions in which hundreds of tiny wounds appear all over Christ's body. See David S. Areford, "The Passion Measured: A Late-Medieval Diagram of the Boy of Christ," in *The Body Broken: Passion Devotion in Late-Medieval Culture*, ed. Alasdair A. MacDonald, Bernhard Ridderbos, Egbert Forsten, and Rita M. Schlusemann (Groningen, Netherlands: Egbert Forsten, 1998).

27. "Columba mea in foraminibus petrae in caverna maceriae ostende mihi faciem tuam sonet vox tua in auribus meis." For biblical citations, I have used *Biblia Sacra Juxta Vulgatam Versionem* 1969. Bestul rightly eschews any attempt to argue decisively for the influence of one text or group of texts on another or to pinpoint the absolute origin of any particular image or image cluster. Given the complexity of medieval manuscript cultures, Bestul argues, "it seems most useful to conceive of these Latin treatises on the Passion as the products of a productive and complex textual community built around mutual relationship and interdependence in which many works reveal the textual traces of many other works, and in which the texts themselves are not static, but, attributed to various authors, subject to revision, recension, and modification." Bestul, *Texts of Passion*, 51.

28. Bernard of Clairvaux, *On the Song of Songs* 3, trans. Kilian Walsh and Irene Edmonds (Kalamazoo, Mich.: Cistercian Publications, 1979), 142; Latin in Bernard of Clairvaux, *Sancti Bernardi Opera* [*SBO*], 8 vols., ed. Jean Leclercq, Charles H. Talbot, and Henri Rochais (Rome: Editiones Cistercienses, 1957–77), 2.61, 149. The Christological reading of the passage can also be found in Cassiodorus (d. c. 580), Rabanus Maurus (d. 856), and Alan of Lille (d. 1202); see Gray, "Five Wounds," 85n19.

29. "Et revera ubi tuta firmaque infirmis requies, nisi in vulneribus Salvatoris? Tanto illic securior habito, quanto ille potentior est ad salvandum." Bernard, *Song* 3, 142–43; *SBO*, 2.61, 150.

30. "Licet mihi sugere mel de petra, oleumque de saxo durissimo, id est gustare et videre quoniam sauvis est Dominus." Bernard, *Song* 3, 143; *SBO*, 2.61, 150. Bernard here characteristically creates a collage of Biblical references. Deuteronomy 32:13: "constituit eum super excelsam terram ut comederet fructus agrorurn ut sugeret mel de petra oleumque de saxo durissimo." Psalm 33:9: "gustate et videte quoniam bonus Dominus."

31. "Patet arcanum cordis per foramina corporis, patet magnum illud pietatis sacramentum, patent VISCERA MISERJCORDIA DEI NOSTRJ, IN QUIBIS VISITAVIT NOS ORJENS EX ALTO. Quidni viscera per vulnera pateant?" Bernard, *Song* 145; *SBO*, 2.61, 150–51. See 1 Timothy 3:16 and Luke 1:78.

32. "Tunc unus ex militibus lancea latus eius aperuit, et exiuit sanguis et aqua. Festina, ne tardeueris, comede fauum cum melle tuo, bibe uinum tuum cum Jacte tuo. Sanguis tibi in uinum uertitur et inebrieris, in lac aqua mutatur ut nutriaris. Fact sunt tibi in petra flumina, in membris eius uulnera, et in maceria corporis eius cauerna, in quibis instar columbae latitans et deosculans singula ex sanguine eius fiant sicut uitta coccinea labia tua, et eloquium tuum dulce." Aelred of Rievaulx, *Treatises and Pastoral Prayer*, trans. Theodore Berkeley, Mary Macpherson, R. Penelope Lawson (Kalamazoo, Mich.: Cistercian Publications, 1971), 90–91; Latin in Aelred of Rievaulx, *Opera Omnia I: Opera Ascetica; Corpus Christianorum Continuatio Mediaevalis*, ed. Anselm Hoste and Charles H. Talbot (Turnhout, Belgium: Brepols, 1971), 671.

33. For a eucharistic reading of this passage, see Marsha L. Dutton, "Eat, Drink, and Be Merry: The Eucharistic Spirituality of the Cistercian Fathers," in *Erudition at God's Service*, ed. John R. Sommerfeldt (Kalamazoo, Mich.: Cistercian Publications, 1987), 1–31. For a reading of the passage in light of medieval devotion to the Blood of Christ, see Caroline Walker Bynum, "The Blood of Christ in the Later Middle Ages," *Church History* 71 (2002): 685–88.

34. See John V. Fleming, *An Introduction to Franciscan Literature of the Middle Ages* (Chicago: Franciscan Herald Press, 1977); and Despres, *Ghostly Sights*.

35. "Ut haurias aquas de fontibus Salvatoris." Bonaventure, *The Works of Bonaventure, Mystical Opuscula* 1, trans. J. de Vinc (Paterson, N.J.: St Anthony Guild Press, 1960), 128; Latin in *Bonaventurae Opera Omnia [BOO]*, ed. P. P. Collegii S. Bonaventurae, 11 vols. (Quaracchi: Collegium S. Bonaventurae, 1882–1902), 8:80, cited by Bestul, *Texts of Passion*, 45.

36. See Bestul, *Texts of Passion*, 47–48, where he cites Bonaventure, *BOO*, 8:188; *Works*, 203–4: "Tandum accendendum est ad cor illud humillimum altissimi Iesu, per ianuam videlicet lateris lanceati." Bestul also points the reader to Bonaventure's *On the Perfection of Life to Sisters:* "non solum mitte manum tuam in latus eius, sed total iter per ostium lateris ingredere usque cor ipsius Iesu [not only put your hand into his side, but enter with your whole being through the door of his side into Jesus's heart itself]." (*BOO* 8:120; *Works* 239). These passages demonstrate particularly clearly an additional source for the devotion to Christ's side wound: the Gospel of John's account of Thomas's doubt that the resurrected Jesus is indeed Jesus. "Deinde dicit Thomae infer digitum tuum hue et vide manus meas et adfer manum tuam et mitte in latus meum et noli esse incredulus sed fidelis. [And then be said to Thomas, 'Put your finger here and see my hands and bring your hand and put it in my side do not be unbelieving but faithful']." John 20:27.

37. Bestul *Texts of Passion*, 56; and Flora Lewis, "The Wound in Christ's Side and the Instruments of the Passion: Gendered Experience and Response," in *Women and the Book: Assessing the Visual Evidence*, ed. Jane H. M. Taylor and Lesley Smith (London: British

Library, 1996), 214. For the text, see James of Milan, *Stimulus Amoris Jacobi Mediolan- ensis*, ed. P. P. Collegii S. Bonaventurae (Quaracchi: Collegium S. Bonaventurae, 1905), 1–132. Wolfgang Riehle and Karma Lochrie go so far as to argue that in James of Milan's text, mystical union is represented as the copulation of two wounds: that of Christ and the female soul. On the one hand, this works to figure Christ's wound as vulvic and vaginal and the interpenetration of wounds as a site of female same-sex eroticism. At the same time, Christ's wound, Lochrie argues, is the "gate of Paradise" evoked by Song of Songs 4:12: "hortus conclusus soror mea sponsa hortus conclusis fons signatus [My sister, my spouse, is a garden enclosed, a garden enclosed, a fountain sealed up]." Often taken as marking the soul or the female religious' virginity, here the enclosed garden signifies Christ, and the soul is invited to penetrate into that protected and protecting space. Lochrie "Mystical Acts, Queer Tendencies," 189; and Wolfgang Riehle, *The Mid- dle English Mystics*, trans. Bernard Standring (London: Routledge, 1981), 46.

38.   The Franciscan Ubertino da Casale's (1259–1329) *Arbor vitae crucifixae Jesu* (1305) commands the reader to join Mary, the mother of Jesus, as she enters Christ's heart through the wound made in his side by the lance. Ludolphus of Saxony's (d. 1377) *Vita Christi*, as Bestul elegantly summarizes, compares "Christ's body pierced by wounds to a dove house where Christians can take refuge in the holes, even building nests in those openings." Bestul, *Texts of Passion*, 57–59. See Ubertino da Casale, *Arbor Vitae Crucifixae Jesu* (Turin, Italy: Bottega d'Erasmo, 1961), 322–35; and Ludolphus of Saxony, *Vita Christi*, 4 vols., ed. L.-M. Rigollot (Paris: Palme, 1870), 2:617. For more on the *Arbor vitae*, see Sandro Sticca, *The Planctus Mariae in the Dramatic Tradition of the Middle Ages*, trans. Joseph R. Berrigan (Athens: University of Geor- gia Press, 1988), 109–11. For more examples of the theme, see Gray, "Five Wounds"; Lewis, "Wound"; and Bestul, *Texts of Passion*, 26–68.

39.   On medieval attention to the dimensions of Christ's side wound, which were believed to be known, see Areford, "Passion Measured," 223–24. On the paradoxical inter- play of narrativization (in the texts dealing with Christ's Passion) and fragmentation (in the images often accompanying these and related texts), see Hollywood, "Acute Melancholia," collected here.

40.   Areford, "Passion Measured," 220. For more on Christ's side wound and its repre- sentation in devotional texts and images, see Lewis, "Wound"; Jeffrey F. Hamburger, *The Visual and the Visionary* (New York: Zone, 1998), 111–48, 197–232; Nigel Mor- gan, "Longinus and the Wounded Heart," *Wiener Jahrbuch für Kunstgeschichte*, 46–47 (1993–94): 507–18, 817–20; and the literature cited by Areford, "Passion Measured," 213–14nn6–8. The wound most often appears surrounded by dispropor- tionately smaller representations of the instruments of Christ's passion—the cross, the whip, the lance, the nails, and other implements by means of which his suffer- ing was accomplished. Hence the synecdoche depends, in part, on a related set of associations between the instruments of the passion and the wounds engendered by them. On the association of the instruments of torture with the tortured body and its pain, see Elaine Scarry, *The Body in Pain: The Making and Unmaking of the World* (Oxford: Oxford University Press, 1985), 13–19.

41. Lewis, "Wound," 204–6.

42. Lochrie, "Mystical Acts, Queer Tendencies," 190–91.

43. Hamburger, *The Visual and the Visionary*, 305.

44. Ibid., 305–6; and Lewis, "Wound," 206.

45. Lewis, "Wound," 206–7.

46. Ibid., 206; Lochrie, "Mystical Acts, Queer Tendencies," 190.

47. Lochrie, "Mystical Acts, Queer Tendencies," 190.

48. Areford, "Passion Measured," 223. Areford goes on to describe the importance of the precise measurement of the side wound for fourteenth- and fifteenth-century devotional practice.

49. Lochrie, "Mystical Acts, Queer Tendencies," 190–91. Although of course not all readers and devotees would have been women, raising the issue of what this form of devotion might have meant to men. See Ibid., 181–86; and Lewis, "Wound," 204.

50. "Medieval authors do not seem to have drawn as sharp a line as we do between sexual responses and affective responses or between male and female. Throughout the Middle Ages, authors found it far easier than we seem to find it to apply characteristics stereotyped as male or female to the opposite sex. Moreover, they were clearly not embarrassed to speak of all kinds of ecstasy in language *we* find physical and sexual and therefore inappropriate to God." Caroline Walker Bynum, *Jesus as Mother: Studies in the Spirituality of the High Middle Ages* (Berkeley: University of California Press, 1982), 162; cited by Lochrie, "Mystical Acts, Queer Tendencies," 182.

51. Caroline Walker Bynum, *Holy Feast and Holy Fast: On the Religious Significance of Food to Medieval Women* (Berkeley: University of California Press, 1987); Bynum, *Fragmentation and Redemption: Essays on Gender and the Human Body in Medieval Religion* (New York: Zone, 1991).

52. Bynum, *Fragmentation*, 182; cited by Lochrie, "Mystical Acts, Queer Tendencies," 183.

53. Caroline Walker Bynum, "Why All the Fuss About the Body?: A Medievalist's Perspective," *Critical Inquiry* 22 (1995): 1–33.

54. Ibid.

55. Richard Rambuss, *Closet Devotions* (Durham: Duke University Press, 1998), 48; and see also Lochrie, "Mystical Acts, Queer Tendencies," 187–88.

56. Cited by Bynum, *Holy Feast and Holy Fast*, 172.

57. Ibid.

58. Lochrie, "Mystical Acts, Queer Tendencies," 183.

59. Ibid., 188.

60. Helen Rodnite Lemay, ed. and trans., *Women's Secrets: A Translation of Pseudo-Albertus Magnus' De Secretis Mulierum with Commentaries* (Albany: State University of New York Press, 1992), 71, 109, 126, 142; see also Charles T. Wood, "The Doctor's Dilemma: Sin, Salvation, and the Menstrual Cycle in Medieval Thought," *Speculum* 54, no. 4 (1981): 710–27.

61. Paulette L'Hermite-Leclercq, "Le lait et le sang de la vierge," in *Le sang au Moyen Âge: Actes du Quatrième International de Montpellier Université Paul-Valéry (27–29 novembre 1997)* (Montpellier: Université Paul Valéry, 1999), 145–62.

62. Irigaray is not the only modern interpreter—or, perhaps better, mimer—of medieval mystical traditions to see a correlation between God and women's sex. Georges Bataille's evocations of female genitals as divine can be elucidated through attention to the divinity of the wound in medieval Christian texts and images. So, in his novel *Madame Edwarda* (closely aligned with his writings on mystical or inner experience from the 1940s), a prostitute exposes her genitals to the unnamed narrator:

You want to see my rags? she said.

My two hands gripping the table, I turned toward her. Seated, she lifted her leg up high: to open her slit better, she pulled the skin apart with her two hands. Thus the "rags" of Edwarda looked at me, hairy and pink, full of life, like a repugnant spider. I stammered softly:

Why are you doing that?

You see, she said, I am GOD . . .

I am mad . . .

But no, you have to look: look!

Her harsh voice softened, she became almost childlike, saying for me, with lassitude, with the infinite smile of abandon: "Oh, how I come [*joui*]."

Bataille, *Oeuvres Complètes*, 12 vols. (Paris: Gallimard, 1970–88), 3:20–21. Angela of Foligno is a key figure for Bataille, a medieval purveyor of that inner, ecstatic experience he seeks to elicit through his own writing and meditative practices. Like Angela, who presses her lips to Christ's side wound, *Madame Edwarda*'s unnamed narrator kisses Edwarda's genitals: "Finally, I knelt, I trembled, and put my lips on the living wound." Bataille, *Oeuvres*, 3:20.

63. Irigaray, "Commodities Among Themselves," in *This Sex Which Is Not One*, trans. Catherine Porter and Carolyn Burke (Ithaca: Cornell University Press, 1985), 192–97, 86–105.

64. Irigaray, *Marine Lover*, 164–90.

65. See Jacques Lacan, *On Feminine Sexuality, the Limits of Love and Knowledge, 1972–73*, in *Encore: The Seminar of Jacques Lacan, Book XX*, trans. Bruce Fink (New York: Norton, 1998).

66. Irigaray, *Sex Which Is Not One*, 105.

67. Ibid., 164–90.

68. There are crucial differences, of course. Most importantly, Irigaray attempts to reconfigure sexuality or eros in nonpenetrative ways, whereas Bynum desexualizes penetration and penetrability, reading them in terms of eating, drinking, decay, and fertility rather than in terms of sexuality. The ramifications of the two moves for sexual identity, sexuality, and gender, however, are very similar.

69. Butler, *Bodies That Matter*, 50–51.

70. See, for example, Dyan Elliott, "The Physiology of Rapture and Female Spirituality," in *Medieval Theology and the Natural Body*, ed. Peter Biller and A. J. Minnis

(Woodbridge: York Medieval Press, 1997), 141–73; and Nancy Caciola, "Mystics, Demoniacs, and the Physiology of Spirit Possession in Medieval Europe," *Comparative Studies in Society and History* 42, no. 2 (April 2000): 268–306.

71.   Irigaray, *Speculum*, 191–202.

72.   Butler demonstrates that Irigaray's *Speculum* also participates in an erotics of inter-penetrative reading, despite Irigaray's explicit claims to the contrary; see Butler, *Bodies That Matter*, 45–46.

8. INSIDE OUT: BEATRICE OF NAZARETH AND HER HAGIOGRAPHER

Parts of this essay were written for two quite different occasions, the first a round-table, "Female Sainthood in the Middle Ages: Methodological and Interpretative Challenges," held at the Berkshire Conference for the History of Women in 1996, and the second a panel on the usefulness of Pierre Bourdieu's work for medieval-ists, held at the International Conference on Medieval Studies in 1997. I am grate-ful to the organizers of both for moving my thinking. Catherine Mooney, who put together the Berkshire roundtable, included this piece in a book inspired by the event, *Gendered Voices: Medieval Women and Their Hagiographers* (1999). I reprint it here because it speaks so directly to other essays in the volume, but the larger argu-ment that runs across *Gendered Voices* remains essential reading.

I would also like to thank Ellen Armour, Dyan Elliott, John King, Cynthia Mar-shall, Catherine Mooney, Walter Simons, and Peter Travis for their helpful com-ments on this essay. Given the range of issues covered here, it is not possible for me to update the bibliography. I leave the essay as it stands.

1.   Talal Asad, *Genealogies of Religion: Discipline and Reasons of Power in Christianity and Islam* (Baltimore: Johns Hopkins University Press, 1993), 62.

2.   Marcel Mauss, "Body Techniques," in *Sociology and Psychology: Essays*, trans. Ben Brewster (London: Routledge, 1979), 97–135.

3.   Pierre Bourdieu, *Outline of a Theory of Practice*, trans. Richard Nice (Cambridge: Cambridge University Press, 1977), 78.

4.   As Louis Althusser argues, subjects are interpellated, called into being as subjects, by those who address them in the name of the law. As Judith Butler explains, "the call is formative, if not performative, precisely because it initiates the individual into the subjected status of the subject." See Louis Althusser, "Ideology and the Ideological State Apparatuses," in *Lenin and Philosophy, and Other Essays*, trans. Ben Brewster (New York: Monthly Review Press, 1971), 170–86; and Judith But-ler, *Bodies That Matter: On the Discursive Limits of "Sex"* (New York: Routledge, 1993), 121.

5.   Asad, *Genealogies*, 77. Sarah Beckwith follows Althusser, Bourdieu, and Žižek in cit-ing the famous lines from Pascal in which he claims that the habit of prayer gives

rise to belief. See Blaise Pascal, *Pensées*, trans. A. J. Krailsheimer (London: Penguin, 1966), 152; Althusser, "Ideology," 158; Pierre Bourdieu, *The Logic of Practice*, trans. Richard Nice (Stanford: Stanford University Press, 1990), 49; Slavoj Žižek, *The Sublime Object of Ideology* (New York: Routledge, 1989), 38–40; and Sarah Beckwith, "Passionate Regulation: Enclosure, Ascesis, and the Feminist Imaginary," *South Atlantic Quarterly* 93 (1994): 811–12.

6. Beckwith, "Passionate Regulation," 819. Caroline Walker Bynum makes the same claim in different ways in "Introduction: The Complexity of Symbols," in *Gender and Religion: On the Complexity of Symbols*, ed. Caroline Walker Bynum, Stevan Harrell, and Paula Richman (Boston: Beacon, 1986), 1–20.

7. Yet while bringing together theories of bodily practice with psychoanalysis, Beckwith does not theorize their relationship.

8. For another critique of some contemporary feminist work on mysticism and the body, see Amy Hollywood, "Beauvoir, Irigaray, and the Mystical," *Hypatia* 9, no. 4 (1994): 158–85.

9. Beckwith, "Passionate Regulation," 818.

10. This claim does not require that we fall back on essentialized conceptions of sexual difference, but merely that we acknowledge the difference between those identified as women within the culture in which they lived and those identified as men. For more on the complexities of this issue, see Amy Hollywood, *The Soul as Virgin Wife: Mechthild of Magdeburg, Marguerite Porete, and Meister Eckhart* (Notre Dame: University of Notre Dame Press, 1995), 36–37.

11. I stress this approach to the material in the slightly different presentation given in Hollywood, *Virgin Wife*, 27–30. There my concern is to show that women's relationship to embodiment is much more complex than modern associations of women with the body suggest. Hence my interest in Beckwith's parallel project. Here I hope to take the discussion a step further, demonstrating the tensions between medieval women's writings and twentieth-century materialist assumptions.

12. For this information and the text of the *vita* in Latin and English, see *The Life of Beatrice of Nazareth, 1200–1268*, trans. Roger De Ganck (Kalamazoo, Mich.: Cistercian Publications, 1991). For the treatise in Dutch, see L. Reypens and J. Van Mierlo, eds., *Seven Manieren van Minne* (Louvain, Belgium: S. V. de Vlaamsche Boekenhalle, 1926).

13. On mystical hagiographies, see Simone Roisin, "L'Efflorescence cistercienne et le courant féminin de piété au XIIIe siècle," *Revue d'Histoire Ecclésiastique* 39 (1943): 342–78; Roisin, *L'Hagiographie cistercienne dans le diocèse de Liège au XIIIe siècle* (Louvain, Belgium: Bibliothèque de l'Université, 1947); Caroline Walker Bynum, *Holy Feast and Holy Fast: The Religious Significance of Food to Medieval Women* (Berkeley: University of California Press, 1987); and Bynum, *Fragmentation and Redemption: Essays on Gender and the Human Body in Medieval Religion* (New York: Zone, 1991).

14. *Life of Beatrice*, 340–41. Ursula Peters questions the attestation of *Seven Manners* to Beatrice of Nazareth, arguing that the differences between it and *Life*, bk. 3, chap.

14, are too great for the latter to be a translation of the former. Yet the similarities in structure, metaphors, and images are exceptionally strong and in my opinion override their divergences. See Ursula Peters, *Religiöse Erfahrung als literarisches Faktum: Zur Vorgeschichte und Genese frauenmystischer Texte des 13. und 14.Jahrhunderts* (Tübingen: Niemeyer, 1988), 32–33.

15. *Life of Beatrice*, 338–39.

16. On the importance of these features to medieval Christian hagiographical literature, see Hippolyte Delehaye, *The Legends of the Saints*, trans. V. M. Crawford (Notre Dame: University of Notre Dame Press, 1961); Thomas J. Heffernan, *Sacred Biography: Saints and Their Biographies in the Middle Ages* (Oxford: Oxford University Press, 1988); and Renate Blumenfeld-Kosinski and Timea Szell, eds., *Images of Sainthood in Medieval Europe* (Ithaca: Cornell University Press, 1991). On the mystical hagiographies of the thirteenth century, see Roisin, "L'Efflorescence"; and Roisin, *L'Hagiographie cistercienne*. For the contested relationship between hagiography and historiography, see Felice Lifshitz, "Beyond Positivism and Genre: 'Hagiographical' Texts as Historical Narrative," *Viator* 25 (1994): 95–113.

17. "Mirentur forsan alij a sanctis antiqui temporis, in signis et virtutibus copiose satis superque patrata miracula; mirentur ab obsessis corporibus fugata demonia., et a motte resuscitata cadauera; necnon et alia quamplurima, vel hijs maiora vel horurn similia:, de quibus loquitur in euangelio dominus dicens ita.: 'Qui credit in me opera que ergo facio et ipse faciet: et maiora horum faciet. Ego vero, pace sanctorurn, beatricis caritatem multis miraculis et signis prefero; de quibus alibi dicitur.: 'signa data sunt non fidelibus sed infidelibus':, presertim cum absque signis ad regnum celorurn multi perueniunt." *Life of Beatrice*, 284–85.

18. The hagiographer's comments and his overall dilemma might also be understood within the context of changing attitudes toward supernaturalism and miracles. See Lifshitz, "Beyond Positivism," 104–5; and Benedicta Ward, *Miracles and the Medieval Mind: Theory, Record, and Event, 1000–1215* (Philadelphia: University of Pennsylvania Press, 1982), 1–24.

19. "Cum autem dicat in euangelio dominus 'Attendite ne iusticiam vestram faciatis coram hominibus vt videamini ab eis.', <e>t rursus alibi 'Sic luceat lux vestra coram hominibus vt videant opera vestra bona [.] et glorificent pattern vestrum qui in celis est': huius vtriusque dominici precepti superficialem discordantiam sic in vnam obeditionis sententiam concordauit, vt et hostis antiqui versutias, secretum suum intra se vigilanter occultando, deluderet., et rursus illud in palam opportune tempore proferendo, proximorum necessitatibus erogaret." *Life of Beatrice*, 4–7.

20. Compare *Life of Beatrice*, bk. 1, chap. 5, pp. 36–37, and *Vita Arnulfu*, in *Acta sanctorum* (Antwerp, 1643; Brussels: Culture et Civilisation, 1965–70), June 30, 24:612–16. See *Life of Beatrice*, x (although the citation he gives there is incorrect).

21. On medieval women's asceticism, see Bynum, *Holy Feast*, 82–87, 103–4, 237–44.

22. This might be understood as a function of the demand for humility, which would preclude the mystic describing her own ascetic heroics. Yet many thirteenth-century mystical writings, such as Beatrice's, take the form of treatises in which the experience

of the soul is described in the third person. If ascetic activity beyond that demanded by monastic and other religious rules was seen as essential to the mystical life, it could certainly be described and prescribed within these kinds of texts. Women's writings after 1300 will begin to do so.

23.   The exceptions are Angela of Foligno's *Book*, an early example of "autohagiography," and some hagiographies written by women. See Hollywood, *Virgin Wife*, 36–38, 231nn49–52.

24.   " . . . quieuisset., magnoque conamine cor suum ad dominum eleuasset. . . . in exces-su\<m\> mentis sue continuo rapta prosilijt." *Life of Beatrice*, 66–69.

25.   "Crucem quippe ligneam, vnius palmi longitudinis, nodoso funiculo sibi stricte colligatam., die noctuque gestabat in pectore; cui tytulum dominice passionis., horrorem extremi iudicij., iudicisque seueritatem inscripserat:, et cetera que iugiter proponebat in memoria retinere. Aliud nichilominus dominice crucis signaculum, in pargameni cedula depictum, etiam gestabat in brachio colligatum:; tercium quo-que coram se, cum scribendi vacabat officio, depictum habebat in assere:, quatenus ad quecumque loca se diuerteret., aut quidquid operis extrinsecus actitaret:, omnis obliuionis effugata caligine, per dominice crucis signaculum, id, de cuius arnissione timebat., impressum cordi suo in memoria firmiter retineret." Ibid., 88–91.

26.   " . . . ad pedes domini crucifixi, coram ipsius ymagine." Ibid., 90–91.

27.   "Exinde vero, per continuum ferme quinquennium, tam firmiter impressum habebat mentis intuitum in memoria dominice passionis., vt vix vmquam ab \<illius\> suaui meditatione recederet:; sed singulis que pro humana salute pati dignatus est, miro deuotionis affectu, iugique meditatione medullitus inhereret." Ibid., 92–93.

28.   The hagiographer does not explicitly compare Beatrice's suffering to that of Christ on the cross, yet the increasing emphasis on her suffering, bloody, and wrenched body suggests the identification. See, for example, ibid., bk. 3, chaps. 1, 2, 3, 4, 14.

29.   "Unde frequenter accidit:, vt, vellet nollet, is quem tolerabat interius mentis iubilus, per aliqua demonstrationis indicia foris erumperet, et vel risu vel tripudio, gestu vel alio quovis indicio se prodendo, quid iubilantis mens pateretur interius, extrinsecus indicaret." Ibid., 94–97.

30.   See ibid., bk. 1, chaps. 11, 13–18; bk. 2, chap. 16; bk. 3, chaps. 2, 4–5, 14.

31.   See ibid., bk. 1, chap. 18; bk. 3, chap. 5.

32.   Ibid., bk. 3, chap. 8.

33.   See ibid., bk. 1, chap. 11; bk. 2, chap. 18; bk. 3, chap. 1, 18.

34.   "In qua liquefactione quid, quantumve spiritualis iocunditatis acceperit., quid senserit., quid gustauerit, et-si verbis explicari non valeat:, ex corporalium tamen defectione sensuum extrinsecus aliquantulum apparebat." Ibid., 238–39.

35.   Beckwith argues for the importance of metaphors of enclosure in the *Ancrene Wisse*. Here the desire to maintain the body's boundaries parallels the desire to maintain the boundaries of the cloister. Beckwith, "Passionate Regulation," 808–12.

36.   *Life of Beatrice*, bk. 2, chaps. 7–9.

37.   This imagery coincides with a cultural tendency to desire an enclosed body, one that does not menstruate or release other problematic fluids. Yet the presence of "good"

emissions—like Beatrice's tears and blood—problematizes any use of Mikhail Bakhtin's distinction between the classical and the grotesque bodies. See Mikhail Bakhtin, *Rabelais and His World*, trans. Hélène Iswolsky (Bloomington: Indiana University Press, 1984). On good and bad emissions, see Claude Carozzi, "Douceline et les autres," in *La Religion populaire en Languedoc du XIIIe siècle à la moitié du XIVe siècle* (Toulouse, France: Privat, 1976), 251–67.

38. *Life of Beatrice*, bk. 2, chap. 16.

39. "Seuen manieren sijn van minnen, die comen vten hoegsten ende <keren> weder ten ouersten," *Seven Manieren*, 3; and "There Are Seven Manners of Loving," trans. Eric Colledge, in *Medieval Women's Visionary Literature*, ed. Elizabeth Alvilda Petroff (Oxford: Oxford University Press, 1986), 200. Translation, including the title, modified.

40. "Sunt igitur hij dilectionis gradus siue status septem numero;, per quos ad dilectum suum, non equalibus quidem passibus., sed nunc vt pedibus incedendo., nunc cursu velocissimo properando., nonnumquam etiam, sumptis agilitatis pennis, pernicius euolando, peruenire promeruit." *Life of Beatrice*, 288–89.

41. There is an implicit hierarchy among the manners, and Beatrice uses the metaphor of ascent, but the dialectic of presence and absence running through and between the seven manners disrupts any easily identified pattern. There is a parallel here with Marguerite Porete's seven states of the soul, which operate in a similarly dialectical manner. See Hollywood, *Virgin Wife*, 87–119; and Michael Sells, *Mystical Languages of Unsaying* (Chicago: University of Chicago Press, 1994), 116–45.

42. As Else Marie Wiberg Pedersen points out, these are the only two instances in which Beatrice uses female imagery to describe the soul. Pedersen, "Image of God-Image of Mary-Image of Woman: The Theology and Spirituality of Beatrice of Nazareth," paper presented at the 28th International Congress on Medieval Studies, Kalamazoo, Mich., May 1993.

43. There is a similar theological movement in Mechthild of Magdeburg. See Hollywood, *Virgin Wife*, 57–86.

44. " . . . te vercrigene ende te wesene in die puerheit ende in die vriheit ende in die edelheit daer si in ghemaket es van haren sceppere na sijn beelde ende na sijn ghelikenesse." *Seven Manieren*, 4; *Seven Manners*, 201.

45. " . . . pro hac de qua mentionem fecimus libertate spiritus obtinenda." *Life of Beatrice*, 290–93.

46. " . . . corporales etiam languores solebat incurrere.; quibus aliquotiens adeo grauabatur in corpore, quod mortem sibi <crederet> imminere?" Ibid., 292–93.

47. Ibid., 294–97.

48. Ibid., 298–99.

49. "Alse aldus har seluen geuuelt in die oueruloedicheit van waelheit ende in die grote volheit van herten, soe wert hare geest altemale in rinnen versinkende ende hore lichame hare ontsinkende hare herte versmeltende, ende al hare macht verderuende. Ende <so> seere wert si verwonnen met minnen, datsi cumelike hare seluen can gedragen ende datsi dicwile ongeweldich wert haerre lede ende al hare sinne.

Ende also gelijc also .i. vat dat voles, alsment ruret, haesteleke oueruloyt ende vut-welt also wert hi haestelec sere gerenen, ende al verwonnen // van der groter uolheit hars herten, so datsi dicwile hars ondanx vut moet breken." *Seven Manieren*, 15–16; *Seven Manners*, 202. Translation modified.

50.   "Fuit etiam in hoc statu tam delicatus sancte mulieris affectus :, vt, liquefacto corde, frequentissime lacrimarum imbre madesceret., et, pre nirnia spiritualis copia delectationis, interdum, virium deficiente presidio, languens et egrotans in lectulo decubaret.

. . . frequenter accidit vt, ad vasis similitudinem quod, cum plenum liquoris fue-rit., impulsum vel modice, mox quod continet eiciendo refundit;, et ipsa, per plurima sancti amoris indicia, quod sentiebat intrinsecus, velut impulsa, refunderet:; aut certe paraliticum quodammodo tremorem incurreret., aut alia queque languoris incom-moda sustineret." *Life of Beatrice*, 304–7. The hagiographer here also follows a famil-iar topos of the genre, tears as a mark of compunction and mystical fervor. See, for example, Jacques de Vitry, *Vita Mariae Oignacensis*, in *Acta Sanctorum* (Antwerp, 1643; Brussels: Culture et Civilisation, 1965–70), June 4, vol. 23, par. 18.

51.   "Ondertusschen so wert minne so onghemate ende so ouerbrekende in der sielen also har seluen so starkeleke ende so verwoedelike <berurt> int herte, dat hare dunct, dat har herte menichfoudeleke wert seere gewont ende dat die wonden dagelix ver-uerschet werden ende verseert, in smerteliker weelicheiden ende in nuer iegenword-icheiden. Ende so dunct hare. dat har adren ontpluken ende hare bloet verwalt ende hare march verswijnt ende hare been vercrencken, ende <hare> borst verbernt ende hare kele verdroget, so // dat hare anscijn ende al har ede gevuelen der hitten van binnen ende des orwoeds van minnen," *Seven Manieren*, 19–20; *Seven Manners*, 203. Translation modified. My thanks to Walter Simons for help with this difficult pas-sage and other suggestions for reading the Dutch text.

52.   This movement can be traced in texts involving the stigmata. While in the early texts describing this phenomenon the visibility of the markings was unimportant, in later ones it takes precedence. On this phenomenon, see Herbert Thurston, *The Physical Phenomenon of Mysticism* (Chicago: Regnery, 1952); and Antoine Imbert-Gourbeyre, *La Stigmatisation: L'Extase divine et les miracles de Lourdes: Réponse aux libres-penseurs*, 2 vols. (Clermont-Ferrand: Librairie Catholique, 1894).

53.   "Siquidem ipsum cor, ad illius inuasionem viribus destitutum, frequenter, ipsa sen-tiente simul et a foris audiente, quasi vas quod // confringitur <sonitum> fractionis emisit:; ipse quoque sanguis, per corporalia membra diffusus, apertis venis exiliens., ebulliuit;, ossibusque contractis ipsa quoque medulla disparuit:, pectoris siccitas ipsius gutturis raucitatem induxit:, et, vt paucis multa concludam., ipse feruor sancti desiderij et amoris omnia membra corporea, mirum in modum sensibiliter estuanti., incendio conflagrauit." *Life of Beatrice*, 308–11.

54.   See ibid., bk. 2, chap. 16; bk. 3, chap. 2.

55.   On the relationship between the human body and divine presence, see Elaine Scarry, *The Body in Pain: The Making and Unmaking of the World* (Oxford: Oxford Univer-sity Press, 1985), 181–243; and Hollywood, *Virgin Wife*, 1–25.

56.   "Fuit enim huius desiderij tam vehemens insolentia:, quod, pre nimia importunitate <vel sensum sui> se putaret interdum amittere vel etiam vite sue dies, pre magna lesione vitalium et cordis angustia, breuiare," *Life of Beatrice*, 324–25.

57.   *Life of Beatrice*, bk. 2, chap. 16; bk. 3, chap. 8.

58.   "Also ontsegt si allen troest dicwile van gode selue ende van sinen creaturen want aile die rasten die hare daer af mogen gescien dat sterket meer hare minne, ende trecket har begerte in een hoger wesen, ende dat uernuwet hare verlancnisse der minnen te plegene ende int gebruken der minnen te wesene ende sonder genuechte in ellenden te leuene. Ende so bliuet si ongesadet ende ongecosteghet in allen ghiften, om datsi noch daruen moet der iegenwordicheit hare minnen." *Seven Manieren*, 34–35; *Seven Manners*, 205. Translation modified.

59.   " . . . sola mentis experientia, non autem verborum affluentia possunt concipi." *Life of Beatrice*, 324–25.

60.   Although there are important exceptions, asceticism and paramystical phenomena clearly are more prominent in the hagiographies of women than in those of men. See, for example, Bynum, *Holy Feast*, 82–87, 103–4, 237–44; André Vauchez, *La Sainteté en Occident aux derniers siècles du moyen âge d'après les procès de canonisation et les documents hagiographiques*, Bibliothèque des Etudes Françaisés d'Athenes et de Rome 241 (Rome: École Française de Rome, 1988), 450–55; and Donald Weinstein and Rudolph M. Bell, *Saints and Society: The Two Worlds of Western Christendom, 1000–1700* (Chicago: University of Chicago Press, 1982), 123–27, 153–57, 236–37. Francis of Assisi and Henry Suso are two famous exceptions, but they remain just that—exceptional. The importance of this trend can be seen in Brenda Bolton's reading of the hagiographies of the *mulieres sanctae* as "desert mothers"—early Christian male models of ascetic heroism are transformed in the later Middle Ages into women. It is precisely the gap between the desert fathers and Beatrice's life and text that creates difficulties for her hagiographer. See Brenda Bolton, "Mulieres Sanctae," in *Women in Medieval Society*, ed. Susan Mosher Stuard (Philadelphia: University of Pennsylvania Press, 1976), 141–58.

61.   On the identification of women with the body, see Joan Ferrante, *Woman as Image in Medieval Literature* (New York: Columbia University Press, 1975), 17–35; Vern Bullough, "Medieval Medical and Scientific Views of Women," *Viator* 4 (1973): 485–501; and Caroline Walker Bynum, "The Female Body and Religious Practice in the Later Middle Ages," in *Fragmentation*, 181–238.

62.   See Petroff, "Introduction," *Medieval Women's Visionary Literature*, 3–86; and Caroline Walker Bynum, *Jesus as Mother: Studies in the Spirituality of the High Middle Ages* (Berkeley: University of California Press, 1982), 247–62. For the authorizing function of visionary experience, see Thomas Aquinas, *Summa Theologiae*, ed. Blackfriars (New York: McGraw Hill, 1964–81), pt. 3, supplement, q. 39, a. 1; and Barbara Newman, *Sister of Wisdom: Saint Hildegard's Theology of the Feminine* (Berkeley: University of California Press, 1987), 34–41.

63.   Elizabeth Castelli's comments about the movement between the visionary and object of vision in *The Martyrdom of Perpetua and Felicitas* helped me to clarify

this point. See Elizabeth Castelli, "Mortifying the Body, Curing the Soul: Beyond Ascetic Dualism in *The Life of Saint Syncletica*," *Differences* 4 (1992): 151n17.

64. Bynum, *Holy Feast and Holy Fast*, 151.

65. Mechthild of Magdeburg, *Mechthild von Magdeburg "Das fleissende Licht der Gottheit": Nach der Einsiedler Handschrift in kritischem Vergleich mit der gesamten Überleiferung*, ed. Hans Neumann (Munich: Artemis Verlag, 1990), bk. 4, chap. 2. There are accounts within the beguine literature, however, that show a movement from spiritual exercise to visionary and ecstatic experience easily read in terms of bodily practice. See especially the visions of Hadewijch in Hadewijch, *The Complete Works*, trans. Mother Columba Hart (New York: Paulist Press, 1981).

66. Sigmund Freud, "The Ego and the Id," in *The Standard Edition of the Complete Psychological Works of Sigmund Freud*, trans. and ed. James Strachey (London: Hogarth, 1953–74), 19:25–26. On the bodily ego, see also Kaja Silverman, *The Threshold of the Visible World* (New York: Routledge, 1996), 9–37; and Beckwith, "Passionate Regulation," 814.

67. Drew Leder, *The Absent Body* (Chicago: University of Chicago Press, 1990), 69–99; and Scarry, *The Body in Pain*, 27–59.

68. See Bynum, *Holy Feast*, 261–76; and Bynum, *Fragmentation*, 181–238; Elizabeth Robertson, "The Corporeality of Female Sanctity in *The Life of Saint Margaret*," in Blumenfeld-Kosinski and Szell, *Images of Sainthood in Medieval Europe*, 268–87; and Robertson, "Medieval Medical Views of Women and Female Spirituality in the *Ancrene Wisse* and Julian of Norwich's *Showings*," in *Feminist Approaches to the Body in Medieval Literature*, ed. Linda Lomperis and Sarah Stanbury (Philadelphia: University of Pennsylvania Press, 1993), 142–67.

69. See Jacques Lacan, *Écrits: A Selection*, trans. Alan Sheridan (New York: Norton, 1977), 1–7. For more on psychoanalytic theories of identification, see Butler, *Bodies That Matter*, 57–120; and Diana Fuss, *Identification Papers* (New York: Routledge, 1996), 1–82.

70. Beckwith, "Passionate Regulation," 817.

71. Ibid., 818.

72. "Hier omme es si in groet verlancnisse ende in starke begerte ute desen ellende te werdene uerledecht, ende van desen lichame ontbonden te sine ende so segtsie die wile met sereleken herten alse die apostel[en] dede die seide. 'Cupio dissolui et esse cum cristo.' Dat es Ic begere ontbonden te sine ende te wesene met kerste." *Seven Manieren*, 33; *Seven Manners*, 205. Translation modified.

73. "Ene salige passie ende .i. scarp torment / ende ene uerlange<n> quale, ende ene mordeleke doet ende steruende leuen." *Seven Manieren*, 34; *Seven Manners*, 205.

74. Beckwith uses Foucault's aphorism at the opening of her essay: "The soul is the prison of the body." See Beckwith, "Passionate Regulation," 803.

75. This use of hagiographies is made evident by the manuscript tradition for Beatrice's own *vita*. Of the four known manuscripts, one is contained in a collection of spiritual writings produced at the request of John of St. Trond, a monk in Villers, when he was the chaplain of the Cistercian convent at Vrouwenpark in Wezemaal. The

manuscript, completed in 1320, was presumably collected for the edification of these Cistercian nuns. Examination of this and similar manuscript collections might further elucidate how hagiographies were read in relationship to other forms of religious writing. For the manuscript information, see *Life of Beatrice*, xxi. These practices are also suggested by the development of hagiographical and autohagiographical writings by women in the fourteenth century. When women's spirituality comes under more stringent ecclesiastical scrutiny, they repeat these hagiographical gestures in their own texts. See Hollywood, *Virgin Wife*, 201–206.

76. It is worth mentioning that Beatrice had early contact with beguines, women who wished to live religious lives in the world. In the reaction against the beguines, their rejection of enclosure and destabilization of the boundaries between inside and outside played a key role. A comparison of the *Ancrene Wisse* with Julian of Norwich's *Showings* in light of Beckwith's reading of the former text would clarify to what extent the anchorite rule was enacted in the ways Beckwith suggests.

77. Butler, *Bodies That Matter*, 76; cited by Beckwith, "Passionate Regulation," 818.

78. Beckwith, "Passionate Regulation," 818–19.

79. For an attempt to bring gender into the genealogy of mysticism, see Grace Jantzen, *Gender Authority and Christian Mysticism* (Cambridge: Cambridge University Press, 1996). For the other major genealogical study, see Michel de Certeau, "Mystique au XVIIe siècle: Le problème du langage mystique," in *L'Homme devant Dieu: Mélanges de Lubac*, 2 vols. (Paris: Aubier, 1964), 2:267–91; and de Certeau, *La Fable mystique, XVIe–XVIIe siècle* (Paris: Gallimard, 1982). For a representative and highly influential attempt to write the history of the modern subject, see Charles Taylor, *Sources of the Self: The Making of Modern Identity* (Cambridge, Mass.: Harvard University Press, 1989). Taylor mentions the work of two women in the text of the book: Hannah Arendt and Iris Murdoch. A few more appear in the notes, although self-consciously feminist scholarship has virtually no impact on his account. See also Michel Foucault, *The History of Sexuality*, vol. 1, *An Introduction*, trans. Robert Hurley (New York: Vintage, 1980) and the voluminous literature emerging from that work, much of it critical of his putative refusal to acknowledge sexual difference. For an introduction to the history of the subject in literary studies, see David Aers, "A Whisper in the Ear of Early Modernists: or, Reflections on Literary Critics Writing the 'History of the Subject,'" in *Culture and History, 1350–1600: Essays on English Communities, Identities and Writing*, ed. David Aers (Detroit: Wayne State University Press, 1992), 177–202. For a brief response to Aers's argument and further literature on the topic, see Valerie Traub, M. Lindsay Kaplan, and Dympna Callaghan, "Introduction," in *Feminist Readings of Early Modern Culture: Emerging Subjects*, ed. Valeria Traub, M. Lindsay Kaplan, and Dympna Callaghan (Cambridge: Cambridge University Press, 1996), 1–4.

80. Denys Turner, *The Darkness of God: Negativity in Christian Mysticism* (Cambridge: Cambridge University Press, 1995), 4.

81. For a better-stated version of this argument, and one that does take into account women's texts, see Sells, *Languages of Unsaying*, 1–13. Jantzen also argues convincingly

for the role of modern Western Protestant theology and philosophy of religion in shaping contemporary conceptions of mysticism. See Jantzen, *Gender Authority and Christian* Mysticism, 304–21.

82.   I cannot speak here to the situation of women south of the Alps. For the complexities of Northern Europe, see Hollywood, *Virgin Wife*, 201–6.

83.   The desire to free body and soul from the demands of corporal and spiritual exercises and the pain they engender is most explicit in Marguerite Porete: "And to the one who would ask them [simple and free souls] what was the greatest torment that a creature could suffer, they would say that it would be to dwell in Love and to be in obedience to the Virtues. For it is necessary to give to the Virtues all that they ask, whatever the cost to Nature. For it is thus that the Virtues demand honor and goods, heart and body and life." The interiorization and annihilation of the simple soul free her from this torment. See Marguerite Porete, *Le Mirouer des simples ames anienties et qui seulement demourent en vouloir et desir d'amour,* ed. Romana Guarnieri and Paul Verdeyen, *Corpus Christianorum: Continuatio Mediaevalis* (Turnhout, Belgium: Brepols, 1986), chap. 8, pp. 28–30.

In this view, a freely given experience of the divine other is the source of the soul's liberating movement. Yet if the experience of the divine other depends on bodily practice, freedom is constrained. And if the theories of Mauss and Asad are correct, without bodily and spiritual exercises, the divine other will not be encountered and unbelief ensues. All this suggests that the mystic's movement may be self-defeating, although a careful reading of Marguerite and Eckhart on this issue may suggest another approach.

9. PERFORMATIVITY, CITATIONALITY, RITUALIZATION

The annual conference of the American Academy of Religion took place in San Francisco in 1997. The Feminist Theory and Religious Reflection Group used that opportunity to invite Judith Butler to respond to a panel on her work. I presented an early draft of this essay there and the final version benefited enormously from that occasion, in the form both of Butler's response and of my engagement with others on the panel. My thanks also to Ellen Armour and Susan St. Ville, who organized the session and edited a subsequent volume in which the essay appeared.

The title was a spell-check nightmare, but I stood by it. Meanwhile, the discussion of performativity, citationality, and ritualization has proceeded at such a pace that my word processing program now accepts the first and the third terms, if not yet the all-important second. I have not tried to update the citations as the field is too vast to survey in any single essay—and my primary point about citationality seems not yet to have been duplicated or challenged in quite the form I make it here. I must point, however, to Judith Butler's *Undoing Gender* (New York: Routledge, 2004) and *Senses of the Self* (New York: Fordham University Press, 2015), both of which contain crucial arguments pertinent to my work here.

1. Judith Butler, *Bodies That Matter: On the Discursive Limits of "Sex"* (New York: Routledge, 1993); and Butler, *Gender Trouble: Feminism and the Subversion of Identity* (New York: Routledge, 1990). For one version of these criticisms, see Susan Bordo, *Unbearable Weight: Feminism, Western Culture, and the Body* (Berkeley: University of California Press, 1993), 289–95.

2. One of the problems is the grammatical injunction that there be a subject either who acts or who is fully determined and acted on. See Butler, *Bodies That Matter*; and Butler, *The Psychic Life of Power: Theories of Subjection* (Stanford: Stanford University Press, 1997).

3. Butler interrogates the concept of materiality without, however, differentiating between different modes of materiality. For this point, my thanks to Saba Mahmood. For an insightful challenge to the liberatory conception of the subject operating within Butler's work, see Saba Mahmood, "Feminist Theory, Embodiment, and, the Docile Agent: Some Reflections on the Egyptian Islamic Revival," *Cultural Anthropology* 16 (2001): 202–35.

4. Butler, *Bodies That Matter*, x.

5. One problem with the term "performativity," as Butler shows in *Bodies That Matter* and *Excitable Speech: A Politics of the Performative* (New York: Routledge, 1997), is the implication, when the theatrical meaning of the term comes to the fore, that the subject intentionally performs. For J. L. Austin, theatrical performance implies utterance without intentionality (or without the intention seemingly indicated by the words spoken). The ritual theorists Caroline Humphrey and James Laidlaw argue that rituals are actions in which apt performance does not depend on intentionality. The example I think of here is the consecrated priest who performs sacraments without belief or right intention, yet the sacrament is still said to be aptly performed. I would argue that in this case intentionality is objective and communal rather than individual. The point to note is that there are distinctions between theatrical and ritual performance, although we might finally want to put them on a continuum rather than opposing them. See Caroline Humphrey and James Laidlaw, *The Archetypal Actions of Ritual: A Theory of Ritual Illustrated by the Jain Rite of Worship* (Oxford: Clarendon, 1994); and Stanley Tambiah, "A Performance Approach to Ritual," in *Culture, Thought, and Social Action: An Anthropological Perspective* (Cambridge, Mass.: Harvard University Press, 1985), 132–34.

6. See, for example, Jacquelyn Zita's review in *Signs* 21 (1996): 786–95; and Caroline Walker Bynum, "Why All the Fuss About the Body?: A Medievalist's Perspective," *Critical Inquiry* 22 (1995): 1–33.

7. Butler, *Bodies That Matter*, 10–11.

8. Butler claims in *Feminist Contentions: A Philosophical Exchange* that *Gender Trouble* does not give an account of the formation of the subject but only of the gendering of the subject. *Bodies That Matter* then might be taken as extending this discussion to the sexed body. Yet I think that all of these theories have implications for a more general account of subjectivity, one toward which Butler herself continually moves. See Butler, "For a Careful Reading," in *Feminist Contentions: A Philosophical Exchange*,

by Seyla Benhabib, Judith Butler, Drucilla Cornell, and Nancy Fraser (New York: Routledge, 1995), 133.

9. Butler, *Gender Trouble*, 136.

10. See Butler, *Excitable Speech*.

11. I will use "signification" as an umbrella term for what both constatives and performatives do. Insofar as they can be separated, constatives have meaning and can be true or false, whereas performatives have force and can be efficacious or not efficacious, felicitous or infelicitous. Despite the complexity of twentieth-century theories of meaning and reference, meaning ultimately seems to depend on reference to something outside of or beyond the utterance itself (even if it be something as illusive as "the truth or falsity of the utterance"). An efficacious performative, however, constitutes that to which it refers. On twentieth-century philosophies, both analytic and continental, of meaning, reference, signification, and performativity, see Benjamin Lee, *Talking Heads: Language, Metalanguage, and the Semiotics of Subjectivity* (Durham: Duke University Press, 1997). Most important for my argument here, Lee describes Austin's discovery "that language cannot be understood without looking for the interplay between indexicality and metaindexicality, between signs whose interpretation is tied to the moment of speaking and signs that represent such signs" (11). Attention to this distinction will be necessary for a more complete account of ritual and bodily practices as performative.

12. Similarly, Butler argues in *Gender Trouble* that gender itself is "the repeated stylization of the body, a set of repeated acts within a highly rigid regulatory frame that congeal over time to produce the appearance of substance, of a natural sort of being" (33).

13. As Butler shows, psychoanalysis offers a useful analysis of some of these norms, particularly as they deal with sexual difference and sexuality. For her arguments about the importance of psychoanalysis to contemporary political theory, see Butler, *Bodies That Matter*, 12–16; and Butler, *The Psychic Life of Power*, 1–30, 83–105, 114.

14. Psychoanalysis deals with this too, although arguably thinkers like Freud and Julia Kristeva more fully than Jacques Lacan. Butler is most interested in the movement between psychic and material bodies. See Butler, *Bodies That Matter*, 72–88.

15. Ibid., x; see also 10, 95, 126, 185.

16. J. L. Austin, *How to Do Things with Words*, ed. J. O. Urmson and Marina Sbisà (Cambridge, Mass.: Harvard University Press, 1962); Jacques Derrida, "Signature, Event, Context," in *Margins of Philosophy*, trans. Alan Bass (Chicago: University of Chicago Press, 1982), 307–30. See, for example, Edmund Leach, "Ritual," in *International Encyclopedia of the Social Sciences* (New York: Macmillan, 1966). The distinction is, of course, too simple and, like that made between performative and constative utterances, ultimately breaks down.

17. This has occurred, I think, because of the problems involved in understanding just how ritual actions signify. See note 5.

18. While Austin leans his conception of the speech act on an untheorized conception of ritual, ritual theorists have turned to Austin's and Searle's accounts of the performative

in order to explain ritual. This is the outcome of the tendency to understand ritual as expressive or symbolic action. Given the bankruptcy of symbolic accounts of ritual, and under pressure to come to an understanding of how the parallel between language and action might operate, Tambiah and others argue that, like illocutions and perlocutions, rituals are not constative but performative. They do not mean, but act. See, for example, Tambiah, "A Performance Approach to Ritual," 128. Lawson and McCauley point to other theorists, like Benjamin Ray, who use speech-act theory to deal only with the linguistic component of ritual. As Lawson and McCauley argue, any good theory of ritual must deal with its multimedia character. This is precisely what Tambiah attempts to do by playing on the multiple meanings of performance. See E. Thomas Lawson and Robert McCauley, *Rethinking Religion: Connecting Cognition and Culture* (New York: Cambridge University Press, 1990), 51–54. Although I agree that rituals are not referential in normally conceived ways, they are intentional (in the sense of having an end or aim—although that end may not always be the one toward which the actor understands herself as moving) and hence cognitive.

19. These theoretical insights might be expanded by an analysis of the changing shape of Christian baptism, a subject of some discussion in Butler insofar as it has to do with naming (see Butler, *Bodies That Matter*, 213–18). In early Christianity and some parts of Protestant Christianity, the importance of bodily practices to the ritual of baptism makes it inexplicable in Butler's purely linguistic terms.

20. Ibid., x.

21. Ibid., 10.

22. Butler uses ritual the same way in *Gender Trouble*, 140: "As in other ritual social dramas, the action of gender requires a performance that is *repeated*." Although it is not clear if repetition is all there is to ritual, it is clearly a key ingredient.

23. Butler, *Bodies That Matter*, 95. The claim that repetition is not performed by the subject but constitutes the subject is also important, although it leads one to ask who or what performs. As I will argue below, Butler's point is that in ritual the performance is itself constitutive of the performer.

24. See Pierre Bourdieu, *Language and Symbolic Power*, trans. Gino Raymond and Matthew Adamson (Cambridge, Mass.: Harvard University Press, 1991).

25. Ibid., 190, quoted in Butler, *Excitable Speech*, 146.

26. Butler, *Excitable Speech*, 147.

27. I think it is possible to read Derrida more generously here, for although he understands ritual in terms of iterability, this is not necessarily to reduce it to language in the narrow sense. Since for Derrida social meanings are generated by iteration, we can extend this to iterated actions as well as linguistic signs (hence to ritual as well as language).

28. Butler, *Excitable Speech*, 150–51.

29. Butler argued in a response to this essay that she ties the force of the performative not to the body of the speaker but through that body to the conventions governing violence. Yet this position seems in danger of returning to the problems represented for Butler by Bourdieu. Shoshana Felman's analysis of the performative is crucial here.

See Shoshana Felman, *The Literary Speech Act: Don Juan with J. L. Austin, or Seduction in Two Languages*, trans. Catherine Porter (Ithaca: Cornell University Press, 1983).

30. Butler, *Excitable Speech*, 155–56.
31. See Pierre Bourdieu, *Outline of a Theory of Practice*, trans. Richard Nice (Cambridge: Cambridge University Press, 1977). Butler calls them rituals (*Excitable Speech*, 152), although Bourdieu does not.
32. Butler, *Excitable Speech*, 155.
33. Butler is closer to Catherine Bell's emphasis on ritualization as a form of practice than to Humphrey and Laidlaw's insistence that ritualization involves action. For Humphrey and Laidlaw, ritual is intentional (and hence involves action) but with intentionality divorced from the individual. See Catherine Bell, *Ritual Theory, Ritual Practice* (Oxford: Oxford University Press, 1992); and Humphrey and Laidlaw, *Archetypal Actions*.
34. Butler, *Excitable Speech*, 159.
35. One might also argue that it is insofar as hate mail points to a veiled but still material and bodily threat that it carries this destructive force. The veiling of the body behind the threat, in fact, makes it all the more potent because its specific parameters are unknown. This suggests that the tie to the body is crucial and yet can perhaps work more effectively when hidden or veiled and hence only loosely tethered to its utterance through writing and the unsigned text.
36. Butler, *Excitable Speech*, 155.
37. If bodily practices are speech acts insofar as they are citational, moreover, we are back with Derrida's position in which what makes ritual and language signify *and* act is iteration.
38. Butler, *Excitable Speech*, 159, quoting Bourdieu.
39. Ibid., 160.
40. See Austin, *How to Do Things with Words*, 5, 18–19.
41. Ibid., 5.
42. Ibid., 14–15.
43. Ibid., 18–19.
44. "Force" is Austin's term. See ibid., 1.
45. Austin later denies that "purely polite conventional ritual phrases" should be included among performatives. Ibid., 84.
46. Ibid., 60.
47. Ibid.
48. Austin makes this even more confusing when he goes on to claim that illocutionary acts are conventional whereas perlocutionary acts are not. This suggests that in illocutionary acts the force of the utterance derives from convention whereas in perlocutionary acts it derives from the speaker, yet Austin never goes so far as to make this claim. Moreover, he goes on in lecture 10 to raise a host of difficulties about our ability easily to distinguish illocutionary and perlocutionary acts. See ibid., 121.

49. Derrida's essay, it should be noted, was performed in the context of a conference on communication presided over by Paul Ricoeur (hermeneutics haunts the piece and is the other pole of reflection on language that runs through it).

50. See, in particular, the work of Searle and the debates between Searle and Derrida: John Searle, *Speech Acts* (Cambridge: Cambridge University Press, 1969); Searle, *Intentionality* (Cambridge: Cambridge University Press, 1983); and Searle, "Reiterating the Differences," *Glyph* 1 (1977): 198–208; and Jacques Derrida, *Limited Inc.* (Evanston, Ill.: Northwestern University Press, 1988).

51. Austin, *How to Do Things with Words*, 18–19, quoted in Derrida, "Signature, Event, Context," 323–24.

52. Stanley Cavell contests this reading. See Stanley Cavell, "What Did Derrida Want of Austin?," in *Philosophical Passages: Wittgenstein, Emerson, Austin, Derrida*, Bucknell Lectures in Literary Theory 12 (Cambridge, Mass.: Blackwell, 1995), 42–65.

53. Derrida, "Signature, Event, Context," 326.

54. This is Butler's phrase. She focuses on the third of these problems, which is her reading of Bourdieu's implicit critique of Derrida. See Butler, *Excitable Speech*, 149–50.

55. See Derrida, "Signature, Event, Context," 310.

56. Ibid., 329–30.

57. Nancy Fraser argues that Butler tends to conflate the break and resignification with critique and positive political change. This valorization of the break is inherited, I think, from Derrida. My reading of Derrida suggests that he, while celebrating deconstruction's break with previous significations, also implies the political and ethical neutrality of the break as such. See Benhabib et al., *Feminist Contentions*, 67–68.

58. Often the fact that participants give many divergent interpretations of the same ritual action is taken to be a problem for symbolic or expressive accounts of ritual. Yet the existence of multiple interpretations of a ritual does not mean that it has no meaning, any more than the possibility of multiple interpretations of a text means it is nonsensical. For this mistake, see Humphrey and Laidlaw, *Archetypal Actions* (see note 5 above). A similar problem occurs if the self-referentiality of ritual is taken as grounds for claiming it is without meaning. For this mistake, see Fritz Staal, "The Meaninglessness of Ritual," *Numen* 26 (1979): 2–22. Lawson and McCauley offer an account of self-reflexive holism to counter these claims. See Lawson and McCauley, *Rethinking Religion*, 137–69.

59. Austin begins by making a clear distinction between constative and performative speech, only to have the distinction blur in the course of his exposition. Finally, what he has described are different ways in which utterances operate, not two radically different forms of utterance. Similarly, ritual actions are both constative and performative—they both signify and do things—although as constitutive acts, the performative comes to the fore.

60. Once again, I think that the confusion in Butler's account stems from her emphasis on speech acts and inattention to the other bodily practices through which subjects are constituted. More attention is given to such issues, however, in *Gender Trouble*.

61. Butler, *Excitable Speech*, 156.

62.   See Talal Asad, *Genealogies of Religion: Discipline and Reasons of Power in Christian-ity and Islam* (Baltimore: Johns Hopkins University Press, 1993), esp. chaps. 2, 3, and 4; and Bell, *Ritual*.

63.   Asad, *Genealogies*, 57.

64.   Ibid., 58. For Asad, this reduction of action to textuality is problematic in that it reduces action to discourse. Yet to see action as meaningful does not necessarily mean to engage in Western imperialist anthropological enterprises, as Asad seems some-times to suggest. (See his critique of Clifford Geertz.) On the contrary, the prob-lem with the expressivist conception of ritual seems to me not to be the claim that actions *mean* as well as *do things* but rather the insistence on reading the "discourse of actions" in terms of psychology or sociology. It is the search for hidden, symbolic meanings that is the problem, for it obscures the semantics of ritual action itself. On this issue, see Daniel Sperber, *Rethinking Symbolism*, trans. A. Morton (Cambridge: Cambridge University Press, 1975); and Lawson and McCauley, *Rethinking Religion*, 37–41.

65.   Asad argues that rites as apt performances presume "a code" but claims that it is a regulatory as opposed to a semantic code. See Asad, *Genealogies*, 62.

66.   Ibid., 131.

67.   Marcel Mauss, *Sociology and Psychology: Essays*, trans. B. Brewster (London: Rout-ledge and Kegan Paul, 1979), 104.

68.   Ibid., 101.

69.   Asad uses Benedict of Nursia's *The Rule of Benedict*—the foundational text for Chris-tian monasticism—to make this claim.

70.   Bell, *Ritual*, 220.

71.   Ibid., 221.

72.   Do rituals and bodily practices then constitute the object of belief as well as its sub-ject? And if so, can we distinguish between fictions and other kinds of realities?

73.   Of course, every account of ritual I have ever read includes some discussion of rep-etition, at the very least as an identificatory criterion. Derrida's work enables us to see what is at stake in ritual repetition and how it is tied to ritual force and meaning. On the power of routinization, see Jonathan Z. Smith, "The Bare Facts of Ritual," in *Imagining Religion: From Babylon to Jonestown* (Chicago: University of Chicago Press, 1981), 53–65.

74.   Bell, *Ritual*, 215. For examples of the theories against which Bell argues, see Bour-dieu, *Outline of a Theory of Practice*; and Maurice Bloch, *Ritual, History and Power: Selected Papers in Anthropology* (London: Athlone, 1989). For more nuanced histori-cized accounts of the relationship between ritual and authority, see Bruce Lincoln, *Discourse and the Construction of Society: Comparative Studies of Myth, Ritual and Classification* (Oxford: Oxford University Press, 1989), 53–74; Lincoln, *Author-ity: Construction and Corrosion* (Chicago: University of Chicago Press, 1994); and Michel de Certeau, *The Practice of Everyday Life*, trans. Steven Rendall (Berkeley: University of California Press, 1984). Lincoln makes a useful distinction between authority, persuasion, and force. Persuasion and force are potentialities implied by

authority, "but once actualized and rendered explicit they signal—indeed, they are, at least temporarily—its negation." Lincoln, *Authority*, 6. If we understand authority as that which is generated through ritual (in keeping with Lincoln's fluid account of authority and my own account of the generative capacities of bodily practice and ritual), then ritual actions mark the participants' complicity in legitimizing authority. However, as with hate speech as analyzed by Butler, the force of the speaker's body (or of the state or army or other body that legitimates authority) always implicitly stands behind authoritative discourse.

75. See Butler, *Excitable Speech*, 5.
76. Bell, *Ritual*, 210.
77. Margaret Thomson Drewal, *Yoruba Ritual: Performers, Play, Agency* (Bloomington: Indiana University Press, 1992), 1–11.

10. PRACTICE, BELIEF, AND FEMINIST PHILOSOPHY OF RELIGION

The essay was written for inclusion in *Feminist Philosophy of Religion: Critical Readings* (2003), edited by Pamela Sue Anderson and Beverley Clack and was reprinted in *Thinking Through Ritual: Philosophical Approaches* (2004), edited by Kevin Schilbrack. I am grateful to Anderson and Clack for the invitation and to all three of the editors for their advice. For an important new intervention in the feminist philosophy of religion and an up-to-date bibliography, see Pamela Sue Anderson, *Re-Visioning Gender in Philosophy of Religion: Religion, Love and Epistemic Locatedness* (2012).

1.   Pamela Sue Anderson, *A Feminist Philosophy of Religion: The Rationality and Myths of Religious Belief* (Oxford: Blackwell, 1998); and Grace Jantzen, *Becoming Divine: Towards a Feminist Philosophy of Religion* (Bloomington: Indiana University Press, 1999). See also Anderson, "Gender and the Infinite: On the Aspiration to Be All There Is," *Journal of Philosophy of Religion* 50 (2001): 191–212; Anderson, "Myth and Feminist Philosophy," in *Thinking Through Myths: Philosophical Perspectives*, ed. Kevin Schilbrack (New York: Routledge, 2002), 101–122; and Anderson, "Feminist Theology as Philosophy of Religion," in *The Cambridge Companion to Feminist Theology*, ed. Susan Frank Parsons (Cambridge: Cambridge University Press, 2002), 40–59. The philosopher Luce Irigaray's work is crucial to both Anderson and Jantzen. See, among other texts, Irigaray, *Speculum of the Other Woman*, trans. Gillian Gill (Ithaca: Cornell University Press, 1985); Irigaray, *An Ethics of Sexual Difference*, trans. Carolyn Burke and Gillian Gill (Ithaca: Cornell University Press, 1993); Irigaray, *Sexes and Genealogies*, trans. Gillian Gill (New York: Columbia University Press, 1993); and Irigaray, *I Love to You*, trans. Alison Martin (New York: Routledge, 1996). For other recent work on feminist philosophy of religion, much of it also influenced by Irigaray, see the special issue of *Hypatia* 9 (1994); Daphne Hampson, *After Christianity* (London: SCM Press, 1996); Amy Hollywood, *Sensible Ecstasy: Mysticism, Sexual Difference, and the Demands of History* (Chicago: University of Chicago Press, 2002); and Sarah Coakley, *Powers and Submissions: Spirituality, Philosophy, and Gender* (Oxford: Blackwell, 2002). A

question that remains unanswered in this literature is that of the relationship between philosophy of religion, philosophical theology, and theology. Like much contemporary analytic philosophy and, arguably, like the work of Irigaray, Anderson and Jantzen are engaged in philosophical theology, a point to which I will return in the chapter.

2. Most introductions to the philosophy of religion define the field in terms of the clarification and justification of religious belief. This is also the case with anthologies for classroom use, which rarely, if ever, include sections on practice or ritual. Even the widespread interest in religious experience and mysticism ultimately reverts to questions of belief and justification, for the central philosophical dispute—the one to which all other questions lead—concerns whether religious experience can provide a means of justification for religious belief. See, for example, Wayne Proudfoot, *Religious Experience* (Berkeley: University of California Press, 1985); William P. Alston, *Perceiving God: The Epistemology of Religious Experience* (Ithaca: Cornell University Press, 1991); and Matthew C. Bagger, *Religious Experience, Justification, and History* (Cambridge: Cambridge University Press, 1999).

3. Jantzen, *Becoming Divine*, 22. Jantzen argues that her work does not focus on belief, yet given the centrality to her work of religious discourse and the symbolic, however broadly conceived, and the absence of any extended discussion of practice or ritual, it is difficult to see how she fully escapes the confines of more traditional forms of analytic philosophy of religion.

4. See my "Performativity, Citationality, Ritualization," included here.

5. Anderson, *Feminist Philosophy of Religion*, 118.

6. Anderson distinguishes fiction, myth, and illusion in the following ways. Fiction she defines, rather flatly, as something that "has been made up." Illusions are defined in a quasi-Freudian way as ideas unconsciously generated "from fear of the contingencies and losses in life." Myths, finally, are complex configurations of narratives and concepts that "constitute a people's meaningful, qualitative identity." Anderson gives considerably attention to myth, articulating its relationship to embodiment, desire, and mimesis in useful ways. Although I think these distinctions require more adequate conceptions of fiction and illusion to be fully convincing, the issue lies beyond the scope of my argument here. See ibid., 118, 127–64.

7. Ibid., 137.

8. Ibid., 213. Hence they are not illusions, as defined by Anderson.

9. Ibid.

10. See Immanuel Kant, *Critique of Pure Reason*, trans. N. K. Smith (London: Macmillan, 1950), 532–70; and Kant, *Critique of Practical Reason*, trans. Lewis White Beck (Indianapolis: Bobbs-Merrill, 1956), 130–38.

11. Jantzen, *Becoming Divine*, 92.

12. Ibid., 223. Essential for Jantzen are the "criteria of trustworthiness and mutual accountability by which aspects of the symbolic can be tested against its fruitfulness in creating a space for the woman subject." Such criteria arguably do not respond to all the problems raised by critics of moral and epistemological relativism, but this issue will have to wait for exploration.

13. Kant, *Critique of Practical Reason*, 136. See Jantzen, "Do We Need Immortality?," in *Contemporary Classics in Philosophy of Religion*, ed. Ann Loades and Loyal D. Rue (La Salle, Ill.: Open Court Press, 1991), 306–8.

14. Van A. Harvey, *Feuerbach and the Interpretation of Religion* (Cambridge: Cambridge University Press, 1995), 110.

15. For more on this issue as it applies to Irigaray's writings on religion and the ambivalent responses to them by feminists, see Hollywood, *Sensible Ecstasy*, 234–235.

16. Marcel Mauss, "Body Techniques," in *Sociology and Psychology: Essays*, trans. Ben Brewer (London: Routledge, 1979), 122, cited by Talal Asad, *Genealogies of Religion: Disciplines and Reasons of Power in Christianity and Islam* (Baltimore: Johns Hopkins University Press, 1993), 76.

17. Asad, *Genealogies*, 77. Or, perhaps better, of differently taught bodies.

18. See, for example, James Samuel Preus, *Explaining Religion: Criticism and Theory from Bodin to Freud* (New Haven: Yale University Press, 1987).

19. Asad, *Genealogies*, 55–79.

20. Mauss, "Body Techniques," 104, cited by Asad, *Genealogies*, 75. I have kept the problematic language of man here, in keeping with Asad's deployment of Mauss.

21. Mauss, "Body Techniques," 101, cited by Asad, *Genealogies*, 75. On the medieval reception of Aristotle and the doctrine of *habitus*, see Cary J. Nederman, "Nature, Ethics, and the Doctrine of 'Habitus': Aristotelian Moral Psychology in the Twelfth Century," *Traditio* 45 (1989–1990): 87–110.

22. Asad, *Genealogies*, 75.

23. Ibid., 131. Put another way, without claims to the primacy of belief over action and hence to the necessarily symbolic nature of ritual action, the distinction between ritual action and instrumental action breaks down and with it the need for a distinction between bodily practices and ritual. All that remains is the distinction between those actions that use the body as the instrument for transforming the body and those actions that use other instruments toward other ends.

24. For more on bodily practices and ritual as performative, see Hollywood, "Performativity, Citationality, Ritualization."

25. Asad, *Genealogies*, 76. Asad cites phrases from Mary Douglas's interpretation of Mauss's essay. Mary Douglas, *Natural Symbols* (London: Barrie and Rockliff, 1970). Asad disagrees deeply with Douglas's account of Mauss and asks how, given his own reading of Mauss's essay, it has been understood as a founding document for symbolic anthropology. "Was it," Asad wonders, "because 'ritual' was already so powerfully in place as symbolic action—that is, as visible behavioral form requiring decoding?" Asad, *Genealogies*, 77.

26. Ibid.

27. Ibid.

28. For an extremely influential proponent of this view, see Elaine Scarry, *The Body in Pain: The Making and Unmaking of the World* (Oxford: Oxford University Press, 1985).

29. From this standpoint, Mauss and Asad seem closer to an Aristotelian conception of practical reason. A longer version of my argument will require attention to both

Aristotle's account of *habitus* and its deployment within medieval moral and sacramental theology. See Nederman, "Nature, Ethics, and the Doctrine of 'Habitus' "; and Marcia Colish, "*Habitus* Revisited," *Traditio* 48 (1993): 77–92.

30. Michel Foucault, *The History of Sexuality*, vol. 2, *The Use Of Pleasure*, trans. Robert Hurley (New York: Vintage, 1986), 25–26.

31. Ibid., 2:29.

32. Ibid.

33. Foucault, "Sexuality and Solitude," in *On Signs*, ed. M. Blonsky (Baltimore: Johns Hopkins University Press, 1985), 367.

34. In the case of Benedictine monasticism, bodily practices and rituals are codified textually; in other instances, prescribed modes of action are passed down through person-to-person interactions (and of course this kind of interaction also plays an essential role in monastic discipline, as the *Rule of Benedict* continually emphasizes).

35. Asad, *Genealogies*, 64. For full discussions of the role of humility in Christian monasticism, see *Genealogies*, 125–67.

36. Margaret Ebner, *The Major Works*, trans. and ed. Leonard P. Hindsley (New York: Paulist Press, 1993), 96; and Philipp Strauch, ed., *Margaretha Ebner und Heinrich von Nördlingen: Ein Beitrag zur Geschichte der Deutschen Mystik* (Freiburg: Mohr, 1882), 20–21.

37. Ebner, *Major Works*, 96; *Margaretha Ebner*, 21. For the kiss of the heart and drinking blood from Christ's side wound/heart, see my "Sexual Desire, Divine Desire" and "'That Glorious Slit,'" in this volume.

38. On this point and the important corrective it provides to the work of Pierre Bourdieu, see Saba Mahmood, "Rehearsed Spontaneity and the Conventionality of Ritual: Disciplines of Ṣalāt," *American Ethnologist* 28 (2001): 837–38.

39. Ebner, *Major Works*, 114; *Margeretha Ebner*, 52.

40. Ebner, *Major Works*, 114; *Margeretha Ebner*, 54.

41. On the salvific power of Christ's blood and the centrality of blood in representations of the Passion, see Hollywood, "Sexual Desire, Divine Desire," in this volume; and Jeffrey F. Hamburger, *The Visual and the Visionary: Art and Female Spirituality in Late Medieval Germany* (New York: Zone, 1998).

42. For the fluidity of gender in the later Middle Ages, see Carolyn Walker Bynum, *Holy Feast and Holy Fast: The Religious Significance of Food to Medieval Women* (Berkeley: University of California Press, 1987); Bynum, *Fragmentation and Redemption: Essays on Gender and the Body in the Later Middle Ages* (New York: Zone, 1991); and Amy Hollywood, *The Soul as Virgin Wife: Mechthild of Magdeburg, Marguerite Porete, and Meister Eckhart* (Notre Dame: Notre Dame University Press, 1995).

43. The Franciscan-authored *Meditations on the Life of Christ*, for example, addressed to women, most often calls for readers to identify with Mary. As Robin O'Sullivan argues, Angela of Foligno, like Ebner, refuses this identification, instead insisting on her oneness with Christ on the cross. See Robin Anne O'Sullivan, "Model, Mirror and Memorial: Imitation of the Passion and the Annihilation of the Imagination in Angela da Foligno's Liber and Marguerite Porete's *Mirouer des simples âmes*"

(PhD diss., University of Chicago Divinity School, 2002); and Hollywood, *Sensible Ecstasy*, 69–74.

44. Henry Suso, *The Exemplar, with Two German Sermons*, trans. Frank Tobin (New York: Paulist Press, 1989), 173–74; and for the German text, Karl Bihlmeyer, ed., *Heinrich Seuse: Deutsche Schriften* (Stuttgart: Kohlhammer, 1907), 154–55.

45. Hamburger writes: "The way in which the young—that is, spiritually immature—Suso so literally imitates Christ's passion bears an uncanny resemblance to the self-inflicted sufferings of numerous nuns." (Hamburger here cites only Elsbeth von Oye, although further examples are readily available from the hagiographical literature.) Hamburger continues: "By contrast in Part 2 of the Life, Suso deliberately distances himself from the extreme asceticism in which he indulged as a novice. The *imitatio Christi* is recast in ritualized, institutionalized forms, governed by texts and enacted through images. Instead of drawing blood, Stagel embroiders in red silk; rather than mortifying her flesh, she emulates her advisor's asceticism by adorning her body in his image." Although I agree with Hamburger that this movement between books 1 and 2 of the Life is decisive, it is crucial also to note that Suso's body remains the source of sanctification. Stagel adorns her flesh, but her flesh never gains the power evinced, still in book 2, by Suso's, a power gained precisely through the ascetic action against which he advises Stagel and his other followers. See Hamburger, *Visual and the Visionary*, 263–66.

46. R. Marie Griffith, *God's Daughters: Evangelical Women and the Power of Submission* (Berkeley: University of California Press, 1997).

47. I follow Griffith here in generalizing about second-wave feminism in the United States, but with full recognition of the enormous variety of positions and practices that exist within it. Griffith seems most interested in the mainstream traditions of liberal feminism most visible to evangelical women and, arguably, most critical of fundamentalist Christian women.

48. Griffith, *God's Daughters*, 27.

49. See Pierre Bourdieu, *Outline of a Theory of Practice*, trans. Richard Nice (Cambridge: Cambridge University Press, 1977).

50. See also Saba Mahmood, "Feminist Theory, Embodiment, and the Docile Subject: Some Reflections on the Egyptian Islamic Revival," *Cultural Anthropology* 16 (2001): 202–36.

11. LOVE OF NEIGHBOR AND LOVE OF GOD: MARTHA AND MARY IN THE CHRISTIAN MIDDLE AGES

This chapter was originally given as a paper as part of the Rockwell Lecture Series at Rice University. I have tried to keep some of the spirit of that public occasion. Notes have been kept to a minimum and refer readers directly to English editions of the cited texts when they are available. These translations will in turn point interested readers to the original texts. My thanks to the Department of Religion at Rice for the invitation to speak, and to my fellow Rockwell lecturers, Catherine Keller and the late Jane Schaberg, for their stimulating discussions of the Magdalen.

1. Katherine Ludwig Jansen, *The Making of the Magdalen: Preaching and Popular Devotion in the Later Middle Ages* (Princeton: Princeton University Press, 2000), 336.

2. For a useful summary of these debates, particularly as they apply to the study of religion, see Elizabeth A. Clark, *History, Theory, Text: Historians and the Linguistic Turn* (Cambridge, Mass.: Harvard University Press, 2004).

3. Jacobus de Voragine, *The Golden Legend: Reading on the Saints*, vol. 1, trans. William Granger Ryan (Princeton: Princeton University Press, 1993), 374–83.

4. Jane Schaberg, *The Resurrection of Mary Magdalene: Legends, Apocrypha, and the Christian Testament* (New York: Continuum, 2002), esp. 65–120. Comparing biblical, apocryphal, and Gnostic texts, Schaberg argues that these conflations worked to efface Mary Magdalen's authority and prophetic power. I do not attend here to Mary Magdelen's powerful presence in Gnostic material, focusing instead on texts important to the Latin Western tradition.

5. "Factum est autem dum irent et ipse intravit in quoddam castellum et mulier quaedam Martha nomine excepit illum in domum suam et huic erat soror nomine Maria quae etiam sedens secus pedes Domini audiebat verbum illius Martha autem satagebat circa frequens ministerium quae stetit et ait Domine non est tibi curae quod soror mea reliquit me solam ministrare dic ergo illi ut me adiuvet et respondens dixit illi Dominus Martha Martha sollicita es et turbaris erga plurima porro unum est necessarium Maria optimam partem elegit quae non auferetur ab ea." Luke 10:38–42, Vulgate.

6. A similar identification of Mary Magdalen as one from whom Jesus cast out seven demons appears in Mark 16:9, following his account of Mary Magdalen, Mary, the mother of James the younger and Joses, and Salome standing at the cross and at Christ's tomb. The longer version of Mark, like the Gospel of John, includes an account of Mary Magdalen as the first to see Christ resurrected. For Mary Magdalen's crucial role in the resurrection narratives, see Mark 16:9–11; Matthew 27:55–56; 28:1–10; Luke 24:1–12; and John 20:1–18.

7. On these traditions, see Jansen, *Making of the Magdalen*, 32–46.

8. The information in this paragraph is informed by Giles Constable, "The Interpretation of Mary and Martha," in *Three Studies in Medieval Religious and Social Thought* (Cambridge: Cambridge University Press, 1995), 14–18. See also Daniel A. Csányi, "Optima pars: Die Auslegungsgeschichte von Lk 10, 38–42 bei den Kirchenvätern der ersten vier Jahrhunderte," *Studia monastica* 2 (1960): 5–78.

9. Clement of Alexandria, *The Rich Man's Salvation*, trans. G. W. Butterworth (Cambridge, Mass.: Harvard University Press, 1953), 291, cited by Constable, "Interpretation," 15.

10. Origen, *Homélies sur S. Luc: Texte latin et fragments grec*, Sources Chrétiennes 87, ed. Henri Crouzel, François Fournier, and Pierre Périchon (Paris: Éditions du Cerf, 1962), frag. 72, pp. 521–22, cited by Constable, "Interpretation," 15–16n57.

11. Origen, *Homélies sur S. Luc*, frag. 72, pp. 521–22 and frag. 80 of the Comm. on John in *Origenes Werke*, ed. Erwin Preuschen, *Die griechischen christlichen Schriftsteller der ersten drei Jahrhunderte* 10 (Leipzig: J. C. Hinrichs, 1903), 547, cited by Constable, "Interpretation," 15.

12. The citations are too numerous to give here, but see Constable, "Interpretation," 15–19; and Anne-Marie de la Bonnardière, "Marthe et Marie, figures de l'Eglise d'après saint Augustin," *La vie spirituelle* 86 (1952): 404–27.

13. Timothy Fry, ed., *RB 1980: The Rule of Benedict in Latin and English with Notes* (Collegeville, Minn.: Liturgical Press, 1981), chap. 42, p. 243, and chap. 73, p. 297.

14. John Cassian, *The Conferences*, trans. Boniface Ramsey (New York: Newman Press, 1997), first conference, chap. 8, p. 47; hereafter cited *Conferences*, conference.ch, p.

15. Ibid., 1.8, 47.

16. Ibid., 1.10, 48.

17. Ibid, 1.10, 48–49.

18. For Gregory's reading of the Lukan passage in light of Genesis, see Constable, "Interpretation," 20–22. Gregory is the first to bring together Luke's female sinner (Luke 7:36–50), Mary of Bethany, sister of Martha, whose brother Lazarus Jesus raised from the dead (John 11:1–45; 12:1–8), and the demonically possessed Mary Magdalen healed by Jesus and subsequently his disciple (Mark 16:9). This Mary Magdalen, then, is easily identified with the Mary of Luke 10:38–42. See Jansen, *Making of the Magdalen*, 32–35.

19. Pope Gregory I, *Sancti Gregorii Magni Homiliae in Hiezechihelem prophetam*, ed. Marcus Adriaen, Corpus Christianorum 142 (Turnhoult: Brepols, 1971), bk. 2, ch. 2, pp. 229–33, cited by Constable, "Interpretation," 21.

20. Pope Gregory I, *Moralia in Job*, Corpus Christianorum 143–143A, ed. Marcus Adriaen (Turnhout: Brepols, 1979), bk. 6, chap. 37, pp. 329–31, cited by Constable, "Interpretation," 20.

21. Constable, "Interpretation," 20.

22. Marbod of Rennes, *Miracula b. Roberti ab. Casae-Dei*, in *Nova bibliotheca manuscriptorum librorum*, vol. 2, ed. Philippe Labbe (Paris, 1657), 652, cited by Constable, "Interpretation," 41.

23. Marbod, *Miracula*, 652, 654, and 655, cited by Constable, "Interpretation," 41.

24. Anselm of Havelberg, *De ordine canonicorum regularium*, Patrologia Latina, ed. J. P. Migne (Paris, 1855), vol. 188, col. 1114c.

25. Anselm of Havelberg, *Apologeticum pro ordine canonicorum regularium*, Patrologia Latina, ed. J. P. Migne (Paris, 1855), vol. 188, col. 1132a. Both passages are discussed, without citations, in André Vauchez, *The Spirituality of the Medieval West: The Eighth to the Twelfth Century*, trans. Colette Friedlander (Kalamazoo, Mich.: Cistercian Publications, 1993), 125. See also Constable, "Interpretation," 49, 69.

26. For interpretative introductions to these changes, see Caroline Walker Bynum, *Jesus as Mother: Studies in the Spirituality of the High Middle Ages* (Berkeley: University of California Press, 1982); Marie-Dominique Chenu, *Nature, Man, and Society in the Twelfth Century*, trans. Jerome Taylor and Lester K. Little (Chicago: University

of Chicago Press, 1968); Giles Constable, *The Reformation of the Twelfth Century* (Cambridge: Cambridge University Press, 1996); Herbert Grundmann, *Religious Movements in the Middle Ages*, trans. Steven Rowan (Notre Dame: University of Notre Dame Press, 1995); Lester K. Little, *Religious Poverty and the Prophet Economy in Medieval Europe* (Ithaca: Cornell University Press, 1978); Bernard McGinn, *The Growth of Mysticism: Gregory the Great Through the Twelfth Century* (New York: Crossroad, 1996); McGinn, *The Flowering of Mysticism: Men and Women in the New Mysticism, 1200–1350* (New York: Crossroad, 1998); and Walter Simons, "New Forms of Religious Life in Medieval Western Europe," in *The Cambridge Companion to Christian Mysticism*, ed. Amy Hollywood and Patricia Z. Beckman (Cambridge: Cambridge University Press, 2012), 80–113. On the history of the term "apostolic," see L. M. Dewailly, "Notes sur l'histoire de l'adjectif 'apostolique,'" *Mélanges de science religieuse* 5 (1948): 141–52.

27.   In "On the Four Degrees of Violent Love," Richard argues that in the fourth degree of love, the soul becomes fruitful, engaged in acts in the worlds just as Christ worked in the world on behalf of humanity. This is very close to what Eckhart will argue in his sermon on the Lukan passage. Richard's text was very likely known by at least Beatrice of Nazareth and Hadewijch, if not by other beguines. See Richard of St. Victor, "On the Four Degrees of Violent Love," trans. Andrew Kraebel, in *On Love: A Selection of Works by Hugh, Adam, Achard, Richard and Godfrey of St. Victor*, ed. Hugh Feiss, OSB (New York: New City Press, 2012), 275–300. For the many relevant citations concerning Mary and Martha, see Constable, "Interpretation," 71.

28.   For Eckhart's relationship to the women's religious movement, see Grundmann, *Religious Movements*, 237–45; Otto Langer, *Mystische Erfahrung und spirituelle Theologie: Zu Meister Eckharts Auseinandersetzung mit der Frauenfrömmigkeit seiner Ziet* (Munich: Artemis, 1987); Bernard McGinn, ed., *Meister Eckhart and the Beguine Mystics: Hadewijch of Brabant, Mechthild of Magdeburg, and Marguerite Porete* (New York: Continuum, 1994); Amy Hollywood, *The Soul as Virgin Wife: Mechthild of Magdeburg, Marguerite Porete, and Meister Eckhart* (Notre Dame: University of Notre Dame Press, 1995); Bernard McGinn, *The Mystical Thought of Meister Eckhart: The Man from Whom God Hid Nothing* (New York: Crossroad, 2001), esp. 9–10; and McGinn, *The Harvest of Mysticism in Medieval Germany* (New York: Crossroads, 2005). Many scholars, especially in Germany, currently downplay the importance of the women's movement for Eckhart, a move with which I cannot agree. See McGinn, *Mystical Thought*; and Jeremiah Hackett, ed., *A Companion to Eckhart* (Leiden: Brill 2013), especially the essay by Lydia Wegener.

29.   On the beguines, see especially Grundmann, *Religious Movements*, 75–201; and Walter Simons, *Cities of Ladies: Beguine Communities in the Medieval Low Countries, 1200–1565* (Philadelphia: University of Pennsylvania Press, 2001).

30.   James of Vitry, "The Life of Mary of Oignies," trans. Margot King, in *Mary of Oignies: Mother of Salvation*, ed. Anneke B. Mulder-Bakker (Turnhout: Brepols, 2006), "Prologue," n. 3, pp. 42–43. Translation slightly modified.

31.   Ibid., "Prologue," n. 4, p. 43.

32. Ibid., "Prologue," n. 6, p. 45. Translation slightly modified.

33. Ibid., "Prologue," n. 7, p. 46. Although written a generation or more after the first outpouring of women's religious devotion in Liège, the writings of the early beguine mystics—Hadewijch's letters, poems, and visions, Mechthild of Magdeburg's *Flowing Light of the Godhead*, and Marguerite Porete's *Mirror of Simple Souls*—emerge out of the religious milieu here first described by James. For English translations, see Hadewijch, *The Complete Works*, trans. Mother Columba Hart (New York: Paulist Press, 1980); Mechthild of Magdeburg, *The Flowing Light of the Godhead*, trans. Frank Tobin (New York: Paulist Press, 1998); Marguerite Porete, *The Mirror of Simple Souls*, trans. Ellen Babinsky (New York: Paulist Press, 1993); and Margaret Porette [sic], *The Mirror of Simple Souls*, trans. Edmund Colledge, J. C. Marler, and Judith Grant (Notre Dame: University of Notre Dame Press, 1999). To these texts one might add the *Life and Revelations* of Agnes Blannbekin (d. 1315), a beguine of Vienna. Although the text has been read as hagiographical, it can also be understood as a collaboratively produced devotional text, closer in its hybrid genre to the work of Mechthild than to thirteenth-century beguine and Cistercian hagiographies. See Ulrike Wiethaus, trans. and ed., *Agnes Blannbekin, Viennese Beguine: Life and Revelations* (Cambridge: D. S. Brewer, 2002), esp. 6–10.

The texts authored by the beguines tell little directly about their external lives. External sources are available only for Marguerite Porete and they give scant evidence concerning her form of religious life. For an overview of the three great beguine mystics, including information about what can be gleaned about their lives from their writings, see McGinn, *The Flowering of Mysticism*, 199–265. For a wonderful reconstruction of what we can—and cannot—say about Marguerite's life and death, see Sean L. Fields, *The Beguine, the Angel, and the Inquisitor: The Trials of Marguerite Porete and Guiard of Cressonessart* (Notre Dame: University of Notre Dame Press, 2012).

34. For a detailed discussion of these texts, see Simons, *Cities of Ladies*, 36–48, 61–90. See also Walter Simon, "Holy Women of the Low Countries: A Survey," in *Medieval Women in the Christian Tradition c. 1100–c.1500*, ed. Alastair Minnis and Rosalynn Voaden (Turnhout: Brepols, 2010), 625–62.

35. Simons, *Cities of Ladies*, 92.

36. Hollywood, *Virgin Wife*, 39–42.

37. Hugh of Floreffe, *Vita Ivetta Reclusa, Acta Sanctorum*, ed. J. Bolland, G. Henschenius et al. (Brussels: Culture et civilisation, 1965–70) January 1, 870n37. On Ivetta, see Anneke Mulder-Bakker, *Lifes of the Anchoresses: The Rise of the Urban Recluse in Medieval Europe*, trans. Myra Heerspink Scholz (Philadelphia: University of Pennsylvania Press, 2005), 51–77.

38. Ibid., 870n37.

39. Ibid., 871n42.

40. On male support for, worries about, and condemnations of the beguines, see Grundmann, *Religious Movements*, 139–52; and Robert Lerner, *The Heresy of the Free Spirit in the Later Middle Ages* (Berkeley: University of California Press, 1972).

41. For medieval medical views of women's bodies and their theological ramifications, see Dyan Elliott, "The Physiology of Rapture and Female Spirituality," in *Medieval Theology and the Natural Body*, ed. Peter Biller and A. J. Minnis (Woodbridge, Suffolk: York Medieval Press, 1997), 141–73; and Nancy Caciola, *Discerning Spirits: Divine and Demonic Possession in the Middle Ages* (Ithaca: Cornell University Press, 2003). For a fuller bibliography, see also my "Feminist Studies," in this volume.

42. Beguine claims to be bringing together the roles of Mary and Martha could themselves be used as evidence against them by those critical of the movement. In his *Dit des Beguines*, the poet Rutebeuf satirizes double claims that he reads as hypocrisy: "If a beguine marries, that is her vocation, because her vows or profession are not for life. Last year she wept, now she prays, next year she'll take a husband. Now she is Martha, then she is Mary; now she is chaste, then she gets a husband. But remember: say only good things of her, because the King would not tolerate otherwise." Rutebeuf, *Oeuvres completes de Rutebeuf*, 2 vols., ed. Edmond Faral and Julia Bastin (Paris: A. and J. Picard, 1959–60), 1:334–35, cited by Simons, *Cities of Ladies*, 119.

43. See Hollywood, *Virgin Wife*, for an extended argument to this effect.

44. Meister Eckhart, *Meister Eckhart: The Essential Sermons, Commentaries, Treatises, and Defense*, trans. Edmund Colledge and Bernard McGinn (New York: Paulist Press, 1981), ser. 2, p. 177; hereafter cited ser., p.

45. For a summary of the scholarship up to 2002, see McGinn, *Meister Eckhart*, 2–19; for more recent work, see Hackett, ed., *Companion to Eckhart*. For an interpretation more in line with my own than those found in Hackett, see Charlotte Radler, " 'In Love I Am More God': The Centrality of Love in Meister Eckhart's Mysticism," *Journal of Religion* 90, no. 2 (2010): 171–98.

46. Simons, *Cities of Ladies*, 85. Simons argues that this was the case particularly among beguine hospital workers. The name "Martha" thereby emphasized their life of humility and service.

47. Eckhart, *Essential*, 2, 177.

48. Ibid.

49. Ibid., 2, 178.

50. For this aspect of Marguerite's work, see Michael Sells, *Languages of Unsaying* (Chicago: University of Chicago Press, 1994), 116–45; and Hollywood, *Virgin Wife*, 97–107.

51. Eckhart, *Essential*, 2, 178–79.

52. Ibid. 6, 186. Translation modified.

53. Ibid., 6, 189.

54. Ibid., 52, 200. Translation modified.

55. See Hollywood, *Virgin Wife*, 120–44.

56. On sermon 86, see Blake R. Heffner, "Meister Eckhart and a Millennium with Mary and Martha," in *Biblical Hermeneutics in Historical Perspective: Studies in Honor of Karlfried Froehlich on His Sixtieth Birthday*, ed. Mark S. Burrows and Paul Rorem (Grand Rapids, Mich.: W. B. Eerdmans, 1991), 117–30; Hollywood, *Virgin Wife*, 166–72; and Hollywood, "Writing as Social Practice in Meister Eckhart," in

Mysticism and Social Transformation, ed. Janet Ruffing (Syracuse: Syracuse University Press, 2001), 76–91.

57. Meister Eckhart, *Meister Eckhart: Teacher and Preacher*, ed. Bernard McGinn with the collaboration of Frank Tobin and Elvira Borgstadt (New York: Paulist Press, 1986), ser. 86, p. 339; hereafter cited ser., p.

58. For a succinct outline of these views, see Porette [sic], *Mirror*, trans. Colledge, Marler, and Grant, chap. 118, pp. 140–46.

59. Eckhart, *Teacher*, 86, 339.

60. Ibid., 86, 342.

61. Eckhart here plays on the language of the Vulgate, which states that Martha "stood and said" ("stetit et ait").

62. Eckhart, *Teacher*, 86, 342.

63. Ibid., 86, 343.

64. Ibid., 86, 344.

65. Ibid.

SOURCES

THE AUTHOR and publisher acknowledge with thanks permission granted to reprint in this volume the following material.

"Acute Melancholia," originally published in *Harvard Theological Review* 99, no. 4 (2006): 381–406.

"Feminist Studies in Christian Spirituality," originally published as "Feminist Studies," in *The Blackwell Companion to Christian Spirituality*, ed. Arthur Holder (Cambridge: Basil Blackwell Press, 2005), 363–86. Copyright © 2005 Blackwell Publishing Ltd.

"Gender, Agency, and the Divine in Religious Historiography," originally published in *Journal of Religion* 84, no. 4 (2004): 514–28. Copyright © 2004 University of Chicago Press. All rights reserved.

"Reading as Self-Annihilation," republished with permission of Taylor and Francis Group LLC, from *Polemic: Critical or Uncritical*, ed. Jane Gallop, Essays from the English Institute, 2004.

"Sexual Desire, Divine Desire; Or Queering the Beguines," originally published in *Theology and Eros: Transfiguring Passion at the Limits of Discipline*, eds. Virginia Burrus and Catherine Keller (New York: Fordham University Press, 2006), 119–33, 404–12. Granted gratis per publication agreement with Amy Hollywood.

"The Normal, the Queer, and the Middle Ages," first published as the article "The Normal, the Queer, and the Middle Ages," by Amy Hollywood, in *Journal of the History of Sexuality* 10, no. 2: 173–79. Copyright © 2001 University of Texas Press. All rights reserved.

"'That Glorious Slit': Irigaray and the Medieval Devotion to Christ's Side Wound," originally published in *Luce Irigaray and Premodern Culture: Thresholds of History*, ed. Elizabeth D. Harvey and Theresa Krier (New York: Routledge, 2005), 105–25.

"Inside Out: Beatrice of Nazareth and Her Hagiographer," originally published in *Gendered Voices: Medieval Saints and Their Interpreters*, ed. Catherine Mooney (Philadelphia: University of Pennsylvania Press, 1999), 78–98. Copyright © 1999 University of Pennsylvania Press. All rights reserved. Some of this material appears in very different form in *SE*.

"Performativity, Citationality, Ritualization," originally published in *History of Religions* 42 (2002): 93–115. Copyright © 2002 University of Chicago Press. All rights reserved. Also reprinted by permission of the publisher from "Toward a Feminist Philosophy of Ritual and Bodily Practices," in *Difference in Philosophy of Religion*, ed. Philip Goodchild (Farnham: Ashgate, 2003), 73–83. Copyright © 2003.

"Practice, Belief, and the Feminist Philosophy of Religion," originally published in *Feminist Philosophy of Religion: Critical Readings*, ed. Pamela Sue Anderson and Beverley Clack (London: Routledge, 2003), 218–33. The chapter also appears in *Thinking Through Ritual: Philosophical Approaches*, ed. Kevin Schilbrack (New York: Routledge, 2004), 52–70.

INDEX

Adams, Henry: attraction to Buddhism, 29, 35; on death of William James, 42; Far East travels of, 29; and Henry James, 42–43; on history, 1; on history *vs.* antiquarianism, 4; on Mary as medieval reality, 1, 2, 4; medieval turn after wife's death, 29; melancholy after wife's death, 41–43, 62; and modern atheism, 3, 272–73n8; rejection of Christianity, 32; wife as absent presence in works after her death, 29, 41–42, 62. See also *Education of Henry Adams, The* (Adams); *Esther* (Adams); grave memorial for Clover Adams; *Mont Saint Michel and Chartres* (Adams)

Adams, Marian Hooper "Clover": Henry's medieval turn after death of, 29; resemblance to Esther in Adams's *Esther*, 32, 35, 37–38; sense of unrealness experienced by, 38; suicide of, 29. *See also* grave memorial for Clover Adams

Aelred of Rievaulx, 178, 187, 329n2

Aers, David, 103–4

affect and emotions in Christian Middle Ages, 313n93; and affective *vs.* speculative mysticism, 113; loss of in modern historiography, 253–54; recent work on, 112

affirmative criticism, Roberts on, 11

afterlife: Christina the Astonishing's account of, 57–58; Esther's rejection of in Adams's

Esther, 33–34, 40; Hadewijch of Brabant on, 302n37; Henry Adams's rejection of, 32; implicit rejection of in Clover Adams's grave memorial, 32; 19th century Protestant conception of, 30–32

Agamben, Giorgio, 312n90

agency: *vs.* critical reflection, Anderson on, 321n33; *vs.* determination or victimization, 318n7; instrumental, 125; separation of from subjectivity, 124–25; spirit possession and, 124–26, 320n16

agency, female: claims of direct inspiration from God and, 118, 125–26, 321n28; Mary Magdalen as model of, 254; submission of will to divine as precondition for, 117; valorization of in feminist history, 321n28

Alexander of Hales, 56

Allen, Amy, 318n7

Althusser, Louis, 347n4

Ancrene Wisse, 191–92, 206, 208

Anderson, Amanda, 321n33

Anderson, Pamela Sue, 233–35, 237, 241, 243–44, 249–50, 364n3

Angela of Foligno, 54, 108, 114, 171–73, 176, 340n11, 346n62

Anselm of Havelberg, 259–60

antibody dualism, and medieval misogyny, 101

antiquarianism, *vs.* history, in Adams, 4

apophasis: and cataphasis, as generative pair,
14–15, 16, 115; Derrida and, 14; and excessive functions of religion, 15–16

aporia, preoccupation with, and trauma
discourse, 47

Aquinas, Thomas, 56

Arbor vitae crucifixae Jesu (Ubertino da
Casale), 344n38

Areford, David S., 179, 182

Armstrong, Nancy, 321n33

Asad, Talal: attack on internalized self by,
210–11; on belief as product of bodily
practice, 191, 192, 195, 205, 239, 240–41,
243–45, 246, 365n23; on cultural variation
in perception of pain, 241; and decoupling
of agency and subjectivity, 124–25; on
habitus, 214; on medieval monastic practice, 244; on reason, 240–41; on ritual,
191, 227–29, 362n64

asceticism, medieval: Beatrice of Nazareth's
efforts to transcend, 209; and doctrine of
the incarnation, 101; as effort to obtain
redeemed body, 208–9

askesis (practice): as component of moral
systems, 242; emotions as product of,
244; and formation of ethical subjects,
242; Kant on, 242–43, 244, 248. *See also*
bodily practice; ritual

atheism, modern inability to think outside of, 3

Augustine: on body-spirit duality, 111, 312n89;
and Christian self-critique, 12; on city of
God, as not fully knowable, 9; Hadewijch
on, 111, 312n89; on Mary and Martha
story, 257; on visionary experience, types
of, 56, 93

Augustinian rule, 260

Auma, Alice, 126

Austin, J. L.: on constative utterances, 219,
223, 361n59; on performatives, 218–21,
224–25, 231, 357n5, 360n48; as source for
Butler, 214–15

authoritarianism, perception of critique as
opposition to, 7–8, 277n34

authority, as term, 319n12

autohagiography: development of after 1300,
103; Ebner's *Revelations* as, 73

autohagiography by women: as capitulation
to male conceptions of sanctity, 104; and
women's spiritual turn inward, 210

Avicenna, 72

Bataille, Georges, 46, 62, 114, 346n62

Beatrice of Nazareth, 69–73; on autonomy
of internal self, 211; Bynum on, 102–3;
hagiography's externalization of Beatrice's
devotion, 69, 70, 72–73; and imaginary
ego generated by ascesis, 208; insistence
on interiority of her experience, 205,
207, 208, 210–11; life of, 193; melancholic
incorporation in, 84, 85, 86; movement
of desire in, 312n90; rebuilding of inner
world by, 85; rejection of association of
women with body, 207–8; and storytelling as incorporation, 87; works by, 193.
See also *Life of Beatrice of Nazareth, The*;
Seven Manners of Loving (Beatrice of
Nazareth)

Beatrice of Ornacieux, 101

Beauvoir, Simone de, 54, 58, 114, 339n5

Beckwith, Sarah, 191–92, 195, 205–6, 208–9,
210–11, 347–48n4

Becoming Divine (Jantzen), 233–34, 236–38,
241, 243–44, 249–50, 364n3

beguines: "bridal mysticism" of, 106, 152;
critics of, 372n42; early, hagiographies
on, 262; James of Vitry on holiness of,
261–62; lifestyle of, 332n14; Marguerite
Porete as, 136; medieval views on women's
susceptibility to sin and, 264; origin of
movement, 261; partial condemnation
of after 1300, 104; queering of gender
identity in works by, 152–62; reaction
against (early 14th century), 219, 355n76;
and tension between contemplative and
active life, 262–64

Behrend, Heike, 126

belief: Anderson on, 233; primacy over practice, in modern anthropology, 239

belief, as product of bodily practice: Asad on, 191, 192, 195, 205, 239, 240–41, 243–45, 246, 365n23; Ebner and, 245–47; Mauss on, 191, 192, 205, 238–39; ritual and, 114–15, 191, 230–31, 233–34, 238–49, 356n83

belief, ontological status of objects of: Anderson on, 234–35, 237; goals of philosophy of religion and, 238; Jantzen on, 233–34, 236–37; Kant on, 235–37; ritual and, 233–34, 238–39

Bell, Catherine, 229–31

Benedict of Nursia, 257

Benes (canon), 179

Benjamin, Walter, 276n19

Bennett, Judith, 149–51, 152, 331n9

Bernard of Clairvaux: on Christ wounds, 176–78; on ecstatic religious experience, 56; on experience in religious life, 94–95; on relationship between soul and God, 153; sex and gender as troubled concepts in, 187; on Song of Songs, 30, 71

Bersani, Leo, 164

Bestul, Thomas, 175, 342n27

Bible: contested meaning of, 8–9; and Western conceptions of critique, 272n6

Bible, critical reading of: history of, 130–33m 322n3; principles of, 130–31; Protestant response to, 132; reason as standard in, 130–31, 131–32, 323n7

Biddick, Kathleen, 103, 104

biology of women, and women's spirituality, 100–101

Blannbekin, Agnes, 371n33

Bodies that Matter (Butler), 213–14, 215, 226, 227, 357n5, 357n8

bodily imagery in women's spiritual writing, as theological, 111

bodily memory, modern research on, 80

bodily practice: conflation of with speech acts, in Butler, 214, 218; constitution of sexual difference through, 244–45;

importance of in medieval worship, 114–15, 191, 356n83. See also *habitus*

bodily practice, belief as product of: Asad on, 191, 192, 195, 205, 239, 240–41, 243–45, 246, 365n23; Ebner and, 245–47; Mauss on, 191, 192, 205, 238–39; ritual and, 114–15, 191, 230–31, 233–34, 238–49, 356n83

body: as sight of enculturation, 191–92, 208, 210–11; as sight of reinvention of social order, 208

body, role in religious life: Anderson on, 243–44; as area of research, 114; *askesis* and, 244; Jantzen on, 243–44

body-mind binary, Christian link to female-male binary, 101, 103–4, 105

body sense, *vs.* body learning, Mauss and, 241

body-spirit binary: Agamben on, 312n90; Augustine on, 111; Paul on, 111

Bolton, Brenda, 353n60

Bonaventure, 178–79

books for and by women, dissemination of as object of study, 109–10

Boswell, John, 163

Bourdieu, Pierre: Butler on, 227; on Derrida's concept of historicity, 224; on force of performative, 216, 226; on *habitus*, 191, 205, 214, 217, 218; on ritual, 225; and undermining of internalized self, 210–11

"bridal mysticism," of beguines, 106, 152

Brown, Judith C., 331n10

Brown, Wendy, 275nn17–18

Buddhism: Esther's attraction to in Adams's *Esther*, 34–36, 37, 38, 41; and grave memorial for Clover Adams, 21, 22, 35, 41; Henry Adams's attraction to, 29, 35

Butler, Judith: on agency *vs.* determination, 318n7; on citationality, 213, 215, 217, 218; conflation of bodily practices and speech acts in, 214, 218; conflation of signification and language in, 225; on critique, 277n34; deconstruction of central theoretical dualism in, 213; on imaginary ego generated by ascesis, 208, 278n45; on Irigaray, 172, 186–87;

Butler, Judith (*continued*)
  on materialization process, 215; on performative subjectivity, 213–14; and primacy of language in subject formation, 214; and queer history, 163; on speech acts as rituals, 215; on subjectivization, 214, 231, 347n4, 357n8. See also *Bodies that Matter* (Butler); *Excitable Speech* (Butler); *Gender Trouble* (Butler); performativity of gender, Butler on
Butler, on body: as constituted by speech acts, 217–18; and *habitus* as speech acts, 214, 218; as location of performative force, 216–17, 221, 226–27, 359n29
Butler, on performatives: body as location of force of, 216–17, 221, 226–27, 359n29; constraints of power on, 215–16; Derrida and, 221–24; force of, 221, 226; and possibilities for resistance, 227; as social ritual, 215, 218, 227; sources underlying, 218–27
Butler, on performativity of gender, 213–14; constraints of power on, 216; extension of to subject formation, 214; gaps and fissures formed in, 213, 215; supplementing of with attention to other bodily practices, 214
Butler, on ritual, 215–18; constraints of power on, 215–16; need for clearer conception of, 218; performatives and, 215, 218; as repetition, 215
Bynum, Caroline Walker: on bodily signs of holiness in hagiography, 204–5; and bridal mysticism, deromanticizing of, 184; on Christ's body, feminization of on cross, 104, 105–6, 149, 152, 184–85; on Christ's side wound, as breast and vagina, 185; and critique of valorization of violence, 104; empowerment thesis of, 101, 103–4; on gender fluidity in medieval worship, 184, 334n36; on individual authorship of medieval texts as issue, 107; influence of, 96, 102; and late-20th-century reevaluation of women's spiritual writings, 117; on male *vs.* female religious imagery, 97–99, 186; on material objects in spiritual practice, 115; on medieval categories of difference, 105;

on modern sexualizing of body imagery, 105, 151–52, 182–85, 330n3, 346n68; on objective analysis of sources, 113, 321n30; on pride, women's avoidance of, 309n77; and radicality of medieval devotional practices, 187; redemptive view of history in, 113; on religious symbols, 98; and same-sex desire, denial of, 105–6, 152, 184; and second-wave feminist theology, 97; use of sources in, 102–3; work on Christian women's spirituality, 96, 97–101
Bynum on women's spirituality: causes of unique characteristics of, 99–101; critique of, 102–7, 113; as different from male form, 98–99, 102; male control of, 104; somatic tendency in, 99, 101, 103–4; valuing of, 114

Cadden, Joan, 166
Cameron, Elizabeth, 42
Canguilhem, Georges, 336n17
capitalism, triumph of, and subaltern history, 123–24
Carlini, Benedetta, 331n10
Carruthers, Mary, 175, 305n50
Caruth, Cathy, 283n92
Cassian, John, 59, 63, 94, 112, 257–58
cataphasis: and apophasis, as generative pair, 14–15, 16, 115; and locative, link between, 15–16
Catherine of Genoa, 102–3
Catherine of Siena, 102–3, 151–52, 182–84
Cavell, Stanley, 11, 15, 277n35
Certeau, Michel de, 310n79
Chakrabarty, Dipesh: on alternative subaltern historiography, 121–24, 126–27, 320n17; on critique, necessity of, 7; on Histories 1 and 2, 123–24, 126; on objective analysis of sources, 321n30; Orsi on, 273n10; and recognition of power of belief, 319n15
Charcot, Jean-Martin, 52, 53
chivalry toward religious faith, 134–35
Chodorow, Nancy, 100
Christ: cross-gender identifications with, as issue, 247–48, 366n43; historical accuracy

of biblical account, as issue, 130–31; touching of, as aspect of medieval spirituality, 168

Christ, feminization of on cross: Bynum on, 104, 105–6, 149, 152, 184–85; disruption of heteronormativity in, 152, 187–88; and medieval metaphorical lesbianism, 149–50; and women as woundedness, 186, 188

Christ, Passion of: Beatrice of Nazareth's experience of, 70–73; internalization of images of, 206; linking of to lovesickness, 71–73, 74–79; Margaret Ebner's experience of, 75–79; meditation on, similarity to traumatic memory, 80–81, 294–95n41. *See also* Passion narratives

Christ, sexualized descriptions of relationship with, 149–50, 152, 329–30nn2–3; disruption of heteronormativity in, 149–51, 152, 153, 156, 157–62, 184–85, 331n4; erotic content of, as issue, 151–52; in Hadewijch of Brabant, 155–58, 160, 161–62, 334n36; in Marguerite Porete, 158–60, 161–62, 335n48; in Mechthild of Magdeburg, 153–55, 160–61

Christ, side wound of, 172–84, *174*, *180*, *181*, *183*, 341n14, 344n40; blood from as cleansing, 173; blood from as garment, 176, *177*; as both breast and vagina, 184–85, 188, 329n2, 330n3; devotions surrounding, 173–74; drinking from, 106, 173, 176, 178, 184, 187, 329n2, 330n3; entry into, 171–72, 173, 178–79, 187; Eucharist and, 178; genitalization of, 149–50, 171, 172, 179–80, 185, 188, 329n2, 330–31nn3–4; Irigaray on, 171; multiple significances of, 173, 178; as objects of devotion, 181–82; as opening to Sacred Heart, 173, 176–78; as symbol of union between soul and Christ, 179; as synecdoche for entire Passion, 179; women's homoerotic relationship with, 182

Christianity: critique within, 8; Esther's rejection of in Adams's *Esther*, 30, 32–34, 36–37, 39–40; feminist critique of, 98; as force in modern world, 4; misperception of as monolithic, 8; origin of critique in, 12, 13, 277n33; reality of both suffering and joy in, 63; as site of critique, 8–9, 11–12

Christian spiritual writings: centrality of sexuality to, 95; centrality of women's writing to, 95, 96; erotic and homoerotic imagery in, 105–7, 149–67, 182–85; individual authorship of, as issue, 107–8, 108–9; methodological issues in study of, 115–16; sex and gender as troubled concepts in, 94, 95, 105–7, 116, 187, 345n50. *See also* erotic imagery in Christian spiritual writing; women's spiritual writings

Christina the Astonishing. See *Life of Christina the Astonishing* (Thomas of Cantimpré)

Christine of Pizan, 110

Chronicon (William of Nangis), 135–36

church, institutional, medieval critique of dependence on lifeless reason, 134, 135

citationality: Butler on, 213, 215, 217, 218; Derrida on, 223–24, 225, 226

Classics of Western Spirituality series, 93–94

Clement of Alexandria, 256

cognition, and affect, in medieval spiritual writings, 112

Colledge, Edmund, 93–94

community contexts for women's spirituality, 108–9

Conferences (Cassian), 59, 257–58

Conflict of the Faculties, The (Kant), 130

Constable, Giles, 258

constative utterances, 358n11; Austin on, 219, 223, 361n59

constructive studies of religion, value of, 11

Cooper, Kate, 95–96

Cornell, Drucilla, 338n2

Council of Vienne (1311), 322n3

Covington, Dennis, 274n14

Crapanzano, Vincent, 134, 328n34

crisis of belief, as function of untaught bodies, in Mauss and Asad, 191

critical detachment, and emancipatory
agency, 321n33
critical reading: effort to define, 129–30, 131,
134; history of term, 130; limitations of,
134–35; and other-than-rational critique,
possibility of, 144–45; variation across
disciplines, 129–30
critical reading, of Bible: history of, 130–33,
322n3; principles of, 130–31; Protestant
response to, 132; reason as standard in,
130–31, 131–32, 323n7
criticism, as term, 323n7
critique: *vs.* agency, Anderson on, 321n33;
balance of objective and ideological in,
113; contingency of Western conceptions
of, 272n6; and imagination, cooperative
effort in discovery of truth, 17; impla-
cable fanaticism of, 12–13; as integral to
history as discipline, 3–4; as obstacle to
understanding, 6–7; as opposition to
authoritarianism, 7–8, 277n34; perception
of as inherently secular, 7–8; refusal to
engage with other-than-rational view-
points, 134, 144–45, 248–49; of religion,
Marx on, 129, 131; religious origin of, 12,
13, 275n18, 277n33; religious practice as
site of, 7, 8–9, 10, 11–12; and tradition, as
irreducible pairing, 16–17, 278n45; and
trauma discourse as negative theology,
46–47, 63–64
critique, and trauma discourse: debilitating
effects of focus on, 63–64; willingness to
credit, 44–45, 46, 47, 50, 55, 59, 61–62, 63
critique, receptive mode of: Mahmoud on,
12–13; Pritchard's critique of, 6–7
Critique of Practical Reason (Kant), 235–36, 237
Critique of Pure Reason (Kant), 235–36
culture, and formation of women's
interiority, 192

Dailey, Patricia, 110–12, 114–15, 283n92,
312n89, 312n90
Dalarun, Jacques, 108

Darkness of God, The (Turner), 209–10
Davis, Lennard, 164–66
deconstruction, Derrida on, 223–24
deities, male, as disempowering for
women, 97
de la Huerta, Jean, 22, *24*
Les démoniaques dans l'art (Charcot and
Richer), 54
Dennett, Daniel, 277n33
Derrida, Jacques: and apophasis/cataphasis,
14, 16, 278n39; Butler on ritual in, 216;
on critique and tradition as irreducible
pairing, 16–17; on historicity, 224; on
performatives, 216, 221–27, 231; and
queer history, 163; and religion, relationship with, 16; repetition as sameness
and difference in, 14, 16; on ritual and
the performative, 221–27, 230–31; and
tradition as both repetition and change,
13–14, 275n17
de Sales, Francis, 94
description *vs.* explanation, of claims of divine
inspiration, 119–21, 124, 318–19n12
De secretis mulierum (pseudo-Albert the
Great), 57, 58
desire: as component of religious belief,
Feuerbach on, 237–38, 249; religious *vs.*
sexual, 152–53; role in religious life, *askesis*
and, 244; same-sex, Bynum's refusal to
recognize, 105–6, 152, 184. *See also* erotic
imagery in Christian spiritual writing
desire, epistemological role of: in Anderson,
235, 243–44, 249–50; in Jantzen, 243–44,
249–50
determination, *vs.* agency, 318n7
de Vries, Hent, 11, 12, 13–14, 277n35, 278n39
differance, and tradition as both repetition
and change, 13–14, 16
Dinshaw, Carolyn, 108, 163–64, 166–69
Dionysius the Areopagite, 14
dissociation following trauma, 45–46
Dit des Beguines (Rutebeuf), 372n42
divine, human access to, 87

doctrine of the incarnation, and medieval asceticism, 101

Dominican movement, 260

Dorothy of Montau, 101

Drewal, Margaret Thomson, 231

Dronke, Peter, 117

Ebner, Margaret: bodily experience of Christ's passion in, 246–47; and bodily practice as source of religious experience, 245–47; ill health of, 74, 291–92n24; melancholic incorporation in, 83, 84, 85, 86; movement of desire in, 312n90; rebuilding of inner world by, 85; and storytelling as incorporation, 87. See also *Revelations* (Ebner)

Eckhart, Meister: and apophasis, 112; critics of, 143, 210; on freedom of soul, 208; on Mary and Martha story, 254, 261, 264–69, 370n27; on virgin souls within married women, 264–66

Education of Henry Adams, The (Adams), 2, 29, 41, 271n1

"The Ego and the Id" (Freud), 82–83, 84–85

Eliade, Mircea, 9

Elliott, Dyan, 56

emancipatory agency, critical detachment and, 321n33

emancipatory project of historiography: alternative projects, as issue, 127; subaltern historiography and, 124, 126, 127

emotions, as product of *askesis*, 244

emotions and affect in Christian Middle Ages, 313n93; and affective *vs.* speculative mysticism, 113; loss of in modern historiography, 253–54; recent work on, 112

Encountering Religion (Roberts), 9–11

enculturation, body as sight of, 191–92, 210–11

Enforcing Normalcy (Davis), 164–65

erotic imagery in Christian spiritual writing, 105, 149–62, 182–85; homoerotic imagery, 105–7, 182–85; and religious *vs.* sexual desire, 152–53; Song of Songs and, 106, 153,

157, 159, 329n2. *See also* Christ, sexualized descriptions of relationship with

Esther (Adams), 1, 32–41; Buddhist tone of Esther's religious impulse, 34–36, 37, 38, 41; on Christianity as selfish, 34; Esther's father's death in, 37–39; Esther's final peace of despair in, 36–37, 41; Esther's love of Hazard in, 36, 37; Esther's physical desire for Hazard, 39, 40–41, 62; Esther's rejection of afterlife in, 33–34, 40; Esther's rejection of Christianity in, 30, 32–34, 36–37, 39–40; Esther's rejection of gender expectations in, 34, 40; Esther's resemblance to Clover Adams in, 32, 35, 37–38; Esther's self-loathing in, 33–34; Esther's sense of unrealness in, 38, 39, 40, 62; Esther's unwillingness to submit to Hazard, 40; Hazard's exploration of mysticism with Esther, 38, 39; Niagara Falls as symbol in, 33, 35, 36, 37, 40, 41; publication of under pseudonym, 32; on resurrection, 33–34, 40, 50; Strong's beliefs in, 36–37; Strong's proposal to Esther, 36; Wharton's experience of unrealness in, 62, 281n77; Wharton's perception of suffering as only reality, 62; Wharton's views on religion in, 36, 39, 41, 281n72, 281n77

eugenics, statistical norms and, 165–66

European philosophy, on inevitable dissolution of religion, 11–12, 275n17

evangelical Christian women, and feminism, bridging gap between, 248–49

Excitable Speech (Butler), 214, 215, 216, 225, 226, 227, 357n5

experientia, 94–95

explanation *vs.* description, in claims of divine inspiration, 119–21, 124, 318–19n12

faith, *vs.* reason, long history of debate on, 133–34

Farmer, Sharon, 105

Fassin, Didier, 44

Fassler, Margot, 114–15

"The Female Body and Religious Practice in the Later Middle Ages" (Bynum), 99, 103–4

female divine, Anderson on, 234

feminism: association of women with body in, Beckwith's critique of, 191–92; critique of male-dominance of religious institutions, 97; and evangelical women, bridging gap between, 248–49; second-wave, ties to Christianity, 97

Feminist Contentions (Butler), 357n8

feminist historiography: goals and methods of, as issue, 253–54; and valorization of female agency, 321n28

feminist philosophy of religion: Anderson on role of passion in, 235; critique of Christianity in, 98; Jantzen on goals of, 233; and relativism, Jantzen on, 237; and ritual, importance of, 234

Feminist Philosophy of Religion, A (Anderson), 233–35, 237, 241, 243–44, 249–50, 364n3

feminist scholarship on Christian spirituality: and balance of objective and ideological, 113; differences between men's and women's writings and, 107; efforts to reclaim women's spiritual writings, 96, 97–101; new directions in, 107–16

Fenellosa, Ernest, 22

Feuerbach, Ludwig: and critique of Christianity, 11, 12, 86, 87; on desire as component of religious belief, 237–38, 249; on divine as projection of human ideal, 236, 237–38

Flowing Light of the Godhead, The (Mechthild of Magdeburg): and flowing of God's grace downward, 118; manuscript history of, 109–10; sexualized descriptions of relationship with Christ in, 153–55, 160–61

La foi qui guérit (Charcot), 53

force, *vs.* persuasion, 362–63n74

Foster, Hal, 44, 62

Foucault, Michel: on critique, 277n34; on formation of ethical subjects, 242; on history as disruption, 320n17; on morality,

three forms of, 241–42; and queer history, 163; on ritual, 228, 231

Fourth Lateran Council (1215), 260–61

Fragmentation and Redemption (Bynum), 99, 100, 102, 107, 151

Fragments (Wilkomirski), 45, 46, 61–62

Franciscan treatises, emphasis on guilt in, 81

Francis of Assisi, 54, 101, 260–61, 353n60

François, Anne-Lise, 283n92

Fraser, Nancy, 361n57

French intellectuals, interest in affective, visionary spirituality, 114

Freud, Sigmund: on construction of interiority, 205; and critique of Christianity, 12; and critique of reason, 132; on hysteria, 54; on internalization of lost loved one, 74, 82–83, 84–85, 86; on melancholy, overestimation of object in, 72; Oedipal nature of internalization in, 83, 84; and religion, reductionistic views on, 86–87; on repression of trauma, 45; on self-critical function as product of melancholic incorporation, 63, 83, 84, 287n133; on superego, 86. *See also* "Mourning and Melancholia" (Freud)

Freudian psychology, and sexual imagery in medieval devotional texts, 151–52

Fulk (archbishop of Toulouse), 261, 262

fundamentalist Christians, refusal to engage with, 134, 248–49, 328n34

Galgani, Gemma, 109

Galton, Francis, 165

gender: and justification of belief, Anderson on, 233; as one of several categories of difference in Middle Ages, 105; and symbol use, 98–99; as troubled concept in Christian spiritual writings, 94, 95, 105–7, 116, 187, 345n50. *See also* queering of gender identity

gender, performativity of in Butler, 213–14; constraints of power on, 216; extension of to subject formation, 214; gaps and fissures formed in, 213, 215; supplementing of with attention to other bodily practices, 214

Gender and Difference in the Middle Ages (Farmer and Pasternack), 105

Gender and Religion (Bynum, Harrell, and Richman), 98

gender binary: Christian link to mind-body binary, 101, 103–4, 105; Irigaray's undermining of in *"La Mystérique,"* 187; as troubled concept in Christian spiritual writings, 94, 95, 105–7, 116, 187, 345n50. *See also* queering of gender identity

gender norms, determination by, 318n7

gender-related symbols, Bynum on polysemic nature of, 98

gender stereotypes, medieval women's responses to, 103

Gender Trouble (Butler), 213–14, 357n8

Gerald of Laveine, 259

Getting Medieval (Dinshaw), 163–64

Gilligan, Carol, 100

Goad of Love, The (Hilton, tr.), 179

goals of historical inquiry, as issue, 127

God: inability to fully know, in Christianity, 14; submission to, as precondition for women's agency, 117

God, existence of: Anderson on, 235; Jantzen on, 236–37; Kant on, 235–36. *See also* women authors, claims of direct inspiration from God

Godfrey of Fontaines, 136

God's Daughters (Griffith), 248–49

Golden Bowl, The (James), 1

Golden Legend, The (Jacob of Voragine), 175, 254

Gospel of Nicodemus, 341n22

grace, and critique and tradition as irreducible pairing, 16–17

Grand chroniques de France, 136

grave memorial for Clover Adams (Saint Gaudens), *20*; Adams's input into design of, 20–22, 35; Buddhist influences on, 21, 22; Henry Adams's commissioning of,

19–21; implicit rejection of afterlife in, 32; implicit rejection of Christianity in, 30, 32; medieval flavor of, 29; and melancholic peace of Buddhism, 35, 41; possible models for, 21–29, *23–28*; theme of *vs.* typical 19th century markers, 29–32, *31*

grave memorials, Christian, characteristic 19th century themes of, 29–32, *31*

Gray, Douglas, 173, 178

Greenspan, Kate, 73, 103

Gregory, Brad, 318–19n12, 319n15

Gregory the Great (pope), 56, 176, 258

Griffith, Marie, 248–49

Griffiths, Paul, 323n7

Guan Yin, 22, *23*, 29, 280n64

Guarnieri, Romana, 136–37

Guha, Ranajit, 121–22, 319n15

Guy of Colmieu (bishop of Cambrai), 136

Guyon, Jean, 54

Habitations of Modernity (Chakrabarty), 126–27

habitus: and anchorite formation of interiority, 191–92; Bourdieu on, 191, 205, 214; day-to-day practices constituting, 218; as formative, Butler on, 217, 218; learned nature of, 249; Mauss on, 191, 214, 218, 228, 239–41, 243–44; as naturalized, 249; and practical reason, 241; reformation of, as challenge, 249–350; and ritual, 231; and spontaneity, modern separation of, 287n133. *See also* bodily practice

Hadewijch of Brabant: on afterlife, 302n37; Augustine and, 312n89; and beguine movement, 371n33; circulation history of works by, 110; and erotic relationship between soul and God, 106; and male theological tradition, 111; Newman on, 110; sexualized descriptions of relationship with Christ in, 155–58, 160, 161–62, 334n36; on suffering with Christ, difficulty of, 101; on union of action and contemplation, 264; will as focus of inner battle in, 203–4 hagiography: reading of as flawed history, 48; reading of in convents, 207, 354–55n85

hagiography of women: greater asceticism and paramysticism in, 353n60; greater emphasis on bodily manifestations in, 204

Hamburger, Jeffrey F., 114–15, 247, 288–99n6, 367n45

Harrell, Stevan, 98

Harvey, Van, 238

hate speech, and force of performative, 217, 360n35

Hawley, John, 98

Hegel, G. W. F., 132

Heidegger, Martin, 123

Henry of Nördlingen, 74, 75, 293n33

Herman, Judith, 44

heteronormativity: author's commitment to those silenced by, 94; challenges to in medieval spiritual writings, 106, 107; sexual metaphors of relationships with Christ and, 149–51, 152, 153, 156, 157–62, 331n4. *See also* queering of gender identity

Hildegard of Bingen, 111

Hilton, Walter, 179

Hindsley, Leonard, 292n30, 293n33

Historia scholastica (Peter Comestor), 175

historicism, postcolonial critiques of, 121–24, 126–27, 320n17

historicity, Derrida on, 224

historiography: modern, and loss of affective possibilities, 253–54; shaping of by ethical and political agendas, 253

historiography, emancipatory project of: alternative projects, as issue, 127; subaltern historiography and, 124, 126, 127

historiography, subaltern: possibility of, 121–24, 126–27, 320n17; potential disruption of naturalist history by, 127

history: *vs.* antiquarianism, in Adams, 4; complex relation to reason, 132; nature of critique in, 3–4, 6; secular, translation of supernatural agents by, 122. *See also* critique

Hollywood, Amy: commitment to those silenced by heteronormativity, 94; death of brother, 87–90; death of great-grandmother, 67–68, 85; as non -Christian, 9; views on religion, 5; views on resurrection, 50

Holsinger, Bruce, 114–15

Holy Feast and Holy Fast (Bynum), 99, 100, 102, 151, 182, 184

Holy Spirit Mobile Forces (HSMF), 126

homosexuality, existence before 19th century, as issue, 164. *See also* same-sex desire

Hugh of Floreffe, 263, 264

human sciences: distinction between real for "them" *vs.* "us," 2–3; nature of critique in, 3–4. *See also* critique

Hume, David, 131

Humphrey, Caroline, 357n5

Huntington, Patricia, 338n2

hysteria: critics' diagnosis of in Christina the Astonishing, 52–53, 54–55, 57, 58, 59; critics' diagnosis of in Ebner, 294n37; medieval association of with spiritual vision, 56; as tool to denigrate women's experience, 54–55

Ida of Nivelles, 196

identities in Middle Ages, categories of difference in, 105

imagination: and critique, cooperative effort in discovery of truth, 17; and imaginary ego of ascesis, 208; religion as product of, as modern assumption, 5; theological, centrality of mourning to, 87

imaginative theology, Newman on, 110

individual authorship of medieval spiritual writings, as issue, 107–8, 108–9

inner worlds: faulty, as cause of pathological melancholy, 85; individual's ability to rebuild, 85

Innocent III (pope), 261

institutions of religion, feminist critique of male-dominance of, 97 instrumental action, *vs.* ritual, 239

instrumental agency, 125

intellectuals: belief in necessary destruction of religion, 134; French, interest in affective, visionary spirituality, 114

intellectual vision: early Christian accounts of, 56; modern instances of, 93

intentionality, and performative power: Austin on, 220–21, 222, 357n5; Derrida on, 222, 223; ritual theory and, 357n5

interiority, formation of: imaginary ego generated by ascesis, 208; psychoanalytic theory on, 205–6; and split in subjectivity, 206, 207; through identification, 206. *See also* subject formation

interiority, formation of in medieval women: association of with pain, 205–6; Beatrice of Nazareth and, 195–97, 206–7; resistance to male prescriptions for, 104, 192; role of interiorization of spiritual life in, 210–11; through bodily practice, 191–92, 205, 206; in women-authored *vs.* men-authored texts, 192

interiority, formation of through bodily practice, 191, 205–6, 210–11; Asad on, 191, 192, 195, 205, 239, 240–41, 243–45, 246, 365n23; Mauss on, 191, 192, 205

internalization of Cross, by Beatrice of Nazareth, 196–97, 206

internalization of lost loved ones, 68, 74, 76; as constitutive of subjectivity, 85–86; by devout persons, 69, 77; Freud on, 74, 82–83, 84–85; as normal part of mourning, Klein on, 84–85; by victims of emotional trauma, 68, 69, 76

inwardness, as term in medieval *vs.* modern discourse, 209–10

Irigaray, Luce: Anderson on, 234; anti-penetrative eros of surfaces in, 172, 186, 188, 346n68; on Christ's side wound as breast, 185; on Christ's side wound as vulva/vagina, 171–72, 179, 185, 331n4; effacing of conceptions of difference in,

338n2; focus on affective spirituality, 114; foreclosure of imaginative possibilities in, 188; on heterosexual matrix in Plato, 186–87; on male appropriate of theory of the subject, 172; and radicality of medieval devotional practices, 187; rejection of Christ's wounds as site of feminine imaginary, 172, 185–86; rejection of female sex as woundedness, 172, 186; temporal dimension to imaginary of, 338n2; and vulva/vagina as basis of feminine imaginary, 171, 338n1. *See also* *"La Mystérique"* (Irigaray); *Speculum and the Other Woman* (Irigaray)

"Is Critique Secular?" (symposium), 7

Ivetta of Huy, 58, 263, 264

Jacob of Voragine, 175, 254

James, Henry, 1, 42–43, 60, 63

James, William, 42, 119

James of Milan, 179, 344n37

James of Vitry, 48–49, 52, 53, 56, 58, 61, 261–62

Janet, Pierre, 45–46

Jansen, Katherine Ludwig, 253, 254–55, 256

Jantzen, Grace, 233–34, 236–38, 241, 243–44, 249–50, 364n3

Jesus as Mother (Bynum), 97, 100, 105

Joan of Arc, 126

John (biblical figure), 257

John (gospel), Mary and Martha story in, 255

John of St. Trond, 179

John the Fearless, tomb of, 22, *24*

Jones, Clair, 114–15

Journal of the American Academy of Religion, 6

joy: as engendered through practice, 60, 63, 287n133; in *Life of Christina the Astonishing*, 59–60, 63

joy, as unspeakable reality, 47; in Christian doctrine, 63; in *Life of Christina the Astonishing*, 59–60; obscuring of in modern critique, 47, 60–63

Julian of Norwich, 93–94, 111

Kannon, 22, *23*, 29

Kano Motonobu, 22, *23*

Kant, Immanuel: on *askesis*, 242–43, 244, 248; and boundaries between disciplines, 130; and critique of Christianity, 11, 12, 132, 275n17, 275n18; on God, existence of, 235–36, 237; on ontological status of religious belief, 235–37

Keller, Mary, 124–26, 320n16

Kempe, Margery: accusations of sexual misconduct against, 167; attempted return to virgin status, 166, 167; Dinshaw's reading of as queer, 164, 166–69; and hysteria, 55; and ideal *vs.* norm in sexual behavior, 167; and modern assumptions about holiness, 168–69, 337nn27–28; queerness of, as modern perception, 169, 337n27; and right to interpret women's body, as issue, 168; use of scribes by, 108

Kieckhefer, Richard, 73, 103

King, Margot, 94

Klein, Melanie, 84–85, 86

Kunigunde (abbess of St George's nunnery), 179

Kwakkel, Erik, 110

Lacan, Jacques, 114, 186, 206, 207, 214–15

LaCapra, Dominick, 46–47, 113

La Farge, John, 19–22

Laidlaw, James, 357n5

language, theological: gendered, 12th–13th century religious practice and, 97; support of social structures by, 97, 98

Largier, Niklaus, 112

Leah (biblical figure), allegorical interpretation of, 257, 258, 262–63, 265

Lears, Jackson, 36, 40–41, 281n72

Lee, Benjamin, 358n11

Legenda aurea (Jacob of Voragine), 175, 254

le Moiturier, Antoine, 22, *24*

lesbianism: existence before 19th century, as issue, 164; medieval, historical evidence for, 149, 150, 331n10

lesbianism, metaphorical: scholarly research on, 149–50; and undermining of heteronormativity, 151; validity of as evidence, 150–51

Lessing, G. E., 130

Leys, Ruth, 44

liberalism, and *habitus*, refusal to recognize embodied nature of, 249

Life of Beatrice of Nazareth, The: and Beatrice's desire for death, 198, 199, 203; on Beatrice's internalization of Cross, 196–97, 206; Beatrice's lack of outward holiness and, 193–94; Beatrice's *Seven Manners* as source of, 193, 198; focus on creation of interiority through bodily practice, 195–97, 205; interplay of inner and outer lives as theme in, 194–95, 197–98, 201; replacement of Beatrice's inner experiences with outward physical signs in, 69, 70, 72–73, 192–93, 194–205, 207, 209; shaping of by hagiographic conventions, 193, 194, 195, 202, 204, 207; 20th century theories of bodily practice and, 193, 195–96; writing of, 193

Life of Christina the Astonishing (Thomas of Cantimpré), 47–61; account of visit to afterlife, 57–58; attribution of hysteria to Christina, 52–53, 54–55, 57, 58, 59; on Christina's choice to return to Earth, 50–51; Christina's moments of unspeakable joy in, 59–60; claimed eyewitness accounts in, 49, 53; historical status of, as issue, 50, 53; joy and suffering as intertwined in, 63; miracles in, as stereotypical, 50, 53; modern willingness to credit reality of suffering in, 50, 55, 59, 61–62; Newman on, 52–54, 55, 57, 58–59, 61; and obscuring of joy in modern critique, 60–62; possible accounts of writing of, 53; reasons for doubting veracity of, 50; religious experience in, as stereotypical, 55–56; resurrection of Christina in, 48–50, 50–51; self-torment by Christina, 49, 51, 52;

theological message of Christina's suffering, 51–52; unbelievable events in, 48; village's assumption of Christina's madness in, 51, 52, 55; and women's right to relate her own experience, as issue, 57–58, 61; writing of, 48–49, 53

Life of Ivetta, The (Hugh of Floreffe), 263, 264

Life of Jesus, The (Schleiermacher), 323n10

Life of Jesus, The (Strauss), 130–31, 132

Life of Lutgard of Aywières (Thomas of Cantimpré), 341n14

Life of Marie of Oignies (James of Vitry), 48–49, 53, 56, 58, 61, 261–62

Life of the Servant (Suso), 247–48, 291n21, 367n45

Lincoln, Bruce, 362–63n74

literalist reading: mainstream biblical scholarship and, 324n14; modern, roots in reasoned critique, 143

literalist reading, inability to escape bounds of: in heresy trial of Echkart, 143; in heresy trial of Marguerite Porete, 142–43

locative function of religion, 9–10; banishment from critical discourse, 11, 13–14; as coeval with utopian form, 10

Lochrie, Karma: on Byrum's desexualization of Passion images, 151–52, 182–85, 186; on Christ's side wound as breast and vagina, 149–51, 179, 185, 329n2, 330n3; on mystical queer, 153; on mystical union as copulation in James of Milan, 344n37; on queering of gender in medieval texts, 149–51, 153, 156

Locke, John, 12, 131

loss of loved ones, sustaining of self despite, 86

Love, as source of higher understanding in Marguerite Porete, 133, 134

loved ones, sustaining of self despite loss of, 86

love of God, *vs.* love of neighbor, in early Christian thought, 258–59, 263

lovesickness: association of with religious visions, 56, 71; linking of to Christ's passion, 71–73, 74–79; medieval association

of with melancholy, 71–72; as symbol of spiritual love, 71

Lukardis of Oberweimar, 101

Luke (gospel), Mary and Martha story in, 254, 255, 256, 260, 264, 267

MacIntyre, Alasdair, 275n17

MacKenzie, Donald, 165

Madame Edwarda (Bataille), 346n62

Madonna of Bruges (Michelangelo), 22, *26*

Maechler, Stefan, 45, 46, 61

Mahmood, Saba: on belief as function of bodily practice, 246; on critique, expanded view of, 12–13; on religion, attitude toward, 5–6; and religious practice as site of critique, 7

Making of the Magdalen, The (Jansen), 253, 254–55, 256

Map Is Not Territory (Smith), 10

Marbod, 259

Margaret of Bavaria, tomb of, 22, *24*

marginalized groups, reading of as victims, 45

Marguerite Porete: and apophasis, 112; on autonomy of internal self, 211; and beguine movement, 371n33; Eckhart's theology and, 266, 267; and erotic relationship between soul and God, 106; on Farnear, 145; life of, 135–36; and queering of gender, 107; rejection of association of women with body, 208; sexualized descriptions of relationship with Christ in, 158–60, 161–62, 335n48; and suffering of desire for God, 159; trial and execution for heresy, 135, 136, 141, 142–43, 143–44, 210; on union of action and contemplation, 264; will as focus of inner battle in, 204. See also *Mirror of Simple Souls, The* (Porete)

Marie of Oignies, 55. See also *Life of Marie of Oignies* (James of Vitry)

Marine Lover of Friedrich Nietzsche (Irigaray), 186

Maritain, Jacques, 109

Maritain, Raïssa, 109

mark, Derrida's theory of, 221

Mark (gospel), Mary and Martha story in, 255–56

Martha, sister of Mary (biblical figure): allegorical associations with, 256–57; as allegorical union of action and contemplation, 267–68; as allegory of active life, 254, 257–60, 262–64; biblical sources on, 254, 255–56; commentators preferring her to Mary/contemplation, 259–60; Eckhart's reading of, 254, 261, 264–69, 370n27; and love of God vs. love of neighbor, 258–59

Marx, Karl: on criticism of religion, 129, 131, 134; and critique of Christianity, 11, 275n17; and critique of reason, 132; on dual history of capitalism, 123

Mary, mother of Jesus (biblical figure): as medieval reality, 1, 2, 4; as model of suffering with Christ, 175; modern skepticism and, 3; as union of contemplative and active life, 260

Mary, sister of Martha (biblical figure): allegorical associations with, 256–57; as allegory of contemplative life, 254, 257–60, 262–64; biblical sources on, 254, 255–56; conflation with Mary Magdalen, 254, 255, 256, 260, 268; Eckhart's reading of, 254, 261, 264–69, 370n27; and love of God vs. love of neighbor, 258–59

Mary Magdalen: biblical sources on, 255–56, 368n6; conflation with Mary, sister of Martha, 254, 255, 256, 260, 268; as model of female agency, 254; modern perspective on, 254; as powerful religious figure, 253, 254; readings of in Middle Ages and late antiquity, 254–55, 256; as union of contemplative and active lives, 254–55

Material Christianity (Bynum), 115

materiality of the body, Butler on, 213, 357n4

materialization process, Butler on, 215

material objects, in medieval spiritual practice, 115

Matthew (gospel), Mary and Martha story in, 255–56

Mauss, Marcel: on belief as product of bodily practices, 191, 192, 205, 238–39; on body as man's first technical means and object, 228, 239, 241; on habitus, 191, 214, 218, 228, 239–41, 243–44; on ritual, 228; and undermining of internalized self, 210

McCutcheon, Russell, 277n33

McDannell, Colleen, 29, 30–32, 31

McGinn, Bernard, 56, 93, 94, 110

Mechthild of Magdeburg: accentuation of humility by, 118; and agency, as issue, 125; and beguine movement, 371n33; and costs of ignoring claims of divine inspiration, 124; and erotic relationship between soul and God, 106; freedom as goal of, 127; lack of preparation for spiritual experience in, 205; Newman on, 110; self-authorization in, 118, 120, 121; sexualized descriptions of relationship with Christ in, 153–55, 160–61; on union of action and contemplation, 264; will as focus of inner battle in, 204. See also Flowing Light of the Godhead, The (Mechthild of Magdeburg)

Medici Madonna (Michelangelo), 22, 27

meditation: on Christ's suffering, similarity to traumatic memory, 80–81, 294–95n41; Passion narratives as aid to, 174–75, 178–79; as type of memory work, 175

melancholia: centrality to theological imagination, 87; as constitutive of subjectivity, 85–86; death of author's great-grandmother from, 67–68, 85; as inherent in tradition, 63; medieval association of with lovesickness, 71–72; overestimation of object in, 72; pathological, as result of inadequate inner world, 85

memory: bodily, modern research on, 80; medieval accounts of, 305n50

memory, traumatic: complexity of, 45–46; meditation on Christ's suffering and, 80–81, 294–95n41 methodological issues: in feminist historiography, 253–54; skepticism about religion and, 3, 4; in study of medieval spirituality, 115–16

Michelangelo, 21, *21*, 22, *26, 27, 28*

Miller, Julie, 104

Mirror of Simple Souls, The (Marguerite Porete): Church efforts to destroy, 136; condemnation of for heresy, 135, 136, 139, 141, 142–43, 143–44; critics' inability to escape literalist reading of, 142–43; Eckhart's theology and, 267; eschewing of visionary mode in, 210; hierarchically-graded explanations in, 138; on Holy Church the Great, 134, 139; on Holy Church the Little, 134, 135, 139, 141, 143; on Love as source of higher understanding, 133, 134; medieval reading practice and, 137, 326–27n24; and other-than-rational critique, possibility of, 144–45; overview of, 133; Porete's anticipations of misreading by Church, 129, 137, 141; on reason as obstacle to true understanding, 133, 134, 137–38, 141–42, 143; on seven modes of being and three deaths, 139, 267; sexualized descriptions of relationship with Christ in, 158–60, 161–62, 335n48; surviving copies of, 136–37, 325nn20–21; on virtues, suffering of those subject to, 140

Mirror of Simple Souls, The, on free annihilated soul, 138–39; as beyond virtues or works, 139–41, 142–43, 335n49, 356n83; characteristics of, 138; process of annihilation, 140–41, 141–42, 159–60, 327–28n31; as without desire or will, 139, 141, 142, 160

mirror stage, Lacan on, 206

misogyny, medieval, and antibody dualism, 101

monastic life, medieval search for alternatives to, 260–61

Monteiro, George, 42

Mont Saint Michel and Chartres (Adams), 1, 29, 41, 62, 281n72

Moore, Brenna, 109

morality: codes and *askesis* as components of, 242; and formation of ethical subjects, 242; Foucault on forms of, 241–42; as obstacle to understanding, 6–7. *See also* belief, as product of bodily practice

moral law, and reason: Jantzen on, 236–37; Kant on, 235–36, 237, 241

mother of Jesse (Michelangelo), 21, *21*

mourning: centrality to theological imagination, 87; incorporation of lost loved ones as normal part of, 84–85

"Mourning and Its Relation to Manic-Depressive States" (Klein), 84–85

"Mourning and Melancholia" (Freud), 81–85

Murk-Jansen, Saskia, 334n36, 334n41

"La Mystérique" (Irigaray): Butler on, 186; Christ in, refusal of gender binaries by, 186; on Christ's side wound, 171–72; on medieval destabilization of gender categories, 185, 187; sources for, 340n10

Mystery of the Hereafter and the Peace of God that Passeth Understanding, The (Saint Gaudens). *See* grave memorial for Clover Adams

mystical queer: in Hadewijch of Brabant, 155–58, 160, 161–62, 334n36; Lochrie on, 153; in Marguerite Porete, 158–60, 161–62, 335n48; in Mechthild of Magdeburg, 153–55, 160–61

Mystical Vine, The (Bonaventure), 179

mysticism, histories of: failure to account for gender difference in, 209–10; and origin of modern subject in women's mysticism, 210–11; and role of body, as issue, 114

myth, *vs.* fiction or illusion, Anderson on, 364n3

narrative, relationship to theory, as issue, 87

natura, as medieval term for judging sexuality, 166

naturalism: account of religion, reasons for questioning, 5; as assumption of Western philosophy, 4–5

negative theology, trauma discourse as, 46–47, 63–64

Newman, Barbara: on Christina the Astonishing and hysteria, 52–54, 55, 57, 58–59, 61; on imaginative theology, 110; and late-20th-century reevaluation of women's spiritual writings, 117; on spirit possession in religious women, 55, 284n102

Niagara Falls: in 19th century imagination, 280n58; as symbol in Adams's *Esther*, 33, 35, 36, 37, 40, 41

Nietzsche, Friedrich, 11, 12, 132

norm(s): etymology of, 166, 336–37n17; and eugenic impulse, 165–66; *vs.* ideal, 165; 19th-century origins of concept, 164–65; sexual, queerness as defiance of, 163–64

normal: etymology of, 166, 336–37n17; use of in Middle Ages, as issue, 166

Notes of a Son and Brother (James), 42

Obeyesekere, Gananeth, 273n10

Obote, Milton, 126

Old Testament, in interpretation of Passion, 176

"On Hiroshima" (Bataille), 46

"On the Four Degrees of Violent Love" (Richard of Saint Victor), 370n27

Origen, 153, 256

origin, pure, inability to know, 14

Orsi, Robert, 6, 273–74n10, 273n10, 274–75n14

otherness, and subaltern history, possibility of, 320n17

pain, cultural variation in perception of, 241

Passional of Abbess Kunigunde of Bohemia, 173, *174*

Passion narratives: as aid to devotional meditation, 174–75, 178–79; sources for rewritings of, 175–76

Pasternack, Carol Braun, 105

Patterson, Lee, 294n37

Paul (apostle), 56, 111

Peregrina Publishing, 94

performative, and ritual: in Austin, 218–20, 221, 224–25, 358–59n18; Bourdieu on, 225; Butler on, 215, 218, 227; in Derrida, 221–27, 230, 362n73

performative actions, 214, 218

performatives, 358n11; Austin on, 218–21, 224–25, 231, 357n5, 360n48; Bourdieu on, 216, 226; Derrida on, 216, 221–27, 231; and separation of bodily from verbal acts, 218; and space for resistance, 231

performatives, Butler on: body as location of force of, 216–17, 221, 226–27, 359n29; constraints of power on, 215–16; Derrida and, 221–24; force of, 221, 226; and possibilities for resistance, 227; as social ritual, 215, 218, 227; sources underlying, 218–27

performative subjectivity, Butler on, 213–14

performativity, as term, 357n5

performativity of gender, Butler on, 213–14; constraints of power on, 216; extension of to subject formation, 214; gaps and fissures formed in, 213, 215; supplementing of with attention to other bodily practices, 214

persuasion, *vs.* force, 362–63n74

Peter (apostle), 257

Peter Comestor, 175

Peter of Abano, 166

Petroff, Elizabeth Alvilda, 94, 117

phantasms, medieval, 312n90

phenomenologists, on construction of interiority, 205–6

philosophy of religion: goal of, as issue, 238; neglect of practice in, 364n2. *See also* feminist philosophy of religion

Pietà (Michelangelo), 22, *27*

Plato, gender identity in, 186–87

Pollitt, Katha, 277n33

Poor, Sara S., 109–10

Poovey, Mary, 321n33

postcolonial critiques of historicism, 121–24, 126–27, 320n17

Post-Traumatic Stress Disorder. *See* trauma

Pot, Philippe, Lord of La Roche-Pot, tomb of (15th c.), 22, *25*

power structures: and formation of women's interiority, 192; ritual and, 215–16, 231

Pritchard, Elizabeth A., 6–7

Promised Bodies (Dailey), 110–12

"The Prose of Counter-Insurgency" (Guha), 121–22

Protestantism: bodily practice as source of religious experience in, 248–49; rejection of ritualism in, 239, 248; response to historical-critical biblical scholarship, 132

Proudfoot, Wayne, 119–21

Provincializing Europe (Chakrabarty), 123

Psalter of Bonne of Luxembourg, 180–81, *181*

pseudo-Albert the Great, 57, 58, 185

psychoanalysis, eugenicist tinge of, 165–66

psychoanalytic criticism, critiques of, 294n37

psychoanalytic theory: on construction of interiority, 205–6; women as woundedness in, 186, 188

psychology of women, and women's spirituality, 100–101

queer historians, task of, 163

queering of gender identity: in feminization of Christ on Cross, 152; historical validity of, as issue, 150; religious language of transcendence and, 152–53; in sexualized descriptions of relationships with Christ/divine, 149–51, 152, 153, 156, 157–62, 331n4. *See also* heteronormativity

queerness: as defiance of sexual norms, 163–64; Dinshaw on historical contingency of, 163; Dinshaw's reading of Margery Kempe and, 166–69; groups included under, as issue, 164; relation to gayness as issue, 164; and transhistorical analysis, 164

queers, identification of with marginal figures of past, 163–64

Quetelet, Adolphe, 164–65

Rachel (biblical figure), allegorical interpretation of, 257, 258, 262–63, 265

Rambuss, Richard, 105–6, 106–7, 151, 152, 182, 184

Raymond of Capua, 182–84, 330n3

reality: of religious experience, openness toward, 5–6; of spiritual beings, meaning of, as issue, 2; for "them," *vs.* truth, 2–3, 44–45. *See also* truth

reason: Asad on, 240–41; as check on belief-based conflict, 5; complex relation to history, 132; *vs.* faith, long history of debate on, 133–34; *habitus* and, 241; limitations of, and value of uncritical reading, 134–35; as obstacle to understanding, in Marguerite Porete's *Mirror*, 133, 134, 137–38, 141–42; as obstacle to understanding religious experience, 5–6; ongoing force of religion despite, 4; power to define, as issue, 276n21; purifactory fervor of, 12; reconciliation with faith, in Schleiermacher, 132–33, 323n7; and rejection of religious experience, 12, 277n33; as standard in critical reading of Bible, 130–31, 131–32; understanding of as historicized, 132

reason, and moral law: Jantzen on, 236–37; Kant on, 235–36, 237, 241

Rechtman, Richard, 44

reductionism, in description *vs.* explanation, 119, 319n12

Reimarus, Hermann Samuel, 130, 131–32

religious experience: compulsion to claim truth of, 3; gendering of in religious traditions, 95–96; impact of accepting truth of, 4–5; rejection of by secularist critics, 12, 277n33; as type of aesthetic experience, in Schleiermacher, 132, 323n7; understanding, necessity of openness for, 5–6

religious faith: author's views on, 5; characterization of as childlike, 272–73n8; elements
not reducible to imagination, as hypothesis, 5; excessive functions of, 10–11, 13,
15–16; Freud on, 86–87; intellectuals'
view of, 134; modern secular tolerance of,
134; ongoing force of in modern world,
4; Orsi on, 273–74n10; reformation of,
habitus and, 249–50; ritual as importance
component of, 238; secularization of, 12;
as site of critique, 7, 8–9, 10, 11–12, 13,
275n18; as source of conflict, 5; utopian
form of, 9–10
repetition, as sameness and difference, in
Derrida, 14, 16
representation, forms of, women's relation
to, 191
repression of trauma, and failure to experience
traumatic event, 45–46
resistance: in medieval women to male
expectations, 104, 192, 210–11; performatives and, 227; ritual and, 231; to women's
association with bodiliness, 50, 114, 210–11
resurrection: author's views on, 50; Esther in
Adams's *Esther* on, 33–34, 40, 50
Revelations (Ebner): as autohagiography,
73; bodily practice as source of religious
experience in, 245–47; critics' diagnosis of
hysteria in Ebner, 294n37; Ebner's bodily
experience of Christ's passion in, 246–47;
on Ebner's devotion to Christ child,
292–93n33; Ebner's meditation on Christ
as induced tramatic memory, 80; Hindsley translation of, 292n30; interaction of
traumatic loss and melancholy in, 68–69;
mingled evocation of Christ's passion,
lovesickness, and melancholia in, 74–79;
mourning as origin of spiritual vision
in, 74, 81; and sin, small role in, 295n49;
stages of spiritual experience in, 77, 79;
traumatic repetition in, 81, 83–84, 295n41,
295n49; and women's internalization of
hagiographic conventions, 73

Richard of St. Victor, 260, 264
Richer, Paul, 54
Richman, Paula, 98
Riehle, Wolfgang, 344n37
ritual: Anderson on, 233–34; Asad on,
227–29, 362n64; Bell on, 229–31;
centrality to medieval spiritual practice,
115; as disciplinary practice, 228; and
engendering of social subjects, 229–30;
as formative bodily practice, 114–15,
191, 230–31, 233–34, 238–49, 356n83;
functionalist theories of, 230; as illocutions, 230–31; as important component
of religion, 238; *vs.* instrumental action,
239; Jantzen on, 233–34; Mauss on,
228; modern understanding of, 227–28;
multiple interpretations of, as issue,
361n58; presumed primacy of belief over,
in modern anthropology, 239; religious
belief as key influence on, 233–34,
238–49; sociological function of, 228;
and space for resistance, 231; symbolic
accounts of, 359n18; theorists' claims
of lack of signification in, 225. See also
askesis (practice)
ritual, and performative: in Austin, 218–20,
221, 224–25, 358–59n18; Bourdieu on,
225; Butler on, 215, 218, 227; in Derrida,
221–27, 230, 362n73
ritual, in Butler, 215–18; constraints of power
on, 215–16; need for clearer conception
of, 218; performatives and, 215, 218, 227; as
repetition, 215
ritualization, Bell on, 229–31
Robert of La Chaise-Dieu, 259
Roberts, Tyler, 9–11, 12, 13, 14, 15, 277n35,
278n39
"Rock of Ages" (hymn), 29–30
Rule of Benedict, The, 191, 193, 244, 257
Rule of Life for a Recluse, The (Aelred of
Reivaulx), 178, 187
Rupert of Deutz, 106, 153
Rutebeuf, 372n42

Saint Gaudens, Augustus. *See* grave memorial for Clover Adams

same-sex desire: Bynum's refusal to recognize, 105–6, 152, 184; in Christian spiritual writing, 105–7. *See also* lesbianism; queering of gender identity

Santal, 124, 320n17

Santner, Eric, 11, 15, 277n35

Sargent, Michael, 143

Schleiermacher, Friedrich, 119, 132–33, 323n10

Schmitt, Carl, 276n19

Sensible Ecstasy (Hollywood), 114

Serafina of San Gimignano, 101

Sermons on the Song of Songs (Bernard of Clairvaux), 187

Serving the Word (Crapanzano), 134

Seven Manners of Loving (Beatrice of Nazareth): absence of external practice in, 195–97, 205; Beatrice's devotions in, as mix of passion, lovesickness, and melancholia, 70–73; on Beatrice's ecstatic experiences, 193; Beatrice's insistence on interiority of her experience, 205, 210–11; on Beatrice's internalization of Christ, 206–7; on Beatrice's longing for death, 198, 199, 200, 202, 203–4, 206–7; Beatrice's meditation on Christ as induced tramatic memory, 80; eschewing of visionary mode in, 210; *The Life*'s replacement of Beatrice's inner experiences with bodily signs, 69, 70, 72–73, 192–93, 194–205, 207, 209; seven manners of loving, described, 199–203; similarity to contemporary works by women, 205; as source for *The Life of Beatrice of Nazareth*, 193, 198; stages of spiritual experience in, 73; traumatic repetition in, 83–84; writing of, 193

sexual difference: constitution of through bodily practice, 244–45; construction of through ritualized repetition, 213–14; as troubled concept in Christian spiritual writings, 94, 95, 105–7, 116, 187, 345n50. *See also* gender; queering of gender identity

Showings (Julian of Norwich), 93–94

"Signature, Event, Context" (Derrida), 221, 225

signification: Derrida on, 223–24; as term, 358n11

Simons, Walter, 262

Sistine Chapel, mother of Jesse in (Michelangelo), 21, *21*

skepticism about religious experience, as methodological assumption, 3, 4

Smith, Frederick, 126

Smith, J. Z., 9–10

"Snakes Alive" (Orsi), 6, 274–75n14

social context of utterance, and performative power: Austin on, 219–20, 221, 224–25; Derrida on, 222–24, 225–26

social structures: impact of women's spirituality, 99–100; theological language's support of, 97, 98

Somerset, Fiona, 112

Song of Songs: in Beatrice of Nazareth's *Seven Manners of Loving*, 71, 199; early commentaries on, 153; in Ebner's *Revelations*, 79; in interpretation of Passion, 176, 178, 341n22, 344n37; and legitimization of erotic imagery in Christian writing, 106, 153, 157, 159, 329n2

Soul as Virgin Wife, The (Hollywood), 118

Speculum of the Other Woman (Irigaray), 171–72, 173, 185–86. See also *"La Mystérique"* (Irigaray)

spirit possession, agency and subjectivity as issues in, 124–26, 320n16

spirituality, definition of, 94

spontaneity, and *habitus*, modern separation of, 287n133

Stagel, Elsbet, 247, 367n45

Staley, Lynn, 108

Stanzas (Agamben), 312n90

statistical analysis, and norm as concept, 164–65

Statistics in Britain, 1865–1930 (MacKenzie), 165

Stout, Jeffrey, 276n21

Stowe, Harriet Beecher, 280n58

Strauss, David Friedrich, 130–31, 132

studies of religion, constructive, value of, 11

subaltern historiography: possibility of, 121–24, 126–27, 320n17; potential disruption of naturalist history by, 127

subject: poststructuralist critique of, trauma discourse and, 44; self-present, Derrida on constitution of, 224

subject formation: Butler on, 214, 231, 347n4, 357n8; modern failure to account for gender difference in, 209; ritual and, 231; through bodily encounters with others, 214; through linguistic performance, 214. See also interiority, formation of

subjectivity: internalization of lost loved ones as constitutive of, 85–86; separation of from agency, 124–25

sublimation, as term, 319n12

suffocation of the womb, medieval views on, 56, 57

Summit, Jennifer, 108

superego, as source of human accomplishment, 86

Suso, Henry, 247–48, 291n21, 353n60, 367n45

Sweetman, Robert, 51

symbols, gendered use of, 98–99

Tambiah, Stanley, 273n10, 359n18

Taylor, Charles, 4

temporality, alternative modes of, and subaltern history, 122, 123

Teresa of Ávila, 54, 114

textual criticism, history of, 130

theological imagination, mourning and melancholia as central to, 87

theological language: gendered, 12th–13th century religious practice and, 97; support of social structures by, 97, 98

theology: imaginative, Newman on, 110; negative, trauma discourse as, 46–47, 63–64; secular, Roberts on, 15; vernacular,

women's participation in, 110; women's spiritual writings and, 110–11, 302n37

theory, relationship to narrative, as issue, 87

Thomas of Cantimpré, 56, 341n14. See also Life of Christina the Astonishing (Thomas of Cantimpré)

Toews, John, 98

Tomb of John the Fearless and Margaret of Bavaria (de la Huerta and le Moiturier), 22, 24

Tomb of Philippe Pot, Lord of La Roche-Pot (15th c.), 22, 25

"Tongues Untied" (Warner), 149

Totem and Taboo (Freud), 287n133

tradition: and critique, as irreducible pairing, 16–17, 278n45; media and arts as modern substitutes for, 15; melancholy inherent in, 63; as passing down and change, 13–14, 275n17

trauma: contemporary theoretical work on, 283n97; dissociation or repression of, 45–46; as founding event, 46; issues in theoretical elevation of, 44–47; and memory, complex relationship between, 45–46

Trauma and Recovery (Herman), 44

trauma discourse: modern focus on, debilitating effects of, 63–64; modern willingness to credit, 44–45, 46, 47, 50, 55, 59, 61–62, 63; as negative theology, 46–47, 63–64; poststructuralist critique of subject and, 44

traumatic memory: modern research on, 80; similarity to meditation on Christ's suffering, 80–81, 294–95n41

Tree of Life (Bonaventure), 178–79

truth: assumptions about, in Western philosophy, 5; cooperative effort of critique and imagination in search for, 17; and critique and tradition as irreducible pairing, 16–17; vs. reality for "them," 2–3, 44–45; of religious experience, impact of accepting, 4–5. See also reality

Turner, Denys, 209–10

Twain, Mark, 22
Twelve Conclusions of the Lollards, 166, 167

Ubertino da Casale, 344n38
uncritical reading: Marguerite Porete's
other-than-rational critique and, 144–45;
religious reading and, 134; value of, 135;
Warner on, 129–30
utopian form of religion, 9–10

vernacular theology, women's participation
in, 110
victimization, *vs.* agency, 318n7
Villers Miscellany, 179–80, *180*
violence: medieval valorization of, as issue,
104; in monastic memory books, 305n50
visionary experience: *vs.* delusion, 3; early
Christian accounts of, 56; in *Life of
Christina the Astonishing*, 56–57; medieval
association of with hysteria, 56; medieval
belief in women's susceptibility to, 56–57;
medieval distinctions between types of,
56–57; of women, right to interpret, as
issue, 57–58
*Vision des Heiligen Bernhard (Sogenanntes
Blutkruzifixus)*, 176, *177*

Wack, Mary, 72
Waldo, Peter, 260
Wallace, David, 108
Walsh, James, 93–94
Warner, Michael, 129–30, 149, 152–53, 336n17
Watson, Nicholas, 110, 159, 160
Weld, Charles Goddard, 22
Western philosophy, naturalism underlying,
4–5
White-robed Bodhisattva of Compassion
(Mano), 22, *23*
Wilkomirski, Binjamin. See *Fragments*
(Wilkomirski)
will, submission of to divine, as precondition
for women's agency in religious sphere, 117
William of Auvergne, 56, 71–72

William of Nangis, 135–36
William of Nogaret, 136
William of Plaisans, 136
William of St. Thierry, 111, 153
Williams, Rowan, 10–11, 14
Wilson, Katharina, 94
women: within Christianity, suppression
of, 95, 96; special graces received by, 95;
susceptibility to visionary experience, in
medieval belief, 56–57. *See also* lesbianism,
medieval
women, as woundedness: in Bataille, 346n62;
Irigaray's rejection of, 172, 186; in Lacan,
186; in psychoanalytic theory, 186, 188
women authors, claims of direct inspiration
from God: and agency as issue, 118,
125–26, 321n28; and alternative subaltern
historiography, 121–24, 127; costs of
ignoring, 118, 120, 124; and description *vs.*
explanation, 119–21, 124; and loss of will,
117; and misogyny of subaltern history,
127; modern ability to take seriously, as
issue, 118; as primary source of legitimacy, 117, 120; privileging of naturalistic
explanations over, 119–21; and separation
of agent and subject, 124–25; women as
passive vessels and, 117
women's agency: claims of direct inspiration
from God and, 118, 125–26, 321n28; Mary
Magdalen as model of, 254; submission
of will to divine as precondition for, 117;
valorization of in feminist history, 321n28
Women's Aglow Fellowship, 248–49
women's association with bodiliness: Beatrice
of Nazareth's rejection of, 207–8; and
formation of women's interiority, 191–92,
205–6; and hagiography, greater emphasis
on bodily manifestations of faith, 204; as
imposed scheme in hagiographies, 209; as
imposed scheme in *Life of Beatrice of Nazareth*, 194–205, 207, 209; resistance to, 50,
114, 210–11. *See also* interiority, formation
of in medieval women

women's bodies: cross-gender identifications
with Christ, as issue, 247–48, 366n43;
right to interpret phenomena of, as issue,
57–58, 61, 168; women's spirituality and,
99, 101, 103–4, 111
women's empowerment: male-dominated
institutions of Christianity and, 97;
men's control of women's spirituality and,
103–4, 112–113, 108–9, 114; special graces
as means of, 95
Women's Secrets (pseudo-Albert the Great),
57, 58, 185
women's spirituality: characteristics of, 99, 113;
community contexts for, 108–9; denigration of, 113–14; men's control of, as issue,
103–4, 108–9, 112–13, 114; social constraints and, 99–100; somatic tendency
in, 99, 101, 103–4, 111; standard periodizations and, 109; women's resistance to male
expectations for, 104, 192, 210–11
women's spirituality as different from men's,
98–99, 102; and affective *vs.* speculative mysticism, 113; causes of unique characteristics,
99–101; critique of, 102–7, 113; importance
to feminist criticism, 107; new directions in
feminist scholarship on, 107–11

women's spiritual writings: absence of
accounts of asceticism before 1300, 103,
104; bodily imagery in as theological, 111;
centrality to Christian tradition, 95, 96; in
Classics of Western Spirituality series, 94;
dissemination of as object of study, 109–
10; feminist efforts to reclaim, 96, 97–101;
formal analysis of, 111; as insight into how
women "think with" gender, 96; interplay
with male writings, 103; late-20th-century
reevaluation of, 117; legitimization and
authorization as issues in, 117; men's control of, as issue, 103, 108–9, 114; in modern
period, 109; notable examples of, 94;
and pride, necessity of avoiding, 309n77;
resistance to modern appropriation,
114; theological innovations in, 302n37;
theological nature of, 110–11; tonal shift
in 12th–13th centuries, 97–98; as typically
mediated, 107–8
*Wounds of Christ with the Symbols of the
Passion, The*, 182, *183*

Young, Allan, 44

Ziarek, Ewa, 338n2

CPSIA information can be obtained
at www.ICGtesting.com
Printed in the USA
LVOW10s2031210417
531676LV00005B/20/P